THE ALLYN & BACON
GUIDE TO WRITING

TOPIC EDITION

JOHN D. RAMAGE • JOHN C. BEAN

PEARSON CUSTOM PUBLISHING

Excerpts taken from:

The Allyn and Bacon Guide to Writing, Second Edition,
by John D. Ramage and John C. Bean
Copyright © 1999, 1997 by Allyn and Bacon
A Pearson Education Company
Needham Heights, Massachusetts 02494

This special edition published in cooperation with
Pearson Custom Publishing.

Printed in the United States of America

10 9 8 7 6 5 4 3 2

Please visit our website at www.pearsoncustom.com

ISBN 0–536–02630–0

BA 990283

PEARSON CUSTOM PUBLISHING
160 Gould Street/Needham Heights, MA 02494
A Pearson Education Company

Brief Contents

PE1408.R18

Contents

Introduction to TOPIC

The English Department of Texas Tech University has established a project to give students in **English 1301** the opportunity to take advantage of the World Wide Web's extraordinary interactive and information-access abilities.

This project is called **TOPIC**, "Texas Tech Online-Print Integrated Curriculum." Allyn & Bacon, the publishers of this textbook, and its authors, Ramage and Bean, have allowed TOPIC to actually change some parts of the book in order to coordinate the book's ideas and writing guidelines with web-based capabilities offered on the Texas Tech's English Department's web server, **english.ttu.edu**.

Many instructors of 1301 will be using the web-based capabilities of TOPIC, and your instructor may be one of them. As you read this textbook, you will occasionally encounter a block of text in a different color under this heading:

TOPIC Guidepost

Those of you whose instructors are participating in TOPIC should follow the instructions provided by these "TOPIC guideposts." They will "point" you and your web browser (*Netscape* or *Internet Explorer*) to web addresses that will engage you in various Internet activities to support your writing.

Is this something different from what usually happens in college writing classrooms? You bet. The activities that TOPIC will be directing you to will engage you directly in the sorts of computer and Internet-based activity that will undoubtedly be a large part of any career you enter as a result of your college education.

Many of you will have your own computers and Internet access (TTUnet, AOL, ARNet, etc.). Others will not. Those who do not have Internet access will have access to computers and the Internet in the ATLC ("Advanced Technology Learning Center") in the basement of the Library or to computers provided by the English Department.

s u p p l e m e n t

TEXAS TECH UNIVERSITY
Policies for English 1301
1999-2000

Instructor: _____

Office/Phone: _____

Office Hours:_____

Telephone Partners (Name and Phone Number):

Class meets on _____ at _____ in Room _____

Texts	Ramage and Bean. *The Allyn & Bacon Guide to Writing, TOPIC Edition* Rosen. *Decisions* (handbook)
Home Web Page	http://english.ttu.edu:5555
Materials Needed	**2 Composition Folders**--pocket folder for drafts and final versions of essays
Course Goals	**In English 1301** you will • focus on the rhetorical elements of writer, reader, and text and place emphasis on writing as communication with self and others; and • develop fluency and effectiveness in your writing
Course Requirements	• Assigned reading • In and out-of-class writing and exercises • Active participation in groups and discussions • Drafts and revisions • **Four formal writing assignments**. Since department policy demands that all final essays be kept on file for one year, please make copies of all final versions before handing them in for grading.

TOPIC Requirements   Some sections of English 1301 will be participating in TOPIC, the "Texas Tech Online-Print Integrated Curriculum." Students in these sections will be engaged in learning activities on the World Wide Web. Look at the beginning of your textbook at the page entitled "Introduction to TOPIC" to find out more, or visit the web site at http://english.ttu.edu:5555

Attendance

Since English 1301 is conducted as a workshop that benefits from the cooperation and collaboration of all present, being on time and attending regularly is in your own best interests. Recent studies have shown that academic success is more often tied to students' time in class than to the time spent studying.

The principal reason students fail 1302 or receive a low grade is excessive absences. If you foresee a necessary absence, please tell the instructor beforehand. If you experience an unforeseen absence, *notify the instructor as soon afterwards as you can.*

Absences that are not explained to the instructor within one week of the absence will not be excused, no matter what documentation you may provide. It is your responsibility to discuss any absences with the instructor within one week of the absence occurring.

University Policy (*Undergraduate Catalog 1996-97*, page 65) states that "The effect of absences on grades is determined by the instructor. . . . Excessive absences constitute cause for dropping a student from class." Also, "In case of an illness that will require absence from class for more than one week, the student should notify his or her academic dean."

After the second TTH or third MWF absence, 5% of your final grade will be deducted per unexcused absence. Your dean will be notified and you will receive a letter acknowledging excessive absences.

The instructor will be the sole judge of whether an absence is excused or not. It is in your best interest to notify the instructor as soon as possible regarding an illness or emergency and to provide legitimate documentation.

Plagiarism

University Policy (*Undergraduate Catalog 1996-97*, page 66) states that "Offering the work of another as one's own, without proper acknowledgment, is plagiarism; therefore, any student who fails to give credit for quotations or essentially identical expression of material taken from books, encyclopedias, magazines, and other reference works, or from the themes, reports, or other writings of a fellow student, is guilty of plagiarism."

Plagiarism can result in a student failing the class and possibly being suspended from the University. Plagiarism is easier to detect than you may think.

Assignments

Final drafts must be turned in by the beginning of the class period in which they are due. Final drafts submitted after this time are considered late. Late drafts can receive no grade higher than 60 (D). Drafts that are never submitted receive a 0, which will severely affect your final grade.

See your instructor regarding late penalties for other course work.

Assignments will be accepted only during class period or during office hours and only by your instructor personally, who will record the work as submitted. Assignments should not be turned in to secretaries, office mates, slipped under doors, or submitted in any other fashion than handed personally to the instructor. Final drafts handed in after the beginning of the class period in which they are due will be considered late.

Exceptions to the above policies must be arranged with the instructor **prior** to the due date and time.

If you have to miss a class, please call your phone partners or group members about missed notes and assignments *before* returning to class.

MISCELLANEOUS

Writing Center

Plan to visit the Writing Center on the third floor of the English building (ROOM 310). Grades often improve dramatically after a session, or several sessions, with a tutor.

Computers

It is recommended that you do all out-of-class writing on a computer. The Advanced Technology Learning Center, or ATLC, in the basement of the Library has a variety of computers for personal use, and tutors there will show you how to use specific systems and word processing programs. Text written on a word processor is much easier to revise. The chances are that you will, in your professional life, have to write on a computer, so this is a good time to learn how.

Disabilities

Any student who, because of a disabling condition, may require some special arrangements in order to meet course requirements should contact the instructor as soon as possible so that the necessary accommodations can be made.

The process of writing is what strengthens your writing, regardless of your current writing ability. Therefore, prompt attendance, contributing to class and group discussions, and your effort on homework are all important and will impact your final grade. Your instructor is readily available during office hours and by appointment to help clarify any issues regarding assignments, attendance, and course policy. If you are confused or troubled about any aspect of the course, you should talk your instructor or the Director of Composition about it promptly.

English 1301 Assignment Schedule

	TOPIC	Readings	Writing Assignments
Week 1	**GuidePost 1**		Take TOPIC Tour Do TOPIC Survey
	GuidePost 2	Chap 1: "Posing Problems: The Demands of College Writing"	Journal Entry 1
Week 2	**GuidePost 3**	Chap 2: "Pursuing Problems: Exploratory Writing and Talking"	Microtheme 0.1
	GuidePost 4	Chap 14: "Working in Groups to Pose and Solve Problems"	Critique 0.1
Week 3	**GuidePost 5**	Handbook: Pages 199-208	TOPIC Mail Interviews
	GuidePost 6	Chap 3: "Solving Content Problems: Thesis and Support"	Write Draft 1.1
Week 4	**GuidePost 7**	Chap 13: "Composing and Revising Open-Form Prose"	Critique of 1.1
	GuidePost 8	Chap 11: "Writing as Problem-Solving Process"	Draft 1.2
Week 5	**GuidePost 9**	Chap 4: "Solving Rhetorical Problems: Purpose, Audience, and Genre"	Critique of 1.2
	GuidePost 10	Handbook: 215-227	Draft 1.3 (Final)
Week 6	**GuidePost 11**	Chap 5: "Seeing Rhetorically: The Writer as Observer"	Journal Responses to 1.3
	GuidePost 12	Handbook: 279-290	Three TOPIC mail messages about something observed
Week 7	**GuidePost 13**	Chap 6: "Reading Rhetorically: The Writer as Strong Reader"	Draft 2.1
	GuidePost 14	Chap 8: "Analyzing Images"	Critique Draft 2.1

Week 8	GuidePost 15	Chap 12: "Nine Lessons in Composing and Revising Closed-Form Prose"	Interactive Tree Diagram
	GuidePost 16	Handbook: 181-190	Draft 2.2
Week 9	GuidePost 17	Handbook: 290-300	Critique of Draft 2.2
	GuidePost 18	Handbook: 243-247	Draft 2.3 (Final)
Week 10	GuidePost 19	Handbook: 255-278	Journal Response to 2.3
	GuidePost 20	Chapter 7: "Writing an Exploratory Essay"	3 TOPIC mail messages
Week 11	GuidePost 21	Handbook: 59-84	Draft 3.1
	GuidePost 22	Reread Chap 7 about "dialectical thinking"	Critique Draft 3.1
Week 12	GuidePost 23	Handbook: 85-131	Draft 3.2 Journal Entry Research for 3.2
	GuidePost 24	Handbook: 313-314	Critique Draft 3.2
Week 13	GuidePost 25	Handbook: 228-236	Draft 3.3 (Final)
	GuidePost 26	Chap 10: "Writing a Classical Argument"	Journal Entry
Week 14	GuidePost 27	Handbook: 209-214	Draft 4.1 Exchange ideas in TOPIC Mail regarding your issue.
	GuidePost 28	Handbook: 308-312	Critique of 4.1 Draft 4.2

Week 15	**GuidePost 29**	Chap 15: "Focusing a Problem and Finding Sources"	Critique 4.2
	GuidePost 30		Draft 4.3 (Final) Journal Entry of Class Notes
Week 16	**GuidePost 31**		Turn in Draft 4.3

TOPIC Guidepost #1

For those using Texas Tech's TOPIC Web-Based assignments:

Direct your web browser to **http://english.ttu.edu:5555**

Here you will be guided on a tour of TOPIC and the English Department's web support for composition. This tour will take about 20 minutes and will provide information that will undoubtedly prove helpful for the rest of the semester. The tour will take roll so that you may be given credit for having participated in it.

TOPIC Guidepost #2

For those using Texas Tech's TOPIC Web-Based assignments:

Direct your web browser to **http://english.ttu.edu:5555**

Guidepost #2 provides full instructions regarding your assignment (Chapter 1) and Journal Entry.

Posing Problems
The Demands of
College Writing

WHAT YOU WILL LEARN IN THIS CHAPTER

In this chapter we show you that writers are questioners and problem posers who focus on two kinds of problems:

- Subject-matter problems, in which they wrestle with the complexities of their topic
- Rhetorical problems, in which they must make decisions about content, organization, and style based on their purpose, audience, and genre

To illustrate subject matter problems, we present a case study of a beginning college writer. To illustrate rhetorical problems, we show you how the rules of writing vary along a continuum from closed to open prose.

> It seems to me, then, that the way to help people become better writers is not to tell them that they must first learn the rules of grammar, that they must develop a four-part outline, that they must consult the experts and collect all the useful information. These things may have their place. But none of them is as crucial as having a good, interesting question.
>
> —Rodney Kilcup, *Historian*

Our purpose in this introductory chapter is to help you see writers as questioners and problem posers—a view of writing that we believe will lead to your greatest growth as a college-level thinker and writer. In particular, we want you to think of writers as people who pose interesting questions or problems and struggle to work out answers or responses to them. As we will show in this chapter, writers pose two sorts of problems: *subject matter* problems (for example, What is the effect of caffeine on a spider's web-making ability? Should the homeless mentally ill be placed involuntarily in mental hospitals?) and *rhetorical* problems (for example, How much background do my readers need on caffeine research? What is my

1

audience's current view about best treatment for the homeless mentally ill? What alternative solutions do I need to address? What form and style should I use?).

We don't mean to make this focus on problems sound scary. Indeed, humans pose and solve problems all the time and often take great pleasure in doing so. Psychologists who study critical and creative thinking see problem solving as a productive and positive activity. According to one psychologist, "Critical thinkers are actively engaged with life. . . . They appreciate creativity, they are innovators, and they exude a sense that life is full of possibilities."* By focusing first on the kinds of problems that writers pose and struggle with, we hope to increase your own engagement and pleasure in becoming a writer.

This chapter opens by showing you some good reasons for taking a writing course with particular emphasis on the relationship between writing and thinking. We then show how writers are engaged with subject matter questions that drive the writing process and bring writers into community with readers interested in the same questions. Since writers also face rhetorical questions, we provide an extended example—what we call the problem of choosing closed versus open forms. The chapter concludes with a brief writing assignment in which you can try your own hand at proposing a subject matter question.

WHY TAKE A WRITING COURSE?

Before turning directly to the notion of writers as questioners and problem posers, let's ask why a writing course can be valuable for you.

For some people, being a writer is part of their identity, so much so that when asked, "What do you do?" they are apt to respond, "I'm a writer." Poets, novelists, script writers, journalists, technical writers, grant writers, self-help book authors, and so on see themselves as writers the way other people see themselves as chefs, realtors, bankers, or musicians. But many people who don't think of themselves primarily as writers nevertheless *use* writing—often frequently—throughout their careers. They are engineers writing proposals or project reports; attorneys writing legal briefs; nurses writing patient assessments; business executives writing financial analyses or management reports; concerned citizens writing letters to the editor about public affairs; college professors writing articles for scholarly journals.

In our view, all these kinds of writing are valuable and qualify their authors as writers. If you already identify yourself as a writer, then you won't need much external motivation for improving your writing. But if you have little interest in writing for its own sake and aspire instead to become a nurse, an engineer, a busi-

*Academic writers regularly document their sources. The standard method for documenting sources in student papers and in many professional scholarly articles is the MLA or APA citation system. By convention, textbook authors usually cite their sources under an "Acknowledgments" section that begins on the copyright page. To find our source for this quotation (or for the quotation from Kilcup at the beginning of this chapter), see the copyright page at the front of the text; acknowledgments continue at the end of the text.

ness executive, a social worker, or a marine biologist, then you might question the benefits of taking a writing course.

What are these benefits? First of all, the skills you learn in this course will be directly transferable to your other college courses, where you will have to write papers in a wide variety of styles. Lower division (general education or core) courses often focus on general academic writing, while upper division courses in your major introduce you to the specialized writing and thinking of your chosen field. What college professors value are the kinds of questioning, analyzing, and arguing skills that this course will help you develop. You will emerge from this course as a better reader and thinker and a clearer and more persuasive writer able to meet the demands of different writing situations.

Effective writing skills are also essential for most professional careers. To measure the importance of writing to career success, researchers Andrea Lunsford and Lisa Ede recently surveyed randomly selected members of such professional organizations as the American Consulting Engineers Counsel, the American Institute of Chemists, the American Psychological Association, and the International City Management Association. They discovered that members of these organizations spent, on the average, 44 percent of their professional time doing writing, including, most commonly, letters, memos, short reports, instructional materials, and professional articles and essays.

Other things being equal, professionals who can write effectively advance further and faster than those who can't. In the workplace, the ability to identify and analyze problems, to propose solutions, and to argue persuasively to different constituencies is critical. Lunsford and Ede report numerous on-the-job situations where written communication skills are crucial. Here, for example, is how one of their respondents—an engineer working as a city planner—described his frustration at not being able to produce adequately persuasive documents:

> After I had been out of school a number of years practicing as a city planner, I had become concerned about why we could develop a good plan for a community and try to explain it to people and they wouldn't seem to understand it. They wouldn't support it for one reason or another. And time and time again we would see a good plan go down the drain because people didn't agree with it or for some reason didn't actively support it.

The city manager describes here a situation often encountered in professional life—the need not only to solve a problem but to sell one's solution to others. As he implies, those who can write clearly and persuasively contribute invaluably to the success of their organizations.

Besides the pragmatic benefits of college and career success, learning to write well can bring you the personal pleasure of a richer mental life. As we show throughout this text, writing is closely allied to thinking and to the innate satisfaction you take in exercising your curiosity, creativity, and problem-solving ability. Writing connects you to others and helps you discover and express ideas that you would otherwise never think or say. Unlike speaking, writing gives you time to think deep and long about an idea. Because you can revise writing, it lets you pursue a problem in stages, with each new draft reflecting a deeper, clearer, or more complex level of thought. In other words, writing isn't just a way to express thought; it is a way to do the thinking itself. The act of writing stimulates, challenges, and stretches your mental powers and, when you do it well, is profoundly satisfying.

◤ SUBJECT-MATTER PROBLEMS: THE STARTING POINT OF WRITING

Having made a connection between writing and thinking, we now move to the spirit of inquiry that drives the writing process. Thus far in your writing career, you may have imagined writing primarily as gathering and assembling information. Someone handed you a broad topic area (for example, contemporary urban America or Renaissance love poetry) or a narrower topic area (homelessness or Shakespeare's sonnets), and you collected and wrote information about that topic. In the process of writing your paper, you may have learned some interesting things about your subject matter. But if you approached your writing in this way, you weren't approximating the thinking processes of most experienced writers. Experienced writers usually see their subject matter in terms of questions or problems rather than broad or narrow topic areas. They typically enjoy posing questions and pursuing answers. They write to share their discoveries and insights with readers interested in the same problems.

Shared Problems Unite Writers and Readers

Everywhere we turn, we see writers and readers forming communities based on questions or problems of mutual interest. Perhaps nowhere are such communities more evident than in academe. Many college professors are engaged in research projects stimulated and driven by questions or problems. At a recent workshop for new faculty members, we asked participants to write a brief description of a question or problem that motivated them to write a seminar paper or article. Here is a sampling of their responses.

A Biochemistry Professor   During periods of starvation, the human body makes physiological adaptations to preserve essential protein mass. Unfortunately, these adaptations don't work well during long-term starvation. After the body depletes its carbohydrate storage, it must shift to depleting protein in order to produce glucose. Eventually, this loss of functional protein leads to metabolic dysfunction and death. Interestingly, several animal species are capable of surviving for extensive periods without food and water while conserving protein and maintaining glucose levels. How do the bodies of these animals accomplish this feat? I wanted to investigate the metabolic functioning of these animals, which might lead to insights into the human situation.

A Nursing Professor   Being a nurse who had worked with terminally ill or permanently unconscious patients, I saw doctors and nurses struggle with the question of when to withdraw life-support systems. I wondered how philosophers and ethicists went about deciding these issues and how they thought physicians and other clinicians should make the decision to withdraw life support. I wanted to answer this question: What is the relationship between the way "experts" say we should solve complex ethical problems and the way it actually happens in a clinical context? So I chose to look at this problem by reading what philosophers said about this topic and then by interviewing physicians and nurses in long-term care facilities (nursing homes) in the United States and the Netherlands—asking them how they made decisions to withdraw life support from patients with no hope of recovery.

   A Journalism Professor   Several years ago, I knocked on the wooden front door of the home of an elderly woman in Tucson, Arizona. Tears of grief rolled down her cheeks as she opened the door. The tears turned to anger when I explained that I was a reporter and wished to talk with her about her son's death in jail. Her face hardened. "What right do you have coming here?" I recall her saying. "Why are you bothering me?" Those questions have haunted me throughout my journalism career. Do journalists have the right to intrude on a person's grief? Can they exercise it any time they want? What values do journalists use to decide when to intrude and violate someone's privacy?

Of course these are not new college students speaking; these are college professors recalling problems that fueled a piece of professional writing. We share these problems with you to persuade you that most college professors value question asking and want you to be caught up, as they are, in the spirit of inquiry.

As you progress through your college career, you will find yourself increasingly engaged with questions. All around college campuses you'll find clusters of professors and students asking questions about all manner of curious things—questions about the reproductive cycles of worms and bugs, the surface structure of metals, the social significance of obscure poets, gender roles among the Kalahari Bushmen, the meaning of Balinese cockfighting, the effect of tax structure on economies, the rise of labor unions in agriculture, the role of prostitutes in medieval India, the properties of concrete, and almost anything else a human being might wonder about. A quick review of the magazine rack at any large grocery store reveals that similar communities have formed around everything from hot rods to model railroads, from computers to kayaks to cooking.

At the heart of all these communities of writers and readers is an interest in common questions and the hope for better or different answers. Writers write because they have something new or surprising or challenging to say in response to a question. Readers read because they share the writer's interest in the problem and want to deepen their understanding.

The Writer as Problematizer

Few writers discover their "answers" in a blinding flash. And even fewer writers produce a full-blown essay in a moment of inspiration. Professionals may require weeks, months, or years of thinking to produce a single piece of writing.

A new insight may start out as a vague sense of uncertainty, an awareness that you are beginning to see your subject (the metabolism of a starving animal, the decision to let a patient die, a grieving mother's anger at a journalist) differently from how others see it. You feel a gap between your view of a topic and your audience's view of the same topic and write to fill these gaps, to articulate your different view. Rarely, however, do writers know at the outset what they will write in the end. Instead, they clarify and refine their thoughts in the act of writing.

One of the most common causes of weak writing is the writer's tendency to reach closure too quickly. It's difficult, of course, to keep wrestling with a question. It's easier simply to ignore alternative views and material that doesn't fit and to grab hold of the first solution that comes to mind. What characterizes a successful writer is the ability to live with uncertainty and to acknowledge the insufficiency of an answer.

One term that describes serious writers is *problematizers;* that is, serious writers are not merely problem solvers, but problem posers, people who problematize their lives. We learned the term *problematize* from South American educator Paulo Freire, who discovered that adult literacy was best taught as a problem-solving activity tied to essential themes in his students' daily lives. Freire's method contrasts starkly with the traditional mode of teaching literacy, which Freire called the banking method. The goal of the banking method is to deposit knowledge in students' memory banks, rather than to teach students to discover or question or act.

The banking method encourages a passive attitude, not only toward learning, but also toward reality. Freire characterized students indoctrinated in such methods as "submerged in reality," unable to distinguish between the way things are and the way things might or should be. When people are taught to read and write by the banking method, they are likely to learn the word *water* by constantly repeating an irrelevant, self-evident sentence, such as "The water is in the well." Using Freire's method of teaching literacy, students might learn the word *water* by asking, "Is the water in our village dirty or clean?" and if the water is dirty, asking, "Why is the water dirty? Who is responsible?" The power of reading and writing lies in making discriminations, in unveiling alternative ways of seeing the world in which we live. By using language to problematize reality, Freire's students learned the meaning of written words because they recognized the power of those words.

Skilled writers, thus, are seekers after alternatives who look deliberately for questions, problems, puzzles, and contradictions. They realize that they can't write anything significant if they don't bring something new or challenging to the reader, something risky enough to spark disagreement or complex enough to be misunderstood. The surest way to improve your writing is to ground your essay in a question or problem that will motivate your thinking and help you establish a purposeful relationship with your audience. In the process, you'll have to live for a while with a sense of incompleteness, ambiguity, and uncertainty—the effects of engagement with any real problem.

Posing a Problem: A Case Study of a Beginning College Writer

So far we have talked about how professional writers pose problems. In this section we show you how student writer Mary Turla posed a problem for an argumentative paper requiring research.

At the start of her process, Mary's general topic area was mail-order brides. Her interest in this subject was sparked by a local newspaper story about an American man who gunned down his Filipina mail-order bride outside the court-room where she was filing for divorce. Although Mary was immediately intrigued by the topic, she didn't initially have a focused question or problem. She began doing library research on the mail-order bride industry and discovered that 75 percent of mail-order brides come from the Philippines. Because Mary is a Filipina American, this statistic bothered her, and she began focusing on the image of Asian women created by the mail-order bride industry. Early in her process, she wrote the following entry in her journal:

Mary's Paper—Early Journal Entry

The mail-order bride industry may create & perpetuate the image of Asian women as commodities, vulnerable, uneducated, subservient; this image is ap-plied to Asian American women or women of Asian descent. . . . Obviously, the mail-order bride is wrong—but what is the statement I want to make about it? Exploits/develops & creates negative image of Asian women. This image passes on to Asian American women. The image makes them sexual objects, "object" period—love as a commodity—exploitation industry—twists our culture—unrealistic expectations. What is the consequence?: domestic violence, unsatis-fied partners, multimillion-dollar industry; subtle consequence: buying/selling people OK; Love/marriage a commodity.

This journal entry helped Mary see the more complex aspects of her subject—especially the connection of the mail-order bride industry to the image of Asian or Asian American women—but she was not yet able to define a central question or problem. Shortly after writing this journal entry, Mary discussed the topic with her classmates. After class, Mary wrote again in her journal.

Mary's Paper—Later Journal Entry

Class was great. We all had a chance to discuss our research so far and give others input on theirs. It was an extremely helpful exercise. A few helpful hints I got from the gang: 1) Define participants (men/women/business); 2) Are some "brides" there because they want to be? 3) *Find* a question! Most everyone (as far as I could tell) felt the mail-order bride industry was comparable to prostitution or trafficking of women. I have to ask: Is it? If it is, is it inherently so? Or, is it something about the mechanics of the industry now that justifies criticism? I could also sense an attitude—a mix of pity and contempt for the women involved.

Shortly thereafter, a conversation between Mary and her mother produced a focusing problem. After Mary complained about the evils of mail-order brides, her mother unexpectedly supported the practice. Women in the Philippines are des-perately poor, her mother explained. Marrying a stranger, she said, may be the only way for some women to escape lives of abject poverty. Although Mary disliked the mail-order bride industry, her mother's response gave her pause. Perhaps being treated like a commodity might be a small price to pay for escaping near starvation and an early death.

Mary was now caught in a dilemma between her own gut-level desire to outlaw the mail-order bride industry and her realization that doing so would end many women's only hope of avoiding a life of poverty. She finally posed her problem this way: Should the mail-order bride industry be made illegal? She was no longer certain about her own answer to this question. Her goal was to make up her mind by learning as much as she could about the industry from the perspectives of the husband, the bride, and the industry itself. We return to Mary's story occasionally throughout this text.

Types of Subject-Matter Questions

Academic researchers often conduct two kinds of research: applied research, in which they try to solve a practical problem in the real world, and pure research, in which they pursue knowledge for its own sake. We can call these two types of research questions *practical application questions* and *pure knowledge questions,* both of which examine what is true about the world. Frequently, writers also explore *values questions,* which focus not on what is true about the world but on how we should act in it. (Mary Turla's question about whether the mail-order bride industry should be made illegal is a values question.) A famous illustration of these kinds of questions involves the development of atomic power:

- **Pure-knowledge question:** Is it possible to split the atom?
- **Practical-application question:** How can we use our knowledge of splitting the atom to build an atomic bomb?
- **Values question:** Should scientists build an atomic bomb? Should the United States drop it on Hiroshima and Nagasaki?

FOR WRITING AND DISCUSSION

Almost any topic area will give rise to pure knowledge questions, practical application questions, and values questions. In this exercise we invite you to generate questions about the topic area "animals." We choose this topic because it is widely studied by university researchers across many disciplines (the metabolism of starvation is just one example; see p. 6) but also because almost everyone has had some experience with animals through owning a pet, observing a hornets' nest, wondering about dinosaurs, or questioning the ethics of stepping on ants.

1. Working in small groups, brainstorm a dozen or so good questions about animals. These should be questions that really puzzle at least

one person in your group and that no one else in your group can answer authoritatively. Try generating questions in each of our three categories, but don't worry if some questions don't fit neatly into a category. Here are some examples of questions about animals:

Pure knowledge questions

- Why did dinosaurs become extinct?
- Why does my dog always bark at people who wear hats but not at anyone else?
- Why does one of my goldfish always swim on its side rather than straight up like the other goldfish?

Practical application questions

- How can I best keep slugs out of my vegetable garden?
- What is the best way to teach a parakeet to talk?
- Can zoos be used to preserve endangered species?

Values questions

- Is saving the spotted owl worth the economic costs?
- Is it cruelty to animals to keep them in zoos?
- Should we tear down several dams on the Columbia River to restore salmon runs?

2. After each group has generated a dozen or more questions, try to reach consensus on your group's three "best" questions to share with the whole class. Be ready to explain to the class why you think some questions are better than others.

◢ RHETORICAL PROBLEMS: REACHING READERS EFFECTIVELY

As we suggested in the introduction, writers wrestle with two categories of problems—subject-matter problems and rhetorical problems. The previous section introduced you to subject-matter problems; we turn now to rhetorical problems.

In their final products, writers need to say something significant about their subjects to an audience, for a purpose, in an appropriate form and style. This network of questions related to audience, purpose, form, and style constitute rhetorical problems, and these problems often loom as large for writers as do the subject-matter problems that drive their writing in the first place. Indeed, rhetorical problems and subject-matter problems are so closely linked that writers can't address one without addressing the other. For example, the very questions you ask about your subject matter are influenced by your audience and purpose. Before you can decide what to say about content, you need to ask: Who am I writing for and why? What does my audience already know (and not know) about my topic? Will the question I pose already interest them, or do I have to hook their interest? What effect do I want my writing to have on that audience? How should I structure my essay and what tone and voice should I adopt?

In Chapter 4, we discuss extensively the rhetorical problems that writers must pose and solve. In this chapter we simply introduce you to one extended example of a rhetorical problem. From a student's point of view, we might call this "the problem of varying rules." From our perspective, we call it "the problem of choosing closed versus open forms."

◢ AN EXAMPLE OF A RHETORICAL PROBLEM: WHEN TO CHOOSE CLOSED VERSUS OPEN FORMS

In our experience, beginning college writers are often bothered by the ambiguity and slipperiness of rules governing writing. Many beginning writers wish that good writing followed consistent rules, such as "Never use 'I' in a formal paper" or "Start every paragraph with a topic sentence." The problem is that different kinds of writing follow different rules, leaving the writer with rhetorical choices rather than with hard and fast formulas for success. To develop this point, we begin by asking you to consider a problem about how writing might be classified.

Read the following short pieces of nonfiction prose. The first is a letter to the editor written by a professional civil engineer in response to a newspaper editorial arguing for the development of wind-generated electricity. The second piece is the opening page of an autobiographical essay by writer Minnie Bruce Pratt about her experiences as a white woman living in a predominantly black neighborhood. After reading the two samples carefully, proceed to the discussion questions that follow.

READINGS

DAVID ROCKWOOD

A LETTER TO THE EDITOR

Your editorial on November 16, "Get Bullish on Wind Power," is based on fantasy   1
rather than fact. There are several basic reasons why wind-generated power can in no way serve as a reasonable major alternative to other electrical energy supply alternatives for the Pacific Northwest power system.

2   First and foremost, wind power is unreliable. Electric power generation is evaluated not only on the amount of energy provided, but also on its ability to meet system peak load requirements on an hourly, daily, and weekly basis. In other words, an effective power system would have to provide enough electricity to meet peak demands in a situation when the wind energy would be unavailable—either in no wind situations or in severe blizzard conditions, which would shut down the wind generators. Because wind power cannot be relied on at times of peak needs, it would have to be backed up by other power generation resources at great expense and duplication of facilities.

3   Secondly, there are major unsolved problems involved in the design of wind generation facilities, particularly for those located in rugged mountain areas. Ice storms, in particular, can cause sudden dynamic problems for the rotating blades and mechanisms which could well result in breakdown or failure of the generators. Furthermore, the design of the facilities to meet the stresses imposed by high winds in these remote mountain regions, in the order of 125 miles per hour, would indeed escalate the costs.

4   Thirdly, the environmental impact of constructing wind generation facilities amounting to 28 percent of the region's electrical supply system (as proposed in your editorial) would be tremendous. The Northwest Electrical Power system presently has a capacity of about 37,000 megawatts of hydro power and 10,300 megawatts of thermal, for a total of about 48,000 megawatts. Meeting 28 percent of this capacity by wind power generators would, most optimistically, require about 13,400 wind towers, each with about 1,000 kilowatt (one megawatt) generating capacity. These towers, some 100 to 200 feet high, would have to be located in the mountains of Oregon and Washington. These would encompass hundreds of square miles of pristine mountain area, which, together with interconnecting transmission facilities, control works, and roads would indeed have major adverse environmental impacts on the region.

5   There are many other lesser problems of control and maintenance of such a system. Let it be said that, from my experience and knowledge as a professional engineer, the use of wind power as a major resource in the Pacific Northwest power system, is strictly a pipe dream.

▼

MINNIE BRUCE PRATT

FROM "IDENTITY: SKIN BLOOD HEART"

1   I live in a part of Washington, D.C. that white suburbanites called "the jungle" during the uprising of the '60s—perhaps still do, for all I know. When I walk the two-and-a-half blocks to H St. NE, to stop in at the bank, to leave my boots off at the shoe-repair-and-lock shop, I am most usually the only white person in sight. I've seen two other whites, women, in the year I've lived here. (This does not count white folks in cars, passing through. In official language, H St., NE, is known as "The H Street Corridor," as in something to be passed through quickly, going from your place, on the way to elsewhere.)

2   When I walk three blocks in a slightly different direction, down Maryland Avenue, to go to my lover's house, I pass the yards of Black folks: the yard of the lady who keeps children, with its blue-and-red windmill, its roses-of-sharon; the yard of the man who delivers vegetables with its stacked slatted crates; the yard of the people next to the Righteous Branch Commandment Church-of-God (Seventh Day) with its tomatoes

in the summer, its collards in the fall. In the summer, folks sit out on their porches or steps or sidewalks; when I walk by, if I lift my head and look toward them and speak, "Hey," they may speak, say, "Hey" or "How you doing?" or perhaps just nod. In the spring, I was afraid to smile when I spoke, because that might be too familiar, but by the end of summer I had walked back and forth so often, I was familiar, so sometimes we shared comments about the mean weather.

I am comforted by any of these speakings for, to tell you the truth, they make me   3
feel at home. I am living far from where I was born; it has been twenty years since I have lived in that place where folks, Black and white, spoke to each other when they met on the street or in the road. So when two Black men dispute country matters, calling across the corners of 8th St—"Hey, Roland, did you ever see a hog catch a rat?"—"I seen a hog catch a *snake*"—"How about a rat? Ever see one catch a *rat?*"—I am grateful to be living within sound of their voices, to hear a joking that reminds me, with a startled pain, of my father, putting on his tales for his friends, the white men gathered at the drugstore.

FOR WRITING AND DISCUSSION

Working in small groups or as a whole class, try to reach consensus on the following specific tasks:

1. What are the main differences between the two types of writing? If you are working in groups, help your recorder prepare a presentation describing the differences between Rockwood's writing and Pratt's writing.
2. Create a metaphor, simile, or analogy that best sums up your feelings about the most important differences between Rockwood's and Pratt's writing: "Rockwood's writing is like . . . , but Pratt's writing is like. . . ."
3. Explain why your metaphors are apt. How do your metaphors help clarify or illuminate the differences between the two pieces of writing?

Now that you have done some thinking on your own about the differences between these two examples, turn to our brief analysis.

Distinctions Between Closed and Open Forms of Writing

David Rockwood's letter and Minnie Pratt's excerpt are both examples of nonfiction prose. But as these examples illustrate, nonfiction prose can vary enormously in form and style. From the perspective of structure, we can place nonfiction prose along a continuum that goes from closed to open forms of writing (see Figure 1.1, on p. 13).

Of our two pieces of prose, Rockwood's letter illustrates tightly closed writing and falls at the far left end of the continuum. The elements that make this writing closed are the presence of an explicit thesis in the introduction (i.e., wind-generated power isn't a reasonable alternative energy source in the Pacific Northwest) and the writer's consistent development of that thesis throughout the body (i.e., "First and foremost, wind power is unreliable. . . . Secondly, there are

Closed Forms──Open Forms

Top-down thesis-based prose
- thesis explicitly stated in introduction
- all parts of essay linked clearly to thesis
- body paragraphs develop thesis
- structure forecast

Thesis-seeking prose
- essay organized around a question rather than a thesis
- essay explores the problem or question
- many ways of looking at problem are expressed
- writer often tells stories to reveal problem's complexity
- writer may or may not arrive at thesis

Thesis as implicit theme
- narrative based
- uses literary techniques
- often called literary nonfiction (belletristic)
- often used to heighten or deepen a problem, show its human significance

Delayed-thesis prose
- thesis appears near end
- text reads as mystery
- reader held in suspense

Thesis as speculation, often highly personalized
- speculative points often emerge out of narrative
- often characterized by digressions and musings
- thesis may only be implied

FIGURE 1.1   A Continuum of Essay Types: Closed to Open Forms

major unsolved [design] problems. . . . Thirdly, . . ."). Once the thesis is stated, the reader knows the point of the essay and can predict its structure. The reader also knows that the writer's point won't change as the essay progresses. Because its structure is transparent and predictable, the success of closed-form prose rests entirely on its ideas, which must "surprise" readers by asserting something new, challenging, doubtful, or controversial. It aims to change the reader's view of the subject through the power of reason, logic, and evidence. Closed-form prose is what most college professors write when doing their own scholarly research, and it is what they most often expect of their students. It is also the most common kind of writing in professional and business contexts.

Pratt's writing falls at the far right of the closed-to-open continuum. It resists reduction to a single, summarizable thesis and leaves the reader in suspense about where it is going. Open-form essays are often organized chronologically; they tell a story rather than support an announced main point. This kind of writing is narrative based rather than thesis based. Narrative-based essays still have a focus, but the focus is more like the theme in a work of fiction than the thesis of an argument. Often the point of a narrative is implied rather than explicitly stated. Readers may argue over the point in the same way that they argue over the meaning of a film or novel.

As you can see from the continuum in Figure 1.1, essays can fall anywhere along the scale. Not all thesis-with-support writing has to be top down, stating its thesis explicitly in the introduction. In some cases writers choose to delay the thesis, creating a more exploratory, open-ended, "let's think through this together" feeling before finally stating the main point late in the essay. In some cases writers explore a problem without *ever* finding a satisfactory thesis, creating an essay that is thesis seeking rather than thesis supporting, an essay aimed at deepening the question, refusing to accept an easy answer. Such essays may replicate their author's process of exploring a problem and include digressions, speculations, conjectures, multiple perspectives, and occasional invitations to the reader to help solve the problem. When writers reach the far right-hand position on the continuum, they no longer state an explicit thesis. Instead, like novelists or short-story writers, they embed their points in plot, imagery, dialogue, and so forth, leaving their readers to *infer* a theme from the text.

Where to Place Your Writing Along the Continuum

Clearly, essays at opposite ends of this continuum operate in different ways and obey different rules. Because each position on the continuum has its appropriate uses, the writer's challenge is to determine which sort of writing is most appropriate for a given situation.

As you will see in later chapters, the kind of writing you choose depends on your purpose, your intended audience, and your genre (a genre is a recurring type of writing with established conventions, such as an academic article, a newspaper feature story, a grant proposal, an article for *Seventeen* or *Rolling Stone,* and so forth). Thus if you were writing an analytical paper for an academic audience, you would typically choose a closed-form structure and your finished product would include such elements as the following:

- an explicit thesis in the introduction
- forecasting of structure
- cohesive and unified paragraphs with topic sentences
- clear transitions between sentences and between parts
- no digressions

But if you were writing an autobiographical narrative about, say, what family means to you, you would probably move toward the open end of the continuum and violate one or more of these conventions (note how extensively Pratt violates them). It's not that open-form prose doesn't have rules; it's that the rules are different, just as the rules for jazz are different from the rules for a classical sonata.

For another perspective on how rules vary, consider two frequently encountered high school writing assignments: the five-paragraph theme and the "What I Did Last Summer" essay. The five-paragraph theme is a by-the-numbers way to teach closed-form, thesis-with-support writing. It emphasizes logical development, unity, and coherence. The five-paragraph structure may emerge naturally if you are writing an argument based on three supporting reasons—an introductory paragraph, three body paragraphs (one for each reason), and a concluding paragraph. Rockwood's letter is a real-world example of a five-paragraph essay, even though Rockwood certainly didn't have that format in mind when writing.

In contrast, the "What I Did Last Summer" assignment calls for a different sort of writing, probably an open-form structure closer to that of Pratt's piece. If you tried to write the "What I Did Last Summer" essay with the thesis-up-front rules of the five-paragraph essay, you would be hamstrung from the start; the summer essay calls not for an argument, but for a well-plotted, vivid story. Whether the writer chooses a closed-form or an open-form approach depends on the intended audience of the piece and the writer's purpose.

FOR WRITING AND DISCUSSION

Do you and your classmates most enjoy writing prose at the closed or more open end of the continuum? Prior to class discussion, work individually by recalling a favorite piece of writing that you have done in the past. Jot down a brief description of the kind of writing this was (a poem, a personal experience essay, a research paper, a newspaper story, a persuasive argument). Then, working in small groups or as a whole class, report one at a time on your favorite piece of writing and speculate where it falls on the continuum from closed to open forms. Are you at your best in closed-form writing that calls for an explicit thesis statement and logical support? Or are you at your best in more open and personal forms?

Is there a wide range of preferences in your class? If so, how do you account for this variance? If not, how do you account for the narrow range?

◪ CHAPTER SUMMARY

This chapter has introduced you to the notion of writers as questioners and problem posers who wrestle with both subject-matter and rhetorical problems. We have shown how writers start with questions or problems about their subject matter, rather than with topic areas, and how they take their time resolving the uncertainties raised by such questions. We saw that writers must ask questions about their rhetorical situation and make decisions about content, form, and style based on their understanding of their purpose, their audience, and their genre. We described how the rules governing writing vary as the writer moves along the continuum from closed to open forms.

The next chapter looks closely at how writers pose problems and pursue them in depth through behind-the-scenes exploratory writing and talking.

BRIEF WRITING PROJECT

We close out this chapter with a brief writing project aimed at helping you appreciate historian Rodney Kilcup's advice to writers: Begin with "a good, interesting question" (see the epigraph to this chapter, p. 1). As you will see later in this text, your brief essay will be similar in structure to the question-posing part of a typical academic introduction.

> Write a one-page (double-spaced) essay that poses a question about animals (or about some other topic provided by your instructor). Besides explaining your question clearly and providing needed background, you will need to help readers understand two things about it: (1) why the question is problematic—that is, what makes it a genuine question or problem; and (2) why the question is significant or worth pursuing—that is, what benefit will come from solving it. Your essay should not answer the question; your purpose is only to ask it.

This assignment builds on the For Writing and Discussion exercise on pages 8 and 9, which asked you to brainstorm questions about animals. For this assignment, choose a puzzling question about animals that interests you. Aim your essay at readers who are not familiar with your question. Your task is to make your question interesting to those readers. To hook their interest, you have to explain what your question is (often providing needed background) and then elaborate on the question by showing two things about it: why the question is problematic and why it is significant. To illustrate what we mean by these terms, we provide the following student essay as an example.

MELISSA DAVIS (STUDENT)
WHY DO SOME DOGS LIKE CATS WHILE OTHERS HATE THEM?

Background story introduces question

Whenever my dog sees a cat, he starts chasing it, barking and snapping his teeth. No matter how much I have tried to teach Sandy to like cats, he chases them ferociously on first sight. However, not all dogs are cat-haters. I often babysit a family that has a dog and two cats. When I let the dog, Willa, into the house, she goes straight towards the cats and starts playing with them. They nudge and cuddle with one another almost as if Willa were their mother. Willa never growls at the cats, but always treats them tenderly.

Statement of question

The contrast between Sandy and Willa makes me wonder why some dogs despise cats and will do any thing to hurt them while others mother them as if they were their own puppies. What causes dogs to react so differently to cats?

Contrasting theories show why question is problematic

One possible theory is genetic; maybe different breeds of dogs have different reactions to cats. My dog is a very small Chihuahua terrier, and Willa is a large chocolate lab. Maybe in this case the difference involves the sizes of the two breeds. Perhaps being small, a Chihuahua is more intimidated by cats while the Lab is so large that the cat is no threat to it.

Yet my friend's big German Shepherds chase and attack cats. Perhaps some breeds are genetically wired to hate cats while others aren't.

Another theory concerns the way dogs are first introduced to cats as puppies. I remember that in the past while visiting relatives Sandy stuck her nose under a bed when a cat reached out and scratched it, sending Sandy howling out of the room. Maybe this memory caused Sandy to hate all cats. In contrast, perhaps Willa was taught to play with cats when she was a puppy. Maybe some kind human being petted Willa and a kitten simultaneously so that cat and dog bonded. Under this theory, hating or liking cats would be a learned experience.

Solving this question might further our knowledge about genetics and the environment in accounting for animal behavior. It might help us discover something useful about the way animals can best be trained.

Suggests significance of question

In this essay, Melissa asks why some dogs hate cats while others don't. Melissa uses her own personal experience—the contrast between her dog Sandy and a neighbor's dog Willa—as background to explain the question clearly to readers. Since most people believe that dogs naturally hate cats, the case of the cat-loving Willa automatically makes her question problematic. (If dogs naturally hate cats, then how do you explain Willa?) She further shows its problematic nature by contrasting several possible theories, none of which is fully satisfactory. Finally she speculates on why this question is significant: Answering it might help us better understand the role of nature versus nurture in animal behavior and lead to better ways of training animals.

With this illustration as a starting point, let's look more closely at what we mean by a problematic and significant question.

Showing Why Your Question Is Problematic

A question is said to be problematic if it has no apparent answers or if the answers that come to a reader's mind can be shown to be unsatisfactory. A question whose answer can be looked up in an encyclopedia or can be completely answered by an expert is not problematic. Problematic questions imply either that the answer is not known or that it is not agreed upon by experts. In other words, problematic questions imply answers that have to be argued for, that have to be justified with reasons and evidence. Some strategies writers use to show that a question is problematic include the following:

- Show how your own (or previous researchers') attempts to solve the problem have failed. (If your problem were "How can I train my dog not to dig holes in the yard?" you could show how your various attempts to solve the problem all failed.)
- Show different ways that people have attempted to answer the question (different theories or hypotheses or competing explanations) and indicate how no one answer is fully adequate. (This is the strategy used by Melissa to show why her question about dogs hating cats is problematic.)

- If you pose a values question, summarize the competing positions on the issue. (For example, if the question concerns the value of saving the spotted owl, the writer can summarize opposing arguments.)
- Show why an expected or "easy" answer isn't satisfactory. (For example, you might show why "to keep itself clean" may not be a satisfactory answer to the question "Why do cats lick themselves?")
- Narrate your own attempts to think through the problem, revealing how none of your possible answers fully satisfied you. You might use the strategy "Part of me thinks this . . . ; but another part of me thinks this. . . ." or "I used to think . . . but now I think. . . ." (For example, if you ask "Is it ethical to eat meat?" you might describe your shifting positions on this issue and show why no single position satisfies you.)

Showing Why Your Question Is Significant

Often a question can be problematic without seeming significant to an audience. A reader might not know why one of your goldfish swims sideways rather than upright and yet not care about it. Thus writers often need to show why a problem is worth pursuing in order to keep the audience from saying "So what?" or "Who cares?" It is easy to show the significance of practical-application questions because their solution will solve real-world problems such as getting one's dog to stop digging holes in the yard, or, in the case of professional applied research, getting rid of acid rain, building a faster microchip, or finding a cure for AIDS. But when you pose a pure-knowledge question, the significance of finding an answer is harder to see. What professional scholars do is show how solving one knowledge question will help us understand another, larger knowledge question. For example, if you understand how Shakespeare uses dog imagery in his plays, you might understand better how he creates other imagery patterns or how his culture regarded the relationship between the human and animal world. Here are two typical ways that writers can show the significance of a problem:

- *Show how solving the problem will lead to practical, real-world benefits.* (For example, finding out what odors trigger the mating of certain insects might lead to an environmentally safe method of controlling their populations.)
- *Show how solving a pure-knowledge problem will help us solve a larger, more important knowledge problem.* (For example, if we understand how spiders "know" how to spin webs, we may be able to understand better how genetic encoding works.)

Planning Your Essay

A premise throughout this book is that a good finished product grows out of a rich exploratory process. We suggest that you talk through your proposed essay with a classmate, explaining your question and showing why it is problematic and significant. Make an informal outline or flowchart for the essay in which you plan out each of the required parts. Here are some examples of student plans that led to successful question-posing essays.

Example 1

I would like to question the ethics of interspecies transplants and show why it is not an easy question to answer.

Illustrate question with case of a man who had a transplant of a baboon heart.

Side One: Interspecies transplants are unethical. It is unethical to "play god" by taking the organs of one species and placing them in another.

Side Two: Interspecies transplants are ethical. They may save lives.

This is a significant problem because it causes us to ask deep questions about what we most value.

Example 2

What can we do about the raccoons that pester our home near Golden Gate Park in San Francisco?

Start by telling story of how horrible the raccoons are—raid our garbage, invade our yards during the day while children are playing, come in the house through the cat door and eat cats' food—most horrible they once ate our kittens.

Nothing seems to work.

Describe our attempts to solve problem: Tried various tricks to discourage raccoons—spraying the hose on them, getting better garbage cans, moving cat food, etc.

Our dilemma: Is it ethical to trap, poison them or otherwise kill them? Wildlife versus humans and domestic animals problem.

Significance: Getting rid of raccoons will increase our quality of life. Answer to ethical question will help us see when human needs should take priority over animals; when is it OK to harm animals? Are raccoons like rodents?

Example 3

Why do starlings change their ordinary behavior and start to swarm?

Describe the strange swarming behavior of starlings.

Show why this behavior is problematic by explaining that starlings don't usually act like this and that no other birds swarm the way starlings do. Explain that I have no theories why this behavior occurs or what triggers it.

This is significant because knowing this answer might tell us something about how the brains of birds have evolved.

TOPIC Guidepost #3

For those using Texas Tech's TOPIC Web-Based assignments:

Direct your web browser to **http://english.ttu.edu:5555**

Guidepost #3 provides full instructions regarding your reading assignment (Chapter 2) and Microtheme 0.1.

Pursuing Problems
Exploratory Writing and Talking

When Ofelya Bagdasaryan completed her first university exam in the United States, she was confident that she would earn a high grade. "I had studied hard, memorized the material and written it perfectly in the examination book," she recalled.

But Ofelya, 26, a recent immigrant from Armenia in the former Soviet Union, was in for a rude shock. When the exams were returned the following week, she discovered that the professor had given her a D. "But I repeated exactly what the textbook said," she told her teaching assistant. "Yes," he replied, "but you didn't tell us your [judgment of what the book said]."

—David Wallechinsky, *Journalist*

My professor said that I received a low grade on this essay because I just gave my opinion. Then she said that she didn't *care* what my *opinion* was; she wanted an *argument*."

—Student overheard in hallway

> "In management, people don't merely 'write papers,' they solve problems,"
> said [business professor Kimbrough Sherman]. . . . He explained that he wanted
> to construct situations where students would have to "wallow in complexity"
> and work their way out, as managers must.
>
> —A. Kimbrough Sherman, *Management Professor*

In the previous chapter, we introduced you to the role of the writer as questioner and problem poser. In this chapter and the next, we narrow our focus primarily to academic writing, which most frequently means closed-form, thesis-based essays and articles. Mastering this kind of writing is necessary to your success in college and requires a behind-the-scenes ability to think deeply and rigorously about problems, pursuing them at length. In this chapter we show you how to use exploratory writing and talking to do this behind-the-scenes work. The strategies explained in this chapter will help you develop powerful thinking and studying habits for every discipline.

◢ WHAT DOES A PROFESSOR WANT?

It is important for you to understand the kind of thinking that most college professors look for in student writing. As the first two chapter-opening quotations indicate, many first-year college students are baffled by their professors' responses to their writing. Ofelya Bagdasaryan mistakenly thought her teachers wanted her to rehash her textbook. The second student thought her teacher wanted her to describe how she felt about a subject (opinion), not why someone else ought to feel the same way (argument). But as management professor A. Kimbrough Sherman explains in the third quotation, college instructors expect students to wrestle with problems by applying the concepts, data, and thought processes they learn in a course to new situations. As Sherman puts it, students must learn to "wallow in complexity" and work their way out.

Learning to Wallow in Complexity

Wallowing in complexity is not what most first-year college students aspire to do. (Certainly that wasn't what we, the authors of this text, had uppermost in our minds when we sailed off to college!) New college students tend to shut down their creative thinking processes too quickly and head straight for closure to a problem. Harvard psychologist William Perry, who has studied the intellectual development of college students, found that few of them become skilled wallowers in complexity until late in their college careers. According to Perry, most students come to college as "dualists," believing that all questions have right or wrong answers, that professors know the right answers, and that the student's job is to learn them. Of course, these beliefs are partially correct. First-year students who hope to become second-year students must indeed understand and memorize mounds of facts, data, definitions, and basic concepts.

But true intellectual growth requires the kind of problematizing we discussed in Chapter 1. It requires students to *do* something with their new knowledge, to apply it to new situations, to conduct the kinds of inquiry, research, analysis, and argument pursued by experts in each discipline. Instead of confronting only questions that have right answers, students need to confront what cognitive psychologists call *ill-structured problems.*

An ill-structured problem is one that may not have a single, correct answer. Often these problems require the thinker to operate in the absence of full and complete data. People face ill-structured problems every day in their personal lives: What should I major in? Should I continue to date person X? Should I take this job or keep looking? Likewise, many decisions in professional and public life are excruciatingly difficult precisely because they concern ill-structured problems that are unsolvable in any clear-cut and certain way: What should be done about homelessness? What public policies will best solve the problem of global warming or the national debt or the lack of affordable health care for our citizens?

Similarly, college professors pursue ill-structured problems in their professional writing. The kinds of problems vary from discipline to discipline, but they all require the writer to use reasons and evidence to support a tentative solution. Because your instructors want you to learn how to do the same kind of thinking, they often phrase essay exam questions or writing assignments as ill-structured problems. They are looking not for one right answer, but for well-supported arguments that acknowledge alternative views. A C paper and an A paper may even have the same "answer" (identical thesis statements), but the C writer may have waded only ankle deep into the mud of complexity, whereas the A writer wallowed in it and worked a way out.

What skills are required for successful wallowing? Specialists in critical thinking have identified the following:

1. The ability to pose problematic questions
2. The ability to analyze a problem in all its dimensions—to define its key terms, determine its causes, understand its history, appreciate its human dimension and its connection to one's own personal experience, and appreciate what makes it problematic or complex
3. The ability (and doggedness) to find, gather, and interpret facts, data, and other information relevant to the problem (often involving library or field research)
4. The ability to imagine alternative solutions to the problem, to see different ways in which the question might be answered and different perspectives for viewing it
5. The ability to analyze competing approaches and answers, to construct arguments for and against alternatives, and to choose the best solution in light of values, objectives, and other criteria that you determine and articulate
6. The ability to write an effective argument justifying your choice while acknowledging counterarguments

We discuss and develop these skills throughout this text.

In addition to these generic thinking abilities, critical thinking requires what psychologists call *domain-specific* skills. Each academic discipline has its own characteristic ways of approaching knowledge and its own specialized habits of mind. The questions asked by psychologists differ from those asked by historians or anthropologists; the evidence and assumptions used to support arguments in literary analysis differ from those in philosophy or sociology.

What all disciplines value, however, is the ability to manage complexity, and this skill marks the final stage of William Perry's developmental scheme. At an intermediate stage of development, after they have moved beyond dualism, students become what Perry calls "multiplists." At this stage students believe that since the experts disagree on many questions, all answers are equally valid. Professors want students merely to have an opinion and to state it strongly. A multiplist believes that a low grade on an essay indicates no more than that the teacher didn't like his or her opinion. Multiplists are often cynical about professors and grades; to them, college is a game of guessing what the teacher wants to hear. Students emerge into Perry's final stages—what he calls "relativism" and "commitment in relativism"—when they are able to take a position in the face of complexity and to justify that decision through reasons and evidence while weighing and acknowledging contrary reasons and counterevidence. The three quotations that open this chapter exemplify Perry's scheme: Whereas the first student sees her task as recalling right answers, the second sees it as forcefully expressing an opinion, and Professor Sherman articulates what is expected at Perry's last stages—wading into the messiness of complexity and working your way back to solid ground.

Seeing Each Academic Discipline as a Field of Inquiry and Argument

When you study a new discipline, you must learn not only the knowledge that scholars in that discipline have acquired over the years, but also the processes they used to discover that knowledge. It is useful to think of each academic discipline as a network of conversations in which participants exchange information, respond to each other's questions, and express agreements and disagreements. The scholarly articles and books that many of your instructors write (or would write if they could find the time) are formal, permanent contributions to an ongoing discussion carried on in print. By extension, your college's or university's library is a huge collection of conversations frozen in time. Each book or article represents a contribution to a conversation; each writer agreed with some of his or her predecessors and disagreed with others.

As each discipline evolves and changes, its central questions evolve also, creating a fascinating, dynamic conversation that defines the discipline. At any given moment, scholars are pursuing hundreds of cutting-edge questions in each discipline. Table 2.1 provides examples of questions that scholars have debated over the years as well as questions they are addressing today.

Of course, students can't immediately address the current, cutting-edge questions of most disciplines, particularly the sciences. But even novice science students

TABLE 2.1 Scholarly Questions in Different Disciplines

Field	Examples of Current Cutting-Edge Questions	Examples of Historical Controversies
Anatomy	What is the effect of a pregnant rat's alcohol ingestion on the development of fetal eye tissue?	In 1628, William Harvey produced a treatise arguing that the heart, through repeated contractions, caused blood to circulate through the body. His views were attacked by followers of the Greek physician Galen.
Literature	To what extent does the structure of a work of literature, for example, Conrad's *Heart of Darkness,* reflect the class and gender bias of the author?	In the 1920s a group of New Critics argued that the interpretation of a work of literature should be based on close examination of the work's imagery and form and that the intentions of the writer and the biases of the reader were not important. These views held sway in U.S. universities until the late 1960s, when they came increasingly under attack by deconstructionists and other postmoderns, who claimed that author intentions and reader bias were an important part of the work's meaning.
Linguistics	Do all the languages of the world descend from the same protolanguage or, in the evolution of humankind, did a variety of languages spring up independently around the globe?	Do humans learn language through behavior modification, as proposed by many learning theorists in the 1950s, or is there an innate language-learning center in the brain that is "hard wired" to learn a language, as proposed by Noam Chomsky?
Psychology	What are the underlying causes of gender identification? To what extent are differences between male and female behavior explainable by nature (genetics, body chemistry) versus nurture (social learning)?	In the early 1900s, under the influence of Sigmund Freud, psychoanalytic psychologists began explaining human behavior in terms of unconscious drives and mental processes that stemmed from repressed childhood experiences. Later, psychoanalysts were opposed by behaviorists, who rejected the notion of the unconscious and explained behavior as responses to environmental stimuli.

can examine historical controversies. Beginning physics students, for example, can wrestle with Archimedes' problem of how to measure the volume of a crown, or with other early problems concerning the mechanics of levers, pulleys, and inclined planes. In the humanities and social sciences, beginning students are often asked to study, explore, and debate some of the enduring questions that have puzzled generations of scholars.

- Is there a rational basis for belief in God?
- Why does Hamlet delay?
- Should Truman have dropped the atomic bomb on Hiroshima?
  On Nagasaki?
- What is the most just economic system?
- Do humans have free will?

As you study a discipline, you are learning how to enter its network of conversations. To do so, you have to build up a base of knowledge about the discipline, learn its terminology, observe its conversations, read its major works, see how it asks questions, learn its methods. To help you get a clearer sense of how written "conversation" works within a discipline—that is, how a writer poses a question and proposes an answer—the next section examines a typical introduction to an academic article.

How a Prototypical Introduction Poses a Question and Proposes an Answer

To illustrate the typical structure of an academic introduction, we will use as our prototype an article by theoretical physicist Evelyn Fox Keller originally published in 1974 in *Harvard Magazine*. (A *prototype* is the most typical or generic instance of class. Thus a prototype dog might be a medium-sized mutt but not a Great Dane or a toy poodle; a prototype bird might be a robin or a blackbird or a crow, but not a hummingbird, a pelican, or an ostrich.) Because *Harvard Magazine* is an alumni publication rather than a specialized science journal, Keller's influential article is free of heavy academic jargon, making it easy to see the question/solution structure of a typical closed-form introduction.

Women in Science: An Analysis of a Social Problem

Are women's minds different from men's minds? In spite of the women's movement, the age-old debate centering around this question continues. We are surrounded by evidence of *de facto* differences between men's and women's intellects—in problems that interest them, in the ways they try to solve those problems, and in the professions they choose. Even though it has become fashionable to view such differences as environmental in origin, the temptation to seek an explanation in terms of innate differences remains a powerful one.

Perhaps the area in which this temptation is strongest is in science. Even those of us who would like to argue for intellectual equality are hard pressed to

Presentation of question

Shows why the question is problematic and significant

explain the extraordinarily meager representation of women in science, particularly in the upper echelons. Some would argue that the near absence of great women scientists demonstrates that women don't have the minds for true scientific creativity. While most of us would recognize the patent fallacies of this argument, it nevertheless causes us considerable discomfort. After all, the doors of the scientific establishment appear to have been open to women for some time now—shouldn't we begin to see more women excelling?

In the last fifty years the institutional barriers against women in science have been falling. During most of that time, the percentage of women scientists has declined, although recent years have begun to show an upswing. Of those women who do become scientists, few are represented in the higher academic ranks. In order to have a proper understanding of these data [the original article includes several tables showing the data], it is necessary to review the many influences that operate. I would like to argue that the convenient explanation that men's minds are intrinsically different from women's is not only unwarranted by the evidence, but in fact reflects a mythology that is in itself a major contribution to the phenomenon observed.

Presentation of thesis

This introduction, like most introductions to academic articles, includes the following prototypical features.

- *Focus on a clear question or problem to be investigated.*   In this case the question is stated explicitly: "Are women's minds different from men's minds?" In many introductions, the question is implied rather than stated directly.
- *Elaboration on the question, showing why it is both problematic and significant.*   In this case, Keller highlights competing explanations for the low number of famous women scientists: innate differences versus environment. The social significance of the problem is implied throughout.
- *The writer's tentative "answer" to this question (the essay's* **thesis),** *which must bring something new, surprising, or challenging to the audience.*   In closed-form articles, the thesis is stated explicitly, usually at the end of the introduction, following the expected sequence of question first and then the answer. Here Keller takes a strong stand in favor of environment over innate differences.
- *[optional] A forecasting statement previewing the content and shape of the rest of the article ("First I will discuss X, then Y, and finally Z").*   Keller's introduction doesn't forecast the structure of her article, but it clearly announces her two purposes: (1) to show that evidence does not support the intrinsic difference theory, and (2) to show that the intrinsic difference myth itself helps explain the paucity of women scientists.

Of course, the body of Keller's article has to present strong arguments to support her controversial thesis. What she presents is a shocking account of the social forces that hindered her professional development as a theoretical physicist: sexual favor seeking and harassment; "isolation, mockery, and suspicion"; "incessant prophecies of failure"; and the pressure to conform to conventional views about women. She concludes that preconceptions about gender roles "serve as strait jackets for men and women alike." Her article is often cited, favorably or unfavorably, by those on all sides of this debate, for the controversy between innate differences and environment in the formation of gender roles still rages today.

We have used Keller's article to show how academic writers—in posing a problem and proposing an answer—join an ongoing conversation. Many of the papers you will be asked to write in college will require you, in some way, to exhibit the same kind of thinking—to pose a problem; to assert a tentative, risky answer (your thesis); and to support it with reasons and evidence. One of the major aims of this book is to teach you how to do this kind of thinking and writing.

In the rest of this chapter we will explain the behind-the-scenes role of exploratory writing and talking. The neatness of Keller's introduction—its statement of a focused problem and its confidently asserted thesis—masks the messiness of the exploratory process that precedes the actual writing of an academic essay. Underneath the surface of finished academic papers is a long process of exploratory writing and talking—periods of intense thinking, reflecting, studying, researching, notebook or journal writing, and sharing. Through this process, the writer defines the question or problem and eventually works out an answer or response. Some of your professors may build opportunities for exploratory writing and talking directly into the course in the form of journals, in-class freewriting, collaborative group work, e-mail exchanges, class discussions and debates, and so forth. Other teachers will spend most of the class time lecturing and leave you on your own to explore ideas. The rest of this chapter presents strategies and techniques that many writers have found useful for exploring ideas.

◼ TECHNIQUES FOR EXPLORATORY WRITING AND TALKING

To use language for exploration, you need to imagine a friendly, nonjudgmental audience with whom you can share ideas in a risk-free environment. Perhaps you can imagine yourself as your audience, or, if you prefer, a friend or classmate. Your purpose is to get ideas down on paper to help you see what you are thinking. Exploratory writing jogs your memory, helps you connect disparate ideas, lets you put difficult concepts into your own words, and invites you to see the relevance of your studies to your own life. In this section we describe four useful techniques for exploratory writing and talking: freewriting, idea mapping, dialectic discussions, and active reading and research.

Freewriting

Freewriting, also sometimes called *nonstop writing* or *silent, sustained writing,* asks you to record your thinking directly. To freewrite, put pen to paper (or sit at your computer screen, perhaps turning *off* the monitor so that you can't even see what you are writing) and write rapidly, *nonstop,* for ten to fifteen minutes at a stretch. Don't worry about grammar, spelling, organization, transitions, or other features of edited writing. The object is to think of as many ideas as possible. Some freewriting looks like stream of consciousness. Some is more organized and focused, although it lacks the logical connections and development that would make it suitable for an audience of strangers.

Many freewriters find that their initial reservoir of ideas runs out in three to five minutes. If this happens, force yourself to keep your fingers moving. If you can't think of anything to say, write "Relax" over and over (or "This is stupid" or "I'm stuck") until new ideas emerge.

What do you write about? The answer varies according to your situation. Often you will freewrite in response to a question or problem posed by your instructor. Sometimes you will pose your own questions and use freewriting to explore possible answers or simply generate ideas. Since the authors are avid freewriters, we can use ourselves for illustration. We use freewriting for many purposes in our scholarly work. We freewrite when we are first becoming engaged with a problem. We often pose for ourselves trigger questions: "What really puzzles me about X?" "Why did I react so strongly to what person A said about X?" "How are my ideas about X different from A's?" We also freewrite extensively when doing scholarly reading. Although our notetaking systems differ, we both react strongly to articles or books we are reading and freewrite our own ideas about them into our notes. (See Chapter 7, in which we explain the process we use for "speaking back" to texts.) Finally, both of us freewrite when we get stuck in the process of writing a draft. If we come to a difficult section and find ourselves blocked, we turn away from the draft itself, find a sheet of scratch paper, and freewrite rapidly just to get the ideas flowing.

Many teachers assign freewriting in the form of journals, invention exercises for a formal essay, or in-class explorations. Mary Turla's journal entries, which you read in Chapter 1 (p. 9), are examples of freewriting. Here is another example of a student's freewrite in response to the prompt "What puzzles you about homelessness?"

> Let's see, what puzzles me about homelessness? Homeless homeless. Today on my way to work I passed a homeless guy who smiled at me and I smiled back though he smelled bad. What are the reasons he was out on the street? Perhaps an extraordinary string of bad luck. Perhaps he was pushed out onto the street. Not a background of work ethic, no place to go, no way to get someplace to live that could be afforded, alcoholism. To what extent do government assistance, social spending, etc, keep people off the street? What benefits could a person get that stops "the cycle"? How does welfare affect homelessness, drug abuse programs, family planning? To what extent does the individual have control over homelessness? This question of course goes to the depth of the question of how community affects the individual. Relax, relax. What about the signs that I see on the way to work posted on the windows of businesses that read, "please don't give to panhandlers it only promotes drug abuse etc" a cheap way of

getting homeless out of the way of business? Are homeless the natural end of unrestricted capitalism? What about the homeless people who are mentally ill? How can you maintain a living when haunted by paranoia? How do you decide if someone is mentally ill or just laughs at society? If one can't function obviously. How many mentally ill are out on the street? If you are mentally ill and have lost the connections to others who might take care of you I can see how you might end up on the street. What would it take to get treatment? To what extent can mentally ill be treated? When I see a homeless person I want to ask, How do you feel about the rest of society? When you see "us" walk by how do you think of us? Do you possibly care how we avoid you?

Note how this freewrite rambles, moving associatively from one topic or question to the next. Freewrites often have this kind of loose, associative structure. The value of such freewrites is that they help writers discover areas of interest or rudimentary beginnings of ideas. When you read back over one of your freewrites, try to find places that seem to you worth pursuing. Freewriters call these places hot spots, centers of interest, centers of gravity, or simply nuggets or seeds. The student who wrote the preceding freewrite discovered that he was particularly interested in the cluster of questions beginning "What about the homeless people who are mentally ill?" and he eventually wrote a research paper proposing a public policy for helping the mentally ill homeless. Because we think this technique is of great value to writers, we suggest that you use it to generate ideas for class discussions and essays.

Idea Mapping

Another good technique for exploring ideas is *idea mapping,* a more visual method than freewriting. To make an idea map, draw a circle in the center of the page and write down your broad topic area (or a triggering question or your thesis) inside the circle. Then record your ideas on branches and subbranches that extend out from the center circle. As long as you pursue one train of thought, keep recording your ideas on subbranches off the main branch. But as soon as that chain of ideas runs dry, go back and start a new branch.

Often your thoughts will jump back and forth between one branch and another. This technique will help you see them as part of an emerging design rather than as strings of unrelated ideas. Additionally, idea mapping establishes at an early stage a sense of hierarchy in your ideas. If you enter an idea on a subbranch, you can see that you are more fully developing a previous idea. If you return to the hub and start a new branch, you can see that you are beginning a new train of thought.

An idea map usually records more ideas than a freewrite, but the ideas are not as fully developed. Writers who practice both techniques report that they can vary the kinds of ideas they generate, depending on which technique they choose. Figure 2.1 (on p. 32) shows a student's idea map made while he was exploring issues related to the grading system.

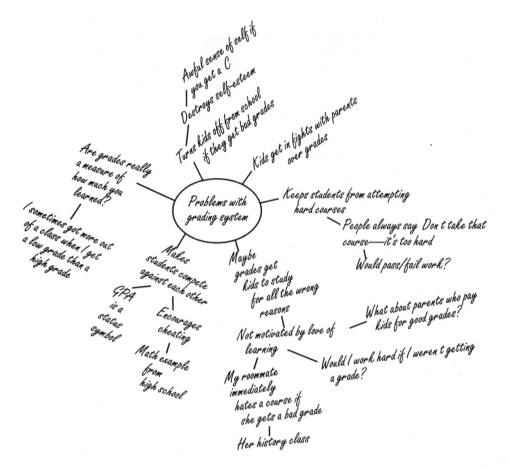

Awful sense of self if
you get a C

Destroys self-esteem

Turns kids off from school
if they get bad grades

Kids get in fights with parents
over grades

Are grades really
a measure of
how much you
learned?

I sometimes got more out
of a class when I get
a low grade than a
high grade

Problems with grading system

Keeps students from attempting
hard courses

People always say Don't take that
course—it's too hard

Would pass/fail work?

What about parents who pay
kids for good grades?

Would I work hard if I weren't getting
a grade?

Makes
students
compete
against each other

GPA
is a
status
symbol

Encourages
cheating

Math example
from
high school

Maybe
grades get
kids to study
for all the wrong
reasons

Not motivated by love of
learning

My roommate
immediately
hates a course if
she gets a bad grade

Her history class

FIGURE 2.1   Idea Map on Problems with the Grading System

Dialectic Discussion

Another effective way to explore the complexity of a topic is through face-to-face discussions with others, whether in class, over coffee in the student union, or late at night in bull sessions. Not all discussions are productive; some are too superficial and scattered, others too heated. Good ones are *dialectic*—participants with differing views on a topic try to understand each other and resolve their differences by examining contradictions in each person's position. The key to dialectic conversation is careful listening, made possible by an openness to each other's views. A dialectic discussion differs from a talk show shouting match or a pro–con debate in which proponents of opposing positions, their views set in stone, attempt to win the argument. In a dialectic discussion, participants assume that each position has strengths and weaknesses and that even the strongest position contains inconsistencies, which should be exposed and examined. When dialectic conversation works well, participants scrutinize their own positions more critically and deeply, and often alter their views. True dialectic conversation implies growth and change, not a hardening of positions. (For more discussion of how to work cooperatively with others through dialectic discussion, see Chapter 20 on working in groups.)

Active Reading and Research

If dialectic discussion engages you in live, face-to-face conversation with others, active reading and research engage you in conversation with others through reading. The key is to become an *active* reader who both listens to a piece of writing and speaks back to it through imaginative interaction with its author. Chapter 6 offers instruction on becoming an active reader, showing you how to read texts both with the grain and against the grain. In addition, Part Four, "A Guide to Research," describes in detail how to use an academic library as well as the Internet to find sources, how to use those sources to stimulate your own thinking, and how to incorporate them purposefully into your own writing.

When you pursue a question through active reading and research, you join the conversation of others who have contemplated and written about your problem. Not all college writing assignments require library or field research, but many do, and most of the rest can benefit by the process. The writing assignments in Part Two of this text involve varying degrees of research, depending on the assignments selected by your instructor and the problems you choose to pursue.

FOR WRITING AND DISCUSSION

The following exercise is a simulation game that asks you to try some of the exploratory writing and talking techniques we have discussed.

The Situation. The city attorney of a large U.S. city* has proposed a "get-tough" policy on "vagrants and panhandlers" in the city's downtown shopping areas. It is time, says the city attorney, to stand up for the rights of ordinary citizens to enjoy their city. Supported by the mayor, the city attorney is ready to present his proposal to the city council, which will vote to pass or reject the proposal. The details of the proposal are outlined in the following newspaper article:

Proposed Law Calls for Fines, Arrests

Proposed public-conduct ordinances before the Seattle
City Council focus on repeated drinking in public, urinating

---

*The actual city is Seattle, Washington, but this proposal is similar to those being debated in many cities across the United States. For the purposes of this simulation game, assume that the city in question is any city close to your college or university where homelessness is a serious problem.

in public, sitting or lying on public streets, aggressive panhandling and public drug trafficking. Among their provisions:

- The second and any subsequent drinking-in-public offense becomes a criminal misdemeanor punishable by up to 90 days in jail, a $1,000 fine and up to one year of probation.

- The second and any subsequent offense of urinating or defecating in public becomes a criminal misdemeanor punishable by up to 90 days in jail, a $1,000 fine and up to one year of probation.

- The purchase, possession or consumption of alcohol by those between ages 18 and 21 becomes a criminal misdemeanor punishable by jail, fine and probation.

- Between 7 a.m. and 9 p.m., it would be unlawful to sit or lie on sidewalks in commercial areas, including Broadway, the University District, other neighborhoods and downtown.

- A tighter definition of "intimidation" would be created to make the present law against aggressive panhandling more effective in prosecution.

- Alleys where drug trafficking occurs could be closed for specific periods of the day or night, except for authorized use. Those who enter without permission could be arrested.

The Task. In class, hold a simulated public hearing on this issue. Assign classmates to play the following roles: (1) a homeless person; (2) a downtown store owner; (3) a middle-class suburban home owner who used to shop downtown but hasn't done so for years because of all the "bums" lying on the streets; (4) an attorney from the American Civil Liberties Union who advocates for the civil rights of the homeless; (5) a college student who volunteers in a homeless shelter and knows many of the homeless by name; (6) a city council member supporting the proposal; (7) a city council member opposing it. Every class member should be assigned to one of these roles; later, all students assigned to a role will meet as a group to select the person to participate in the actual simulation.

The Procedure. (1) Begin with five minutes of freewriting. Class members should explore their own personal reactions to this ordinance. (2) Class members should freewrite again, this time from the perspective of the character they have been assigned to play in the simulation. (3) Classmates should meet in groups according to assigned roles in the simulation, share freewrites, and make a group idea map exploring all the arguments that the group's assigned character might make. Group members can choose a person to play the role; those not chosen can play members of the city council. (4) Allow time for people playing the roles to develop their arguments fully and to exchange views. (5) After each participant has spoken, the remaining members of the class, acting as city council members, should sit in a circle and hold a dialectic discussion (listening carefully to each other rather than conducting a shouting match), trying to decide whether to accept or reject the city attorney's proposal. (6) Finally, the class should hold a vote to see whether the proposal is accepted or rejected.

◿ HOW TO MAKE EXPLORATORY WRITING AND TALKING WORK FOR YOU

All of the formal writing assignments in Part II of this text have built-in opportunities for exploratory writing and talking, but we hope you will use the techniques in this chapter for all of your college courses. In this final section of the chapter we will discuss some of the habits you can cultivate to make exploratory writing and talking a regular part of your intellectual life.

Make Marginal Notes on Readings

Experienced scholars often make extensive notes in the margins of books and articles. (If you don't own the book, you will need to write your notes in a journal or reading log.) In Chapter 6 we discuss this technique in detail, showing how critical readers regularly write two kinds of marginal notations: (1) *summarizing notes* that help them understand and recall the gist of the text, and (2) *responding notes* that help readers "speak back" to the text by agreeing or disagreeing, posing questions, drawing connections to other ideas, supplying new examples from their own experience, and so forth. See pages 108–23 for further elaboration of this method.

Keep a Journal or Learning Log

Another good exploratory strategy is to keep a *journal* or *learning log*. Many teachers assign journals in their courses and provide guidance about topics to explore. Most professional writers keep regular journals, since they know that ideas for formal pieces often take root in a journal as they record daily observations, play with ideas, and reflect thoughtfully upon the "stuff" of their lives. You can keep a journal or learning log for any of your courses by posing questions about course material and then writing out exploratory answers.

Discuss Your Ideas with E-Mail Correspondents

At a number of institutions, teachers use electronic mail (e-mail) to connect students with each other. The great advantage of e-mail is that it facilitates dialogue in a leisurely, nonthreatening atmosphere. You and classmates can share questions and insights, rehearse your understanding of course material, and try out new ideas. In many situations, the teacher can also enter the conversation, asking questions and stimulating further dialogue.

If your teacher doesn't set up an e-mail network for your course, you can set up your own by finding classmates with e-mail accounts. Sometimes, too, if you are doing research on a particular problem, you can find an international network of people interested in the same topic through an Internet Listserv, news group, or chat room (see Chapter 23).

Join Focused Study Groups

A focused study group, unlike a bull session, is a collection of individuals who voluntarily come together to study for a course. Many students do their best work by alternating between private and communal study. Focused study groups work best if members prepare for them in advance by creating lists of questions about course material and focusing first on comprehension. If parts of the material are confusing to everyone in your study group, then you can formulate questions to ask the teacher. Focused study groups also help you predict the kinds of critical thinking questions teachers are apt to ask on exams. When they function effectively, study groups can stimulate thinking about course material and send you back to private study with more confidence and an enhanced appreciation for complexity.

Participate Effectively in Class Discussions

Class discussion provides an excellent opportunity for exploratory talking. The key is learning to listen to classmates' ideas and to tie your own contributions to what others have said. Often students are so busy rehearsing what they want to say in a class discussion that they fail to listen carefully to other points of view, thus diminishing their sense of the topic's complexity. Because it is difficult to take class notes on a good discussion (ideas are flying everywhere, and you don't know what is important and what isn't), many students don't take notes in class but summarize what they got out of discussion as soon as class ends.

◼ CHAPTER SUMMARY

In this chapter we looked at the kind of wallowing in complexity that professors expect from students and introduced techniques for exploratory writing and talking that will help you become fully engaged in an academic problem. We saw how an academic essay contributes to a conversation by posing a question and then offering a tentative and risky answer. We also saw how an academic essay is preceded by a long process of thinking, reflecting, studying, researching, and talking. The starting point for such an essay is exploratory writing and talking. We explained four strategies for exploring ideas—freewriting, idea mapping, dialectic conversation, and active reading and research—and then offered suggestions for making exploratory writing and talking a regular habit throughout your academic career.

BRIEF PROJECT

One of the best ways to dwell with a problem is to play what writing theorist Peter Elbow calls the "believing and doubting game." This game helps you appreciate the power of alternative arguments and points of view by urging you to formulate and explore alternative positions. To play the game, you imagine a possible answer to a problematic question and then systematically try first to believe that answer and then to doubt it.

Playing the Believing and Doubting Game

Play the believing and doubting game with two of the following assertions (or other assertions provided by your instructor). For one of the assertions, play the game by freewriting your believing and doubting responses (following the example on pages 36–37). For your second assertion, use the idea-mapping method. Label one side of your center circle "Believe" and the other side "Doubt." Spend approximately twenty minutes believing and doubting each assertion for a total of about forty minutes for the whole assignment.

1. State and federal governments should legalize hard drugs.
2. Grades are an effective means of motivating students to do their best work.
3. If I catch someone cheating on an exam or plagiarizing a paper, I should report that person to the instructor.
4. The city council should pass a get-tough policy on vagrants (see For Writing and Discussion, pp. 31–33).
5. In recent years advertising has made enormous gains in portraying women as strong, independent, and intelligent.
6. For grades 1 through 12, the school year should be extended to eleven months.
7. It is a good idea to make children take music lessons.
8. States should legalize marriage for gays and lesbians.
9. Cutting off welfare payments for single mothers will reduce teenage pregnancy.
10. Hate speech should be forbidden on college campuses.

When you play the believing side of this game, you try to become sympathetic to an idea or point of view. You listen carefully to it, opening yourself to the possibility that it is true. You try to appreciate why the idea has force for so many people; you try to accept it by discovering as many reasons as you can for believing it. It is easy to play the believing game with ideas you already believe in, but the game becomes more difficult, sometimes even frightening and dangerous, when you try believing ideas that seem untrue or disturbing.

The doubting game is the opposite of the believing game. It calls for you to be judgmental and critical, to find fault with an idea rather than to accept it. When you doubt a new idea, you try your best to falsify it, to find counterexamples that disprove it, to find flaws in its logic. Again, it is easy to play the doubting game with ideas you don't like, but it, too, can be threatening when you try to doubt ideas that are dear to your heart or central to your own worldview.

Student Example

Here is how one student played the believing and doubting game with the following assertion from professional writer Paul Theroux that emphasizing sports is harmful to boys.

> Just as high school basketball teaches you how to be a poor loser, the manly attitude towards sports seems to be little more than a recipe for creating bad marriages, social misfits, moral degenerates, sadists, latent rapists and just plain louts. I regard high school sports as a drug far worse than marijuana.

Believe

Although I am a woman I have a hard time believing this because I was a high school basketball player and believe high school sports are *very* important. But here goes. I will try to believe this statement even though I hate it. Let's see. It would seem that I wouldn't have much first-hand experience with how society turns boys into men. I do see though that Theroux is right about some major problems. Through my observations, I've seen many young boys go through humiliating experiences with sports that have left them scarred. For example, a 7-year-old boy, Matt, isn't very athletic and when kids in our neighborhood choose teams, they usually choose girls before they choose Matt. I wonder if he sees himself as a sissy and what this does to him? I have also experienced some first-hand adverse affects of society's methods of turning boys into men. In our family, my dad spent much of his time playing football, basketball, and baseball with my brother. I've loved sports since I was very young so I was eager to play. In order to play with them, I had to play like a boy. Being told you threw or played like a girl was the worst possible insult you could receive. The phrase, "be tough" was something I heard repeatedly while I was growing up. Whenever I got hurt, my dad would say, "Be tough." It didn't matter how badly I was hurt, I always heard the same message. Today, I think, I have a very, very difficult time opening up and letting people get to know me, because for so long I was taught to keep everything inside. Maybe sports does have some bad effects.

Doubt

I am glad I get to doubt this too because I have been really mad at all the sports bashing that has been going on in class. I think much of what Theroux says is just a crock. I know that the statement "sports builds character" is a cliché, but I really believe it. It seems to me that the people who lash out at sports clichés are those who never experienced these aspects of athletics and therefore don't understand them. No one can tell me that sports didn't contribute to some of my best and most meaningful friendships and growing experiences. I am convinced that I am a better person because through sports I have had to deal with failure, defeat, frustration, sacrificing individual desires for the benefit of the team, and so on. After my last high school basketball game when after many years of mind games, of hating my coach one minute and the next having deep respect for him, of big games lost on my mistakes, of hours spent alone in the gym, of wondering if the end justifies the means, my coach put his arm around me and told me he was proud. Everything, all the pain, frustration, anxiety, fear, and sacrifice of the past years seemed so worthwhile. You might try to tell me that this story is hackneyed and trite, but I won't listen because it is a part of me, and something you will never be able to damage or take away. I think athletes share a special bond. They know what it is like to go through the physical pain of practice time and again. They understand the wide variety of emotions felt (but rarely expressed). They also know what a big role the friendships of teammates and coaches play in an athlete's life.

We admire this writer a great deal—both for the passion with which she defends sports in her doubting section and for the courage of walking in a sports basher's shoes in the believing section. This exercise clearly engaged and stretched her thinking.

This brief writing assignment asks you to stretch your own thinking by choosing any two of the assigned assertions and practicing believing and doubting each in turn. Use freewriting to explore your first assertion. Spend ten minutes believing the assertion and ten minutes doubting it for a total of twenty minutes. Then choose a second assertion, but this time use idea mapping. Spend ten minutes entering reasons for believing the assertion and then ten minutes for doubting it (or move back and forth between believing and doubting, since an idea map gives you this flexibility), again for a total of twenty minutes. The total assignment should take forty minutes.

TOPIC Guidepost #6

For those using Texas Tech's TOPIC Web-Based assignments:

Direct your web browser to **http://english.ttu.edu:5555**

Guidepost #6 provides full instructions regarding your reading assignment (Chapter 3) and Draft 1.1.

c h a p t e r 3

Solving Content Problems

Thesis and Support

WHAT YOU WILL LEARN IN THIS CHAPTER:

In this chapter you will learn the importance of drafting as a problem-solving process in which writers seek a surprising thesis and convincing support. In particular, you will learn the following:

- How to create a thesis statement aimed at changing your readers' view of the topic
- How to give your thesis tension
- How to support your thesis with a network of points and particulars

By seeing how points convert information to meaning, you will understand essential structural principles behind closed-form prose that will help you revise your drafts, write summaries, and move easily up and down the scale of abstraction.

> The commonsense, conventional understanding of writing is as follows. Writing is a two-step process. First you figure out your meaning, then you put it into language. . . . This idea of writing is backwards. . . . Meaning is not what you start out with but what you end up with.
>
> —Peter Elbow, *Writing Teacher and Theorist*

Chapter 2 explained how to use exploratory writing and talking to discover and develop ideas. This chapter and the next describe the kinds of problems that experienced writers try to solve as they move beyond exploratory writing and talking to produce a formal finished product. This chapter explains how writers of academic essays seek a final product that poses a good question, has a surprising thesis, and supports that thesis with strong arguments and convincing detail. Chapter 4 shifts from subject-matter problems to rhetorical problems and demonstrates that what writers say and how they say it are controlled by their purpose, intended audience, and genre. In these two chapters we temporarily separate subject-matter problems from rhetorical problems for the sake of instructional clarity. But, like the classic problem of the chicken and the egg, it is impossible to say which should or can be addressed first, subject-matter problems (What's my thesis? What's my supporting evidence?) or rhetorical problems (Who's my audience? What's my purpose?). Throughout the writing process, writers wrestle simultaneously and recursively with both subject-matter problems and rhetorical problems.

■ DRAFTING AND REVISING AS A PROBLEM-SOLVING PROCESS

Beginning writers often don't appreciate the extent to which experienced writers struggle when they compose. Unlike beginning writers, who often think of revision as cleaning up errors in a rough draft, experienced writers use the writing process to "wallow in complexity." The more experienced the writer, the more likely that he or she will make large-scale, global revisions in a draft rather than local, sentence-level changes. Experienced writers, in fact, often dismantle their first constructions and start fresh. They build on what they learned the first time to create a more appropriate structure the second time around. Chapter 10 describes this writing process in more detail.

Our point in this chapter is that writers often need multiple drafts because early in the writing process they may be unsure of what they want to say or where their ideas are headed. As Peter Elbow puts it (in the epigraph for this chapter), "Meaning is not what you start out with but what you end up with." To appreciate Elbow's point, consider the following partial transcript of a writing center conference in which the student writer is responding to a political science assignment: Is U.S. involvement in Central America a case of imperialism?

TUTOR: If I said, tell me whether or not this is imperialism, what's your first gut reaction?...

WRITER: There's very strong arguments for both. It's just all in how you define it.

TUTOR: Okay, who's doing the defining?

WRITER: Anybody. That's just it, there's no real clear definition. Over the time it's been distorted. I mean, before, imperialism used to be like the British who go in and take Hong Kong, set up their own little thing that's their own British government. That's true imperialism. But the definition's been expanded to include indirect control by other means, and what exactly that is, I guess you have to decide. So I don't know. I don't think we really have control in Central America, so that part of me says no that's not imperialism. But other parts of me say we really do control a lot of what is going on in Central America by the amount of dollars and where we put them. So in that essence, we do have imperialism....

TUTOR: So you're having a hard time making up your mind whether it is or isn't imperialism?

WRITER: Yes! The reason why I'm undecided is because I couldn't create a strong enough argument for either side. There's too many holes in each side. If I were to pick one side, somebody could blow me out of the water. . . .

This student writer is blocked because she thinks she has to make up her mind about her issue before she starts writing. The assigned problem requires her both to define imperialism and to argue whether U.S. activity in Central America meets the definition. What we admire about this student is that she is "wallowing in complexity," fully aware of the problem's difficulty and actively confronting alternative views. The best way for her to think through these complexities, we would argue, is to start doing exploratory writing—freewriting, idea mapping, or another of the strategies described in Chapter 2. This exploratory writing can then evolve into a first draft. Our point here is that the act of writing generates thought. The more she writes, the more she will clarify her own ideas. Her first drafts may have to be dismantled once she finally commits herself to a position. But the discarded drafts won't have been wasted; they will have helped her to manage the complexity of the assignment.

This writer needs to realize that her difficulty is a sign of strength. A good thesis statement is a risky one. Knowing that a skeptical reader might "blow you out of the water" motivates you to provide the best support possible for your thesis while acknowledging the power of opposing views. Perhaps this writer hopes that a miraculous insight will give her the "correct" solution, which she can then write out effortlessly. "In your dreams," we reply. Or perhaps she thinks that her present difficulty is a sign of her own inadequacy. To the contrary, her awareness of complexity and risk means that she is on the right track.

◢ TAKING RISKS: SEEKING A SURPRISING THESIS

As we have seen, most academic writing is thesis based. By *thesis based* we mean that the writer aims to support a main point or thesis statement, which is the writer's one-sentence summary answer to the problem or question that the paper addresses. The writer supports the thesis with reasons and evidence because he or she assumes that the audience will regard it skeptically and will test it against other possible answers. As the quotation from Peter Elbow implies, many writers do not formulate their final arguments until quite late in the writing process because they are constantly testing their ideas as they draft. The underlying motivation for multiple drafting is the search for a strong argument headed by a strong thesis.

But what makes a thesis strong? For one thing, a strong thesis always contains an element of uncertainty, risk, or challenge. A strong thesis implies a counter thesis. According to Elbow, a thesis has "got to stick its neck out, not just hedge or wander. [It is] something that can be quarreled with." Elbow's sticking-its-neck-out metaphor is a good one, but we prefer to say that a strong thesis *surprises* the reader with a new, unexpected, different, or challenging view of the writer's topic. In this section, we present two ways of creating a surprising thesis: (1) trying to change your reader's view of your subject and (2) giving your thesis tension.

Try to Change Your Reader's View of Your Subject

To change your reader's view of your subject, you must first imagine how the reader would view the subject *before* reading your essay. Then you can articulate how you aim to change that view. A useful exercise is to write out the "before" and "after" views of your imagined readers.

Before reading my essay, my readers think this way about my topic:

_____.

After reading my essay, my readers will think this different way about my

topic: _____.

You can change your reader's view of a subject in several ways.* First, you can enlarge it. Writing that enlarges a view is primarily informational; it provides new ideas and data to add to a reader's store of knowledge about the subject. For example, a research paper on wind-generated electricity might have the following thesis: "The technology for producing wind-generated electricity has improved remarkably in recent years." (Before reading my essay, the reader has only limited, out-of-date knowledge of wind-power technology; after reading my essay, the reader will have up-to-date knowledge.)

Second, you can clarify your reader's view of something that was previously fuzzy, tentative, or uncertain. Writing of this kind often explains, analyzes, or interprets. Engineers, for example, in comparing the environmental impact of dams versus wind towers might be uncertain how to calculate the environmental impact of dams when their costs (loss of fish runs, destruction of streams and natural habitats) are weighed against their benefits (flood control, irrigation, power generation). An economist might write an article that would clarify this problem. (Before reading my article, engineers and politicians will be uncertain how to measure the environmental costs of dams. After reading my article, these persons will have a clearer understanding of how to calculate these costs.)

Still another kind of change occurs when an essay actually restructures a reader's whole view of a subject. Such essays persuade readers to change their minds or make decisions. They can be threatening to a reader's identity because they shake up closely held beliefs and values. For example, in Chapter 1 we printed a letter to the editor written by a civil engineer who argued that "wind-generated power can in no way serve as a reasonable major alternative [to hydro, coal-fired, or nuclear power]." (Before reading my letter, the reader believes that

---

*Our discussion of how writing changes a reader's view of the world is indebted to Richard Young, Alton Becker, and Kenneth Pike, *Rhetoric: Discovery and Change* (New York: Harcourt Brace & Company, 1971).

wind-generated power is a solution to our energy crisis; after reading my letter, the reader will believe that wind-generated power is a pipe dream.) One person we know—a committed environmentalist with high hopes for wind energy—said that this letter persuaded him that large-scale harnessing of wind energy wouldn't work. He was visibly dismayed; the engineer's argument had knocked his view of wind energy off its props. (We aren't saying, of course, that the engineer is *correct*. We are saying only that his letter persuaded at least one of our acquaintances to change his mind about wind energy.)

Surprise, then, is the measure of change an essay brings about in a reader. (Of course, to bring about such change requires more than just a surprising thesis; the essay itself must persuade the reader that the thesis is sound as well as novel. In the last part of this chapter we talk about how writers support a thesis through a network of points and particulars.)

Give Your Thesis Tension

Another element of a surprising thesis is tension. By *tension* we mean the reader's sensation of being stretched from a familiar, unsurprising idea to a new, surprising one or of being twisted by two ideas pushing in opposing directions.

Theses that induce stretching are compelling because they continually give the reader something new to consider. Often the purpose of these essays is to inform, explain, or analyze. They are satisfying because they fill gaps in knowledge as they take the reader on a journey from old, familiar ground into new territory—stretching the reader, as it were, into a new place. Stretching theses teach readers something they didn't already know about a subject.

A thesis designed to twist a reader sets up an opposition between the writer's claims and various counterclaims. The reader is asked to choose among alternative ways of looking at a topic. Twisting theses argue for a particular view of the subject in the face of alternative or countering views.

One of the best ways to create tension in a thesis statement is to begin the statement with an *although* or *whereas* clause: "Whereas most people believe X, this essay asserts Y." The *whereas* or *although* clause summarizes the reader's "before" view of your topic or the counterclaim that your essay opposes; the main clause states the surprising view or position that your essay will support. You may choose to omit the *although* clause from your actual essay, but formulating it first will help you achieve focus and surprise in your thesis. The examples that follow illustrate the kinds of tension we have been discussing and show why tension is a key requirement for a good thesis.

Question	What effect has the telephone had on our culture?
Thesis Without Tension	The invention of the telephone has brought many advantages to our culture.
Thesis with Tension	Although the telephone has brought many advantages to our culture, it may also have contributed to the increase of violence in our society.

Question	Do reservations serve a useful role in contemporary Native American culture?
Thesis Without Tension	Reservations have good points and bad points.
Thesis with Tension	Although my friend Wilson Real Bird believes that reservations are necessary for Native Americans to preserve their heritage, the continuation of reservations actually degrades Native American culture.

In the first example, the thesis without tension (telephones have brought advantages to our culture) is a truism with which everyone would agree and hence lacks surprise. The thesis with tension places this truism (the reader's "before" view) in an "although" clause and goes on to make a risky or contestable assertion. The surprising idea that the telephone contributes to violence shakes up our old, complacent view of the telephone as a beneficent instrument, and gives us a new way to regard telephones.

In the second example, the thesis without tension may not at first seem tensionless because the writer sets up an opposition between good and bad points. But *almost anything* has good and bad points, so the opposition is not meaningful, and the thesis offers no element of surprise. Substitute virtually any other social institution (marriage, the postal service, the military, prisons), and the statement that it has good and bad points would be equally true. The thesis with tension, in contrast, is risky. It commits the writer to argue that reservations have degraded Native American culture and to oppose the counterthesis that reservations are needed to *preserve* Native American culture. The reader is twisted by the tension between two opposing views.

We have used the terms *stretching* and *twisting* to help you see various ways in which a thesis can have tension, but it is not important to make sharp distinctions between the two. Frequently, a thesis stretches and twists simultaneously. What *is* important is that you see that the writer's goal is to surprise the reader in some way, thereby bringing about some kind of change in the reader's view. A thesis can surprise a reader by doing the following:

- giving the reader new information or clarifying a confusing concept
- posing a dilemma by juxtaposing two or more differing answers to the same question or by finding paradoxes or contradictions in an area that others regard as nonproblematic
- identifying an unexpected effect, implication, or significance of something
- showing underlying differences between two concepts normally thought to be similar or underlying similarities between two concepts normally thought to be different
- showing that a commonly accepted answer to a question isn't satisfactory or that a commonly rejected answer may be satisfactory
- opposing a commonly accepted viewpoint, supporting an unpopular viewpoint, or otherwise taking an argumentative stance on an issue
- providing a new solution for a problem

FOR WRITING AND DISCUSSION

It is difficult to create thesis statements on the spot because a writer's thesis grows out of an exploratory struggle with a problem. However, through brief exploratory writing and talking it is sometimes possible to arrive at a thesis that is both surprising and arguable. Working individually, spend ten minutes freewriting on one of the following topics chosen by your class or the instructor:

competitive sports   mathematics education
commuting by automobile   television talk shows
homelessness   sex-education classes
gangs   zoos

Then, working in small groups or as a whole class, share your freewrites, looking for elements in each person's freewrite that surprise other members of the class. From the ensuing discussion, develop questions or problems that lead to one or more surprising thesis statements. Each thesis should be supportable through personal experiences, previous reading and research, or critical thinking; for example:

Topic	Competitive Sports.
Question	Is it psychologically beneficial to participate in competitive sports?
Surprising Thesis	Although we normally think that playing competitive sports is good for us psychologically, the psychological traits that coaches try to develop in athletes are like anorectic dieting.

◢ SUPPORTING A THESIS: POINTS AND PARTICULARS

Of course, a surprising thesis is only one aspect of an effective essay. An essay must also persuade the reader that the thesis is sound as well as surprising. Although tabloid newspapers have shocking headlines ("Thigh cream found to be a cheap alternative to fossil fuel!" "Elvis captains UFO that buzzes home of Dennis Rodman!"), skepticism quickly replaces surprise when we discover that within the articles the claims are unsupported. A strong thesis, then, must both surprise a reader and be supported with convincing particulars.

In fact, the particulars are the flesh and bone of writing and comprise most of the sentences. A principle of closed-form prose is that these particulars are always connected clearly to points and that the points precede the particulars. In this section, we want to help you understand this principle more fully because it will give you a powerful conceptual understanding of what effective closed-form writing does.

How Points Convert Information to Meaning

When particulars are clearly related to a point, that point converts information to meaning. To put it another way, a point's function is to state a meaning. A particular's function is to support a point: Particulars constitute the evidence, data, details, specifics, examples, explanations, and so forth that develop a point and make it convincing. By themselves, particulars are inert information—mere data without meaning.

You can see this difference for yourself in the following exercise. Here is a short list of information about a room in Dorkfinkster Hall.

- Dingy paint is peeling from the walls.
- Several light bulbs are burned out.
- The windows are dirty.

To convert this list of information into a meaningful unit, you need to make a point. What point might a writer have in mind if she wanted to mention peeling paint, burned-out light bulbs, and dirty windows? Although lots of variations are possible, she might solve the problem like this:

> The rooms in Dorkfinkster Hall are poorly maintained. Dingy paint is peeling from the walls, several light bulbs are burned out, and the windows are dirty.

Here her opening sentence makes a point and thus gives meaning to the list of information.

Now try a variation of the same exercise. Consider the same list of information about a room in Dorkfinkster Hall. Add several more pieces of information that could also be plausibly true about the room.

Since all the particulars on the list imply poor maintenance, most people continue with this meaning as they invent new particulars for the list:

- There are dead flies on the window sills.
- The floors have stained splotches.
- Some of the desks are sticky with spilled pop.

However, the exercise itself doesn't specify "poor maintenance" information; it asks for any kind of information. So the following data about the room would also fit the task:

- The room is rectangular and contains fifty movable desks.
- The wall clock has black hands on a white face.
- The window frames are two inches wide.

Obviously, once people start listing raw information, they can keep going forever. But reasonable people don't like lists of raw information; they like meanings. Hence our minds naturally intuited "poor maintenance" in the original list and continued with poor maintenance data. In closed-form prose, writers need to state those meanings explicitly in point sentences. What we should see is that the point sentence "The rooms in Dorkfinkster Hall are poorly maintained" is not an individual datum about the room, but rather a writer-created generalization that states a meaning found in some of the data about the room—the burned-out light bulbs, the peeling paint, the filthy windows—but not in the other equally true data concerning the number of desks or the width of the window frames.

These examples should make clear that a sentence like "The rooms in Dorkfinkster Hall are poorly maintained" is fundamentally different from a sentence like "There are fifty moveable desks in the room." The first sentence is a *point,* whereas the second is a *particular*—that is, a specific piece of information, a fact. Obviously, reasonable people seek some kind of coordination between points and particulars, some sort of weaving back and forth between them. Writing teachers use a number of nearly synonymous terms for expressing this paired relationship: points/particulars, generalizations/specifics; claims/evidence; ideas/details; interpretations/data, meaning/support.

By definition, the highest-level point sentence in an essay is called its *thesis statement* and the highest-level point sentence in a paragraph is its *topic sentence.* But in reality essays have many more levels of points than just the thesis statement and the topic sentences of paragraphs. Several paragraphs can work together to support a single major point while an individual paragraph might have several subpoints. As an example of how small blocks of meaning (a point with its supporting particulars) get nested into a larger essay, consider how our little miniparagraph on Dorkfinkster Hall could function as part of a larger essay with this thesis: "The Administration at this college doesn't care about its students." Our hypothetical essay could have the following outline:

Thesis: The Administration at this college doesn't care about its students.

I.   Registration day is absolute chaos.
        [Particulars about problems with registration day]
II. Student services are inadequate.
        [Particulars about bad student services]
III. The physical plant is in bad shape.

   A. The Student Union Building is falling apart.

      1. Broken tables in the cafeteria

      2. Moldy smell in the game room

      3. Restrooms have leaky plumbing

   B. Dorkfinkster Hall is poorly maintained.

      1. Peeling paint on the walls

      2. Burned out light bulbs

      3. Windows dirty

As this outline shows, the writer has three complaints: registration day is chaos, student services are inadequate, and the physical plant is in bad shape. Our miniparagraph on Dorkfinkster Hall now functions as support for the writer's last main point.

How Removing Particulars Creates a Summary

What we have shown, then, is that skilled writers weave back and forth between generalizations and specifics. The generalizations form a network of higher-level and lower-level points that develop the thesis; the particulars (specifics) support each of the points and subpoints in turn. In closed-form prose, the network of points is easily discernible because points are clearly highlighted with transitions and main points are placed prominently at the heads of paragraphs. (In open-form prose, generalizations are often left unstated, creating gaps where the reader must actively fill in meaning.)

If you remove most of the particulars from a closed-form essay, leaving only the network of points, you will have written a summary or abstract of the essay. As an example, reread the civil engineer's letter to the editor arguing against the feasibility of wind-generated power (pp. 10–11). The writer's argument can be summarized in a single sentence:

> Wind-generated power is not a reasonable alternative to other forms of power in the Pacific Northwest because wind power is unreliable, because there are major unsolved problems involved in the design of wind generation facilities, and because the environmental impact of building thousands of wind towers would be enormous.

What we have done in this summary is remove the particulars, leaving only the high-level points that form the skeleton of the argument. The writer's thesis remains surprising and contains tension, but without the particulars the reader has no idea whether to believe the generalizations or not. The presence of the particulars is thus essential to the success of the argument.

FOR WRITING AND DISCUSSION

Compare Rockwood's original letter with the one-sentence summary just given and then note how Rockwood uses specific details to support each point. How do these particulars differ from paragraph to paragraph? How are they chosen to support each point?

How to Use Your Knowledge About Points and Particulars When You Revise

The lesson to learn here is that in closed-form prose writers regularly place a point sentence in front of detail sentences. When a writer begins with a point, readers interpret the ensuing particulars not as random data, but rather as *evidence* in support of that point. The writer depends on the particulars to make the point credible and persuasive.

This insight may help you clarify two of the most common kinds of marginal comments that readers (or teachers) place on writers' early drafts. If your draft has a string of sentences giving data or information unconnected to any stated point, your reader is apt to write in the margin, "What's your point here?" or "Why are you telling me this information?" "How does this information relate to your thesis?" Conversely, if your draft tries to make a point that isn't developed with particulars, your reader is apt to write marginal comments such as "Evidence?" "Development?" "Could you give an example?" and "More details needed."

Don't be put off by these requests; they are a gift. It is common in first drafts for main points to be unstated, buried, or otherwise disconnected from their details and for supporting information to be scattered confusingly through the draft or missing entirely. Having to write point sentences obliges you to wrestle with your intended meaning: Just what am I trying to say here? How can I nutshell that in a point? Likewise, having to support your points with particulars causes you to wrestle with the content and shape of your argument: What particulars will make this point convincing? What further research do I need to do to find these particulars? In Part Three of this text, which is devoted to advice about composing and revising, we show how the construction and location of point sentences are essential for reader clarity. Part Three also explains various composing and revising strategies that will help you create effective networks of points and particulars.

Moving Up and Down the Scale of Abstraction

We have said, then, that writers weave back and forth between points and particulars. But the distinction between points and particulars is a matter of context: A point in one context can be a particular in another. For example, the sentence "The rooms in Dorkfinkster Hall are poorly maintained" is a point in relationship to the specific details about dirty windows and burned out light bulbs, but it is a particular in relationship to the larger point "This college doesn't care about its students." What matters is the relative position of sentences along a scale of abstraction. As an illustration of such a scale, consider the following list of words, descending from the abstract to the specific:

living creature

animal

mammal

cow

Holstein

Twyla

old sleepy-eyed Twyla chewing her cud

This scale takes you from a general word that encompasses all living creatures down to a specific phrase, the details of which represent one specific cow—old sleepy-eyed Twyla.

In descriptive and narrative prose, writers often use sensory details very low on the scale of abstraction. Note how shifting down the scale improves the vividness of the following passage:

Mid-scale	The awkward, badly dressed professor stood at the front of the room.
Low on the scale	At the front of the room stood the professor, a tall, gawky man with inch-thick glasses, an enormous Adam's apple, wearing a manure brown jacket, burgundy and gray plaid pants, a silky vest with what appeared to be "scenes from an aquarium" printed on it, and a polka dot blue tie.

The details in the more specific passage help you experience the writer's world. They don't just tell you that the professor was dressed weirdly; they *show* you.

Academic or professional prose also often uses particulars that are low on the scale of abstraction—statistics, facts, quotations, or specific examples. Civil engineer David Rockwood uses low-on-the-scale numerical data about the size and number of wind towers to convince readers that wind generation of electricity entails environmental damage. But particulars don't always have to be concrete sensory details (such as the colors of the professor's tie and jacket) or highly specific factual or numerical data (such as those used in Rockwood's letter). Some kinds of writing remain at fairly high levels of abstraction, especially in academic prose on theoretical or philosophical topics. Yet even the most theoretical kind of prose will include several layers on the scale. Each of the assignment chapters in Part Two of this text gives advice on finding the right kinds and levels of particulars to support each essay.

FOR WRITING AND DISCUSSION

Working as individuals, what kinds of particulars could you use to support each of the provided points? Share your results as a whole class or in small groups. This exercise is a warm-up for the brief writing assignment at the end of this chapter.

1. The weather was beautiful yesterday.
2. I was shocked by the messiness of Bill's dorm room.
3. Advertising in women's fashion magazines creates a distorted and unhealthy view of beauty.
4. Although freewriting looks easy, it is actually quite difficult.
5. At the introductory level, chemistry is much more abstract than physics.

▧ CHAPTER SUMMARY

In this chapter, we have highlighted the importance of drafting as a problem-solving process in which the writer seeks a surprising thesis and convincing details. To achieve surprise, the writer develops a thesis aimed at changing the reader's view of a topic. A surprising thesis is characterized by tension, created either from stretching the reader's understanding in a new direction or from twisting the reader's beliefs in a contrary direction. In addition to presenting a surprising thesis, a writer needs to support the thesis through a network of points, each point backed up by particulars. By omitting the particulars, a writer can create a summary of a closed-form piece. Writers weave back and forth between generalizations and specifics by moving up and down the ladder of abstraction.

BRIEF WRITING PROJECT

The brief writing assignment for this chapter gives you practice generating particulars to support a point. To make it easier, we've supplied the point sentence. This assignment teaches an essential concept: effective closed-form writing supports points with particulars.

> Write one full paragraph that uses specific details to support the provided point sentence. Begin your paragraph with the point sentence and then use the body of the paragraph to provide specific supporting details. Your paragraph should be between 150 and 250 words in length. For your point sentence, choose any one of the following (or another point sentence provided by your instructor):
>
> - Directly or indirectly, anyone who is not a vegetarian causes animals to suffer.
> - Although the college library looks as though it is a good place to study, it has many distractions that lure you from your work.
> - Although doing X looks easy, it actually requires remarkable skill. (For X, substitute any activity of your choice; for example, "Although playing center midfielder in soccer looks easy, it actually requires remarkable athletic skill.")
> - Although X works reasonably well, it has one major problem—_____. (For X substitute anything of your choice, e.g., "Although the interior of my new car is generally well designed, it has one major problem—awkward controls." or "Although the registration system at our school works reasonably well, it has one major problem: Most students find it almost impossible to locate their advisor." The idea is to use convincing details to persuade readers that a problem exists.
> - The most memorable trait of (person's name) is X. (e.g., "The most memorable trait of my grandfather was his sense of humor." or "The most memorable trait of my sister is her incredible athletic ability." Then use specific details to illustrate the trait.)

The purpose of this assignment is to help you appreciate the difference between generalizations and specifics. This assignment provides you with a generalization or the frame for a generalization that you can apply to your own topic. Your task is to provide the supporting particulars that convince the reader of the truth of the generalization. For this assignment, your particulars will probably take the form of specific observations, facts, or examples. Here is a student paragraph written for this assignment.

Student Example

Although my new stereo receiver produces a pleasant sound and has ample power and volume, it has one major problem: poor design of the controls. The on/off switch in the upper left-hand corner is small and easy to confuse with two switches that control the main and remote speakers. If you hit the main speaker switch instead of the on/off switch, the sound will go off and you will think you have turned off the amplifier. When you try to turn it on again (by hitting the on/off switch), you will not hear any sound and will think the system is broken. This problem wouldn't be so bad if the tuning dial were always lit—that way you would know if the amplifier was turned on or not. But no light appears on the face of the receiver unless it is set in the "tuner" mode. Another problem with the controls is that the preset tuning buttons for radio stations are so small and close together that you have to use your little finger to push them. In the dark, they aren't lit, so I have to keep a little flashlight next to the amplifier to change radio stations at night. Finally, the volume control isn't gradual enough. The slightest movement of the knob changes the volume dramatically so that it is very difficult to adjust the sound to just the right level. (236 words)

Main point sentence

First subpoint: on/off switch confused with other switches

Details supporting first subpoint

Second subpoint: tuning buttons are too hard to use

Details supporting second subpoint

Third subpoint: volume controls not gradual

TOPIC Guidepost #9

For those using Texas Tech's TOPIC Web-Based assignments:

Direct your web browser to **http://english.ttu.edu:5555**

Guidepost #9 provides full instructions regarding your reading assignment (Chapter 4) and Critique of Draft 1.2.

Solving Rhetorical Problems
Purpose, Audience, and Genre

WHAT YOU WILL LEARN IN THIS CHAPTER

In this chapter you will learn how writing is motivated by both internal and external factors. When you analyze your rhetorical situation, you discover how decisions about your purpose, audience, and genre affect the content, structure, and style of what you write. In particular, you will learn the following:

- How to write for different purposes
- How to analyze your audience
- How to recognize different genres
- How to make decisions about structure and style based on analysis of your purpose, audience, and genre
- How to vary your style and construct an appropriate voice

It is amazing how much so-called writing problems clear up when the student really cares, when he is realistically put into the drama of somebody with something to say to somebody else.

—James Moffett, *Writing Teacher and Theorist*

In Chapter 3, we characterized composing as a problem-solving process requiring multiple drafts. We focused on subject-matter problems, in particular, the writer's struggle to find a surprising thesis and convincing details. In this chapter we explore ways in which writers' structural and stylistic choices are influenced by their rhetorical situations. We begin by discussing occasions that impel people to write. We then analyze three key variables of rhetorical context—purpose, audience, and genre—and show how these variables affect choices about structure and style.

◢ MOTIVATING OCCASIONS, OR WHY AM I WRITING THIS PIECE?

We said in Chapter 1 that people naturally enjoy posing and pursuing subject-matter problems. It is less clear whether people naturally enjoy writing about those problems. It is interesting to ask yourself when putting words on paper, "Why am I sitting here writing an essay when I could be doing something else?"

If asked, Why *do* you write? many of you might well answer, "Because teachers like you tell me to." Perhaps from first grade on, writing—or at least writing for school—has not been pleasant for you. Left to your own desires, you might have avoided school writing as diligently as you avoided canned spinach or bad hair days.

For others, writing school essays may have been—at least on occasion—deeply satisfying. Perhaps there was something about the assignment, the subject matter, or the environment created by the teacher that engaged you. On those occasions you may have immersed yourself in the writing project, written with care, and rewritten until you had fulfilled standards higher than those you would have set on your own. Even when there is an element of compulsion in the writing situation, you can claim ownership of the project and grow in the act of writing.

What we are suggesting is that there are two different motivations for writing—an external compulsion and an internal creative desire. Many of you might think that the first of these motivations—compulsion or coercion—is peculiar to school situations in which teachers assign papers and set deadlines. But you should know that the element of external compulsion felt so keenly in school writing is present in nearly every writing situation. Even poets report that writing can be a laborious process, provoked as often by ego, dumb habit, publishers' deadlines, or even greed, as by a burning vision. Eighteenth-century English writer Samuel Johnson, regarded by many as the first professional writer in Western culture, claimed that "No man but a blockhead ever wrote but for money." Yet he managed to write compellingly and artfully on everything from politics to language.

Most writing, whether it's done by students, artists, or businesspeople, is the product of mixed motives, some more or less voluntary, others downright coercive. Consider a middle manager requested by a company vice-president to write a report explaining why his division's profits are down. The manager is motivated by several factors: he wants to provide sound causal explanations for the financial decline, which will help the company set a course to remedy the situation; he wants to avoid looking bad or at least appearing to be solely responsible for the dip in profits; he wants to impress the vice-president in the hope that she will promote him to upper management; he wants to understand and articulate for himself just how this lamentable state of affairs came about; he wants each sentence to say just what he wants it to say; and so on.

College students' motivations for writing are often as complex as those of our hypothetical middle manager. Perhaps your writing is occasioned by an assignment and a deadline set by an instructor. But that rarely tells the whole story. In part, you write because you are engaged by an intellectual problem and want to say something significant about that problem; in part, you want to produce a well-written essay; in part, you want to please the teacher and get a good grade; in part, you want to improve your writing, and so forth. However arbitrary or artificial a college writing assignment might seem, it is really no more so than the writing occasions you will encounter outside college, when you must often write on tight deadlines for purposes specified by others. Given this fact, we believe that your best chance of writing successfully in college is to become engaged with the intellectual problem specified in the assignment. When you care about your ideas, you begin to imagine readers who care about them also (as opposed to imagining a teacher looking for mistakes), and you write to have an impact on those readers. The external motivations for writing are real and inescapable, but developing an internal motivation for writing—the desire to say something significant about your topic to an audience for a purpose—will help you produce your best work.

FOR WRITING AND DISCUSSION

Think of a time when you actually wanted to write something. What did you write and why did you find it satisfying? If this experience was a school assignment, what was it about the assignment, the subject matter, the classroom environment, the teacher, or you that awakened in you an internal motivation for writing? Prior to class discussion, spend several minutes freewriting about the occasion, exploring what made you feel internally motivated to write. Then, working in small groups or as a whole class, share your experiences with classmates. As a class, can you make any generalizations about the kinds of occasions or experiences that make a person want to write something? (If you cannot recall such an occasion, then recall the most hideous writing experience you've had and recount the elements that made it particularly gruesome. Why did the occasion fail to motivate you internally?)

THE ELEMENTS OF RHETORICAL CONTEXT: PURPOSE, AUDIENCE, AND GENRE

We have said that the best motivation for writing is the desire to say something significant about a substantive problem to an audience that cares about your ideas. But while writing you must also wrestle with rhetorical problems. What you say about your topic, how you organize and develop your ideas, what words you choose, and what voice and tone you adopt are all determined by your rhetorical context. In this section, we discuss in detail three important components of rhetorical context—purpose, audience, and genre.

Purpose

In analyzing your rhetorical context, you should start by asking: What is my purpose? Or, to put it another way: What effect do I want to have on my readers? What change do I want to bring about in their understanding of my subject? In most instances, you can write a one-sentence, nutshell answer to your question about purpose.

My purpose is to share with my reader my successful struggle with dyslexia.

My purpose is to raise serious doubts in my reader's mind about the value of the traditional grading system.

My purpose is to inform my reader about the surprising growth of the marijuana industry in the midwestern farm states.

My purpose is to explain how Northrop Frye's view of *Hamlet* fails to account for several key features of the text.

My purpose is to convince readers that the potential bad consequences of mail-order marriages require governments to regulate the mail-order bride industry.

My purpose is to persuade the general public that wind-generated electricity is not a practical energy alternative in the Pacific Northwest.

In closed-form academic articles, technical reports, and other business and professional pieces, writers typically place explicit purpose statements in the introduction. In most other forms of writing, they formulate purpose statements behind the scenes—the writer keeps a purpose statement in mind and uses it to achieve focus and direction, but seldom states it explicitly.

Writers' purposes generally fall into six broad categories. Situating your writing project within one or more of these categories can help you understand how to approach your task.

Writing to Express or Share (Expressive Purpose)

When you adopt this general purpose, you place your own life—your personal experiences and feelings—at the center of your reader's attention. You express in words what it is like to be you, to see or feel the world your way. Writing expressively in a diary, journal, or personal notebook has therapeutic value because it gives you the opportunity to vent your feelings and explore your thoughts. Often, however, you may choose to write expressively to move or touch a reader, to share your experiences and feelings with others—with friends or relatives through letters or with strangers through formal autobiographical essays or personal reflections.

Expressive writing usually follows the impulse to share rather than to argue or disagree. It says, in effect, "While you read my story or my reflections, you can momentarily cease being you and become me for a while, seeing the world through my eyes. My words might cause you to see the world differently, but my goal isn't to change you, just to help you appreciate the uniqueness of my experience." Instead of creating surprise through an argumentative thesis, expressive writing achieves surprise by offering the reader access to the private experiences of another human being.

Expressive writing usually falls near the open end of our closed-to-open continuum. When an expressive purpose is joined to a literary one (which we will describe shortly) the writer produces autobiographical pieces that function in a literary way, using image, plot, character, and symbol.

Writing to Inquire or Explore (Exploratory Purpose)

Although exploratory writing is closely linked to expressive writing, it usually focuses more on subject-matter problems than on the writer's life. You use exploratory writing to wade into complexity via freewriting, idea mapping, journal keeping, note taking, e-mail exchanges, letter writing, drafting, and any other writing that probes a subject and deepens your thinking. Its goal is to help you ask questions, explore possible answers, consider opposing views, pursue conflicting trains of thought, expand and clarify your thinking, and generally delay closure on a question in order to work your way through the complexity of your subject.

Exploratory writing is usually unfinished, behind-the-scenes work not intended to be read by others, but it sometimes results in a formal, finished product. In these cases, the writing aims to *pose* or *deepen a problem*, to muddy waters that the reader thought were clear. It doesn't *support* a thesis; it *seeks* a thesis. It perplexes the reader by revealing new questions about a topic, by showing how various approaches to that topic are unsatisfactory or how certain aspects of a topic are more problematic than previously supposed. Because exploratory writing often takes a narrative shape, dramatizing the process of the writer's thinking about a subject, it usually falls toward the open end of the closed-to-open continuum.

Writing to Inform or Explain (Informative Purpose)

When your purpose is informative, you see yourself as more knowledgeable than your reader about your topic. You create surprise by enlarging the reader's view of a topic, providing new ideas and information based on your own experiences or research. When you write to inform, you adopt the role of teacher in relation to your reader. You imagine that the reader will trust your authority and not dispute what you say. Although informative writing usually has a closed-form structure, it may fall anywhere along the continuum from closed to open.

Writing to Analyze or Interpret (Analytical Purpose)

When your purpose is analytical, you examine aspects of a subject that puzzle your reader and offer tentative ways to resolve these puzzles. Analytical writing requires you to think critically about a problematic text, set of data, or other phenomenon. Your goal is to clarify your reader's understanding of this problematic subject. You surprise your reader with a new or more illuminating way of seeing, thinking about, or understanding the subject.

Analytical writing, often laced with informative elements, constitutes the most common kind of academic prose. It typically takes a closed-form structure. The introduction poses a question, and the body presents the writer's solution. The reader generally regards the solution as *tentative,* so the writer must support it with reasons and evidence or other justifying arguments. Unlike informative writing, which positions the writer as an expert, analytical writing generally assumes that writer and reader are equally well informed and equally engaged with the puzzling phenomenon. Analytical writing presupposes a more skeptical audience than does informative prose. The writer might not expect readers to argue back, but will certainly expect them to test his or her ideas against their own experience and hypotheses.

Writing to Persuade (Persuasive Purpose)

When your purpose is persuasive, you enter a conversation in which people disagree with each other about answers to a given question. You think of your audience as judges, jurors, or other decision makers, who must be convinced that your answer to the question is sounder than other answers. Persuasive writing addresses a controversial problem, to which there are several alternative answers with supporting reasons and evidence. When you write to persuade, you aim to surprise the reader with your own reasons and evidence or other appeals that will change the reader's beliefs or actions.

Persuasive writing can fall anywhere along the closed-to-open continuum. It may have a closed-form structure of reasons and evidence set out in a logical point-by-point format, or it may have a very open structure—a powerful story or a collage of emotionally charged scenes might be extremely persuasive in influencing a reader's views on an issue.

When writing persuasively, writers usually imagine skeptical readers vigorously questioning their claims. The only way they can effectively anticipate and respond to these questions is to understand alternative positions on the issue—including understanding the values, assumptions, and beliefs of the people who hold alternative views—and either refute these views, concede to them, or compromise with them. This emphasis on countering or accommodating alternative views and on appealing to the values and beliefs of the reader distinguishes persuasive writing from most analytical writing.

Writing to Entertain or Give Aesthetic Pleasure (Literary Purpose)

Sometimes writers focus not on themselves (expressive prose), nor on the subject matter (exploratory, informative, and analytical prose), nor on the reader (persuasive prose), but on the artistic shaping of language. When you adopt a literary purpose, you treat language as a medium, such as paint or clay. You explore its properties and its sound and rhythms. We typically think of literary writing as fiction or poetry, but nonfiction prose can also use literary techniques. Such prose is often called *literary nonfiction* or *belletristic prose.* Literary nonfiction usually combines a literary purpose with one or more other purposes, for example, an expressive purpose (an autobiographical essay about a turning point in your life) or an exploratory purpose (your contemplation of the cosmic meanings of a spider web).

FOR WRITING AND DISCUSSION

As a class, choose one of the following topic areas or another provided by your instructor. Then imagine six different writing situations in which a hypothetical writer would compose an essay about the selected topic. Let each situation call for a different purpose. How might a person write about the selected topic with an expressive purpose? An exploratory purpose? An informative purpose? An analytical purpose? A persuasive purpose? A literary purpose? How would each essay surprise its readers?

baseball	cats	hospices or nursing homes
homelessness	garbage	dating or marriage
advertising	newspapers	gays in the military

Working on your own or in small groups, create six realistic scenarios, each of which calls for prose in a different category of purpose. Then share your results as a whole class. Here are two examples based on the topic "hospices."

| Expressive Purpose | Working one summer as a volunteer in a hospice for dying cancer patients, you befriend a woman whose attitude toward death changes your life. You write an autobiographical essay about your experiences with this remarkable woman. |
| Analytic Purpose | You are a hospice nurse working in a home-care setting. You and your colleagues note that sometimes family members cannot adjust psychologically to the burden of living with a dying person. You decide to investigate this phenomenon. You interview "reluctant" family members in an attempt to understand the causes of their psychological discomfort so that you can provide better counseling services as a possible solution. You write a paper for a professional audience analyzing the results of your interviews. |

Audience

In our discussion of purpose, we have already had a lot to say about audience. What you know about your readers—their familiarity with your subject matter, their reasons for reading, their closeness to you, their values and beliefs—affects most of the choices you make as a writer.

In assessing your audience, you must first consider what to them is old information and what is new information. You'll ask questions like these: What in my essay will be old and familiar and what will be new, challenging, and surprising? How much background will my readers need? What can I assume they know and don't know? What is their current view of my topic that I am trying to change?

On a related note, you will also need to consider your audience's methods and reasons for reading. Imagine that you are a marketing manager and you want to persuade your harried boss to increase your research budget. You picture your boss sitting at her desk, people waiting to see her, phone ringing, a pile of memos, reports, and proposals in the in box. Consequently, you fashion a budget request with a tightly closed structure. Your document must be clear, concise, and well designed for her immediate comprehension and assent. The same reader in a different mood and setting may turn to a different kind of prose. In the evening, your harried boss might relax in an easy chair, sip a cup of tea, and reach for her favorite magazine. Is she most concerned now with speedy comprehension and quick access to needed information? Probably not. She's more likely to be interested in leisurely reading, perhaps an open-form piece on, say, bicycling in Italy. And she may well savor the way a passage is written, pausing to reflect on the scene it evokes.

Now consider how a change in audience can affect the content of a piece. Suppose you want voters in your city to approve a bond issue to build a new baseball stadium. If most members of your audience are baseball fans, you can appeal to their love of the game, the pleasure of a new facility, and so forth. But non–baseball fans won't be moved by these arguments. To reach them, you must tie the new baseball stadium to their values. You can argue that a new stadium will bring new tax revenues to the city, clean up a run-down area, revitalize local businesses, or stimulate the tourist industry. Your purpose remains the same, to persuade taxpayers to fund the stadium, but the content of your argument changes if your audience changes.

A change in audience can change a writer's purpose as well. A graduate student we know who studies wildlife management developed a technique for using a net gun to capture mountain goats so that researchers could place radio collars around their necks. He wrote several articles based on his expertise. For fellow specialists who studied mountain goats, he wrote a scientific article showing that capturing mountain goats with a net gun was more effective than drugging them with a dart gun (informative and analytical purposes). For the audience of a popular outdoors magazine, he wrote a personal-action narrative about shooting a net gun from a hovering helicopter (expressive and literary purpose). And because he was also concerned with preserving natural habitats for mountain goats, he wrote letters to legislators using data gathered from the radio collars to argue for restrictions on wilderness development (persuasive purpose).

In college, you are often writing for an audience of one—your instructor. However, most instructors try to read as a representative of a broader audience. To help college writers imagine these readers, many instructors try to design writing assignments that provide a fuller sense of audience. They may ask you to write for the readers of a particular magazine or journal, or they may create case assignments with a built-in audience (for example, "You are an accountant in the firm of Numbers and Fudge; one day you receive a letter from . . . "). If your instructor does not specify an audience, you can generally assume what we like to call the generic academic audience—student peers who have approximately the same level of knowledge and expertise in the field as you do, who are engaged by the question you address, and who want to read your writing to be surprised in some way.

Assessing Your Audience

In any writing situation, you can use the following questions to help you make decisions about content, form, and style:

1. Who is going to read what I write? A specific individual? A specific group with special interests? Or a general readership with wide-ranging interests and backgrounds?
2. What relationship do I have with these readers? Do I and my readers have an informal, friendly relationship or a polite, formal one? Is my readers' expertise in my general subject area greater, less, or equal to mine?
3. How much do my readers already know about the specific problem I address? How much background will I have to provide?
4. How much interest do my readers bring to my topic? Do I need to hook readers with a vivid opening and use special techniques to maintain their interest throughout? Or are they interested enough in the problem I am examining that the subject matter itself will drive their reading? (In persuasive writing, particularly in writing that proposes a solution to a problem, you may need to shock your readers into awareness that the problem exists.)
5. What are my audience's values, beliefs, and assumptions in relation to my topic? If I am writing on a controversial issue, will my readers oppose my position, be neutral to it, or support it? To which of their values, beliefs, or assumptions can I appeal? Will my position unsettle or threaten my audience or stimulate a strong emotional response? (Because a concern for audience is particularly relevant to persuasive writing, we will treat these questions in more depth in Chapter 9.)

Posing these questions will not lead to any formulaic solutions to your writing problems, but can help you develop strategies that will appeal to your audience and enable you to achieve your purpose.

FOR WRITING AND DISCUSSION

Working on your own, imagine that you enjoyed a fun party last weekend. (a) Describe that party in a letter to a close friend, inventing the details needed to show your friend how great the party was. (b) Describe the same party in a letter to a parent (or some other person whose differences from your friend would lead to a different description.) Note: You may substitute any other event or phenomenon that you would describe in different ways to different audiences.

Then, in small groups or as a class, share excerpts from your two letters. What changes did you make in your description as a result of changes in your audience?

Genre

The term *genre* refers to broad categories of writing that follow certain conventions of style, structure, and approach to subject matter. Literary genres include the short story, the novel, the epic poem, the limerick, the sonnet, and so forth. Nonfiction prose has its own genres: the business memo, the technical manual, the scholarly article, the scientific report, the popular magazine article (each magazine, actually, has its own peculiar conventions), the five-paragraph theme (a school genre), the newspaper editorial, the cover letter for a job application, the legal contract, the advertising brochure, and so forth.

The concept of genre creates strong reader expectations and places specific demands on writers. How you write any given letter, report, or article is influenced by the structure and style of hundreds of previous letters, reports, or articles written in the same genre. If you wanted to write for *Reader's Digest,* for example, you would have to use the conventions that appeal to its older, conservative readers: simple language, subjects with strong human interest, heavy reliance on anecdotal evidence in arguments, an upbeat and optimistic perspective, and an approach that reinforces the conservative ethos of individualism, self-discipline, and family. If you wanted to write for *Seventeen* or *Rolling Stone,* however, you would need to use quite different conventions.

To illustrate the relationship of a writer to a genre, we sometimes draw an analogy with clothing. Although most people have a variety of different types of clothing in their wardrobe, the genre of activity for which they are dressing (Saturday night movie date, job interview, wedding) severely constrains their choice and expression of individuality. A man dressing for a job interview might express his personality through choice of tie or quality and style of business suit; he probably wouldn't express it by wearing a bicycle helmet and mismatched shoes. Even when people deviate from a convention, they tend to do so in a conventional way. For example, teenagers who do not want to follow the genre of "teenager admired by adults" form their own genre of purple hair and pierced body parts. The concept of genre raises intriguing and sometimes unsettling questions about the relationship of the unique self to a social convention or tradition.

These same kinds of questions and constraints perplex writers. For example, academic writers usually follow the genre of the closed-form scholarly article. This highly functional form achieves maximum clarity for readers by orienting them quickly to the article's purpose, content, and structure. Readers expect this format, and writers have the greatest chance of being published if they meet these expectations. In some disciplines, however, scholars are beginning to publish more experimental, open-form articles. They may slowly alter the conventions of the scholarly article, just as fashion designers alter styles of dress.

The genre of the scholarly article varies enormously from discipline to discipline, both in the kinds of questions that specialists pose about their subject matter and in the style and structure of articles. As a specific example of a genre that many college students regularly encounter, we introduce you here to the *experimental report*. This genre is commonly used in fields that conduct empirical research, such as the physical or social sciences, nursing, medicine, business, engineering, education, and other fields.

The Experimental Report

An experimental report, sometimes called a scientific or technical report, is a formal paper addressed primarily to professionals who are interested in the results of an investigation: Its readers want to know why the investigation was undertaken, how it was conducted, what was learned, and whether the findings are significant and useful. Experimental reports usually follow a standard five-part format:

1. *Introduction.*   This section explains the purpose of the investigation, what problem was addressed and what makes the problem both problematic and significant. The introduction often includes a review of the literature, which summarizes previous research addressing the same or a related problem. In many scientific disciplines, it is conventional to conclude the introduction with a hypothesis, a tentative answer to the question, which the investigation confirms or disconfirms.

2. *Methods.*   Sometimes called *methodology* or *procedures,* the methods section details in cookbook fashion how the investigators conducted the research. It provides enough details so that other researchers can replicate the investigation. This section usually includes the following subsections: (a) research design, (b) apparatus and materials, and (c) procedures followed.

3. *Findings (results).*   This section presents the empirical results of the investigation, the data discovered in the experiment. The findings may be displayed in figures, tables, graphs, or charts. Usually, the findings are not interpreted in this section.

4. *Discussion of findings.*   This section is the main part of the experimental report. It explains the significance of the findings by relating what was discovered back to the problem set out in the introduction and detailing how the investigation did or did not accomplish its original purpose, that is, whether it answered the questions outlined in the introduction. (Did it confirm/disconfirm the writer's hypothesis?) This section also discusses the usefulness and significance of the findings and explores new questions raised by the experiment.

5. *Conclusions and recommendations.*   This last section focuses on the main points learned from the investigation and, in some cases, on the practical applications of the investigation. If the investigation was a pure research project, this section often summarizes the most important findings and recommends areas for further research. If the investigation was aimed at mak-

ing a practical decision (for example, an engineering design decision), this section recommends appropriate actions.

You can tell from this description that the experimental report has a very closed form. Note, however, that the thesis is delayed until the discussion section, which reveals through the writer's analysis of the findings whether the original hypothesis was confirmed or disconfirmed.

FOR WRITING AND DISCUSSION

1. On page 61, we offered you a brief description of the conventions governing *Reader's Digest* articles, which appeal mainly to older, conservative readers. For this exercise, prepare similar descriptions of the conventions that govern articles in several other magazines, such as *Rolling Stone, Sports Illustrated, Cosmopolitan, Details, The New Yorker,* or *Psychology Today.* Each person should bring to class a copy of a magazine that he or she enjoys reading. The class should then divide into small groups according to similar interests. Your instructor may supply a few scholarly journals from different disciplines. In preparing a brief profile of your magazine, consider the following:

   - Scan the table of contents. What kinds of subjects or topics does the magazine cover?
   - Look at the average length of articles. How much depth and analysis are provided?
   - Consider the magazine's readership. Does the magazine appeal to particular political or social groups (liberal/conservative, male/ female, young/old, white collar/blue collar, in-group/general readership)?
   - Look at the advertisements. What kinds of products are most heavily advertised in the magazine? Who is being targeted by these advertisements? What percentage of the magazine consists of advertisements?
   - Read representative pages, including introductions, of some articles. Would you characterize the prose as difficult or easy? Intellectual or popular? Does the prose use the jargon, slang, or other language particular to a group? Are the paragraphs long or short? How are headings, inserts, visuals, and other page-formatting features used? Is the writing formal or informal?
   - Think about what advice you would give a person who wanted to write a freelance article for this magazine.

2. Imagine that someone interested in hospices (see the example in the For Writing and Discussion exercise on p. 58) wanted to write an article about hospices for your chosen magazine. What approach would the

writer have to take to have a hospice-related article published in your magazine? There may be no chance of this happening, but be creative. Here is an example:

Ordinarily *Sports Illustrated* would be an unlikely place for an article on hospices. However, *SI* might publish a piece about a dying athlete in a hospice setting. It might also publish a piece about sports memories of dying patients or about watching sports as therapy.

▨ RHETORICAL CONTEXT AND DECISIONS ABOUT STRUCTURE

So far in this chapter we have examined purpose, audience, and genre as components of a writer's rhetorical context. In this section and the next, our goal is to help you appreciate how these variables influence a writer's choices regarding structure and style. Although there is no formula that allows you to determine an appropriate structure and style based on particular purposes, audiences, and genres, there are some rules of thumb that can help you make decisions. Let's look first at structure.

Because most academic, business, and professional writing uses a closed-form structure, we spend a significant portion of this text advising you how to write such prose. However, you also need to be able to open up your prose on occasion, and to that end you need to practice writing at different positions on the continuum. The following advice will help you decide when closed or open forms are more appropriate.

When is closed-form prose most appropriate?

- When your focus is on the subject matter itself and your goal is to communicate efficiently to maximize clarity. In these cases, your purpose is usually to inform, to analyze, or to persuade.
- When you imagine your audience as a busy or harried reader who needs to be able to read quickly and process ideas rapidly. Closed-form prose is easy to summarize; moreover, a reader can speed read closed-form prose by scanning the introduction and then glancing at headings and the openings of paragraphs, where writers place key points.
- When the conventional genre for your context is closed-form writing, and you choose to meet, rather than break, readers' expectations.
- When you encounter any rhetorical situation that asks you to assert and support a thesis in response to a problem or question.

When is a more open form desirable?

- When you want to delay your thesis rather than announce it in the introduction, for example, to create suspense. A delayed thesis structure is less combative and more friendly; it conveys an unfolding "let's think through this together" feeling.

- When your purpose is expressive, exploratory, or literary. These purposes tend to be served better through narrative rather than through thesis-with-support writing.
- When you imagine your audience reading primarily for enjoyment and pleasure. In this context you can often wed a literary purpose to another purpose.
- When the conventional genre calls for open-form writing, for example, autobiographical narratives, character sketches, or personal reflective pieces. Popular magazine articles often have a looser, more open structure than do scholarly articles or business reports.
- When you are writing about something that is too complex or messy to be captured in a fixed thesis statement, or when you feel constrained by the genre of thesis with support.

RHETORICAL CONTEXT AND DECISIONS ABOUT STYLE

Writers need to make choices not only about structure but also about style. By *style*, we mean the choices you make about how to say something. Writers can say essentially the same thing in a multitude of ways, each placing the material in a slightly different light, subtly altering meaning, and slightly changing the effect on readers. In this section we illustrate more concretely the many stylistic options open to you and explain how you might go about making stylistic choices.

Factors that Affect Style

As we shall see, style is a complex composite of many factors. We can classify the hundreds of variables that affect style into four broad categories.

1. *Ways of shaping sentences:* long/short, simple/complex, many modifiers/few modifiers, normal word order/frequent inversions or interruptions, mostly main clauses/many embedded phrases and subordinate clauses.
2. *Types of words:* abstract/concrete, formal/colloquial, unusual/ordinary, specialized/general, metaphoric/literal, scientific/literary.
3. *The implied personality projected by the writer (often called* **persona***):* expert/layperson, scholar/student, outsider/insider, political liberal/conservative, neutral observer/active participant.
4. *The writer's implied relationship with the reader and the subject matter (often called* **tone***):* intimate/distant, personal/impersonal, angry/calm, browbeating/sharing, informative/entertaining, humorous/serious, ironic/literal, passionately involved/aloof.

Recognizing and Creating Style or "Voice"

When discussing style, writing teachers often use the terms *style* and *voice* interchangeably. We can distinguish the two terms by thinking of style as analyzable textual features on the page (number of words in a sentence, number of main and subordinate clauses, use of active or passive voice, use of first, second, or third person, and so forth) and of voice as the reader's impression of the writer projected from the page—a combination of the image that you try to portray and the attitude you take toward your subject matter. Through your stylistic choices, you create an image of yourself in your reader's mind. This image, sometimes called a *persona,* can be cold or warm, humorous or serious, stuffy or lively, and so forth. It is your persona that readers like or dislike, trust or distrust. It is your tone (that is, your implied attitude toward your audience and subject) that engages and interests your readers or turns them off, that inspires or antagonizes them.

An Example of Varying Voices and Styles

To help you get a sense of different voices and styles, we try our hand at illustrating a few. In this section, rather than drawing examples from published sources, we imitate different styles and voices ourselves—both to show you that doing so can be fun and to let you see how stylistic variations on the same subject matter can produce different effects. Imagine the following scenario: One Farrago Pomp, a rising light in the educational community, has developed a new teaching method that he calls the critical visionary method of instruction. He has conducted several studies to demonstrate its effectiveness, and now other scholars are beginning to join the conversation that Pomp has initiated. First we present the introduction to a hypothetical scholarly article written in a formal academic style by a critic of Pomp, one Dr. Elwit Morganthorpe.

Formal Academic Style

Variations in pedagogical methodology are widely reported in the literature, and it is to be assumed that such variations will continue so long as empirical research yields less than unanimous consensus concerning the psychological and environmental factors that influence learning and cognition. Nevertheless, the work of F. Pomp (see especially 1989; 1992b; 1995) has firmly established the trance-inducing methodology embodied in his "Critical Visionary Method of Instruction" as among the most influential of the last two decades. Indeed, a recent review of the literature reveals that eighty-four articles—virtually all of which make elaborate claims for the efficacy of Pomp's approach—were published in the last three years alone.

Yet Pomp's work is being called increasingly into question. Shovit (1994) and Stuffit (1995) recently questioned a number of Pomp's underlying premises, while Ehrbag's (1994) pioneering empirical study raised serious doubts about Pomp's methodology. For that reason a rigorous research agenda was undertaken to put Pomp's claims to a definitive test in 26 college classrooms around the country. The results of this study are reported herein. The findings, while confirming a few of Pomp's less ambitious claims, show significantly sparser learning gains overall than those claimed in the literature.

—Elwit Morganthorpe, "Dimming the Vision: A Critical
Evaluation of Pomp's 'Visionary Method of Instruction'"

Next is the introduction to a conference presentation by another Pomp skeptic, Elmira Eggwhite, addressed to an academic audience. It is still an academic paper, but in a conversational rather than a formal style.

Informal Academic Style

A lot of teachers these days have been experimenting with Farrago Pomp's Visionary Method, and many have reported good results. (I am told that more than eighty articles supporting Pomp's work have been published in the last three years.) So I decided to try out some of Pomp's methods myself—with disastrous results. I admit that I have no weighty evidence to support my own less than enthusiastic assessment of VM—just one semester's experience with thirty first-year students in a writing class at Weasel College. I sincerely tried to make the method work. I read Pomp meticulously and tried to follow his suggestions exactly when I induced the trances, including use of drums, mantras, and synthetic sea music. In short, I employed Pomp's method with as much conviction as a normally credulous human being could muster.

As I'll show in the rest of this paper, Pomp's method had dismal effects on my students' writing and evoked extremely negative reactions to the more evangelical aspects of the approach. As one of my students put it: "Trances are for summer camp, not the classroom."

—Elmira Eggwhite, "Waking Up from Pomp's Trance"

In our final example, we switch all three variables of rhetorical context: purpose, audience, and genre. In this example the writer's purpose is not to analyze or evaluate Pomp's methods, but to write an informative piece on the visionary method movement. The audience consists of general readers rather than scholars. The genre is an upbeat popular magazine aimed at a youthful audience.

Popular Magazine Style

What's new in the college classroom these days? Retro hairdos and plastic pumps, you say. Tattoos and nose rings? True true, but what are people actually doing in those classrooms? Anything new about the way today's students are being taught?

Most definitely, say our campus correspondents. The latest rage is Vision. Or, more properly, Visionary Method.

According to Farrago Pomp, the man who invented the Visionary Method, his approach will be the mainstay of the 21st century classroom.

The tall, bearded Pomp explained the genesis of his approach at an early morning interview between numerous cups of double espresso.

"The idea for the Visionary Method hit me," says Pomp, "during a drum ceremony in my men's group."

"I realized that the old methods—tedious studying, often in weary isolation—didn't work. Knowledge should be imbibed, or quaffed in heady drafts, amidst chanting circles of fellow Visionaries," said Pomp, gesturing frantically for another espresso.

It appears, however, that not all of Pomp's colleagues are beating the same drum. Professor Elwit Morganthorpe has been leading a pack of educators throwing sand and water on Pomp's sacred campfires. "Pomp's methods are bogus," says Morganthorpe, citing his own comprehensive investigation of the Visionary Method. "Drum ceremonies can never replace old-fashioned studying."

In the meantime, thousands of college students are chanting their way through their college courses. Heady stuff indeed for those of us who got through college by memorizing textbooks and solving equations. What we wouldn't have given to be able to walk into our philosophy class and chug-a-lug some Spinoza. . . .

—"Drum Rolls, Please: Learning in the New Age"

FOR WRITING AND DISCUSSION

Working in small groups or as a whole class, analyze the differences in the styles of these three samples. How do the differences in styles create different voices—that is, what features of the writing make each voice sound different? How are differences in style a result of differences in the writer's purpose, audience, or genre?

TOPIC *Guidepost #10*

For those using Texas Tech's TOPIC Web-Based assignments:

Direct your web browser to **http://english.ttu.edu:5555**

Guidepost #10 provides full instructions regarding your reading assignment (Handbook pages 215-227) and the final draft 1.3.

TOPIC *Guidepost #11*

For those using Texas Tech's TOPIC Web-Based assignments:

Direct your web browser to **http://english.ttu.edu:5555**

Guidepost #11 provides full instructions regarding your reading assignment (Chapter 5) and Journal Entry.

Seeing Rhetorically
The Writer as Observer

ABOUT SEEING RHETORICALLY

One time-honored way to begin a writing course is to have students observe a scene and describe it in dense, sensory language. On the surface, this seems a simple and pleasurable enough exercise. But consider what happens to this traditional task when it is given a rhetorical twist. Suppose we asked you to write *two* descriptions of the same scene from different angles of vision (for example, different perspectives, moods, or rhetorical purposes) and then to analyze how the two descriptions differed. We could then ask you to reflect on the extent to which any description of a scene is influenced by the prior experiences, beliefs, moods, and purposes of the observer. Recast in this way, the task requires you to reflect on your degree of responsibility for what you see and to acknowledge the impossibility of arriving at a single, objective account of the scene.

We take this self-reflective twist as our point of departure for this chapter. As soon as you realize that your perceptions of the world shape as well as record that world, you are ready to play a more active role in the learning process and to use writing as a way of seeing and a mode of learning. Your writing assignment for this chapter falls into a category that we call *writing to learn.* Such assignments seldom result in self-contained essays. More often they result in thought exercises that help you learn a concept and then reflect on your learning.

One goal of this writing assignment is to raise the issue of angle of vision versus objectivity in writing. Angle of vision is a factor in all kinds of writing, not just in description. Consider an example from the world of statistics. At one point in a recent baseball season, the Seattle Mariners had the following twelve-game sequence of wins and losses: seven consecutive losses; two wins; one loss; two wins. On the same day in the local papers, two different sports writers summed up the Mariners' record as follows:

Reporter 1   The surging Mariners have now won four out of their last five games.

Reporter 2   The struggling Mariners have won only four of their last twelve games.

These two accounts raise some interesting questions. Are they equally factual? Are they equally true? Is there a term that would sum up the Mariners' recent record more accurately than "surging" or "struggling"? (By "recent" do we mean the last five games or the last twelve? Why not the last eight or the last eighteen?)

This example illustrates what we mean by *seeing rhetorically*. To see something rhetorically is to interpret it, that is, to see it as meaningful. To see data as meaningful entails asserting a point about it ("The Mariners are struggling" or "The Mariners are surging") and identifying data that account for that conclusion (to go back twelve games, which explains "struggling," or to go back five games, which explains "surging"). Before we develop this explanation in more detail, we would like you to experience for yourself the dilemma of having to see rhetorically.

◢ EXPLORING RHETORICAL OBSERVATION

You are an assistant professor of management in the School of Business at Ivy Lite College. One day you receive a letter from a local bank requesting a confidential evaluation of a former student, one Neal Weasel, who has applied for a job as a management trainee. The bank wants your assessment of Weasel's intelligence, aptitude, dependability, and ability to work with people. You haven't seen Neal for several years, but you remember him well. Here are some of the facts and impressions you recall about Mr. Weasel.

- Very temperamental student, seemed moody, something of a loner.
- Long hair and very sloppy dress—seemed like a misplaced street person; often twitchy and hyperactive.
- Absolutely brilliant mind; took lots of liberal arts courses and applied them to business.
- Wrote a term paper relating different management styles to modern theories of psychology—the best undergraduate paper you ever received. You gave it an A+ and remember learning a lot from it yourself.
- Had a strong command of language—the paper was very well written.
- Good at mathematics; could easily handle all the statistical aspects of the course.
- Frequently missed class and once told you that your class was boring.
- Didn't show up for the midterm. When he returned to class later, he said only that he had been out of town. You let him make up the midterm, and he got an A.
- Didn't participate in a group project required for your course. He said the other students in his group were idiots.
- You thought at the time that Weasel didn't have a chance of making it in the business world because he had no talent for getting along with people.
- Other professors held similar views of Weasel—brilliant, but rather strange and hard to like; an odd duck.

You are in a dilemma because you want to give Weasel a chance (he's still young and may have had a personality transformation of some sort), but you also don't want to damage your own professional reputation by falsifying your true impression.

Working individually at your desk for ten minutes or so, compose a brief letter assessing Weasel; use details from the list to support your assessment. Try to convey a positive impression, but remain honest. Then, working in small groups or as a whole class, share your letters. Pick out representative examples ranging from most positive to least positive and discuss how the letters achieve their different rhetorical effects. To what extent does honesty compel you to mention some or all of your negative memories? Is it possible to mention negative items without emphasizing them? How?

WRITING PROJECT

Your writing project for this chapter is to write two descriptions and an analysis. The assignment has two parts.*

Part A: Find a place on or near campus where you can sit and observe for fifteen or twenty minutes in preparation for writing a focused description of the scene that will enable your readers to see what you see. Here is the catch. You are to write *two* descriptions of the scene. Your first description must convey a favorable impression of the scene, making it appear pleasing or attractive. The second description must convey a negative, or unfavorable, impression, making the scene appear unpleasant or unattractive. Both descriptions must contain only factual details and must describe exactly the same scene from the same location at the same time. It's not fair, in other words, to describe the scene in sunny weather and then in the rain or otherwise to alter factual details. Each description should be one paragraph long (approximately 125–175 words).

Part B: Attach to your two descriptions an analysis (approximately 400–500 words) that explains how your two equally factual descriptions create two contrasting impressions of the same subject. What did you do differently to create the contrasting effects in the two descriptions? In the conclusion of your analysis, address the question "So what?" by exploring what you have learned about reading and writing from composing your two descriptions. Help your readers see what is significant about your thought exercise.

Part A of the assignment asks you to describe the same scene in two different ways, giving your first description a positive tone and the second description a

---

*For this assignment, we are indebted to two sources: (1) Richard Braddock, *A Little Casebook in the Rhetoric of Writing* (Englewood Cliffs, NJ: Prentice-Hall, 1971), and (2) Kenneth Dowst, "Kenneth Dowst's Assignment," in William E. Coles, Jr., and James Vopat (eds.), *What Makes Writing Good?* (Lexington, MA: D. C. Heath, 1985), pp. 52–57.

negative one. You can choose from any number of scenes: the lobby of a dormitory or apartment building, a view from a park bench or from your dormitory or apartment window, the entrance to campus, a crowd at a basketball game, a busy street, a local eating or drinking spot, a scene in a lecture hall, a person studying at a library table, whatever. Part B of the assignment asks you to reflect on what you did to convey a positive or negative impression. Did you include details in one scene that you omitted from the other? Did you choose words with different connotations or use different figures of speech? Did you arrange details in different order or alter sentence structure for different emphasis? The assignment concludes by prompting you to reflect further on what you learned from this exercise about seeing rhetorically.

More discussion of this assignment, as well as a student example of two contrasting descriptions, occurs later in this chapter. As we noted earlier, this assignment results in a thought exercise rather than in a self-contained essay that requires an introduction, transitions between parts, and so forth. You can label your sections simply "Descriptions" and "Analysis."

UNDERSTANDING OBSERVATIONAL WRITING

In this section we explore the extent to which the writer's angle of vision shapes the language he or she chooses, or, to put it inversely, how the chosen language creates an angle of vision. We also explore the complex relationship between perception and belief by showing how previous knowledge, cultural background, interests, values, and beliefs may influence perceptions.

How Observational Writing Reflects an Angle of Vision

To see how observational or descriptive writing reflects an angle of vision, let's look at several examples. Our first is the opening of a newspaper feature article in which a freelance writer describes his bicycle tour through the Prudhoe Bay area of Alaska.

> The temperature is 39 degrees. The going is slow but finally I am in motion. The bike churns through big rocks and thick gravel that occasionally suck the wheels to a dead halt.
>
> Sixty miles to the east lies the Arctic National Wildlife Refuge, a place ARCO describes as "a bleak and forbidding land where temperatures plunge to more than 40 degrees below zero and the sun is not seen for nearly two months each year." To me, the refuge is 19.5 million acres of unspoiled wilderness believed to contain crude oil and natural gas fields.
>
> Prudhoe Bay production is on the decline, and oil corporations are salivating over the prospect of drilling on the 125-mile-long stretch of coastal plain within the refuge.
>
> This area is the principal calving ground for the 180,000-member porcupine caribou herd that annually migrates to this windswept plain, seeking relief from insects.

The refuge also provides habitat for grizzlies, wolves, musk oxen, wolverines and arctic foxes. Polar bears hunt over the ice and come ashore. Millions of waterfowl, seabirds and shorebirds nest here.

—Randal Rubini, "A Vicious Cycle"

The opening of this article juxtaposes the author's view of the Arctic National Wildlife Refuge (ANWR) and ARCO's view. ARCO, a major oil-refining company, describes the ANWR as a "bleak and forbidding land where temperatures plunge to more than 40 degrees below zero and the sun is not seen for nearly two months each year." In contrast, Rubini describes it as "unspoiled wilderness," the habitat of caribou, grizzly bears, shorebirds, and other wildlife.

FOR WRITING AND DISCUSSION

Working as a whole class or in small groups, address the following questions:

1. How does each description reflect an angle of vision that serves the political interests of each party? (Hint: How does ARCO's description make the ANWR seem like a good place to drill for oil? How does Rubini's description make it seem like a bad place to drill for oil?)
2. What is the rhetorical effect of the word "salivating" in the third paragraph? How does Rubini's choice of that word serve his interests?

Appreciating how a writer's choice of words and selection of details reflects an angle of vision can help you read any text from a position of strength. One key is to pay attention to what is *omitted* from a text as well as to what is included. For example, ARCO's descriptive passage about the ANWR omits reference to the animals, keeping the reader focused on the bleak and frigid landscape. In contrast, Rubini's description of the ANWR omits references to the Alaskan economy or the U.S. need for domestic oil, keeping the reader focused instead on the ANWR's beauty and wildlife. Neither perspective is necessarily dishonest; each is true in a limited way. In any writing, writers necessarily—whether consciously or unconsciously—include some details and exclude others. Their choices are driven by their sense of audience and purpose and most important, by their "situatedness" in the world, which creates a predisposition toward a particular perspective or angle of vision. By noting what is *not there,* a reader can begin to detect that angle of vision and analyze it. The reader sees the piece of writing not as the whole truth, but as a constructed piece with a rhetorical effect (that is, with a persuasive power) created by its angle of vision.

The rhetorical effect of observational writing is even more clear in our next example, consisting of excerpts from the works of two female anthropologists studying the role of women in the !Kung* tribe of the African Kalahari (sometimes called

---

*The word *!Kung* is preceded by an exclamation point in scholarly work to indicate the unique clicking sound of the language.

the Bushmen). Anthropologists have long been interested in the !Kung because they still hunt and forage for food in the manner of their prehistoric ancestors.

Here is how anthropologist Lorna Marshal describes !Kung women's work:

Marshal's Description

Women bring most of the daily food that sustains the life of the people, but the roots and berries that are the principal plant foods of the Nyae Nyae !Kung are apt to be tasteless, harsh and not very satisfying. People crave meat. Furthermore, there is only drudgery in digging roots, picking berries, and trudging back to the encampment with heavy loads and babies sagging in the pouches of the karosses: there is no splendid excitement and triumph in returning with vegetables.

—Lorna Marshal, *The !Kung of Nyae Nyae*

And here is how a second anthropologist describes women's work:

Draper's Description

A common sight in the late afternoon is clusters of children standing on the edge of camp, scanning the bush with shaded eyes to see if the returning women are visible. When the slow-moving file of women is finally discerned in the distance, the children leap and exclaim. As the women draw closer, the children speculate as to which figure is whose mother and what the women are carrying in the karosses. [. . .]

!Kung women impress one as a self-contained people with a high sense of self-esteem. There are exceptions—women who seem forlorn and weary—but for the most part, !Kung women are vivacious and self-confident. Small groups of women forage in the Kalahari at distances of eight to ten miles from home with no thought that they need the protection of the men or of the men's weapons should they encounter any of the several large predators that also inhabit the Kalahari.

—P. Draper, "!Kung Women: Contrasts in Sexual Egalitarianism in Foraging and Sedentary Contexts"

As you can see, these two anthropologists "read" the !Kung society in remarkably different ways. Marshal's thesis is that !Kung women are a subservient class relegated to the heavy, dull, and largely thankless task of gathering vegetables. In contrast, Draper believes that women's work is more interesting and requires more skill than other anthropologists have realized. Her thesis is that there is an egalitarian relationship between men and women in the !Kung society.

The source of data for both anthropologists is careful observation of !Kung women's daily lives. But the anthropologists are clearly not seeing the same thing. When the !Kung women return from the bush at the end of the day, Marshal sees their heavy loads and babies sagging in their pouches, whereas Draper sees the excited children awaiting the women's return.

So, which view is correct? That's a little like asking whether the Mariners are surging or struggling or whether the ANWR is bleak or teeming with animals. All writers necessarily present their own perspectives on their subjects; the alternative would be to list only facts—but even then you would have to decide which facts to list and in what order. As soon as you begin interpreting the facts—making inferences, reaching judgments, asserting meanings—you create a view of your subject from your own angle of vision. As a reader you should realize that all texts filter reality by privileging some aspects of the subject and suppressing others. When you realize that no text gives you the whole truth, but only the author's version of the truth, you can learn to read more critically, to be aware of the writer's point of view, and to be alert to how the writer's choice of words, use of metaphor, style, and arrangement of text urge you to narrow your view of the subject until it coincides with the writer's own angle of vision.

This doesn't mean that there is no such thing as truth. It means that no one writer can give you the complete picture and that you must actively seek alternative points of view, do further research, ask more questions, and confront the subject's complexity. If you wanted to do further study of women's roles in !Kung society, for example, some additional questions you might want to ask are the following: Were the two anthropologists studying the same !Kung groups at the same time? Are there aspects of male and female behaviors in !Kung society on which most anthropologists agree? What other information about male and female roles would be helpful and how could it be obtained? Should some terms, such as *male dominance* and *subservient role,* be defined more clearly?

Conducting a Simple Rhetorical Analysis

Our discussion of two different views of the ANWR and two different views of the role of women in !Kung society shows how a seemingly objective description of a scene reflects a specific angle of vision that can be revealed through analysis. Rhetorically, a description subtly persuades the reader toward the author's angle of vision. This angle of vision isn't necessarily the author's "true self" speaking, for authors *create* an angle of vision through rhetorical choices they make while composing.

We hope you will discover this insight for yourself while doing the assignment for this chapter. This assignment asks you first to compose two contrasting descriptions of the same scene (Part A) and then to explain how your two equally true descriptions create contrasting rhetorical effects (Part B). This latter task constitutes a rhetorical analysis of your two descriptions. In this section we describe five textual strategies writers often use (consciously or unconsciously) to create the persuasive effect of their texts. Each strategy creates textual differences that you can discuss in your rhetorical analysis.

Strategy 1: Writers Can State Their Meaning or Intended Effect Directly

Often writers state their point or angle of vision openly so that readers do not need to infer the writer's meaning or intentions. For example, the first anthropologist says that "there is only drudgery in digging roots" while the second anthropologist says "!Kung women impress one as a self-contained people with a high sense of self-esteem." The first writer announces her meaning directly—women's work is drudgery; in contrast, the second writer announces a more positive meaning.

Strategy 2: Writers Can Select Details that Convey Their Intended Effect and Omit Those that Don't

Another strategy for creating an angle of vision (and therefore influencing a reader's view) is to select details that further the writer's purpose and omit those that do not. For example, the details selected by Marshal, the first anthropologist, focus on the tastelessness of the vegetables and the heaviness of the women's loads, creating an overall impression of women's work as thankless and exhausting. The details chosen by Draper, the second anthropologist, focus on the excitement of the children awaiting their mothers' return and the fearlessness of the women as they forage "eight to ten miles from home," creating an impression of self-reliant women performing an essential task. As a specific example, Marshal includes the detail "babies sagging in the pouches of the karosses" while Draper includes "clusters of children standing on the edge of camp." The different details create different rhetorical effects.

Strategy 3: Writers Can Choose Words with Connotations that Convey Their Intended Effect

Writers can also influence readers through their choice of words. Because words carry emotional connotations as well as denotative meanings, any given word is a kind of lens that filters its subject in a certain way. Marshal chooses words connoting listlessness and fatigue, such as *drudgery, trudging, heavy,* and *sagging.* In contrast, Draper chooses words connoting energy: the children *scan* the bush, *leap and exclaim,* and *speculate,* while the women *forage.*

Strategy 4: Writers Can Use Figurative Language that Conveys Their Intended Effect

Figurative language—metaphors, similes, and analogies that compare or equate their subject to something else—can profoundly affect perception of a subject. When Rubini writes that oil companies are "salivating" for new oil-drilling opportunities, the reader's negative image of drooling dogs is transferred subconsciously to the oil companies. If those same companies were said to be "exploring new paths toward American independence from foreign oil," the reader might see them in a quite different light.

Strategy 5: Writers Can Create Sentence Structures that Convey Their Intended Effect

Another subtle way to control the rhetorical effect of a passage is through sentence structure. By placing key words and phrases in emphatic positions (for example, at the end of a long sentence, in a short sentence surrounded by long sentences, or in a main clause rather than a subordinate clause), writers can emphasize some parts of the passage while de-emphasizing others. Consider the difference in emphasis of these two possible sentences for a letter of recommendation for Neal Weasel (from the exercise on pp. 70–71).

Although Neal Weasel was often moody and brusque in my classes, he is surely a genius.

Although Neal Weasel is surely a genius, he was often moody and brusque in my classes.

Most readers will agree that the first version emphasizes Neal's brilliance and the second version emphasizes his less than peachy personality. The passages are equally factual—they both contain the same information—but they subtly convey different impressions.

Next consider how the first anthropologist, Marshal, uses sentence structure to create a negative feeling about !Kung women's plant-gathering role:

> Women bring most of the daily food that sustains the life of the people, but the roots and berries that are the principal plant foods of the Nyae Nyae !Kung are apt to be tasteless, harsh and not very satisfying. People crave meat.

Here the writer's emphasis is on meat as highly desirable (the short sentence, "People crave meat," in an environment of long sentences is especially emphatic) and on vegetables as "tasteless, harsh and not very satisfying" (these words occur in the stress position at the end of a long sentence). We could rewrite this passage, keeping the same facts, but creating a quite different rhetorical effect.

> Although the !Kung people crave meat and consider the plant food of the Kalahari tasteless, harsh, and not very satisfying, the women nevertheless provide most of the daily food that sustains the life of the people.

In this version, the emphasis is on how the women sustain the life of the people—a point presented in a nonstressed position in the original passage.

FOR WRITING AND DISCUSSION

What follows is a student example of two contrasting descriptions written for the assignment in this chapter. Read the descriptions carefully. Working individually, analyze the descriptions rhetorically to explain how the writer has created contrasting impressions through overt statements of meaning, selection and omission of details, word choice, figurative language, and sentence structure. You will do the same thing for your own two descriptions in Part B of your assignment. Spend approximately ten minutes freewriting your analysis. Then, working in small groups or as a whole class, share your analyses, trying to reach agreement on examples of how the writer has created different rhetorical effects by using the five strategies just described.

Description 1—Positive Effect

Light rain gently drops into the puddles that have formed along the curb as I look out my apartment window at the corner of 14th and East John. Pedestrians layered in sweaters, raincoats, and scarves and guarded with shiny rubber boots and colorful umbrellas sip their steaming hot triple-tall lattes. Some share smiles and pleasant exchanges as they hurry down the street, hastening to work where it is warm and dry. Others, smelling the aroma of French roast espresso coming from the coffee bar next to the bus stop, listen for the familiar rumbling sound that will mean the 56 bus has arrived. Radiant orange, yellow, and red leaves blanket the sidewalk in the areas next to the maple trees that line the road. Along the curb a mother holds the hand of her toddler, dressed like a miniature tugboat captain in yellow raincoat and pants, who splashes happily in a puddle.

Description 2—Negative Effect

A solemn grayness hangs in the air, as I peer out the window of my apartment at the corner of 14th and East John. A steady drizzle of rain leaves boot-drenching puddles for pedestrians to avoid. Bundled in rubber boots, sweaters, coats, and rain-soaked scarves, commuters clutch Styrofoam cups of coffee as a defense against the biting cold. They lift their heads every so often to take a small sip of caffeine, but look sleep-swollen nevertheless. Pedestrians hurry past each other, moving quickly to get away from the dismal weather, the dull grayness. Some nod a brief hello to a familiar face, but most clutch their overcoats and tread grimly on, looking to avoid puddles or spray from passing cars. Others stand at the bus stop, hunched over, waiting in the drab early morning for the smell of diesel that means the 56 bus has arrived. Along the curb an impatient mother jerks the hand of a toddler to keep him from stomping in an oil-streaked puddle.

Using Rhetorical Knowledge to Become a Strong Reader

Knowing how to analyze a text rhetorically can help you become a stronger reader. The more you understand how a text works, the more you can appreciate its particular point of view. Learning to ask what is *not* in the text, why the text is constructed *this* way and not *that* way, or why the writer took this particular point of view and not another enables you to identify the forces that shape what a writer sees and opens up the possibility for you to challenge and speak back to the text.

Reading written texts in this way prepares you to "read" many other human artifacts—body language, advertising images, architecture, classroom seating arrangements, party behaviors—in a similar way. You can learn to ask questions like the following:

What news items are *not* included on page 1 of today's paper? What belief or value system (and whose) causes this story to be front-page news while relegating that story to page 4?

When I read *Mademoiselle* or *Seventeen*, what products are *not* being advertised in its pages? Why?

Why does a party in the Philippines typically include all the host's neighbors and relatives whereas a party in the United States typically includes just one social group (for example, teens, but not uncles, aunts, and neighbors)? How do differences in who is invited or not invited to parties reflect differences in cultures?

We return to such questions in subsequent chapters. For now, keep in mind that the exercise of creating two different descriptions of the same scene can open up new ways of asking questions about countless things in the world around you.

Which Comes First, Perception or Interpretation?

So far we have been examining how writers, in observing a certain scene from their unique angle of vision, create a rhetorical effect through language choices. What we have saved for last is a crucial chicken-and-egg question: Which comes first, the writer's perception or the writer's interpretation? For example, did the two anthropologists begin their observations of the !Kung people with no preconceived theories or notions, letting their interpretations arise from their observations, or did they start with a theory or hypothesis, which in turn determined what they saw? This is a truly knotty problem, for, as we try to show in this section, it is difficult to draw a clear line between observation and interpretation; what you see and what you are predisposed to see are complexly intertwined.

On the face of it, terms such as *observation, perception,* and *seeing* seem nonproblematic. Objects are objects, and the process of perceiving an object—assuming that you aren't imbibing mind-altering drugs—is immediate and automatic. However, perception is never a simple matter. Consider what we call the expert–novice phenomenon. Experts on any given subject notice details about that subject that a novice overlooks. An experienced birdwatcher can distinguish dozens of kinds of swallows by subtle differences in size, markings, and behaviors, whereas a non-birdwatcher sees only a group of birds of similar size and shape. Similarly, people observing an unfamiliar game (for example, an American watching cricket or a Nigerian watching baseball) don't know what actions or events have meaning and hence don't know what to look for. Psychologists have found that after observing an inning of baseball, avid baseball fans remember numerous details about plays on the field, but people unfamiliar with the game remember none of these details, although they may have vivid recollections of people in the stands or of a player's peculiar mannerisms. In short, prior knowledge or absence of it causes people to see different things.

Cultural differences also affect perception. An American watching two Japanese business executives greet each other might not know that they are participating in an elaborate cultural code of bowing, eye contact, speech patterns, and timing of movements that convey meanings about social status. An Ethiopian newly arrived in the United States and an American sitting in a doctor's office will see different things when the nurse points to one of them to come into the examination room. The American notices nothing remarkable about the scene; he or she may remember what the nurse was wearing or something about the wallpaper. The Ethiopian, however, is likely to remember the nurse's act of pointing, a gesture of rudeness used in Ethiopia only to beckon children or discipline dogs. Again, observers of the same scene see different things.

Sometimes your beliefs and values are so powerful that they create blind spots. You won't notice data that contradict them. You may perceive contradictory data at some level, but if they don't register on your mind as significant, you disregard them. In this vein, a syndicated columnist explains why people who favor gun control and people who oppose it have trouble communicating with each other; they each filter out information that contradicts their own beliefs.

> The gun control advocates keep large files on every case of careless gun use they can find.
> But they don't have any records of people successfully defending themselves against criminals.
> At the same time, the National Rifle Association has thick files on honest citizens using guns to kill, wound or capture criminals.
> But under F in its file cabinets, there is nothing about family gun tragedies.
>
> —Mike Royko, *Chicago Tribune*

The lesson here is that people note and remember whatever is consistent with their worldview much more readily than they note and remember whatever is inconsistent with that view. What you believe is what you see.

To really see something that is familiar to you, to get beyond your beliefs about a subject in order to recognize aspects of it that are inconsistent with those beliefs, you may need to "defamiliarize" it, to make it strange. Many artists try to defamiliarize familiar objects by seeing them from unfamiliar perspectives, sometimes even distorting the object to disrupt ordinary ways of seeing. An artist might draw something upside down, or a writer might write about an event from the point of view of someone he or she considers loathsome—whatever it takes to wipe away "the film of habit" from the object. The writing project for this chapter will get you to see your scene in unfamiliar ways.

▨ COMPOSING YOUR ESSAY

Since the assignment for this chapter has two parts—Part A, calling for two contrasting descriptions, and Part B, calling for a rhetorical analysis—we will address each part separately.

Generating and Exploring Ideas for Your Two Descriptions

When you think about description, it sometimes helps to imagine yourself as the companion of a recently blinded person. Suppose that you were to become that person's eyes, describing your scene so fully that your blind companion could share your experience of seeing it. Then your blind companion, having a newly heightened sense of hearing, touch, and smell, could enrich your own perceptions so that the two of you, pooling your perceptions, could work together to create a richly detailed description of the scene. In your writing, good description should also be packed with sensory detail—sights, sounds, smells, textures, even on occasion tastes—all contributing to a dominant impression that gives the description focus.

After you have chosen a subject for your two descriptions, observe it intensely for fifteen or twenty minutes. One way to train yourself to notice sensory details is to create a sensory chart, with one column for your pleasant description and one column for your unpleasant description.

Pleasant Impression	Unpleasant Impression
Sight/eyes	Sight/eyes
Sound/ears	Sound/ears
Odor/nose	Odor/nose
Touch/fingers	Touch/fingers
Taste/tongue	Taste/tongue

As you observe your scene, note details that appeal to each of the senses and then try describing them first positively (left column) and then negatively (right column). One student, observing a scene in a local tavern, made these notes in her sensory chart:

Taste/tongue	Taste/tongue
salted and buttered popcorn	salty, greasy popcorn
frosty pitchers of beer	half-drunk pitchers of stale, warm beer
big bowls of salted-in-the-shell peanuts on the tables	mess of peanut shells and discarded pretzel wrappers on tables and floor

Sound/ears	Sound/ears
hum of students laughing and chatting	din of high-pitched giggles and various obnoxious frat guys shouting at each other from across the room
the juke box playing oldies but goodies from the early Beatles	juke box blaring out-of-date music

Shaping and Drafting Your Two Descriptions

Once you have observed your scene and made your sensory chart, compose your two descriptions. You will need to decide on an ordering principle for your descriptions. It generally makes sense to begin with an overview of the scene to orient your reader.

> From the park bench near 23rd and Maple, one can watch the people strolling by the duck pond.

> By 8:00 on any Friday night, Pagliacci's Pizzeria on Broadway becomes one of the city's most unusual gathering places.

Then you need a plan for arranging details. There are no hard and fast rules here, but there are some typical practices. You can arrange details in the following ways:

- by spatially scanning from left to right or from far to near
- by using the written equivalent of a movie zoom shot; begin with a broad overview of the scene, then move to close-up descriptions of specific details

Compose your pleasant description, selecting and focusing on details that convey a positive impression. Then compose your unpleasant description. Each description should comprise one fully developed paragraph (125–175 words).

Using *Show* Words Rather than *Tell* Words

In describing your scenes, use *show* words rather than *tell* words. *Tell* words interpret a scene without describing it. They name an interior, mental state, thus telling the reader what emotional reaction to draw from the scene.

Tell Words

There was a *pleasant* tree in the back yard.

There was an *unpleasant* tree in the back yard.

In contrast, *show* words describe a scene through sensory details appealing to sight, sound, smell, touch, and even taste. The description itself evokes the desired effect without requiring the writer to state it overtly.

Show Words

A *spreading elm* tree *bathed* the back yard with *shade*.   *[evokes positive feelings]*

An *out-of-place elm, planted too close to the house, blocked our view* of the *mountains*.)   *[evokes negative feelings]*

Whereas show words are particulars that evoke the writer's meaning through sensory detail, tell words are abstractions that announce the writer's intention directly (strategy 1 on p. 85). An occasional tell word can be useful, but show words operating at the bottom of the "scale of abstraction" (see Chapter 3, pp. 50–51) are the flesh and muscle of descriptive prose.

Inexperienced writers often try to create contrasting impressions of a scene simply by switching tell words.

Weak: Overuse of *Tell* Words

The smiling merchants happily talked with customers trying to get them to buy their products.   *[positive purpose]*

The annoying merchants kept hassling customers trying to convince them to buy their products.   *[negative purpose]*

In this example, the negative words *annoying* and *hassling* and the positive words *smiling* and *happily* are tell words; they state the writer's contrasting intentions, but they don't describe the scene. Here is how the student writer revised these passages using show words.

Strong: Conversion to *Show* Words

One of the merchants, selling thick-wooled Peruvian sweaters, nodded approvingly as a woman tried on a richly textured, blue cardigan in front of the mirror.   *[positive purpose]*

One of the merchants, hawking those Peruvian sweaters that you find in every open-air market, tried to convince a middle-aged woman that the lumpy, oversized cardigan she was trying on looked stylish.   *[negative purpose]*

Here are some more examples taken from students' drafts before and after revision:

Draft with *Tell* Words	**Revision with *Show* Words**
Children laugh and point animatedly at all the surroundings.	Across the way, a small boy taps his friend's shoulder and points at a circus clown.
The wonderful smell of food cooking on the barbecue fills my nose.	The tantalizing smell of grilled hamburgers and buttered corn on the cob wafts from the barbecue area of the park, where men in their cookout aprons wield forks and spatulas and drink Budweisers.
The paintings on the wall are confusing, dark, abstract, demented, and convey feelings of unhappiness and suffering.	The paintings on the wall, viewed through the smoke-filled room, seem confusing and abstract—the work of a demented artist on a bad trip. Splotches of black paint are splattered over a greenish-yellow background like bugs on vomit.

Revising Your Two Descriptions

The following revision hints will help you improve your first draft.

1. ***Do the two descriptions focus on the same scene at the same time?***   The rules for the assignment ask you to use only factual details observable in the same scene at the same time. It violates the spirit of the assignment to have one scene in the rain and another in the sunshine, or to have one scene at a winning basketball game and another at a losing game.
2. ***Do you use plenty of "show" words and few "tell" words?***   Inexperienced writers tend to rely on tell words rather than show words. Go through your draft identifying words that describe internal mental states (*pleasant, happy, depressing, annoying, pretty, ugly,* and so forth). These are tell words, most of which should be eliminated. Rewrite the passages by actually describing what you see, hear, smell, touch, and taste.

3. *Can the focus on a dominant impression be improved through more effective word choice?*   Can you improve the focus on each description's dominant impression by choosing naming and action words with stronger connotations? For example, consider synonyms for the generic word *shoe*. Most people wear shoes, but only certain people on certain occasions wear wing tips or pumps or sandals. Among words for kinds of sandals, *Birkenstocks* carries a different connotation from *Tevas* or *thongs* or *strappy espadrilles with a faux-metallic finish*. Search your draft for places where you could substitute more colorful or precise words for a generic word to convey your dominant impression more effectively.

Generating and Exploring Ideas for Your Rhetorical Analysis

Part B of the assignment asks you to write a rhetorical analysis of your two descriptions in which you explain the strategies you used to create different rhetorical effects. Your analysis should answer questions like these:

1. Did you state your intended meaning overtly in each description through the use of "tell" words? Give examples.
2. Did you include different details in each description? Why? Illustrate.
3. Did you select words with positive connotations in one description and negative connotations in the other? Illustrate.
4. Did you use figurative language differently in the two descriptions? Why? Illustrate?
5. Did you vary sentence structure in the two descriptions to emphasize positive details in one and negative details in the other? Illustrate.
6. What other strategies did you use?

Your rhetorical analysis should be organized as a brief essay with a thesis statement and good paragraph structure. One effective approach is to begin with a thesis statement that forecasts the rhetorical strategies you used. Then illustrate your analysis with examples and brief quotations from your two descriptions.

The last part of the rhetorical analysis should be your reflection on what you learned from doing this assignment. In effect, you are answering your reader's "So what?" question. "So you wrote two different descriptions," your reader might say. "Why are you telling me this? What's your point?" Your reader needs an answer to this question to understand the larger implications—the value—of what he or she has read. In sharing your two descriptions of a scene, what larger point do you want to make about writing and reading? What is the surprise (new knowledge? new understanding about description?) that you want to bring your reader?

What did you learn? To help you generate ideas for this section, try freewriting your responses to the following questions:

1. What are the most important things you learned from reading this chapter and writing your two descriptions?

2. How has reading this chapter and doing this writing project affected the way you now read other texts, for example, the newspaper or readings from your other courses?

3. Did the need to slant your descriptions affect the way you observed? How so? Do you think you could write a single objective description of your scene that would be better than the two paragraphs you wrote? Why?

4. What are the most important questions that this chapter raises in your mind? What does it make you think about?

Freewriting for several minutes in response to each of these questions should give you enough material for your final reflection on what you learned.

Shaping and Drafting Your Rhetorical Analysis

The structure of your analysis is prescribed by the assignment: (a) a rhetorical analysis of the difference between your two descriptions, and (b) a final reflection on what you learned.

Revising Your Rhetorical Analysis

When you have written a draft of your rhetorical analysis, share it with your classmates to get insights about how best to revise it. Your goal at the revision stage is to discover the ideas that you want to communicate and then to make those ideas as clear as possible for readers. The following guidelines for peer reviewers should be helpful.

g u i d e l i n e s
for Peer Reviewers

Instructions for peer reviews, including use of these guidelines, are provided in Chapter 10, pages 195–202. To write a peer review for a classmate, use your own paper, numbering your responses to correspond to the questions on the guidelines. At the head of your paper place the author's name and your own name, as shown.

Author's Name: _____

Peer Reviewer's Name: _____

I. Read the draft at a normal reading speed from beginning to end. As you read, do the following:

A. Place a wavy line in the margin next to any passages that you find confusing, that contain something that doesn't seem to fit, or that otherwise slow down your reading.

B. Place a "Good!" in the margin next to any passages where you think the writing is particularly strong or interesting.

II. Read the draft again slowly and answer the following questions by writing brief explanations of your answers.

A. The two descriptions:

1. Are there differences in the time or place of the two descriptions or other differences in "fact" (change in the weather, in what people are doing, or so forth)? If so, alert the writer to redo at least one of the descriptions.

2. Are the two descriptions clearly of the same scene but from different angles of vision? Could the two descriptions be made more parallel, sketched more boldly, or made more detailed and vivid?

3. Where does the writer use show words effectively? How many of the five senses are appealed to? Where could the writer replace tell words with show words or improve the specificity of show words?

4. If the writer has relied primarily on one or two methods of creating contrast (overt interpretation, selection or omission of details), how might he or she use other methods (contrasting word choice, contrasting figurative language, changes in sentence structure)?

B. Analysis section:

1. How might the writer improve the ideas or structure of the analysis?

2. Does the analysis show how the writer has used several or all of the five strategies explained on pages 75–77? Are there strategies used that the writer doesn't discuss?

3. Where could the writer use more or better examples to illustrate differences in overt commentary, selection or omission of details, word choice, figurative language, and sentence structure?

4. What could be added or changed in the analysis?

C. "So what?" section:

1. Has the writer explained what he or she has learned from seeing rhetorically? Do the insights seem interesting? Are they clear?

2. Which, if any, of the writer's points could be better developed or illustrated?

D. Sum up what you see as the chief strengths and problem areas of this draft.

1. Strengths

2. Problem areas

III. Read the draft one more time. Place a check in the margin wherever you notice problems in grammar, spelling, or mechanics (one check per problem).

TOPIC Guidepost #12

For those using Texas Tech's TOPIC Web-Based assignments:

Direct your web browser to **http://english.ttu.edu:5555**

Guidepost #12 provides full instructions regarding your reading assignment (Handbook pages 279-290) and TOPIC Mail messages.

TOPIC Guidepost #13

For those using Texas Tech's TOPIC Web-Based assignments:

Direct your web browser to **http://english.ttu.edu:5555**

Guidepost #13 provides full instructions regarding your reading assignment (Chapter 6) and Draft 2.1.

chapter 6

Reading Rhetorically
The Writer as
Strong Reader

ABOUT READING RHETORICALLY

Many new college students are surprised by the amount, range, and difficulty of reading they have to do in college. Every day they are challenged by reading assignments ranging from scholarly articles and textbooks on complex subject matter to primary sources, such as Plato's dialogues or Darwin's *Voyage of the Beagle.*

The goal of this chapter is to help you become a more powerful reader of academic texts, prepared to take part in the conversations of the disciplines you study. To this end, we explain two kinds of thinking and writing essential to your college reading: first, your ability to listen carefully to a text, to recognize its parts and their functions, and to summarize its ideas; and second, your ability to formulate strong responses to texts by interacting with them, either by agreeing with, interrogating, or actively opposing them.

To interact strongly with texts, you must learn how to read them both with and against the grain. When you read *with the grain* of a text, you see the world through its author's perspective, open yourself to the author's argument, apply the text's insights to new contexts, and connect its ideas to your own experiences and personal knowledge. When you read *against the grain* of a text, you resist it by questioning its points, raising doubts, analyzing the limits of its perspective, or even refuting its argument. We say that readers who respond strongly to texts in this manner read *rhetorically;* that is, they are aware of the effect a text is intended to have on them, and they critically consider that effect, entering into or challenging the text's intentions.

EXPLORING RHETORICAL READING

As an introduction to rhetorical reading, we would like you to read Dr. Andrés Martin's "On Teenagers and Tattoos," which appeared in the *Journal of the American Academy of Child and Adolescent Psychiatry,* a scholarly publication. Before reading the article, complete the following opinion survey. Answer each question using a 1–5 scale, with 1 meaning "strongly agree" and 5 meaning "strongly disagree."

1. For teenagers, getting a tattoo is like following any other fad, such as wearing the currently popular kind of shoe or hairstyle.
2. Teenagers get tattoos primarily as a form of asserting independence from parents and other adults.
3. Teenagers get tattoos on the spur of the moment and usually don't consider the irreversibility of marking their skin.
4. Teenagers who get tattoos are expressing deep psychological needs.
5. A psychiatry journal can provide useful insights into teen choices to tattoo their bodies.

When you have finished rating your degree of agreement with these statements, read Martin's article, using whatever notetaking, underlining, or highlighting strategies you normally use when reading for a class. When you have finished reading, complete the exercises that follow.

READING

ANDRÉS MARTIN, M.D.
ON TEENAGERS AND TATTOOS

The skeleton dimensions I shall now proceed to set down are copied verbatim from my right arm, where I had them tattooed: as in my wild wanderings at that period, there was no other secure way of preserving such valuable statistics.

—Melville/Moby Dick CII

1   Tattoos and piercings have become a part of our everyday landscape. They are ubiquitous, having entered the circles of glamour and the mainstream of fashion, and they have even become an increasingly common feature of our urban youth. Legislation in most states restricts professional tattooing to adults older than 18 years of age, so "high end" tattooing is rare in children and adolescents, but such tattoos are occasionally seen in older teenagers. Piercings, by comparison, as well as self-made or "jailhouse" type tattoos, are not at all rare among adolescents or even among schoolage children. Like hairdo, makeup, or baggy jeans, tattoos and piercings can be subject to fad influence or peer pressure in an effort toward group affiliation. As with any other fashion statement, they can be construed as bodily aids in the inner struggle toward identity consolidation, serving as adjuncts to the defining and sculpting of the self by means of external manipulations. But unlike most other body decorations, tattoos and piercings are set apart by their irreversible and permanent nature, a quality at the core of their magnetic appeal to adolescents.

Adolescents and their parents are often at odds over the acquisition of bodily dec- 2
orations. For the adolescent, piercings or tattoos may be seen as personal and beautifying statements, while parents may construe them as oppositional and enraging
affronts to their authority. Distinguishing bodily adornment from self-mutilation may indeed prove challenging, particularly when a family is in disagreement over a teenager's
motivations and a clinician is summoned as the final arbiter. At such times it may be
most important to realize jointly that the skin can all too readily become but another
battleground for the tensions of the age, arguments having less to do with tattoos and
piercings than with core issues such as separation from the family matrix. Exploring
the motivations and significance underlying tattoos (Grumet, 1983) and piercings can
go a long way toward resolving such differences and can become a novel and additional way of getting to know teenagers. An interested and nonjudgmental appreciation
of teenagers' surface presentations may become a way of making contact not only in
their terms but on their turfs: quite literally on the territory of their skins.

The following three sections exemplify some of the complex psychological under- 3
pinnings of youth tattooing.

Identity and the Adolescent's Body

Tattoos and piercing can offer a concrete and readily available solution for many 4
of the identity crises and conflicts normative to adolescent development. In using such
decorations, and by marking out their bodily territories, adolescents can support their
efforts at autonomy, privacy, and insulation. Seeking individuation, tattooed adolescents can become unambiguously demarcated from others and singled out as unique.
The intense and often disturbing reactions that are mobilized in viewers can help to effectively keep them at bay, becoming tantamount to the proverbial "Keep Out" sign
hanging from a teenager's door.

Alternatively, [when teenagers feel] prey to a rapidly evolving body over which they 5
have no say, self-made and openly visible decorations may restore adolescents' sense
of normalcy and control, a way of turning a passive experience into an active identity.
By indelibly marking their bodies, adolescents can strive to reclaim their bearings within
an environment experienced as alien, estranged, or suffocating or to lay claim over their
evolving and increasingly unrecognizable bodies. In either case, the net outcome can
be a resolution to unwelcome impositions: external, familial, or societal in one case; internal and hormonal in the other. In the words of a 16-year-old girl with several facial
piercings, and who could have been referring to her body just as well as to the position
within her family. "If I don't fit in, it is because *I* say so."

Incorporation and Ownership

Imagery of a religious, deathly, or skeletal nature, the likenesses of fierce animals 6
or imagined creatures, and the simple inscription of names are some of the time-tested
favorite contents for tattoos. In all instances, marks become not only memorials or re-
cipients for clearly held persons or concepts: they strive for incorporation, with images
and abstract symbols gaining substance on becoming a permanent part of the individual's skin. Thickly embedded in personally meaningful representations and object relations, tattoos can become not only the ongoing memento of a relationship, but at
times even the only evidence that there ever was such a bond. They can quite literally
become the relationship itself. The turbulence and impulsivity of early attachments and
infatuations may become grounded, effectively bridging oblivion through the visible
reality of tattoos.

7   *Case Vignette.* A, a 13-year-old boy, proudly showed me his tattooed deltoid. The coarsely depicted roll of the dice marked the day and month of his birth. Rather disappointed, he then uncovered an immaculate back, going on to draw for me the great "piece" he envisioned for it. A menacing figure held a hand of cards: two aces, two eights, and a card with two sets of dates. A's father had belonged to "Dead Man's Hand," a motorcycle gang named after the set of cards (aces and eights) that the legendary Wild Bill Hickock had held in the 1890s when shot dead over a poker table in Deadwood, South Dakota. A had only the vaguest memory of and sketchiest information about his father, but he knew he had died in a motorcycle accident: the fifth card marked the dates of his birth and death.

8   The case vignette also serves to illustrate how tattoos are often the culmination of a long process of imagination, fantasy, and planning that can start at an early age. Limited markings, or relatively reversible ones such as piercings, can at a later time scaffold toward the more radical commitment of a permanent tattoo.

The Quest for Permanence

9   The popularity of the anchor as a tattoo motif may historically have had to do less with guild identification among sailors than with an intense longing for rootedness and stability. In a similar vein, the recent increase in the popularity and acceptance of tattoos may be understood as an antidote or counterpoint to our urban and nomadic lifestyles. Within an increasingly mobile society, in which relationships are so often transient—as attested by the frequencies of divorce, abandonment, foster placement, and repeated moves, for example—tattoos can be a readily available source of grounding. Tattoos, unlike many relationships, can promise permanence and stability. A sense of constancy can be derived from unchanging marks that can be carried along no matter what the physical, temporal, or geographical vicissitudes at hand. Tattoos stay, while all else may change.

10   *Case Vignette.* A proud father at 17, B had had the smiling face of his 3-month-old baby girl tattooed on his chest. As we talked at a tattoo convention, he proudly introduced her to me, explaining how he would "always know how beautiful she is today" when years from then he saw her semblance etched on himself.

11   The quest for permanence may at other times prove misleading and offer premature closure to unresolved conflicts. At a time of normative uncertainties, adolescents may maladaptively and all too readily commit to a tattoo and its indefinite presence. A wish to hold on to a current certainty may lead the adolescent to lay down in ink what is valued and cherished one day but may not necessarily be in the future. The frequency of self-made tattoos among hospitalized, incarcerated, or gang-affiliated youths suggests such motivations: a sense of stability may be a particularly dire need under temporary, turbulent, or volatile conditions. In addition, through their designs teenagers may assert a sense of bonding and allegiance to a group larger than themselves. Tattoos may attest to powerful experiences, such as adolescence itself, lived and even survived together. As with Moby Dick's protagonist Ishmael, they may bear witness to the "valuable statistics" of one's "wild wandering(s)": those of adolescent exhilaration and excitement on the one hand; of growing pains, shared misfortune, or even incarceration on the other.

12   Adolescents' bodily decorations, at times radical and dramatic in their presentation, can be seen in terms of figuration rather than disfigurement, of the natural body being through them transformed into a personalized body (Brain, 1979). They can often be understood as self-constructive and adorning efforts, rather than prematurely

subsumed as mutilatory and destructive acts. If we bear all of this in mind, we may not only arrive at a position to pass more reasoned clinical judgment, but become sensitized through our patients' skins to another level of their internal reality.

References

Brain, R. (1979). *The Decorated Body.* New York: Harper & Row.

Grumet, G. W. (1983). Psychodynamic implications of tattoos. *Am J Orthopsychiatry* 53:482–492.

Postreading Exercises

1. Summarize in one or two sentences Martin's main points.
2. Freewrite your response to this question: In what way, if any, has Martin's article caused me to reconsider my answers to the opinion survey?
3. Working in small groups or as a whole class, compare the notetaking strategies you used while reading this piece. (a) How many people wrote marginal notes? How many underlined or highlighted? (b) Compare the contents of these notes. Did people highlight the same passage or different passages? (c) Individually, look at your annotations and highlights and try to decide why you wrote or marked what you did. Share your reasons for making these annotations. The goal of this exercise is to make you more aware of your thinking processes as you read.
4. Working as a whole class or in small groups, share your responses to the questionnaire and to the postreading questions. To what extent did this article change people's thinking about the reasons teenagers choose to tattoo their bodies? What were the most insightful points in this article?
5. Assume that you are looking for substantial, detailed information about teenagers and tattooing. What parts of this article leave you with unanswered questions? Where would you like to have more explanation or examples?

WRITING PROJECT

Write a "summary/strong response" essay that includes: (a) a summary (approximately 150–250 words) of a reading specified by your instructor and (b) a strong response to that reading in which you speak back to that reading from your own critical thinking, personal experience, and values. As you formulate your own response, consider both the author's ideas and the author's rhetorical choices concerning audience, purpose, genre, and style. Think of your response as your analysis of how the text tries to influence its readers rhetorically and how your wrestling with the text has expanded and deepened your thinking about its ideas.

The skills this assignment develops are crucial for academic writers. You will learn how to summarize an article, including how to quote brief passages, how to use attributive tags to cue your reader that you are reporting someone else's ideas rather than your own, and how to cite the article using (in this case) the Modern Language Association (MLA) documentation system. You will use these skills any time you write a research paper, term paper, or any other scholarly work that uses sources. But you will also learn how to contribute your own ideas to a conversation. Weak readers passively report what other people have said. Strong readers see themselves as contributors to the conversation, capable of analyzing and evaluating texts, speaking back to other authors, and thinking actively for themselves.

◢ UNDERSTANDING RHETORICAL READING

In this section we contrast the kinds of difficulties college students encounter when they read academic texts with the fluent reading practices of experts. We then show you how to read a text both with the grain and against the grain—skills you will need to summarize a text and respond to it strongly.

What Makes College-Level Reading Difficult

The difficulty of college-level reading stems in part from the complexity of the subject matter. Whatever the subject—from international monetary policies to cold fusion—you have to wrestle with new and complex materials that might perplex anyone. But in addition to the daunting subject matter, several other factors contribute to the difficulty of college-level reading.

Vocabulary

Many college-level readings—especially primary sources—contain unfamiliar technical language. The Martin text, for example, assumes that you understand such technical terms as *identity consolidation, normative, individuation,* and *object relations.* In some contexts you can look up a difficult word in the dictionary. But in academia, words often carry specialized meanings that evoke a whole history of conversation and debate that may be inaccessible even through a specialized dictionary. *Existentialism, Neoplatonic, postmodernism, Newtonian,* and *Keynesian,* for example, are code words for attitudes or positions in a complex conversation. No dictionary could capture all the nuances of meaning that these words carry in those conversations. You will not fully understand them until you are initiated into the disciplinary conversations that gave rise to them.

Unfamiliar Rhetorical Context

Another cause of difficulty, especially in primary materials, is lack of familiarity with the text's original rhetorical context. As we explained in Part One, writers write to an audience for a purpose; the purpose results from some motivating occasion or event. Unless you know something about a text's purpose, occasion, and intended audience (that is, unless you know the conversation to which the text belongs), you may well be left floundering. Sometimes the rhetorical context is easy to figure out, as in the case of the Martin article (he is offering advice to psychiatrists about how to counsel tattooed teens and their families effectively). But why did Plato write his dialogues? What conversation was Freud joining when he began interpreting dreams? Whom was Einstein opposing when he proposed his theory of relativity? The more you can learn about a text's rhetorical context, through internal clues or through outside research, the easier it is to read and respond to the text.

Unfamiliar Genre

In Chapter 4 we discussed genre in our analysis of a writer's rhetorical context. In your college reading you will encounter a wide range of genres, such as textbooks, scholarly articles, scientific reports, historical documents, newspaper articles, op-ed pieces, and so forth. Each of these genres makes different demands on readers and requires a different reading strategy. An unfamiliar genre adds to the difficulty of reading.

Lack of Background Knowledge

Writers necessarily make assumptions about what their readers know. If you lack background knowledge, you may have trouble interpreting the writer's ideas and fully understanding the text. Your understanding of Martin, for example, would be more complete if you had a background in adolescent psychology and psychiatric therapy.

FOR WRITING AND DISCUSSION

The importance of background knowledge can be easily demonstrated any time you dip into past issues of a news magazine or try to read articles about an unfamiliar culture. Consider the following passage from a 1986 *Newsweek* article. How much background knowledge do you need before you can fully comprehend this passage? What cultural knowledge about the United States would a student from Ethiopia or Indonesia need?

Throughout the NATO countries last week, there were second thoughts about the prospect of a nuclear-free world. For 40 years nuclear weapons have been the backbone of the West's defense. For almost as long American presidents have ritually affirmed their desire to see the world rid of them. Then, suddenly, Ronald Reagan and Mikhail Gorbachev came close to actually doing it. Let's abolish all nuclear ballistic missiles in the next 10 years, Reagan said. Why not all nuclear weapons, countered Gorbachev. OK, the president responded, like a man agreeing to throw in the washer-dryer along with the house.

What if the deal had gone through? On the one hand, Gorbachev would have returned to Moscow a hero. There is a belief in the United States that the Soviets need nuclear arms because nuclear weapons are what make them a superpower. But according to Marxist-Leninist doctrine, capitalism's nuclear capability (unforeseen by Marx and Lenin) is the only thing that can prevent the inevitable triumph of communism. Therefore, an end to nuclear arms would put the engine of history back on its track.

On the other hand, Europeans fear, a nonnuclear United States would be tempted to retreat into neo-isolationism.

—Robert B. Cullen, "Dangers of Disarming," *Newsweek*

Working in small groups or as a class, identify words and passages in this text that depend on background information or knowledge of culture for complete comprehension.

Reading Processes Used by Experienced Readers

In Chapter 10, we describe the difference between the writing processes of experts and those of beginning college writers. There are parallel differences between the reading processes of experienced and inexperienced readers, especially when they encounter complex materials. In this section we discuss some of the skills used by experienced readers.

Varying Strategies to Match Reading Goals

Unlike novices, experienced readers vary their reading speed and strategies according to their goals. Experienced readers sometimes scan texts for a piece of information and other times scrutinize every word. Robert Sternberg, a cognitive psychologist, asked subjects to read four different passages for four different purposes: (1) scanning for a piece of information, (2) skimming for main ideas, (3) reading for complete comprehension, and (4) reading for detailed analysis. The researcher discovered that experienced readers varied their reading speed appropriately, spending the most time with passages they had to analyze in detail and the least time with those requiring only scanning or skimming. Inexperienced readers, in contrast, read all four passages at the same speed, spending too much or too little time on three of the four readings.

FOR WRITING AND DISCUSSION

Suppose you are doing a research project on a question of interest to you. So far you have located several books and a dozen or so articles on your topic. Working in small groups or as a whole class, create hypothetical scenarios in which you would, on different occasions, read material at all four reading speeds. When would you scan material? When would you skim for main ideas only? When would you read a text carefully from beginning to end? When would you pore over a text line by line?

Varying Strategies to Match Genre

Experienced readers also match their reading strategies to the genre of the piece being read. They use conventions of the genre to select the portions of the text that are most important to their purposes. To illustrate, let's look at how experienced readers read scientific or technical reports, a genre described in Chapter 4. Such reports typically contain five sections: introduction, methods (procedures), findings, discussion of findings, and conclusions and recommendations.

Experts seldom read a scientific report from beginning to end. A common approach is to read the introduction section (which explains the research question being examined, often reviews the literature surrounding the question, and presents the hypothesis), move to the discussion section, and then read the conclusions and recommendations section. These sections carry the study's argument by showing to what extent the findings help answer the research question. Most experts would turn to the methods and findings sections only after determining that the research was relevant to their work and generally helpful. They would read these sections primarily to determine how carefully and thoughtfully the research was done. (Debates about scientific research often focus on the research design and methodology.)

Other genres, too, demand special ways of reading, which you will develop through experience. For now, it is important simply to recognize that different genres use different conventions, which, in turn, invite different ways of reading.

Adopting a Multidraft Reading Process

Just as people may mistakenly believe that experienced authors compose effortlessly in one sitting, they also may mistakenly believe that expert readers comprehend a text perfectly with one rapid reading. Deceived by speed-reading advertisements, many students push themselves to read more quickly rather than more carefully. Experts, however, adjust their reading speed to the text's level of difficulty. As they read, they struggle to make the text comprehensible. They hold confusing passages in mental suspension, having faith that later parts of the essay may clarify earlier parts. They "nutshell" passages, often writing gist statements in the margins. A gist statement is a brief indication of the paragraph's function or purpose in the argument or a brief summary of the paragraph's content. Experts reread difficult texts two and three times, treating their first pass as an approximation or rough draft. They interact with the text by asking questions, expressing disagreement, and linking the text with other readings or with personal experience.

Students often don't allot enough study time for this kind of careful reading and rereading, thus depriving themselves of the challenges that will help them grow as readers. The rest of this chapter will show you how to struggle effectively with a challenging text.

Improving Your Own Reading Process

Here are some general strategies you can use to improve your ability to read any kind of college-level material.

1. *Slow down or speed up, depending on your goals.*   First, decide why you are reading the material and what you will need to do with it. If you are

looking through several articles to find those that relate to a specific research topic, then you probably want to skim quickly through them. But many of your assignments will demand close, detailed reading. In these instances, follow the strategies of experts, reading with pen in hand and allotting time to reread a text if it is particularly difficult, treating first readings as first drafts.

2. *Reconstruct the rhetorical context.*   Train yourself to ask questions such as these: Who is this author? What audience is the author targeting? What occasion prompted this writing? What is the author's purpose? Any piece of writing makes more sense if you think of its author as a real person writing for some real purpose within a real historical context. Often you can reconstruct the rhetorical context from clues within the text. Encyclopedias and biographical dictionaries can also help you establish a rhetorical context.

3. *Join the text's conversation by exploring your views on the issues before reading.*   To determine the text's issues before reading it through, note the title, read the first few paragraphs carefully, and skim the opening sentences of all paragraphs. Try to appreciate from the outset what conversation the text is joining and consider your own views on the issue. This sort of personal exploration at the prereading stage both increases your readiness to understand the text and enhances your ability to enjoy it. We tried to create this experience for you by designing the brief prereading questionnaire for the Martin piece.

4. *Lose your highlighter; find your pen.*   Relying on those yellow highlighters or underlining with a pen or pencil can be a good strategy when your sole concern is to note main ideas, but in other cases it can make you too passive. When you read for full comprehension and detailed analysis, highlighting can lull you into thinking that you are reading actively when you aren't. Next time you get the urge to highlight a passage, write in the margin why you think it's important. Is it a major new point in the argument? A significant piece of support? A summary of the opposition? A particularly strong or particularly weak point? Use the margins to summarize, protest, question, or assent—but don't just color the pages. If you are reading a text that you can't write in (for example, a library book), make your "marginal notes" in a reading log keyed to the text's pages.

5. *Get the dictionary habit.*   Get in the habit of looking up words when you can't tell their meaning from context. One strategy is to make small tick marks next to words you're unsure of and look them up after you've finished reading so that you don't break your concentration.

6. *Recognize when lack of background information is the source of your difficulty.*   Sometimes you simply have to live a while with fuzzy passages that refer to concepts or phenomena that you don't understand. Write a question in the margin to make note of the concept, term, or reference you can't understand and then continue to do the best you can with the rest of the text. After you finish your reading, you can consult encyclopedias, other library resources, or knowledgeable peers to fill gaps in your knowledge.

7. ***Try "translating" difficult passages.*** When you stumble over a difficult passage, try translating it into your own words. Converting the passage into your own language will force you to focus on the precise meanings of words. Although your translation may not be exactly what the author intended, you will see more clearly where the sources of confusion lie and what the likely range of meanings might be.

8. ***Read both with the grain and against the grain.*** When you read with the grain, you are a compliant reader who tries to read the text the way the author intended. When you read against the grain, you are a resistant reader who asks unanticipated questions, pushes back, and reads the text in ways unforeseen by the author. Using the believing/doubting game introduced in Chapter 2 as a metaphor, reading with the grain means to believe the text; reading against the grain means to doubt it. When you share the author's belief system, it is sometimes difficult to resist the text; when you oppose the author's belief system, it is sometimes hard to be compliant. Nevertheless, strong readers try to develop their ability to read in both ways. A good strategy is to write in the margins what the text prompts you to think as you read—your surprises, insights, questions, and objections.

9. ***Continue the conversation after you read.*** After you've read a text, try completing the following statements in a journal:
    - Before reading this text, I believed this about the topic:

      _____

    - But after reading the text, my view has changed in these ways:

      _____

    - Although the text has persuaded me that _____,
      I still have these doubts: _____
    - The most significant questions this text raises for me are these:

      _____

    - The most important insights I have gotten from reading this text are these:

      _____

How to Write a Summary

In the rest of this chapter, we are going to show you how to apply these active reading skills to writing about complex texts. One of the skills you will need and use most in your college courses—and later in your career and life as a citizen— is the ability to produce accurate, thoughtful, and informed responses to what you have read. Writing a summary fosters a close encounter between you and the text and demonstrates your understanding of it.

We turn now to the nuts and bolts of reading a text when your goal is a full and detailed comprehension of its arguments. When you write a summary, you practice reading with the grain of a text. In summarizing, you "listen" actively to the text's author, showing that you understand the author's point of view by re-stating his or her argument as completely and fairly as possible. Sometimes you will need to compose a stand-alone summary of your own piece of writing, as when professionals are asked to write *abstracts* or *executive summaries* of an experimental report, proposal, or paper to be presented at a scholarly conference. Most commonly, however, you will need to summarize the views of other writers, particularly when you imagine readers who have not read a text that you want to refer to in your own writing. The summary gives your readers a condensed view of the other writer's argument, which you can then use as support for your own views or as a starting point for analysis or disagreement.

The process for summarizing outlined in the following steps will help you read more actively and accurately. As you become a more experienced reader and writer, you'll follow these steps without thinking about them.

Reading for Both Structure and Content

Step 1: The first time through, read the text fairly quickly for general meaning. If you get confused, keep going; later parts of the text might clarify earlier parts.

Step 2: Reread the text carefully. As you read, write gist statements in the margins for each paragraph. A *gist statement* is a brief indication of the paragraph's function or purpose in the text or a brief summary of the paragraph's content. Sometimes it is helpful to think of these two kinds of gist statements as "what it does" statements and "what it says" statements.* A "what it does" statement specifies the paragraph's function—for example, "summarizes an opposing view," "introduces another reason," "presents a supporting example," "provides statistical data in support of a point," and so on. A "what it says" statement captures the main idea of a paragraph by summarizing the paragraph's content.

When you first practice detailed readings of a text, you might find it helpful to write complete *does* and *says* statements on a separate sheet of paper rather than in the margins until you develop the internal habit of appreciating both the function and content of parts of an essay. Here are *does* and *says* statements for selected paragraphs in Andres Martin's essay on teenage tattooing (pp. 89–92).

Paragraph 1: Does: Introduces the subject and sets up the argument. *Says:* The current popularity of tattoos and piercings is partly explained as an aid toward finding an identity, but the core or their appeal is their irreversible permanence.

Paragraph 2: Does: Narrows the focus and presents the thesis. *Says:* To counsel families in disagreement over tattoos, psychiatrists should exhibit a nonjudgmental appreciation of teen tattoos and use them to understand teenagers better.

Paragraph 4: Does: Discusses the first complex motivation behind youth tattooing. *Says:* Teens use tattoos to handle identity crises and to establish their uniqueness from others.

---

*For our treatment of "what it does" and "what it says" statements, we are indebted to Kenneth A. Bruffee, *A Short Course in Writing*, 2nd ed. (Cambridge, MA: Winthrop, 1980).

Paragraph 5: Does: Elaborates on the first motivation, the identity issue. *Says:* Tattoos provide teens with a sense of control over their changing bodies and over an environment perceived as adverse and domineering.

Paragraph 11: Does: Complicates the view of teens' use of tattoos to find permanence and belonging. *Says:* Although tattoos may unrealistically promise the resolution to larger conflicts, they may at least record the triumphs and miseries of adolescent turbulence, including gang and prison experience.

Paragraph 12: Does: Sums up the perspective and advice of the article. *Says:* Psychiatrists should regard adolescent tattoos positively as adornment and self-expression and employ tattoos to help understand teens' identities and sense of reality.

You may occasionally have difficulty writing a *says* statement for a paragraph because you may have trouble deciding what the main idea is, especially if the paragraph doesn't begin with a closed-form topic sentence. One way to respond to this problem is to formulate the question that you think the paragraph answers. If you think of chunks of the text as answers to a logical progression of questions, you can often follow the main ideas more easily. Rather than writing *says* statements in the margins, therefore, some readers prefer writing *says* questions. *Says* questions for the Martin text may include the following: What is the most constructive approach clinicians can take to teen tattooing when these tattoos have become the focus of family conflict? What psychological needs and problems are teenagers acting out through their tattoos? Why does the permanence of tattoos appeal to young people?

No matter which method you use—*says* statements or *says* questions—writing gist statements in the margins is far more effective than underlining or highlighting for helping you recall the text's structure and argument.

Step 3:   After you have analyzed the article paragraph by paragraph, try locating the article's main divisions or parts. In longer closed-form articles, writers often forecast the shape of their essays in their introductions or use their conclusions to sum up main points. Although Martin's article is short, it uses both a forecasting statement and subheads to direct readers through its main points. The article is divided into several main chunks as follows:

■ Introductory paragraphs, which establish the problem to be addressed and narrow the focus to a clinical perspective (paragraphs 1–2)

■ A one-sentence organizing and predicting statement (paragraph 3)

■ A section explaining how tattoos may help adolescents establish a unique identity (paragraphs 4–5)

■ A section explaining how tattoos help teens incorporate onto their bodies a symbolic ownership of something important to them (paragraphs 6–8)

■ A section explaining how tattoos represent and satisfy teens' search for permanence (paragraphs 9–11)

■ A conclusion that states the thesis explicitly and sums up Martin's advice to fellow psychiatrists (paragraph 12)

Instead of listing the sections, you might prefer to make an outline or tree diagram of the article showing its main parts.

Writing Your Summary

Once you have written gist statements or questions in the margins and clarified the text's structure by creating an outline or diagram, you are ready to write a summary. Typically, summaries range from 100 to 250 words, but sometimes writers compose summaries as short as one sentence. The order and proportions of your summary can usually follow the order and proportions of the text. However, if the original article has a delayed thesis or other characteristics of open-form writing, you can rearrange the order and begin with the thesis. With prose that has many open-form features, you may also have to infer points that are more implied than expressed.

A summary of another author's writing—when it is incorporated into your own essay—makes particular demands on you, the writer. A successful summary should do the following:

- Represent the original article accurately and fairly.
- Be direct and concise, using words economically.
- Remain objective and neutral, not revealing your own ideas on the subject but rather only the original author's points.
- Give the original article balanced and proportional coverage.
- Use your own words to express the original author's ideas.
- Keep your reader informed through attributive tags (such as *according to Martin* or *Martin argues that*) that you are expressing someone else's ideas, not your own.
- Possibly include quotations for a few key terms or ideas from the original, but quote sparingly.
- Be a unified, coherent piece of writing in its own right.
- Be properly cited and documented so that the reader can find the original text.

Some of these criteria for a successful summary are challenging to meet. For instance, to avoid interjecting your own opinions, you will need to choose your words carefully, including the verbs you use in attributive tags. Note the subtle differences between these pairs of verbs: *Smith argues* versus *Smith rants; Jones criticizes* versus *Jones attacks; Brown asserts* versus *Brown leaps to the conclusion*. In each pair, the second verb, by moving beyond neutrality, reveals your own judgment of the author's ideas.

When you incorporate a summary into your own writing, it is particularly important to distinguish between the author's ideas and your own—hence the importance of frequent attributive tags, which tell the reader that these ideas belong to Smith or Jones or Brown rather than you. If you choose to copy any of the author's words directly from the text, you need to use quotation marks and cite the quotation using an appropriate documentation system.

The following example, which summarizes Martin's article on teenagers and tattoos, uses the MLA documentation system.

Summary of Martin Article

Identification of the article, journal and author

In "On Teenagers and Tattoos," published in The American Academy of Child and Adolescent Psychiatry, Dr. Andrés Martin advises fellow

Thesis of article

psychiatrists to think of teenage tattooing not as a fad or as a form of self-mutilation but as an opportunity for clinicians to understand

Attributive tag

teenagers better. Martin examines three different reasons that teenagers

Transition

get tattoos. First, he argues that tattoos help teenagers establish

Attributive tag

unique identities by giving them a sense of control over their evolving

Transition and attributive tag

bodies and over an environment perceived as adverse and domineering. Second, he believes that a tattooed image often symbolizes the teen's relationship

Transition and attributive tag

to a significant concept or person, making the relationship more visible

Inclusion of short quotation from article. MLA documentation style; number in parentheses indicates page number of original article where quotation is found

and real. Finally, says Martin, because teens are disturbed by modern society's mobility and fragmentation and because they have an "intense longing for rootedness and stability" (861), the irreversible nature of tattoos may give them a sense of permanence. Martin concludes that tattoos can be a meaningful record of survived teen experiences. He

Attributive tag

Attributive tag

Another short quotation

encourages therapists to regard teen tattoos as "self-constructive and adorning efforts," rather than as "mutilatory and destructive acts" (861)

Brackets indicate that the writer changed the material inside the brackets to fit the grammar and context of the writer's own sentence

and suggests that tattoos can help therapists understand "another level of [teenagers'] internal reality" (861). [195 words]

Works Cited

Martin article cited completely using MLA documentation form; in a formal paper, the "works cited" list begins on a new page

Martin, Andrés. "On Teenagers and Tattoos." Journal of the American Academy of Child and Adolescent Psychiatry 36 (1997): 860-61.

FOR WRITING AND DISCUSSION

Imagine that the context of a research paper you are writing calls for a shorter summary of the Martin article than the one presented here (which is approximately 195 words, including attributive tags). To practice distilling the main ideas of an article to produce summaries of different lengths, first write a 100-word summary of "On Teenagers and Tattoos." Then reduce your summary further to 50 words. Discuss the principles you followed in deciding what to eliminate or how to restructure sentences to convey the most information in the fewest number of words.

How to Write a Strong Response

In college and professional life, you will often need more than a clear understanding of the main ideas you have read. You will also need to engage with this reading at a deeper level by writing strong responses. To respond strongly to a text means to carry on an interactive dialogue with it in a conscious and purposeful manner. You can interact strongly with a text by reading it with the grain, against the grain, or anywhere along a continuum ranging from enthusiastic agreement and assimilation to outright anger and disbelief.

When you read with the grain of a text, you practice what psychologist Carl Rogers calls *empathic listening,* in which you try to see the world through the author's eyes, role-playing as much as possible the author's intended audience, adopting its beliefs and values, and acquiring its background knowledge. Reading with the grain requires your willingness to extend the author's project, to support the author's thesis or point of view or method with new evidence from your own personal experiences, other readings, or research; you focus on how this text endows you with a new understanding of this subject.

When you read against the grain of a text, you challenge, question, resist, and perhaps even rebut the author's ideas. Your strong response often consists of pointed queries to the author that challenge the author's reasoning, sources, examples, or choice of language. Your talking back to the text might take the form of counterexamples, a mentioning of the points that the author has overlooked or omitted, and alternative lines of reasoning.

Most often, a strong response to a text will consist of both with-the-grain and against-the-grain interactions. Perhaps you find that you agree with parts of the text and disagree with others. Perhaps the text poses questions you have never considered. Such texts can stretch your thinking and, if you allow them to, can cause you to grow and change. When we say that a strong response involves speaking back to a text, we don't necessarily mean opposing it. We mean adding your voice to the conversation the text is part of.

What Should a Strong Response Do?

In a strong response you speak back to an author as if you were joining him or her in a conversation. The key is to think of several main points you want to add to the conversation, sketch out those points in an initial thesis statement, and prepare to develop those points one at a time. A strong response is truly strong when it includes both rhetorical points (points about why, to whom, and how the text is written) and subject matter points.

When you join an author in conversation, you need to have a good sense of the context, purpose, and style of the original reading. At least one of your main points should consider how the author tries to influence his or her audience. You should look first at what the author of the text is trying to accomplish. You can then comment on the author's purpose, audience, genre, and stylistic choices. You can read with the grain by affirming the effectiveness of the author's rhetorical strategies, or you can read against the grain by questioning and challenging these strategies from your own perspective. Consider questions such as these:

■   What is the author's purpose in writing the text?
■   Who is the intended audience?
■   What is the genre and how does that genre restrict/limit readership, style and purpose?
■   What change does the author hope to make in the audience's view of the topic?
■   What persuasive strategies does the author use (amount of and kinds of evidence, strategies of reasoning, selection/omission of details, word choices, figurative language, and stylistic choices)?

In some cases, your strong response might consist entirely of a rhetorical analysis, especially if the text you are analyzing is particularly interesting or complex rhetorically. But often you will want to respond to the text in other ways as well. The strong response gives you an opportunity to add your own voice to the conversation of ideas stimulated by the text. (Think of the text as having thrown you a ball and now you have to throw it back.) Here are some examples of the kinds of ways you can speak back to the author's ideas:

■   Agree with one of the author's points and support it using new evidence from personal experience or knowledge.
■   Identify a new insight you have gotten from the text and illustrate it, perhaps by applying it to a different context.
■   Disagree with or raise doubts about one of the author's points by using counter-evidence from your own personal experience or knowledge.
■   Fill in a gap in the text by adding your own theory, hypothesis, explanation, or analysis; show the value of adding something that the author overlooked or left out.
■   Develop one or more questions, issues, or problems raised for you by the text. How does the text cause you to question your own understanding of the text's subject matter or to question your own values, assumptions, or beliefs?

■ Evaluate the usefulness of the text, its applicability to other contexts, its limitations based on the writer's bias or narrowness, or the potential consequences of its ideas.

Student Example of a "Summary/Strong Response" Essay

Before giving you some tips on how to discover ideas for your strong response, we show you an example of a student essay for this chapter: a "summary/strong response" essay. Note that the essay begins by identifying the question under discussion: Why do teenagers get tattoos? It then summarizes the article by Andrés Martin.* Immediately following the summary, the student writer states his thesis, followed by the strong response, which contains both rhetorical and subject matter points.

Why Do Teenagers Get Tattoos? A Response to Andrés Martin
Sean Barry (student)

My sister has one. My brother has one. I have one. Just take a stroll downtown and you will see how commonplace it is for someone to be decorated with tattoos and hung with piercings. In fact, hundreds of teenagers, every day, allow themselves to be etched upon or poked into. What's the cause of this phenomenon? Why do so many teenagers get tattoos?

Introduces topic and sets context

Dr. Andrés Martin has answered this question from a psychiatrist's perspective in his article "On Teenagers and Tattoos," published in *The American Academy of Child and Adolescent Psychiatry*. Martin advises fellow psychiatrists to think of teenage tattooing as a constructive opportunity for clinicians to understand teenagers better. Martin examines three different reasons that teenagers get tattoos. First, he argues that tattoos help teenagers establish unique identities by giving them a sense of control over their evolving bodies and over an environment perceived as adverse and domineering. Second, he believes that a tattooed image often symbolizes the teen's relationship to a significant concept or person, making the relationship more visible and real. Finally, says Martin, because teens are disturbed by modern society's mobility and fragmentation and because they have an "intense longing for rootedness and stability" (103), the irreversible nature of tattoos may give them a sense of permanence. Martin concludes that tattoos can be a meaningful record of survived teen experiences.

Summary of Martin's article

Although Martin's analysis has relevance and some strengths, I think he overgeneralizes and over-romanticizes teenage tattooing, leading him to overlook other causes of teenage tattooing such as commercialization and teenagers' desire to identify with a peer group as well as achieve an individual identity.

Thesis statement

Some of Martin's points seem relevant and realistic and match my own experiences. I agree that teenagers sometimes use tattoos to establish their own identities. When my brother, sister, and I all got our tattoos, we were partly asserting our own independence from our parents. Martin's point about the symbolic significance of a tattoo image also connects with my experiences. A Hawaiian guy in my dorm has a fish tattooed on his back, which he says represents his love of the ocean and the spiritual experience he has when he scuba dives.

With-the-grain point in support of Martin's ideas

*In this essay the student writer uses a shortened version of his 195-word summary used as an illustration on page 105.

Rhetorical point
about Martin's
audience, purpose,
and genre that has
both with-the-
grain and against-
the-grain elements

Martin, speaking as a psychiatrist to other psychiatrists, also provides psychological insights into the topic of teen tattooing even though this psychological perspective brings some limitations, too. In this scholarly article, Martin's purpose is to persuade fellow psychiatrists to think of adolescent tattooing in positive rather than judgmental terms. Rather than condemn teens for getting tattoos, he argues that discussion of the tattoos can provide useful insights into the needs and behavior of troubled teens (especially males). But this perspective is also a limitation because the teenagers he sees are mostly youths in psychiatric counseling, particularly teens struggling with the absence of or violent loss of a parent and those who have experience with gangs and prison-terms. This perspective leads him to over-generalize. As a psychological study of a specific group of troubled teens, the article is informative. However, it does not apply as well to most teenagers who are getting tattoos today.

Against-the-grain rhetorical point: Barry analyzes Martin's use of quotations from Moby Dick

Besides over-generalizing, Martin also seems to romanticize teenage tattooing. Why else would a supposedly scientific article begin and end with quotations from *Moby Dick*? Martin seems to imply a similarity between today's teenagers and the sailor hero Ishmael who wandered the seas looking for personal identity. In quoting *Moby Dick*, Martin seems to value tattooing as a suitable way for teenagers to record their experiences. Every tattoo, for Martin, has deep significance. Thus, Martin casts tattooed teens as romantic outcasts, loners, and adventurers like Ishmael.

Transition to writer's own analysis

→ In contrast to Martin, I believe that teens are influenced by the commercial nature of tattooing, which has become big business aimed at their age group. Every movie or television star or beauty queen who sports a tattoo sends the commercial message that tattoos are cool: "A tattoo will help you be successful, sexy, handsome, or attractive like us." Tattoo parlors are no longer dark dives in seedy, dangerous parts of cities, but appear in lively commercial districts; in fact, there are several down the street from the university. Teenagers now buy tattoos the way they buy other consumer items.

Against-the-grain point: writer's alternative theory

Against-the-grain point: writer's second theory

Furthermore, Martin doesn't explore teenagers' desire not only for individuality but also for peer group acceptance. Tattooing is the "in" thing to do. Tattooing used to be defiant and daring, but now it is popular and more acceptable among teens. I even know a group of sorority women who went together to get tattoos on their ankles. As tattooing has become more mainstreamed, rebels/trendsetters have turned to newer and more outrageous practices, such as branding and extreme piercings. Meanwhile, tattoos bring middle-of-the-road teens the best of both worlds: a way to show their individuality and simultaneously to be accepted by peers.

Conclusion and summary

In sum, Martin's research is important because it examines psychological responses to teen's inner conflicts. It offers partial explanations for teens' attraction to tattoos and promotes a positive, noncritical attitude toward tattooing. But I think the article is limited by its overgeneralizations based on the psychiatric focus, by its tendency to romanticize tattooing, by its lack of recognition of the commercialization of tattooing, and by its under-emphasis on group belonging and peer pressure. Teen tattooing is more complex than even Martin makes it.

Works Cited

Complete citation of article in MLA format

Martin, Andrés. "On Teenagers and Tattoos." *Journal of the American Academy of Child and Adolescent Psychiatry* 36 (1997): 860–61. Rpt. in *The Allyn and Bacon Guide to Writing.* John D. Ramage and John C. Bean. 2nd ed. Boston, MA: Allyn and Bacon, 2000. 101–104.

How to Think of Ideas for Your Strong Response

In the student example just shown, Sean Barry makes a number of points. He analyzes the rhetorical context of Martin's original article by pointing out some of the limitations of a psychiatric point of view and exploring the implications of the *Moby Dick* references; he supports two of Martin's points using his own personal examples; and he argues that Martin—perhaps influenced by his romantic view of tattoos—fails to appreciate the impact on teenagers of the commercialization of tattooing and the importance of peer group acceptance. Clearly, Sean Barry illustrates what we mean by being a strong reader.

How can you develop the aptitude and habits of strong reading? Here are some strategies you can practice when preparing to write your own summary/strong response essay.

Make Strong Marginal Notations as You Read

A strong reader thinks actively while reading. She not only tries to understand the author's ideas but also interacts with the text (as if in dialogue with the author) and records ideas and reactions while reading. A portion of Sean Barry's annotations of the Martin article, showing both with- and against-the-grain reading comments is shown in Figure 6.1.

Identify "Hot Spots" in the Text

Most texts will create "hot spots" for you (each reader's hot spots are apt to be different). By "hot spot" we mean a quotation or passage that you especially notice, either because you agree or disagree with it or because it triggers memories or other associations. Or perhaps the hot spot strikes you as particularly thought provoking. Perhaps it raises a problem or is confusing yet suggestive. Go back through the text and copy out short quotations that intrigue you (or place an asterisk next to longer passages); then freewrite your responses to these hot spots.

Write Out Questions Triggered by the Text

Almost any text triggers questions as you read. A good way to begin formulating a strong response is simply to write out several questions that the text caused you to think about. Then explore your responses to those questions through freewriting. Sometimes the freewrite will trigger more questions.

Consent to the Text's Perspective

As you read, try to suspend your own belief system and enter fully into the author's position. Put into play the believing part of the believing and doubting game discussed in Chapter 2. Consider what thinking about the subject in this way enables you to perceive that you haven't thought of before. Write comments back to the text that acknowledge the points where this text surprises you, enriches your thinking, or enlarges your perspective. Brainstorm for examples from your own personal experience or knowledge that support the author's argument. Read intensely with the grain.

▼

ANDRÉS MARTIN, M.D.

ON TEENAGERS AND TATTOOS

Quotation from a novel?

The skeleton dimensions I shall now proceed to set down are copied verbatim from my right arm, where I had them tattooed: as in my wild wanderings at that period, there was no other secure way of preserving such valuable statistics.

—*Melville/Moby Dick Cll*

A strange beginning for a scientific article

What do 19th-century sailors have to do with late 20th-century teens?

Idea here: the body as a concrete record of experience?

Larger tattooing scene?

Tattoos and piercings have become a part of our everyday landscape. 1 They are ubiquitous, having <u>entered the circles of glamour</u> and the <u>mainstream of fashion,</u> and they have even become an increasingly common feature of our urban youth. Legislation in most states restricts professional tattooing to adults older than 18 years of age, so "high end" tattooing is rare in children and adolescents, but such tattoos are occasionally seen in older teenagers. Piercings, by comparison, as well as self-made or "jailhouse" type tattoos, are not at all rare among adolescents or even among schoolage children. Like hairdo, makeup, or baggy jeans, tattoos and piercings can be subject to fad influence or peer pressure in an effort toward group affiliation. As with any other fashion statement, they can be construed as bodily aids in the inner struggle toward identity consolidation, serving as adjuncts to <u>the defining and sculpting of the self</u> by means of external manipulations. But unlike most other body decorations, tattoos and piercings are set apart by their irreversible and permanent nature, a quality at the core of their magnetic appeal to adolescents.

This idea is surprising and interesting. It merits lots of discussion.

I like the phrase "the defining and sculpting of the self"—sounds creative, like art

Which teenagers? All teenagers?

Adolescents and their parents are often at odds over the acquisition of 2 bodily decorations. For the adolescent, piercings or tattoos may be seen as personal and beautifying statements, while parents may construe them as oppositional and enraging affronts to their authority. Distinguishing <u>bodily adornment</u> from <u>self-mutilation</u> may indeed prove challenging, particularly when a family is in disagreement over a <u>teenager's motivations</u> and a clinician is summoned as the final arbiter. At such times it may be most important to realize jointly that the skin can all too readily become but another battleground for the tensions of the age, arguments having less to do with tattoos and piercings than with core issues such as separation from the family matrix. Exploring the motivations and significance belying tattoos (Grumet, 1983) and piercings can go a long way toward resolving such differences and can become a novel and additional way of getting to know teenagers. An interested and nonjudgmental appreciation of teenagers' surface presentations may become a way of making contact not only in their terms but on their turfs: quite literally on the territory of their skins.

These terms show the main opposing views on tattoos.

Is he speaking only to psychiatrists? Does this clinical perspective have other applications?

Good open-minded, practical approach to teen tattoos

I like Martin's focus on complexity

The following three sections exemplify some of the complex psycho- 3 logical underpinnings of youth tattooing.

FIGURE 6.1   Student Marginal Notes on Martin's Text

Deny the Text's Perspective

Now, reading again, remain skeptical of the text and resist its argument. Put into play the doubting side of the believing and doubting game. Show what might be harmful or dangerous in adopting the author's perspective. Brainstorm for examples from your own personal experience or knowledge that raise doubts about the author's argument. Question the author's values, beliefs, or assumptions. Read intensely against the grain.

Articulate Your Difference from the Intended Audience

In some cases you can read strongly by articulating how you differ from the text's intended audience. As we show in Chapter 4, experienced writers try to imagine their audience. They ask: What are my audience's values? How interested in and knowledgeable about my topic is my audience? Eventually, the author makes decisions about audience, in effect "creates" the audience, so that the text reveals both an image of the author and of its intended reader.

Your own experiences, arising from your gender, class, ethnicity, sexual orientation, political and religious beliefs, interests, values, and so forth, may cause you to feel estranged from the author's imagined audience. If the text seems written for straight people and you are gay, or for Christians and you are a Muslim or an atheist, or for environmentalists and you grew up in a small logging community, you may well resist the text. Sometimes your sense of exclusion from the intended audience makes it difficult to read a text at all. For example, a woman student of our acquaintance once brought a class to a standstill by slamming the course anthology on her desk and exclaiming, "How can you people stand reading this patriarchal garbage!" She had become so irritated by the authors' assumption that all readers shared their male-oriented values that she could no longer bear to read the selections.

When you differ significantly from the text's assumed audience, you can often use this difference to question the author's underlying assumptions, values, and beliefs.

FOR WRITING AND DISCUSSION

What follows is a short passage by writer Annie Dillard in response to a question about how she chooses to spend her time. This passage often evokes heated responses from our students.

> I don't do housework. Life is too short. . . . I let almost all my indoor plants die from neglect while I was writing the book. There are all kinds of ways to live. You can take your choice. You can keep a tidy house, and when St. Peter asks you what you did with your life, you can say, "I kept a tidy house, I made my own cheese balls."

Individual task: Read the passage and then briefly freewrite your reaction to it. *Group task:* Working in groups or as a whole class, develop answers to the following questions:

1. What values does Dillard assume her audience holds?
2. What kinds of readers are apt to feel excluded from that audience?
3. If you are not part of the intended audience for this passage, what in the text evokes resistance?

Articulate Your Own Purpose for Reading

You may sometimes read a text against the grain if your purposes for reading differ from what the author imagined. Normally you read a text because you share the author's interest in a question and want to know the author's answer. In other words, you usually read to join the author's conversation. But suppose that you wish to review the writings of nineteenth-century scientists to figure out what they assumed about nature (or women, or God, or race, or capitalism). Or suppose that you examine a politician's metaphors to see what they reveal about his or her values, or analyze *National Geographic* for evidence of political bias. In these cases, you will be reading against the grain of the text. In a sense, you would be "blindsiding" the authors—while they are talking about topic X, you are observing them for topic Y.

You can see this strategy at work in literary critic Jane Tompkins' " 'Indians': Textualism, Morality, and the Problem of History" (see pp. 177–85). Tompkins, assigned to teach a course in early American literature, wanted to find out as much as she could about the relationship between Puritans and Native Americans in colonial New England. So she turned to a famous 1950s scholarly work by Perry Miller on the Puritan mind. Here is her brief account of her reading experience:

> My research began with Perry Miller. Early in the preface to *Errand into the Wilderness*, while explaining how he came to write his history of the New England mind, Miller writes a sentence that stopped me dead. He says that what fascinated him as a young man about his country's history was "the massive narrative of the movement of European culture into the vacant wilderness of America." "Vacant?" Miller, writing in 1956, doesn't pause over the word "vacant," but to people who read his preface thirty years later, the word is shocking. In what circumstances could someone proposing to write a history of colonial New England *not* take into account the Indian presence there?

This experience—reading a sentence that "stopped [her] dead"—sets Tompkins off on her own research project: "How do historians examining colonial New England portray Indians?" As she reads historian after historian, her interest isn't in the research problems posed by the authors but in her own research problem: How does this author portray Indians? This method of resistant reading is very common in academia.

Ask Generic Strategic Questions

The essence of reading strongly, then, is to read critically and to pose questions. Here are generic strategic questions you can ask to generate ideas for your strong response:

- How is the author trying to change his or her intended readers' view of the topic? What rhetorical strategies does the author use to influence the intended audience?

- How has this author changed my view of this topic? What do I have to give up or lose in order to change my view? What do I gain? How do the author's rhetorical strategies affect me?

- What is excluded from this author's text? All writers must select certain details to include in their texts and others to exclude. By looking at what is omitted from a text, you can often ascertain something about the author's value system.

- How can I question this author's data, evidence, and supporting arguments? If I am not persuaded by the author's data and evidence, why not? What is missing? What can be called into question?

- How can I question the author's values, beliefs, and assumptions, both stated and unstated? Conversely, how does this text cause me to question my own values, beliefs, and assumptions?

- How can I use this author's ideas for my own purposes? What new insights have I gained? What new ways of thinking can I apply to another context?

Consider Your Purpose(s) for Writing

In imagining possibilities for different kinds of strong responses, consider again the various purposes for writing that we developed in Chapter 4. Most of these purposes suggest approaches you might take in composing your strong response: to express, to explore, to inform, to analyze, and to persuade. (In fact, potentially a strong response could even take the form of a poem or short story: that is, have a literary purpose.)

For a strong response essay, you most likely will be doing some or all of the following: expressing your personal reaction to the text from the perspective of your own life, exploring your ideas and questions prompted by the text, informing readers of new or different data related to the text's subject matter, analyzing the author's ideas and rhetorical choices, and persuading a reader to think as you do about the text. You may focus primarily on one of these purposes, or you may choose to encompass and combine several purposes.

◪ COMPOSING YOUR SUMMARY/STRONG RESPONSE ESSAY

Generating and Exploring Ideas for Your Summary

Once you have selected the piece you will use for this assignment, your first task is to read it carefully to get as accurate an understanding of the article as you can. Remember that summarizing is the most basic and preliminary form of reading with the grain of a text.

1. The first time through, read the piece for general meaning. Follow the argument's flow without judgment or criticism, trying to see the world as the author sees it.
2. Reread the piece slowly, paragraph by paragraph, writing "what it does" or "what it says" gist statements in the margins for each paragraph or writing out the question that you think each paragraph answers. We recommend that you supplement these marginal notations by writing out a complete paragraph-by-paragraph *does/says* analysis modeled after our example on pages 99–100.
3. After you've analyzed the piece paragraph by paragraph, locate the argument's main divisions or parts and create an outline or tree diagram of the main points.

Shaping, Drafting, and Revising Your Summary

Once you have analyzed the article carefully paragraph by paragraph and understand its structure, you are ready to write a draft. If the piece you are summarizing is closed form, you can generally follow the order of the original article, keeping the proportions of the summary roughly equivalent to the proportions of the article. Begin the essay by identifying the question or problem that the reading addresses. Then state the article's purpose or thesis and summarize its argument point by point. If the article has a delayed thesis or some features of open-form prose, then you may have to rearrange the original order to create a clear structure for readers.

Count the number of words in your first draft to see if you are in the 150–250 word range specified by the assignment. When you revise your summary, follow the criteria presented on page 113.

Generating and Exploring Ideas for Your Strong Response

After you have written your summary, your next step is to engage with the text on a deeper level. Read more deeply with the grain—beyond merely understanding the article—by believing its values and applying its principles to other contexts. Then read against the grain. Your strong response will most likely include both with-the-grain and against-the-grain observations and will discuss both the author's ideas and his or her other rhetorical strategies.

1. Begin by making strong marginal notations in the text. Identify and praise interesting points; relate the text to your own ideas and experiences; note your reactions, especially where you are surprised or disturbed by "hot spots"; doubt evidence, raise problems, jot down counterexamples.
2. List questions that the text raises in your mind or identify several hot spots that particularly attracted your notice (see p. 107). Pick the most promising of these questions or hot spots and freewrite your responses to them.
3. Do a rhetorical analysis of the text by exploring your answers to the questions on page 116 describing the "rhetorical analysis" component of a strong response.
4. For some texts, it is useful to articulate the differences between you and the text's intended audience. How does your "position"—in terms of gender, class, ethnicity, sexual orientation, or value system—make you different from the reader the text assumes? Also identify your purpose for reading the text if your purpose differs from that of the original author's intended audience. (For example, Andrés Martin imagined an audience of psychiatrists whose purpose for reading was to improve their ability to counsel teenagers with tattoos. In contrast, student writer Sean Barry's purpose was to get insights on the broad social question of why teenagers get tattoos.)
5. Freewrite your responses to the generic strategic questions listed on pages 110–111.

Shaping and Drafting Your Strong Response

Based on these explorations, draft a strong response to the reading. Typically, a strong response will be organized as follows:

- *Thesis statement* (one- or two-sentence assertion of the main points you want to make in response to the article). Your thesis may appear at the end of the summary paragraph or may be placed in its own mini-paragraph following the summary.
- A series of developed strong response points, including your response to the author's ideas and rhetorical choices. This section typically contains both with-the-grain and against-the-grain elements. At least one of your points should address the author's rhetorical choices and strategies. Your strong response constitutes your own voice in the conversation raised by the text.

Revising Your Strong Response

In revising your strong response, you will find that peer reviews are especially helpful, both in generating ideas and in locating places that need expansion and development. As you revise, think about how well you have incorporated ideas from your initial explorations and how you can make your essay clearer and more meaningful to readers.

TOPIC Guidepost #20

For those using Texas Tech's TOPIC Web-Based assignments:

Direct your web browser to **http://english.ttu.edu:5555**

Guidepost #20 provides full instructions regarding your reading assignment (Chapter 7) and TOPIC Mail Messages.

Writing an Exploratory Essay

ABOUT EXPLORATORY WRITING

In Chapter 1, we said that to grow as a writer you need to love problems—
to pose them and to live with them. Most academic writers testify that writing
projects begin when they become engaged with a question or problem and commit themselves to an extensive period of exploration. During exploration, writers
may radically redefine the problem and then later alter or even reverse their initial thesis.

As we noted in Chapters 2 and 3, however, inexperienced writers tend to trun-
cate this exploratory process, committing themselves hastily to a thesis to avoid
complexity. College professors say this tendency hinders their students' intellectual growth. Asserting a thesis commits you to a position. Asking a question, on
the other hand, invites you to contemplate multiple perspectives, entertain new
ideas, and let your thinking evolve. As management professor A. Kimbrough
Sherman puts it, to grow as thinkers students need "to 'wallow in complexity' and
work their way back out" (see p. 21).

To illustrate his point, Sherman cites his experience in a management class
where students were asked to write proposals for locating a new sports complex
in a major U.S. city. To Sherman's disappointment, many students argued for a location without first considering all the variables—impact on neighborhoods,
building costs and zoning, availability of parking, ease of access, attractiveness to
tourists, aesthetics, and so forth—and without analyzing how various proposed
locations stacked up against the criteria they were supposed to establish. The students reached closure without wallowing in complexity.

The assignment for this chapter asks you to dwell with a problem, even if you
can't solve it. You will write an essay with an exploratory purpose; its focus will
be a question rather than a thesis. The body of your paper will be a narrative account of your thinking about the problem—your attempt to examine its complexity, to explore alternative solutions, and to arrive at a solution or answer. Your
exploration will generally require outside research, so many instructors will assign
sections of Part Four, "A Guide to Research," along with this chapter. The paper

will be relatively easy to write because it will be organized chronologically, but you will have nothing to say—no process to report—unless you discover and examine the problem's complexity.

◢ EXPLORING EXPLORATORY WRITING

Through our work in writing centers, we often encounter students disappointed with their grades on essay exams or papers. "I worked hard on this paper," they tell us, "but I still got a lousy grade. What am I doing wrong? What do college professors want?"

To help you answer this question, consider the following two essays written for a freshman placement examination in composition at the University of Pittsburgh, in response to the following assignment:

> Describe a time when you did something you felt to be creative. Then, on the basis of the incident you have described, go on to draw some general conclusions about "creativity."

How would you describe the differences in thinking exhibited by the two writers? Which essay do you think professors rated higher?

Essay A

I am very interested in music, and I try to be creative in my interpretation of music. While in high school, I was a member of a jazz ensemble. The members of the ensemble were given chances to improvise and be creative in various songs. I feel that this was a great experience for me, as well as the other members. I was proud to know that I could use my imagination and feelings to create music other than what was written.

Creativity to me means being free to express yourself in a way that is unique to you, not having to conform to certain rules and guidelines. Music is only one of the many areas in which people are given opportunities to show their creativity. Sculpting, carving, building, art, and acting are just a few more areas where people can show their creativity.

Through my music I conveyed feelings and thoughts which were important to me. Music was my means of showing creativity. In whatever form creativity takes, whether it be music, art, or science, it is an important aspect of our lives because it enables us to be individuals.

Essay B

Throughout my life, I have been interested and intrigued by music. My mother has often told me of the times, before I went to school, when I would "conduct" the orchestra on her records. I continued to listen to music and eventually started to play the guitar and the clarinet. Finally, at about the age of twelve, I started to sit down and to try to write songs. Even though my instrumental skills were far from my own high standards, I would spend much of my spare time during the day with a guitar around my neck, trying to produce a piece of music.

Each of these sessions, as I remember them, had a rather set format. I would sit in my bedroom, strumming different combinations of the five or six chords I could play, until I heard a series which sounded particularly good to me. After this, I set the music to a suitable rhythm (usually dependent on my mood at the time), and ran through the tune until I could play it fairly easily. Only after this section was complete did I go on to writing lyrics, which generally followed along the lines of the current popular songs on the radio.

At the time of the writing, I felt that my songs were, in themselves, an original creation of my own; that is, I, alone, made them. However, I now see that, in this sense of the word, I was not creative. The songs themselves seem to be an oversimplified form of the music I listened to at the time.

In a more fitting sense, however, I *was* being creative. Since I did not purposely copy my favorite songs, I was, effectively, originating my songs from my own "process of creativity." To achieve my goal, I needed what a composer would call "inspiration" for my piece. In this case the inspiration was the current hit on the radio. Perhaps, with my present point of view, I feel that I used too much "inspiration" in my songs, but, at that time, I did not.

Creativity, therefore, is a process which, in my case, involved a certain series of "small creations" if you like. As well, it is something the appreciation of which varies with one's point of view, that point of view being set by the person's experience, tastes, and his own personal view of creativity. The less experienced tend to allow for less originality, while the more experienced demand real originality to classify something a "creation." Either way, a term as abstract as this is perfectly correct, and open to interpretation.

Working as a whole class or in small groups, analyze the differences between Essay A and Essay B. What might cause college professors to rate one essay higher than the other? What would the writer of the weaker essay have to do to produce an essay more like the stronger?

WRITING PROJECT

Choose a question, problem, or issue that genuinely perplexes you. At the beginning of your exploratory essay, explain why you are interested in this chosen problem and why you have been unable to reach a satisfactory answer. Then write a first-person, chronologically organized, narrative account of your thinking process as you investigate your question ~~through library research~~, talking with others, and doing your own reflective thinking. You might also wish to interview people, if appropriate, and to draw on your own personal experiences, memories, and observations. Your goal is to examine your question, problem, or issue from a variety of perspectives, assessing the strengths and weaknesses of different positions and points of view. By the end of your essay, you may or may not have reached a satisfactory solution to your problem. You will be rewarded for the quality of your exploration and thinking processes. In other words, your goal is not to answer your question, but to report on the process of wrestling with it.

This assignment asks you to dwell with a problem—and not necessarily to solve that problem. Your problem may shift and evolve as your thinking progresses. What matters is that you actively engage with your problem and demonstrate why it is problematic.

Your instructor may choose to combine this writing project with a subsequent one (for example, a research paper based on one of the assignments in the remaining chapters in Part Two) to create a sustained project in which you write two pieces on the same topic. If so, then the essay for this chapter will prepare you to write a later analytical or persuasive piece. Check with your instructor to make sure that your chosen question for this project will work for the later assignment.

◢ UNDERSTANDING EXPLORATORY WRITING

As we have explained, this assignment calls for an essay with an *exploratory purpose* (see our discussion of purposes in Chapter 4, pp. 55–58). Exploratory writing generally has an open-form structure; the writer cannot assert a thesis and forecast a structure in the introduction (typical features of closed-form prose) because the thesis is unknown as the essay opens. Instead of following a closed-form, points-first structure, the essay narrates chronologically the process of the author's thinking about the problem.

The Essence of Exploratory Prose: Considering Multiple Solutions

The essential move of an exploratory essay is to consider multiple solutions to a problem or multiple points of view on an issue. The writer defines a problem, poses a possible solution, explores its strengths and weaknesses, and then *moves* on to consider another possible solution.

To show a mind at work examining multiple solutions, let's return to the two student essays you examined in the previous exploratory activity (pp. 116–17). The fundamental difference between Essay A and Essay B is that the writer of Essay B treats the concept of "creativity" as a true problem. Note that the writer of Essay A is satisfied with his or her initial definition.

> Creativity to me means being free to express yourself in a way that is unique to you, not having to conform to certain rules and guidelines.

The writer of Essay B, however, is *not* satisfied with his or her first answer and uses the essay to think through the problem. This writer remembers an early creative experience—composing songs as a twelve-year-old.

> At the time of the writing, I felt that my songs were, in themselves, an original creation of my own; that is, I, alone, made them. However, I now see that, in this sense of the word, I was not creative. The songs themselves seem to be an oversimplified form of the music I listened to at the time.

This writer distinguishes between two points of view: "On the one hand, I used to think this, but now, in retrospect, I think that." This move forces the writer to go beyond the initial answer to think of alternatives.

The key to effective exploratory writing is to create a tension between alternative views. When you start out, you might not know where your thinking process will end up; at the outset you might not have formulated an opposing, countering, or alternative view. Using a move such as "I used to think . . . , but now I think" or "Part of me thinks this . . . , but another part thinks that . . ." forces you to find something additional to say; writing then becomes a process of inquiry and discovery.

The second writer's dissatisfaction with the initial answer initiates a dialectic process that plays one idea against another, creating a generative tension. In contrast, the writer of Essay A offers no alternative to his or her definition of creativity. This writer presents no specific illustrations of creative activity (such as the specific details in Essay B about strumming the guitar), but presents merely space-filling abstractions ("Sculpting, carving, building, art, and acting are just a few more areas where people can show their creativity."). The writer of Essay B scores a higher grade, not because the essay creates a brilliant (or even particularly clear) explanation of creativity; rather, the writer is rewarded for thinking about the problem dialectically.

We use the term *dialectic* to mean a thinking process often associated with the German philosopher Hegel, who said that each thesis ("My act was creative") gives rise to an antithesis ("My act was not creative") and that the clash of these opposing perspectives leads thinkers to develop a synthesis that incorporates some features of both theses ("My act was a series of 'small creations' "). You initiate dialectic thinking any time you play Elbow's believing and doubting game (see Chapter 2, pp. 35–37) or use other strategies to place alternative possibilities side by side.

Essay B's writer uses a dialectic thinking strategy that we might characterize as follows:

1. Regards the assignment as a genuine problem worth puzzling over.
2. Considers alternative views and plays them off against each other.
3. Looks at specifics.
4. Continues the thinking process in search of some sort of resolution or synthesis of the alternative views.
5. Incorporates the stages of this dialectic process into the essay.

FOR WRITING AND DISCUSSION

1. According to writing theorist David Bartholomae, who analyzed several hundred student essays in response to the placement-examination question on p. 166, almost all the highest scoring essays exhibited a similar kind of dialectic thinking. How might the writer of the first

essay expand the essay by using the dialectic thinking processes just described?

2. Working individually, read each of the following questions and write out your initial opinion or one or two answers that come immediately to mind.

   ■ Given the easy availability of birth-control information and the ready availability of condoms, why do you think there are so many teenage pregnancies?

   ■ Why do U.S. students, on the average, lag so far behind their European and Asian counterparts in scholastic achievement?

   ■ Should women be assigned to combat roles in the military?

   ■ The most popular magazines sold on college campuses around the country are women's fashion and lifestyle magazines such as *Glamour, Seventeen, Mademoiselle,* and *Cosmopolitan.* Why are these magazines so popular? Is there a problem with these magazines being so popular? (Two separate questions, both of which are worth exploring dialectically.)

3. Choose one of these questions or one assigned by your instructor and freewrite for five or ten minutes using one or more of the following moves to stimulate dialectic thinking.

   I used to think _____, but now I think _____.

   Part of me thinks _____, but another part of me thinks _____.

   On some days I think _____, but on other days I think _____.

   The first answers that come to mind are _____, but as I think further I see _____.

   My classmate thinks _____, but I think _____.

   Your goal here is to explore potential weaknesses or inadequacies in your first answers, and then to push beyond them to think of new or different answers. Feel free to be wild and risky in posing possible alternative solutions.

4. As a whole class, take a poll to find out what the most common first-response answers were for each of the questions. Then share alternative solutions generated by class members during the freewriting. The goal is to pose and explore answers that go beyond or against the grain of the common answers. Remember, there is little point in arguing for an answer that everyone else already accepts.

◢ COMPOSING YOUR EXPLORATORY ESSAY

Generating and Exploring Ideas

Your process of generating and exploring ideas is, in essence, the *subject matter* of your exploratory paper. This section should help you get started and keep going.

Keeping a Research Log

Since this assignment asks you to create a chronologically organized account of your thinking process, you will need to keep a careful, detailed record of your investigation. The best tool for doing so is a research log or journal in which you take notes on your sources and record your thinking throughout the process.

As you investigate your issue, keep a chronologically organized account that includes notes on your readings, interviews, and significant conversations, plus explorations of how each of these sources, new perspectives, or data influence your current thinking. Many writers keep a double-entry notebook that has a "notes" section, in which you summarize key points, record data, copy potentially usable quotations verbatim, and so forth, and a "reflections" section, in which you write a strong response to the reading exploring how it advanced your thinking, raised questions, or pulled you in one direction or another. (For an example, see "Sam's Notes on *Newsweek* Article" on pages 123–124.)

As you write your exploratory essay, your research log will be your main source for details—evidence of what you were thinking at regular intervals throughout the process.*

Exploring Possible Problems for Your Essay

Your instructor may assign you a specific problem to explore. If not, then your first step is to choose a question, problem, or issue that currently perplexes you. Perhaps a question is problematic to you because you haven't studied it (How serious is the problem of global warming? How can we keep pornography away from children on the Internet?) or because the available factual data seem conflicting and inconclusive (Should postmenopausal women take supplemental estrogen?), or because the problem or issue draws you into an uncomfortable conflict of values (Should we legalize drugs? Where do I stand on abortion?).

The key to this assignment is to choose a question, problem, or issue *that truly perplexes you.* The more clearly readers sense your personal engagement with the problem, the more likely they are to be engaged by your writing. Note: If your instructor pairs this assignment with a later one, be sure that your question is appropriate for the later assignment. Check with your instructor.

---

*For those of you majoring in science or engineering, this research log is similar to the laboratory notebooks that are required parts of any original research in science or industry. Besides recording in detail the progress of your research, these notebooks often serve as crucial data in patent applications or liability lawsuits. Doctors and nurses keep similar logs in their medical records file for each patient. This is a time-honored practice. In Mary Shelley's early nineteenth-century novel *Frankenstein*, the monster learns about the process of his creation by reading Dr. Frankenstein's laboratory journal.

Here are several exercises to help you think of ideas for this essay.

Exploration Exercise 1.   In your research log, make a list of issues or problems that both interest and perplex you. Then choose two or three of your issues and freewrite about them for five minutes or so, exploring questions such as these: Why am I interested in this problem? What makes the problem problematic? What makes this problem significant? Share your list of questions and your freewrites with friends and classmates. Discussing questions with friends often stimulates you to think of more questions yourself or to sharpen the focus of questions you have already asked.

Exploration Exercise 2.   If your exploratory essay is paired with a subsequent assignment, look at the invention exercises for that assignment to help you ask a question that fits the context of the final paper you will write.

Exploration Exercise 3.   A particularly valuable kind of problem to explore for this assignment is a public controversy. Often such issues involve complex disagreements about facts and values that merit careful, open-ended exploration. This assignment invites you to explore and clarify where you stand on such complex public issues as gay marriages, overcrowded prisons, the Endangered Species Act, funding of Medicare or Social Security, public funding of the arts, and so forth. These issues make particularly good topics for persuasive papers or formal research papers, if either is required in your course. For this exercise, look through a current newspaper or weekly newsmagazine and in your research log make a list of public issues that you would like to know more about. Use the following trigger question:

I don't know where I stand on the issue of _____.

Share your list with classmates and friends.

Formulating a Starting Point

After you've chosen a problem or issue, write a research-log entry identifying the problem or issue you have chosen and explaining why you are perplexed by and interested in it. You might start out with a sharp, clearly focused question (for example, "Should the United States eliminate welfare payments for single mothers?"). Often, however, formulating the question turns out to be part of the *process* of writing the exploratory paper. Many writers don't start with a single, focused question but rather with a whole cluster of related questions swimming in their heads. This practice is all right—in fact, it is healthy—as long as you have a direction in which to move after the initial starting point. Even if you do start with a focused question, it is apt to evolve as your thinking progresses.

For this exercise, choose the question, problem, or issue you plan to investigate and write a research-log entry explaining how you got interested in that question and why you find it both problematic and significant. This will be the *starting point* for your essay; it might even serve as the rough draft for your introduction. Many instructors will collect this exploration as a quick check on whether you have formulated a good question that promises fruitful results.

Here is how one student, Sam, wrote the starting-point entry for his research log.

Sam's Starting Point Research-Log Entry

I want to focus on the question of whether women should be allowed to serve in combat units in the military. I became interested in the issue of women in combat through my interest in gays in the military. While I saw that gays in the military was an important political issue for gay rights, I, like many gays, had no real desire to be in such a macho organization. But perhaps that was just the point—we had the opportunity to break stereotypes and attack areas most hostile to us.

Similarly, I wonder whether feminists see women in combat as a crucial symbolic issue for women's rights. (I wonder too whether it is a *good* symbol, since many women value a less masculine approach to the world.) I think my instinct right now is that women should be allowed to serve in combat units. I think it is wrong to discriminate against women. Yet I also think America needs to have a strong military. Therefore, I am in a quandary. If putting women in combat wouldn't harm our military power, then I am fully in favor of women in combat. But if it would hurt our military power, then I have to make a value judgment. So I guess I have a lot to think about as I research this issue. I decided to focus on the women issue rather than the gay issue because it poses more of a dilemma for me. I am absolutely in favor of gays in the military, so I am not very open-minded about *exploring* that issue. But the women's issue is more of a problem for me.

Continuing with Research and Dialectic Thinking

After you have formulated your starting point, you need to proceed with research, keeping a research log that records both your reading notes and your strong-response reflections to each reading.

After Sam wrote his starting-point entry, he created an initial bibliography by searching his college library's INFOTRAC. He decided to try keeping his research log in a double-entry format. What follows is his research-log entry for the first article he read, a piece from *Newsweek*.

Sam's Notes on *Newsweek* Article

Notes

Hackworth, David H. "War and the Second Sex." *Newsweek* 5 Aug. 1991: 24–28.

- Ideals in conflict are equality and combat readiness.
- Acknowledges women's bravery, competence, and education (uses the Gulf War as an example). Admits that there are some women as strong and fit as the strongest men (gives some examples), but then argues that allowing even these women in combat is the type of experimentation that the army doesn't need right now. (He says women already have plenty of jobs open for them in noncombat units).

- Biggest problem is "gender norming"—having different physical standards for men and women. A 22-year-old female is allowed three more minutes than a 22-year-old male to run two miles; men have to climb a 20-foot rope in 30 seconds; women can take 50 seconds.
- One of Hackworth's big values is male bonding. He points to "male bonding" as a key to unit cohesion. Men have been socialized to think that women must be protected. He uses Israel as an example:

  "The Israeli Army put women on the front lines in 1948. The experiment ended disastrously after only three weeks. It wasn't that the women couldn't fight. It was that they got blown apart. Female casualties demoralized the men and gutted unit cohesion." (pp. 26–27)

- Another major problem is pregnancy causing women to leave a unit. He says that 10 to 15 percent of servicewomen wear maternity uniforms in a given year. During the Gulf War, pregnancy rates soared. 1200 pregnant women were evacuated from the gulf (p. 28) during the war. On one destroyer tender, 36 female crew members got pregnant (p. 28). These pregnancies leave vacancies in a unit that can destroy its effectiveness.
- He claims that women soldiers themselves had so many complaints about their experiences in the Gulf War (fraternization, sexual harassment, lack of privacy, primitive living conditions) that they said "don't rush to judgment on women in combat" (p. 28).

Reflections

Some challenging points, but not completely convincing. His biggest reason for opposing women in combat is harm to unit morale, but this isn't convincing to me. The Israeli example seems like unconvincing evidence seeing how those soldiers' attitudes in 1948 reflected a much different society.

Issue of pregnancy is more convincing. A pregnant woman, unlike a father-to-be, cannot continue to fill her role as a combat soldier. I was shocked by the number of pregnancies during the Gulf War and by the extent (although Hackworth doesn't give statistics) of the fraternization (he says the army passed out over a million condoms—p. 28).

I am also bothered by the gender-norming issue. It seems to me that there ought to be some absolute standards of strength and endurance needed for combat duty and the military ought to exclude both men and women who don't meet them. This would mean that a lower percentage of women than men would be eligible, but is that discrimination?

Where do I now stand? Well, I am still leaning toward believing that women should be allowed to serve in combat, but I see that there are a number of subquestions involved. Should physical standards for combat positions be the same for men and women? Will the presence of women really hurt morale in a mostly male unit? Should women be given special consideration for their roles as mothers? How serious a problem is pregnancy? I also see another problem: Should physically eligible women be *required* (e.g., drafted) to serve in combat the same way men are drafted into combat positions? And I still want to know whether this is a crucial issue for the women's rights movement.

In the next section we see how Sam converts material from his research log into a draft of his exploratory essay.

Shaping and Drafting

Your exploratory essay should offer accounts of your search procedures (useful conversations with friends, strategies for tracking down sources, use of indexes or computer searches, strokes of good fortune at stumbling on good leads, and so forth) and your thought processes (what you were discovering, how your ideas were evolving). Drawing on your research log, you can share your frustration when a promising source turned out to be off the mark or your perplexity when a conversation with a friend over late-night espresso forced you to rethink your views. Hook your readers by making your exploratory essay read like a detective story. Consider giving your account immediacy by quoting your thoughts at the very moment you wrote a log entry. The general shape of an exploratory essay can take the following pattern:

1. Starting point: you describe your initial problem, why you are interested in it, why it is problematic, why it is worth pursuing.
2. New input: you read an article, interview someone, pose an alternative solution.
    a. Summarize, describe, or explain the new input.
    b. Discuss the input, analyzing or evaluating it, playing the believing and doubting game with it, exploring how this input affects your thinking.
    c. Decide where to go next—find an alternative view, pursue a subquestion, seek more data, and so forth.
3. More new input: you repeat step 2 for your next piece of research.
4. Still more new input.
5. Ending point: you sum up where you stand at the point when the paper is due, how much your thinking about the issue has changed, whether or not you've reached a satisfactory solution.

Here is how Sam converted his starting-point entry (see p. 123) and his first research entry (pp. 123–24) into the opening pages of his exploratory essay.

Should Women Be Allowed to Serve in Combat Units?

Sam Scofield

At first, I wanted to explore the issue of gays in the military. But since I am a gay man I already knew where I stood on that issue and didn't find it truly problematic *for myself*. So I decided to shift my question to whether women should be allowed to serve in combat units. I wasn't sure whether feminists see the issue of women in combat the same way that gays see the military issue. Is it important to the feminist cause for women to be in combat? Or should feminists seek a kind of political order that avoids combat and doesn't settle issues through macho male behavior? In my initial thinking, I was also concerned about maintaining our country's military strength. In my "starting point" entry of my research log, I recorded the following thoughts:

> If putting women in combat wouldn't harm our military power, then I am fully in favor of women in combat. But if it would hurt our military power, then I have to make a value judgment.

So I decided that what I should do first is find some general background reading on the women in combat question. I went to the library, plugged the key words "woman and combat" into our online INFOTRAC database, and found a dozen entries just for the last two years. I went to the stacks and found the most familiar magazine in my initial list: *Newsweek.*

I began with an article by a retired Air Force colonel, David H. Hackworth. Hackworth was opposed to women in combat and focused mainly on the standard argument I was expecting—namely that women in combat would destroy male bonding. He didn't provide any evidence, however, other than citing the case of Israel in 1948.

> The Israeli Army put women on the front lines in 1948. The experiment ended disastrously after only three weeks. It wasn't that the women couldn't fight. It was that they got blown apart. Female casualties demoralized the men and gutted unit cohesion. (26–27)

However, this argument wasn't very persuasive to me. I thought that men's attitudes had changed a lot since 1948 and that cultural changes would allow us to get used to seeing both men and women as *people* so that it would be equally bad—or equally bearable—to see either men or women wounded and killed in combat.

But Hackworth did raise three points that I hadn't anticipated, and that really set me thinking. First he said that the military had different physical fitness requirements for men and women (for example, women had three minutes longer to run two miles than did men [25]). As I said in my research log, "It seems to me that there ought to be some absolute standards of strength and endurance needed for combat duty and the military ought to exclude both men and women who don't meet them." A second point was that an alarming number of female soldiers got pregnant in the Gulf War (1200 pregnant soldiers had to be evacuated [28]) and that prior to the war about 10–15 percent of female soldiers were pregnant at any given time (28). His point was that a pregnant woman, unlike a father-to-be, cannot continue to fill her role as a combat soldier. When she leaves her unit, she creates a dangerous gap that makes it hard for the unit to accomplish its mission. Finally, Hackworth cited lots of actual women soldiers in the Gulf War who were opposed to women in combat. They raised issues such as fraternization, sexual harassment, lack of privacy, and primitive living conditions.

Although Hackworth didn't turn me against wanting women to be able to serve in combat, he made the issue much more problematic for me. I now realized that this issue contained a lot of sub-issues, so I decided to focus first on the two major ones for me: (1) How important is this issue to feminists? This concern is crucial for me because I want to support equal rights for women just as I want to do so for gays or ethnic minorities. And (2) How serious are the pregnancy and strength-test issues in terms of maintaining military strength?

As I read the rest of the articles on my list, I began paying particular attention to these issues. The next article that advanced my thinking was. . . .

Revising

Because an exploratory essay describes the writer's research and thinking in chronological order, most writers have little trouble with organization. When they revise, their major concern is often to improve their essay's interest level by keeping it focused and lively. Exploratory essays grow tedious if the pace crawls too slowly or if extraneous details appear. They also tend to become too long, so that condensing and pruning become key revision tasks. The draft here is actually Sam's second draft; the first draft was a page longer and incorporated many more details and quotations from the Hackworth article. Sam eliminated these because he realized that his purpose was not to report on Hackworth, but to describe the evolution of his own thinking. By condensing the Hackworth material, Sam saved room for the ideas he discovered later.

Peer reviewers can give you valuable feedback about the pace and interest level of an exploratory piece. They can also help you achieve the right balance between external details (how you did the research, to whom you talked, where you were) and mental details (what you were thinking about). As you revise, make sure you follow proper stylistic conventions for quotations and citations.

TOPIC Guidepost #14

For those using Texas Tech's TOPIC Web-Based assignments:

Direct your web browser to **http://english.ttu.edu:5555**

Guidepost #14 provides full instructions regarding your reading assignment (Chapter 8) and Critique of Draft 2.1.

c h a p t e r 8

Analyzing Images

◢ ABOUT ANALYZING IMAGES

This chapter asks you to analyze the persuasive power of images. We are surrounded by images that have designs on us, that urge us to buy things, go places, believe ideas, and so forth. Often the messages of these images are fairly subtle. Information brochures rely on carefully shot photographs of people and places to enhance a subject's image (consider the photographs of the campus included in your college catalog); news photographs editorialize their content (during the Vietnam War a newspaper photograph of a naked Vietnamese child running screaming toward the photographer turned many Americans against the war); and paintings and visual arts cause us literally to see new things ("There was no yellow fog in London until Turner painted it," according to Oscar Wilde). But the most powerful and pervasive images in our culture come to us through the medium of magazine and television advertisements. This chapter focuses on helping you learn to analyze the persuasive nature of these images.

By *images* we mean both the advertisements' pictures themselves and also the images of self and society that they project. When we discuss the persuasive nature of ads we can ask both: How does this ad persuade me to buy this product? and How does this ad persuade me to be a certain kind of person, to adopt a certain self-image, or to strive for certain values?

This chapter is the first of four chapters on writing to analyze. As you may recall from Chapter 4, when you write to analyze you apply your own critical thinking to a puzzling object or to puzzling data. Your goal is to raise interesting questions about the object or data being analyzed—questions that perhaps your reader hasn't thought to ask—and then to provide tentative answers to those questions through close examination of the object or data. The word *analysis* derives from a Greek word meaning "to dissolve, loosen, or undo." Metaphorically, analysis means to divide or dissolve the whole into its constituent parts, to examine these parts carefully, to look at the relationships among them, and then to use this understanding of the parts to better understand the whole—how it functions or what it means. Synonyms for writing to analyze might be writing to interpret, to clarify, or to explain.

What you will develop through this chapter is the ability to understand and explain the persuasive power of advertisements. We will look at the constituent parts of these advertisements—setting, furnishings, and props; characteristics of the models, including their clothes, gestures, hair, facial expressions, and poses; camera angle and lighting; the interplay between the visual images and the verbal copy—and ask how all these parts working together contribute to the rhetorical effect of the advertisement. Along the way, we raise questions about how advertisements shape our sense of who we are and what we value.

Because advertising is such a broad and complex subject, any discussion of it raises numerous interconnected questions concerning the ethics of advertising, the nature of a consumer economy, the complexity and challenge of running a successful business, and what modern critics sometimes call the "social construction of the self," that is, the way messages in the culture create our sense of self and others. Critics of advertising point to its harmful effects (hooking young women on dieting, inciting young men to steal in order to buy $150 basketball shoes), while supporters of advertising point to its benefits (making capitalism work, funding radio and television, undermining communist economies by creating a longing for Western consumer products). All these are areas for exploration and debate.

◢ EXPLORING IMAGE ANALYSIS

Working on your own, freewrite your responses to the following questions:

1. Can you recall a time when a magazine or TV advertisement directly influenced you to buy a product? Describe the occasion and try to recall the specifics of how the ad influenced you.
2. According to a communications professor, Sut Jhally, many critics of advertising claim that "it is a tool whereby consumers are controlled and manipulated by the producers of goods (on whose behalf advertising is waged) to desire things for which they have no real need." To what extent has advertising made you desire things that you don't need? Give some examples. How did the advertisements work on you? What techniques did they use?
3. Has advertising ever influenced your values or your image of what you want to be? For example, an ad may not have caused you to buy a product (a particular perfume or brand of coffee), but has an ad made you long for certain values or experiences (to ride a horse through the pounding surf, to have a romantic encounter in a European café)? As a specific example, one of the authors of this text remembers one summer morning when he and his seven-year-old daughter ate their breakfast cereal on their front porch, cereal bowls cupped in their hands, as a direct result of a Grapenuts advertisement. Can you think of similar experiences?

In small groups or as a whole class, share your freewrites. From the ensuing discussion, create a list of specific ways in which magazine or TV advertisements have been successful in persuading members of your class (a) to buy a product, (b) to value something they didn't need, and (c) to embrace particular values or long for certain experiences.

For further exploration, read the following introduction to a brief article with the headline "Attention Advertisers: Real Men Do Laundry." This article appeared in a recent issue of *American Demographics,* a magazine that helps advertisers target particular audiences based on demographic analysis of the population.

> Commercials almost never show men doing the laundry, but nearly one-fifth of men do at least seven loads a week. Men don't do as much laundry as women, but the washday gap may be closing. In the dual-career 1990's laundry is going unisex.
>
> Forty-three percent of women wash at least seven loads of laundry a week, compared with 19 percent of men, according to a survey conducted for Lever Brothers Company, manufacturers of Wisk detergent. Men do 29 percent of the 419 million loads of laundry Americans wash each week. Yet virtually all laundry-detergent advertising is aimed at women.

Working in small groups, create an idea for a laundry detergent ad to be placed in a men's magazine such as *Playboy, Sports Illustrated, Field and Stream,* or *Esquire.* Draw a rough sketch of your ad that includes the picture, the placement of words, and a rough idea of the content of the words. Pay particular attention to the visual features of your ad—the models, their age, ethnicity, social status or class, and dress; the setting, such as a self-service laundry or a home laundry room; and other features. When you have designed a possible approach, explain why you think your ad will work.

WRITING PROJECT

Choose two magazine or TV advertisements that sell the same kind of product but appeal to different audiences (for example, a car advertisement aimed at men and one aimed at women; a cigarette ad aimed at upper-middle-class consumers and one aimed at working-class consumers; a clothing ad from *The New Yorker* and one from *Rolling Stone*). Describe the ads in detail so that an audience can easily visualize them without actually seeing them. Analyze the advertisements and explain how each appeals to its target audience. To what values does each ad appeal? How is each ad constructed to appeal to those values? In addition to analyzing the rhetorical appeals made by each ad, you may also wish to evaluate or criticize the ads, commenting on the images they convey of our culture.

This assignment asks you to analyze two different advertisements that are for the same kind of product but appeal to different audiences. Seeing the contrasts in the ads will heighten your awareness of how advertisers vary their appeals to reach different target audiences. For example, Budweiser beer and Pyramid ale are aimed at two different segments of the beer market and the kinds of appeals they use are very different. Companies often vary their appeals for the same product by gender. The Coors beer advertisements in *Glamour* or *Redbook* often differ from the Coors advertisements in *Playboy* or *Sports Illustrated.* Similarly, advertisers often vary their appeals to reach African-American, Hispanic, or Asian markets. This assignment asks you to explain how these appeals are targeted and created.

◪ UNDERSTANDING IMAGE ANALYSIS

Advertisements use images in subtle ways. Although some advertisements are primarily informational—explaining why the company believes its product is superior—most advertisements involve parity products, such as soft drinks, deodorants, breakfast cereals, toothpaste, and jeans. *Parity* products are products that are roughly equal in quality to their competitors and can't be sold through any rational or scientific proof of superiority.

Advertisements for parity products usually use psychological and motivational strategies to associate a product with a target audience's (often subconscious) dreams, hopes, desires, and wishes. The ads play on the idea that the product will magically dispel subconscious fears and anxieties or magically deliver on values, desires, and dreams. Using sophisticated research techniques, advertisers study how people's fears, dreams, and values differ according to their ethnicity, gender, educational level, socioeconomic class, age, and so forth; this research allows advertisers to tailor their appeals precisely to a target audience.

Every feature of an expensive ad, down to the tiniest detail, is the result of conscious choice. Therefore, you must pay close attention to every detail: Why is the hair this way rather than that way? Why these clothes rather than other clothes? Why these body positions rather than other body positions? Why this facial expression rather than another facial expression? Why these words rather than other words? Why this camera angle rather than another camera angle? And so forth.

Targeting Specific Audiences

Much of the market research on which advertisers rely is based on an influential demographic tool developed by SRI Research called the VALS™ (*values and lifestyle system*).* This system divides consumers into three basic categories, with further subdivisions.

1. *Needs-driven consumers.* Poor, with little disposable income, these consumers generally spend their money only on basic necessities.
   - *Survivors:* Live on fixed incomes or have no disposable income. Advertising seldom targets this group.

---

*Our discussion of the VALS™ is adapted from Harold W. Berkman and Christopher Gibson, *Advertising*, 2nd ed. (New York: Random House, 1987), pp. 134–37.

- *Sustainers:* Have very little disposable income, but often spend what they have impulsively on low-end, mass-market items.
2. ***Outer-directed consumers.*** These consumers want to identify with certain in-groups, to "keep up with the Joneses" or to surpass them.
   - *Belongers:* Believe in traditional family values and are conforming, non-experimental, nostalgic, and sentimental. They are typically blue collar or lower middle class, and they buy products associated with mom, apple pie, and the American flag.
   - *Emulators:* Are ambitious and status conscious. They have tremendous desire to associate with currently popular in-groups. They are typically young, have at least moderate disposable income, are urban and upwardly mobile, and buy conspicuous items that are considered "in."
   - *Achievers:* Have reached the top in a competitive environment. They buy to show off their status and wealth and to reward themselves for their hard climb up the ladder. They have high incomes and buy top-of-the-line luxury items that say "success." They regard themselves as leaders and persons of stature.
3. ***Inner-directed consumers.*** Marching to their own drummers, these consumers are individualistic and buy items to suit their own tastes rather than to symbolize their status.
   - *I-am-me types:* Are young, independent, and often from affluent backgrounds. They typically buy expensive items associated with their individual interests (such as mountain bikes, stereo equipment, or high-end camping gear), but may spend very little on clothes, cars, or furniture.
   - *Experiential types:* Are process-oriented and often reject the values of corporate America in favor of alternative lifestyles. They buy organic foods, make their own bread, do crafts and music, value holistic medicine, and send their children to alternative kindergartens.
   - *Socially conscious types:* Believe in simple living and are concerned about the environment and the poor. They emphasize the social responsibility of corporations, take on community service, and actively promote their favorite causes. They have middle to high incomes and are usually very well educated.

No one fits exactly into any category, and most people exhibit traits of several categories, but advertisers are interested in statistical averages, not individuals. When a company markets an item, it enlists advertising specialists to help target the item to a particular market segment. Budweiser is aimed at belongers, expensive imported beers at achievers, and microbrewery beers at either experiential types or emulators (if microbeers are currently "in"). To understand more precisely the fears and values of a target group, researchers can analyze subgroups within each of these VALS segments by focusing specifically on women, men, children, teenagers, young adults, or retirees or on specified ethnic or regional minorities. Researchers also determine what kinds of families and relationships are valued in each of the VALS segments, who in a family initiates demand for a product, and who in a family makes the actual purchasing decisions. Thus ads aimed at belongers depict traditional families; ads aimed at I-am-me types may depict more ambiguous relationships. Advertisements aimed at women can be particularly complex because of women's conflicting social roles in our society. When advertisers target the broader category of gender, they sometimes sweep away VALS distinctions and try to evoke more deeply embedded emotional and psychological responses.

FOR WRITING AND DISCUSSION

You own a successful futon factory that has marketed its product primarily to experiential types. Your advertisements have associated futons with holistic health, spiritualism (transcendental meditation, yoga), and organic wholesomeness (all-natural materials, gentle people working in the factory, incense and sitar music in your retail stores, and so forth). You have recently expanded your factory and now produce twice as many futons as you did six months ago. Unfortunately, demand hasn't increased correspondingly. Your market research suggests that if you are going to increase demand for futons you have to reach other VALS segments.

Working in small groups, develop ideas for a magazine or TV advertisement that might sell futons to one or more of the other target segments in the VALS system. Your instructor can assign a different target segment to each group, or each group can decide for itself which target segment constitutes the likeliest new market for futons.

Groups should then share their ideas with the whole class.

Analyzing an Advertisement

When you analyze an advertisement, you need to examine it in minute detail. Here are some suggestions for analyzing magazine advertisements. The same strategies can be applied to television advertisements, but TV ads are more complex because they add dialogue, multiple scenes, music, and so forth.

1. *Examine the setting, furnishings, and props.*
   a. List all furnishings and props. If the ad pictures a room, look carefully at such details as the kind and color of the rug; the subject matter of paintings on the walls; the styles of picture frames, curtains, and furniture; the objects on tables; the general arrangement of objects (Is the room neat and tidy or does it have a lived-in look?); the room's feeling (Is it formal? Warm? Casual?); and so forth. Almost all details are purposely chosen; almost nothing is accidental.
   b. What social meanings and values are attached to the objects you listed in (a)? In a den, for example, duck decoys and fishing rods have a connotation different from that of computers and fax machines. It makes a difference whether a dog is a Labrador retriever, an English sheepdog, a toy poodle, or a mutt. What symbolic meanings or associations do vari-

ous props have? A single rose connotes romance or elegance, a bouquet of daisies suggests freshness, and a hanging fuchsia suggests earthy naturalness. Always ask why the ad maker includes one particular prop rather than another.

2. *Consider the characters, roles, and actions.*

   a. Create the story of the ad. Who are the people? What are their relationships? Why are they here? What are they doing? Note details about the clothing and accessories of all the models; pay special attention to hairstyles, because popular culture invests hair with great significance (hence the anxiety created by a bad hair day). Note the poses and gestures of models as well as their positioning and relative sizes. For further advice on what to look for when analyzing the people in advertisements, consult Gillian Dyer's discussion of the manner and actions of characters in ads (pp. 143–145).

   b. Ask what social roles are being played and what values appealed to. Are the gender roles traditional or nontraditional? Are the relationships between people romantic, erotic, friendly, formal, uncertain? What are the power relationships between characters? In most ads, men are larger than women and occupy a stronger position (the woman looking up at the man, the man looking directly at someone or into the camera while the woman averts her eyes), but sometimes these roles are reversed. Either choice is deliberate.

3. *Examine the photographic effects.*   Some advertisements use highly artistic photographic techniques. Parts of the ad may be in crisp focus and others slightly blurred; camera angle or filters may have been used to create special effects. Why? Frequently, photographs are cropped so that only parts of a body are shown. Research suggests that women's bodies are more often cropped than are men's. It is not unusual to see photographs of women's arms, feet, ears, lips, or eyes, but it is rare to see similar photographs of men. What does this difference suggest about the culture's view of men and women? Many ads consist of a large picture with a small insert picture at the top or bottom; the insert often includes one of the characters from the large picture in a different role or pose. Ask how the insert comments on the large picture or how the insert and the large picture otherwise interrelate.

4. *Analyze words and copy.*   The words in advertisements are chosen with extreme care, and special attention is given to connotations, double entendres, and puns. In well-made ads the words and pictures combine for a unified effect. Pay attention to both the message of the words and their visual effect on the page (placement, relative size, and so forth).

Sample Analysis of an Advertisement

As an example of how a specific ad persuades, consider the contrast between the beer ads typically aimed at men (showing women in bikinis fulfilling adolescent male sexual fantasies or men on fishing trips or in sports bars) with the "Sam

Sam and Me.

Me and Sam? We're just friends. Best friends, actually, since Mrs. Ainsley's first grade class when I let the hamster loose and Sam took the rap for me. I mean Sam's seen me in braces and I've seen him eat pizza. There's just way too much history here. Sam's my friend. The one I go to when I really need someone to talk to. I bring the Coors Light and Sam brings his shoulder. And sometimes it's Sam bringing the Coors Light and I'm doing the listening. Me and Sam? Together? I've never even thought about it. Okay, so I've thought about it.

Coors Light.
Just between friends.

and Me" Coors Light ad (above), which ran in a variety of women's magazines. Rather than associating beer drinking with a wild party, this ad associates beer drinking with the warm friendship of a man and woman and with just a hint of potential romance. The ad shows a man and a woman, probably in their early to mid-twenties, in relaxed conversation; they are sitting casually on a tabletop, with their legs resting on chair seats. The woman is wearing casual pants, a summery cotton top, and informal shoes. Her braided, shoulder-length hair has a healthy, messed appearance, and one braid comes across the front of her shoulder. She is turned away from the man, leans on her knees, and holds a bottle of Coors Light. Her sparkling eyes are looking up, and she smiles happily, as if reliving a pleasant memory. The man is wearing slacks, a cotton shirt with the sleeves rolled up, and scuffed tennis shoes with white socks. He also has a reminiscing smile on his face, and he leans on the woman's shoulder. The words "Coors Light. Just between friends" appear immediately below the picture next to a Coors Light can.

This ad appeals to women's desire for close friendships and relationships. Everything about the picture signifies long-established closeness and intimacy— old friends rather than lovers. The way the man leans on the woman shows her strength and independence. Additionally, the way they pose, with the woman slightly forward and sitting up more than the man, results in their taking up equal space in the picture. In many ads featuring male-female couples the man appears larger and taller than the woman; this picture signifies mutuality and equality.

The words of the ad help you interpret the relationship. Sam and the woman have been friends since the first grade, and they are reminiscing about old times. The relationship is thoroughly mutual. Sometimes he brings the Coors Light and sometimes she brings it; sometimes she does the listening and sometimes he does; sometimes she leans on his shoulder and sometimes he leans on hers. Sometimes the ad says, "Sam and me"; sometimes it says "me and Sam." Even the "bad grammar" of "Sam and me" (rather than "Sam and I") suggests the lazy, relaxed absence of pretense or formality.

These two are reliable old buddies. But the last three lines of the copy leave just a hint of potential romance. "Me and Sam? Together? I've never even thought about it. Okay, so I've thought about it." Whereas beer ads targeting men portray women as sex objects, this ad appeals to women's desire for relationships and for romance that is rooted in friendship rather than sex.

And why the name Sam? Students in our classes have hypothesized that Sam is a "buddy" kind of name rather than a romantic hero name. Yet it is more modern and more interesting than other buddy names such as Bob or Bill or Dave. "A Sam" said one of our students, "is more mysterious than a Bill." Whatever associations the name strikes in you, be assured that the ad makers spent hours debating possible names until they hit on this one. For an additional example of an ad analysis, see the sample student essay (pp. 146–148).

FOR WRITING AND DISCUSSION

Examine any of the other magazine ads reprinted in this chapter, or ads brought to class by students or your instructor, and analyze them in detail, paying particular attention to setting, furnishings, and props; characters, roles, and actions; photographic effects; and words and copy. Prior to discussion, freewrite your own analysis of the chosen ad.

Cultural Issues Raised by Advertisements

There isn't space here to examine in depth the numerous cultural issues raised by advertisements, but we can introduce you to a few of them and provide several tasks for exploratory writing and talking.

In 1979, the influential sociologist and semiotician* Erving Goffman published a book called *Gender Advertisements,* arguing that the way in which women are pictured in advertisements removes them from serious power. In many cases, Goffman's point seems self-evident. Women in advertisements are often depicted in frivolous, childlike, exhibitionistic, sexual, or silly poses that would be considered undignified for a man, such as the "Of Sound Body" Zenith ad (p. 139). Women in advertisements are often fun to look at or enthralling to "gaze" at, but seldom call for serious attention. What distinguishes Goffman's work is his analysis of apparently positive portrayals of women in advertisements. He points out tiny details that differentiate the treatment of men from that of women. For example, when men hold umbrellas in an ad, it is usually raining, but when women hold umbrellas, it is for decoration; men grip objects tightly, but women often caress objects or cup them in a gathering in or nurturing way. Female models dance and jump and wiggle in front of the camera (like children playing), whereas male models generally stand or sit in a dignified manner. Even when trying to portray a powerful and independent woman, ads reveal cultural signs that the woman is subordinate.

FOR WRITING AND DISCUSSION

To see what Goffman is getting at, we invite you to explore this issue in the following sequence of activities, which combine class discussion with invitations for exploratory writing.

1. Bring to class advertisements for clothing, perfumes, or accessories from recent fashion and beauty magazines, such as *Glamour, Elle, Mademoiselle,* and *Vogue.* Ask male students to assume the postures of the women in the ads. How many of the postures, which look natural for women, seem ludicrous when adopted by men? To what extent are these postures really natural for women? Freewrite your responses to this exercise.

2. Examine the Zenith advertisement on page 139. How might Erving Goffman argue that this ad subordinates women? Do you agree that this ad reflects the inferior status of women in U.S. culture? Why or why not? Freewrite your response in preparation for class discussion.

3. A highly popular advertisement for cognac that ran several years ago shows three male business executives, ranging in age from the early thirties to early fifties, sitting in an upscale bar overlooking a subway

---

*A *semiotician* is a person who studies the meanings of signs in a culture. A *sign* is any human-produced artifact or gesture that conveys meaning. It can be anything from a word to a facial expression to the arrangement of chairs at a dinner table.

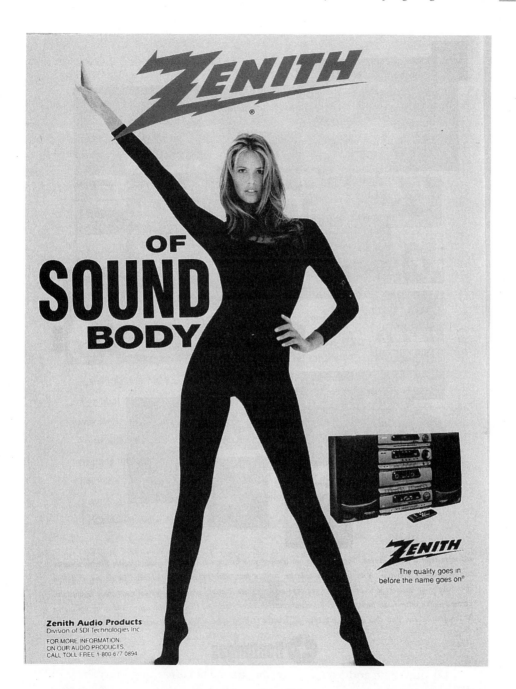

station (see the "The World's Most Civilized Spirit" Hennessy ad, p. 140). The men are wearing power suits; one man has removed his jacket and rolled up the sleeves on his striped oxford shirt, revealing

his power tie and expensive suspenders. He is reaching for cashew nuts in a cut-glass bowl. The three men are sipping cognac from expensive brandy snifters. The copy at the top of the ad reads, "When the 8:05 isn't leaving until 8:55." What the ad reveals, then, are powerful business leaders at the end of a business day, which is—conspicuously—

close to 8:00 p.m., not 5:00. Since the 8:05 train has been delayed, the men relax, enjoy each other's company, and sip fine cognac.

Freewrite or discuss your responses to this question: Would this ad work if you replaced the male business executives with female executives? Why or why not?

4. Imagine a comparable ad featuring female models that appeals to women's desire to be seen as competent, empowered corporate leaders in today's business environment. Freewrite your ideas for such an ad, addressing the following questions: (a) What product would the ad be selling? (b) What kind of model or models would you choose for your ad? Of what age? From what ethnic group? With what look? (c) What setting and props would you use? (d) How would the models be dressed? What would their hairstyles be? How would they pose? What would they be doing? (e) What might the ad copy say? (f) In what magazines would you publish your ad?

5. Bring to class examples of advertisements that portray women in a particularly positive and empowered way—ads that you think couldn't be deconstructed even by Erving Goffman, to show the subordination of women in our culture. Share your examples with the class and see if they agree that these ads place women on a par with men.

6. After everyone in the class has examined several recent advertisements in a variety of magazines, ask individuals or groups to look at some advertisements from magazines from the 1950s. (Most college libraries have old copies of *Time* or *Life*.) Then hold a class debate on the following question:

> RESOLVED: In recent years advertising has made enormous gains in portraying women as strong, independent, intelligent, and equal with men in their potential for professional status.

READINGS

Vance Packard's *The Hidden Persuaders* is one of the most significant books ever written on advertising. Published in 1957, it brought to public awareness the extent to which advertisers were applying findings from psychological studies in their attempts to influence consumer behavior. In a chapter entitled "Marketing Eight Hidden Needs," Packard provided convincing evidence that advertisers were trying to manipulate the middle class by appealing to eight psychological needs: emotional security, reassurance of worth, ego gratification, something for moms to love once their kids are grown, a sense of power, a sense of roots, a sense of immortality, and creative outlets. The excerpt that follows focuses on this last need—creative outlets. Although Packard was not a feminist, his observations reveal many of the subtle expectations and limitations that society placed on the roles of middle-class women during the *I Love Lucy,* and *Leave It to Beaver* era. *The Hidden Persuaders* laid the groundwork for subsequent studies of gender and advertising and remains a standard reference for those who pursue this fascinating subject.

VANCE PACKARD
FROM *THE HIDDEN PERSUADERS*

Selling creative outlets.   The director of psychological research at a Chicago ad agency mentioned casually in a conversation that gardening is a "pregnancy activity." When questioned about this she responded, as if explaining the most obvious thing in the world, that gardening gives older women a chance to keep on growing things after they have passed the child-bearing stage. This explains, she said, why gardening has particular appeal to older women and to men, who of course can't have babies. She cited the case of a woman with eleven children who, when she passed through menopause, nearly had a nervous collapse until she discovered gardening, which she took to for the first time in her life and with obvious and intense delight.

Housewives consistently report that one of the most pleasurable tasks of the home is making a cake. Psychologists were put to work exploring this phenomenon for merchandising clues. James Vicary made a study of cake symbolism and came up with the conclusion that "baking a cake traditionally is acting out the birth of a child" so that when a woman bakes a cake for her family she is symbolically presenting the family with a new baby, an idea she likes very much. Mr. Vicary cited the many jokes and old wives tales about cake making as evidence: the quip that brides whose cakes fall obviously can't produce a baby yet; the married jest about "leaving a cake in the oven"; the myth that a cake is likely to fall if the woman baking it is menstruating. A psychological consulting firm in Chicago also made a study of cake symbolism and found that "women experience making a cake as making a gift of themselves to their family," which suggests much the same thing.

The food mixes—particularly the cake mixes—soon found themselves deeply involved in this problem of feminine creativity and encountered much more resistance than the makers, being logical people, ever dreamed possible. The makers found themselves trying to cope with negative and guilt feelings on the part of women who felt that use of ready mixes was a sign of poor housekeeping and threatened to deprive them of a traditional source of praise.

In the early days the cake-mix packages instructed, "Do not add milk, just add water." Still many wives insisted on adding milk as their creative touch, overloaded the cakes or muffins with calcium, and often the cakes or muffins fell, and the wives would blame the cake mix. Or the package would say, "Do not add eggs." Typically the milk and eggs had already been added by the manufacturer in dried form. But wives who were interviewed in depth studies would exclaim: "What kind of cake is it if you just need to add tap water!" Several different psychological firms wrestled with this problem and came up with essentially the same answer. The mix makers should always leave the housewife something to do. Thus Dr. Dichter counseled General Mills that it should start telling the housewife that she and Bisquick *together* could do the job and not Bisquick alone. Swansdown White Cake Mix began telling wives in large type: "You Add Fresh Eggs . . ." Some mixes have the wife add both fresh eggs and fresh milk.

5   Marketers are finding many areas where they can improve sales by urging the prospective customer to add his creative touch. A West Coast firm selling to home builders found that although its architects and designers could map houses to the last detail it was wise to leave some places where builders could add their own personal touch. And Dr. Dichter in his counseling to pharmaceutical houses advised them that in merchandising ready-mixed medical compounds they would be wise to leave the doctors ways they could add personal touches so that each doctor could feel the compound was "his own."

Thinking Critically About *The Hidden Persuaders*

1. Packard's explanation of how Bisquick advertisers used psychological research to make their ads more effective suggests both the complexity and the sophistication of the "science" of advertising. Bring to class examples of contemporary advertisements that use psychological motivations in subtle ways. Share your examples with classmates and discuss the strategies employed in the ads.
2. Very few advertisements for stereo equipment are found in women's magazines, although women now constitute a large segment of stereo buyers. Why don't the ads for stereo equipment found in men's magazines, such as *GQ* and *Esquire,* appeal to women? How might you design a stereo advertisement with a strong appeal to women?

Many of the points addressed in our earlier discussion about analyzing advertisements are explained in greater detail in an influential book published in 1982, *Advertising as Communication,* by Gillian Dyer, a British professor of communication. The following excerpt from that book focuses on what models' nonverbal behaviors are meant to communicate. Again, although Dyer is attempting merely to present observations rather than to promote a feminist point of view, the findings inevitably hone in on gender distinctions and their societal implications. The citations of Erving Goffman refer to the book we mentioned earlier, *Gender Advertisements* (p. 138).

GILLIAN DYER
ON MANNER AND ACTIVITY

Manner

1   Manner indicates behaviour or emotion at any one time, and is manifest in three main codes of non-verbal communication.

2   1. *Expression.* The face and facial expression are a particular focus of attention in ads. Most expressions are based on socially learned, conventionalized cultural codes, which vary from culture to culture. The expression is meant to underwrite

the appeal of a product and arouse our emotions. Normally the expression of the "actor" will be positive, contented, purposeful, delighted, happy, gleeful, etc. There is considerable empirical evidence to suggest that in our society women smile more than men—both in reality and in commercial scenes. Women are often depicted in a childlike state of expectation and pleasure. They frequently seem to be too easily pleased in ads, as Goffman suggests:

> If television commercials are to be believed, most American women go into uncontrollable ecstasies at the sight and smell of tables and cabinets that have been lovingly caressed with long-lasting, satin-finish, lemon-scented, spray-on furniture polish. Or they glow with rapture at the blinding whiteness of their wash—and the green-eyed envy of their neighbours . . . (1979, p. 68).

In cosmetic ads in glossy fashion magazines the model's look might be cool and naughty as she looks the reader in the eye. Other typical expressions in ads may be seductive, alluring, coy, kittenish, inwardlooking, thoughtful, pensive, carefree, out-going, comic, maternal or mature.

2. *Eye contact.* The attention of the actor in an ad is significant whether it be directed   3
   towards audience/camera (person to viewer eye contact), at an object (product), towards other people in the ad or to the middle-distance (detached, distant). Goffman discusses the ritual of withdrawing one's gaze, mental drifting and social dissociation under the general description *licensed withdrawal.* He remarks that

> Women more than men . . . are pictured engaged in involvements which remove them psychologically from the social situation at large leaving them unoriented in it and to it, and presumably, therefore, dependent on the protectiveness and good will of others who are (or might come to be) present. (1979, p. 57)

Covering the face or mouth with the hands is one way of hiding an emotion like remorse, fear, shyness or laughter. The aversion of the eyes and lowering of the head can indicate withdrawal from a scene and symbolize dependency and submissiveness. In many advertisements women are shown mentally drifting while in close physical contact with a male as if his mental and physical alertness were enough for both of them. Women may focus their attention on the middle distance, on some object (like the product) or on a piece of the man's clothing. Women are sometimes seen with a dreamy luxuriating look in their eyes. Eyes may be covered up or shaded by hair, hats, hands, dark glasses. Similarly, blinking or winking have great cultural significance. However, an equally important feature in ads is the shielding of everything but the eyes so that the person can observe an event without actually participating in it; some ads show women coyly peeping from behind fans, curtains, objects or products.

3. *Pose.* This can be static or active and sometimes corresponds to expression.   4
   Poses can be composed, relaxed, leisurely, passive, leaning, seductive, snuggling. Bodies can be vertical or horizontal. An individual can use another to act as a shield or as an object to lean against, or rest hands or legs on. Pose is also related to social position and status, hence women are often seen in a lower position than the man, for instance sitting at their feet.

4. *Clothes.* These are obviously extremely important carriers of meaning in ads,   5
   even when they are not the object being sold. They can range from the formal

(regimental or work costume), to the informal (leisure, relaxation, sports wear), and can be smart, sophisticated, glamorous, elegant, trendy or comfortable and casual. They can of course sum up a "look," e.g. the "twenties" look.

Activity

6   Body gestures, movement and posture can be related to what the actor is doing.

7   1. *Touch.* The finger brought to the mouth or face can signify thoughtfulness but of a dissociated kind; women and children are often shown with the tips of their fingers in the mouth. Finger to finger touching similarly implies dissociation. Women more than men are pictured touching, or delicately fingering objects, tracing their outline, caressing their surfaces. This ritualistic touching is different from functional touching like grasping or holding. Hand-holding can be a significant gesture in ads and often is used to allow the man to protect or direct the woman. Self-touching is again something that women do more than men; it conveys the impression of narcissism, admiring one's own body and displaying it to others, so that everyone can share the admiration of this delicate and precious thing. Sometimes the act of touching is displaced onto things—sun, wind or water on the naked body when sunbathing or swimming. The feel of clothes against the skin—satins, silks, furs—is conveyed as a pleasurable thing.

8   2. *Body movement.* This might be quite functional, i.e. simply related to what the actor is doing—cleaning the kitchen floor, making beds, filling up the car with petrol, playing football, gardening. These movements may be exaggerated, ridiculous or child-like, calling into question the competence of the performer. Bodies, particularly women's, are often not treated seriously, either through what Goffman calls "ritual subordination" (that is lowering the body in front of others more superior, lying or sitting down, ritually bending the knee or lowering the head) *or* through puckishness and clowning. An example of body movement is where two people are engaged in "mock assault" and this is sometimes seen in advertisements, men usually playing these games on women.

9   3. *Positional communication.* The relationships between actors and actors, actors and objects are extremely significant, and are shown by their position within the frame of a picture. Superiority, inferiority, equality, intimacy and rank can be signified by people's position, size, activity and their relationship to the space around them, the furniture and to the viewer/consumer. Close-up shots, for instance, are meant to signify more intimacy and identification than long-shots.

Thinking Critically About "On Manner and Activity"

1. Your instructor will choose an advertisement for analysis. Observe the ad closely, paying attention to expression, eye contact, pose, clothes, touch, body movement, and positional communication. How would a change in any of these features affect the ad's impact and "meaning"?

2. Dyer explains that the manner and activity of males and females in advertisements differ significantly. What are some of these differences? Can you find these differences illustrated in the advertisements that you and your classmates have been examining?

3. Do you agree with Dyer and Goffman that these differences are culturally significant, that is, that they reveal (and subtly reinforce) a cultural belief that women are subordinate to men?

The final reading is a student essay written in response to the assignment in this chapter. It contrasts the strategies of two different cigarette ads to make smoking appear socially desirable despite public sentiment to the contrary.

STEPHEN BEAN (STUDENT)
HOW CIGARETTE ADVERTISERS ADDRESS THE STIGMA AGAINST SMOKING: A TALE OF TWO ADS

Any smoker can tell you there's a social stigma attached to smoking in this country. With smokers being pushed out of restaurants, airports, and many office buildings, how could anyone not feel like a pariah lighting up? While never associated with the churchgoing crowd, smoking is increasingly viewed as lower class or as a symbol of rebellion. Smoking has significantly decreased among adults while increasing among teenagers and young adults in recent years—a testament to its growing status as an affront to middle- and upper-class values. Cigarette advertisers are sharply tuned into this cultural attitude. They must decide whether to overcome the working-class/rebellious image of smoking in their advertisements or use it to their advantage. The answer to this question lies in what type of people they want an ad to target—the young? the rich? the poor?—and in what values, insecurities, and desires they think this group shares. Two contrasting answers to these questions are apparent in recent magazine ads for Benson and Hedges cigarettes and for Richland cigarettes.

The ad for Benson and Hedges consists of a main picture and a small insert picture below the main one. The main picture shows five women (perhaps thirty years old) sitting around, talking, and laughing in the living room of a comfortable and urbane home or upscale apartment. The room is filled with natural light and is tastefully decorated with antique lamps and Persian rugs. The women have opened a bottle of wine, and a couple of glasses have been poured. They are dressed casually but fashionably, ranging from slightly hip to slightly conservative. One woman wears a loose, black, sleeveless dress; another wears grungesque boots with a sweater and skirt. One of the women, apparently the hostess, sits on a sofa a bit apart from the others, smiles with pleasure at the conversation and laughter of her friends, and knits. Two of the women are smoking, and three aren't. No smoke is visible coming from the cigarettes. Underneath the main picture is a small insert photograph of the hostess—the one knitting in the main picture—in a different pose. She is now leaning back in pleasure, apparently after the party, and this time she is smoking a cigarette. Underneath the photos reads the slogan "For people who like to smoke."

The ad for Richland cigarettes shows a couple in their late twenties sitting in a diner or perhaps a tavern off the freeway. The remains of their lunch—empty burger and fries baskets, a couple of beer bottles—lie on the table. They seem to be talking leisurely,

1

2

3

sharing an after-meal smoke. The man is wearing black jeans and a black T-shirt. The woman is wearing a pinkish skirt and tank top. Leaning back with her legs apart she sits in a position that signals sexuality. The slogan reads, "It's all right here." And at the bottom of the ad, "Classic taste. Right price." Outside the window of the diner you can see a freeway sign slightly blurred as if from heated air currents.

4   Whom do these different advertisements target? What about them might people find appealing? Clearly the Benson and Hedges ad is aimed at women, especially upper-middle-class women who wish to appear successful. As the media have noted lately, the social stigma against smoking is strongest among middle- and upper-class adults. My sense of the B&H ad is that it is targeting younger, college-educated women who feel social pressure to quit smoking. To them the ad is saying, "Smoking makes you no less sophisticated; it only shows that you have a fun side too. Be comfortable doing whatever makes you happy."

5   What choices did the advertisers make in constructing this scene to create this message? The living room—with its antique lamps and vases, its Persian rugs and hard-cover books, and its wall hanging thrown over what appears to be an old trunk—creates a sense of comfortable, tasteful, upscale living. But figuring out the people in the room is more difficult. Who are these women? What is their story? What brought them together this afternoon? Where did their money come from? Are these professional women with high-paying jobs, or are they the wives of young bankers, attorneys, and stockbrokers? One woman has a strong business look—short hair feathered back, black sleeveless dress—but why is she dressed this way on what is apparently a Saturday afternoon? In contrast, another woman has a more hip, almost grunge look—slightly spiky hair that's long in the back, a loose sweater, a black skirt, and heavy black boots. Only one woman wears a wedding ring. It seems everything about these women resists easy definition or categorization. The most striking image in the ad is the hostess knitting. She looks remarkably domestic, almost motherly, with her knees drawn close, leaning over her knitting and smiling to herself as others laugh out loud. Her presence gives the scene a feeling of safety and old-fashioned values amidst the images of independence. Interestingly, we get a much different image of the hostess in the second insert picture placed just above the B&H logo. This picture shows the hostess leaning back pleasurably on the couch and smoking. The image is undeniably sexual. Her arms are back; she's deeply relaxed; the two top buttons of her blouse are open; her hair is slightly mussed; she smokes languidly, taking full pleasure in the cigarette, basking in the party's afterglow.

6   The opposing images in the advertisement (knitting/smoking, conservative/hip, wife/career, safe/independent, domestic/sexual) mean that these women can't easily be defined—as smokers or as anything else. For an ad promoting smoking, the cigarettes themselves take a back seat. In the main picture the cigarettes are hardly noticeable; the two women holding cigarettes do so inconspicuously and there is no visible smoke. The ad doesn't say so much that it is good to smoke, but that it is okay to smoke. Smoking will not make you less sophisticated. If anything, it only shows that you have an element of youth and fun. The slogan, "For people who like to smoke," targets nonsmokers as much as it does smokers—not so much to take up smoking but to be more tolerant of those who choose to smoke. The emphasis is on choice, independence, and acceptance of others' choices. The ad attacks the social stigma against smoking; it eases the conscience of "people who like to smoke."

7   While the B&H ad hopes to remove the stigma attached to smoking, the Richland ad feasts on it. Richland cigarettes aren't for those cultivating the upper-class look. The ad goes for a rebellious, gritty image, for beer drinkers, not wine sippers. While the story

of the women in the B&H ad is difficult to figure out, the Richland ad gives us a classic image: a couple on the road who have stopped at a diner or tavern. Here the story is simpler: a man and woman being cool. They are going down the freeway to the big city. I picture a heavy American cruising car parked out front. Everything about the ad has a gritty, blue-collar feel. They sit at a booth with a Formica tabletop; the walls are bare, green-painted wood. The man is dressed in black with a combed-back, James Dean haircut. The woman wears a pink skirt with a tank top; her shoulder-length hair hasn't been fussed over, and she wears a touch of makeup. Empty baskets and bottles cluttering the table indicate they had a classic American meal—hamburgers, fries, and a beer—eaten for pleasure without politically correct worries about calories, polyunsaturated fats, cruelty to animals, or cancer. While the sexual imagery in the B&H ad is subtle, in the Richland ad it is blatant. The man is leaning forward with his elbows on the table; the woman is leaning back with her legs spread and her skirt pushed up slightly. Her eyes are closed. They smoke leisurely, and the woman holds the cigarette a couple of inches from her expecting lips. The slogan, "It's all right here," is centered beneath the woman's skirt. Smoking, like sex, is about pure pleasure—something to be done slowly. Far from avoiding working-class associations with smoking, this ad aims to reinforce them. The cigarettes are clearly visible, and, unlike the cigarettes in the B&H ad, show rings of rising smoke. This ad promotes living for the moment. The more rebellious, the better.

So we see, then, two different ways that cigarette companies address the stigma against smoking. The B&H ad tries to eliminate it by targeting middle-class, college-educated women. It appeals to upscale values, associating cigarette smoking with choice, and showing that "people who like to smoke" can also knit (evoking warm, safe images of domestic life) or lean back in postparty pleasure (evoking a somewhat wilder, more sexual image). In contrast, the Richland ad exploits the stigma. It associates smoking with on-the-road freedom, rebellion, sexuality, and enjoyment of the moment. The smoke visibly rising from the cigarettes in the Richland ad and noticeably absent from the Benson and Hedges ad tells the difference.

8

Thinking Critically About "A Tale of Two Ads"

1. Stephen Bean argues that the Benson and Hedges and the Richland ads use very different appeals to encourage their target audiences to smoke. What are the appeals he cites? Do you agree with Stephen's analysis?
2. Collect a variety of cigarette ads from current magazines and analyze their various appeals. How do the ads vary according to their intended audience? Consider ads targeted at men versus women or at audiences from different VALS segments.
3. What do you see as the strengths and weaknesses of Stephen's essay?

◼ COMPOSING YOUR ESSAY

Generating and Exploring Ideas

Your first task is to find two ads that sell the same general product to different target audiences or that make appeals to noticeably different value systems.

Look for ads that are complex enough to invite detailed analysis. Then, analyze the ads carefully, using the strategies suggested in Analyzing an Advertisement (pp. 220–21) and Dyer's ideas from "On Manner and Activity" (pp. 229–31). The sample student essay (pp. 232–34) provides an example of the kind of approach you can take.

If you get stuck, try freewriting your responses to the following questions: (a) What attracted your attention to this ad? (b) Whom do you think this ad targets? Why? (c) What props and furnishings are in this ad, and what values or meanings are attached to them? (d) What are the characters like, what are they doing, and why are they wearing what they are wearing and posed the way they are posed? (e) Is there anything worth noting about camera angle or photographic effects? (f) How do the words of the ad interplay with the picture? (g) How would the ad be less effective if its key features were changed in some way? (h) Overall, to what fears, values, hopes, or dreams is this ad appealing?

Shaping and Drafting

Your essay should be fairly easy to organize at the big-picture level, but each part will require its own organic organization depending on the main points of your analysis. At the big-picture level, you can generally follow a structure like this:

I. Introduction (hooks readers' interest, gives background on how ads vary their appeals, asks the question your paper will address, and ends with initial mapping in the form of a purpose or thesis statement)
II. General description of the two ads
   A. Description of ad 1
   B. Description of ad 2
III. Analysis of the two ads
   A. Analysis of ad 1
   B. Analysis of ad 2
IV. Conclusion (returns to the big picture for a sense of closure; makes final comments about the significance of your analysis or touches in some way on larger issues raised by the analysis)

We recommend that you write your rough draft rapidly, without worrying about gracefulness or about correctness or even about getting all your ideas said at once. Many people like to begin with the description of the ads and then write the analysis before writing the introduction and conclusion. After you have written your draft, put it aside for a while before you begin revising. We recommend that you ask classmates for a peer review of your draft early in the revising process.

Revising

Most experienced writers have to make global changes in their final drafts when they revise, especially when they are doing analytical writing. The act of writing a rough draft generally leads to the discovery of more ideas. You may also realize that many of your original ideas aren't clearly developed or that the draft feels scattered and unorganized.

g u i d e l i n e s

for Peer Reviewers

Instructions for peer reviews, including use of these guidelines, are provided in Chapter 10, pages 195–202. To write a peer review for a classmate, use your own paper, numbering your responses to correspond to the questions on the guidelines. At the head of your paper place the author's name, and your own name, as shown.

Author's Name: _____

Peer Reviewer's Name: _____

I. Read the draft at a normal reading speed from beginning to end. As you read, do the following:
   A. Place a wavy line in the margin next to any passages that you find confusing, that contain something that doesn't seem to fit, or that otherwise slow down your reading.
   B. Place a "Good!" in the margin next to any passages where you think the writing is particularly strong or interesting.
II. Read the draft again slowly and answer the following questions by writing brief explanations of your answers.
   A. Introduction:
      1. Is the title appropriate for an academic analysis? Does it suggest the thesis and focus of the paper and pique your interest? How might the title be improved?
      2. What does the writer do to capture your interest, provide needed background, and set up the question to be addressed?
      3. Does the thesis statement, purpose statement, or forecasting statement provide the big picture for both the description and the analysis of the two ads? How might the writer improve the introduction?
   B. Description of the ads:
      1. Does the writer describe the ads in an interesting and vivid manner? How could this description help you "see" the ads more clearly?
      2. In what ways do the ads appeal to different audiences or have different value systems? What makes the ads complex enough to justify an analysis?
   C. Analysis of the ads:
      1. How does the analysis of the ads shed light on and build on the description of the ads?

2. How many of the following features does the writer discuss? Which could be added to deepen and complicate the analysis?
   a. Setting, props, and furnishings: how they indicate lifestyle and socioeconomic status; appeal to certain values; carry certain cultural associations or meanings; serve as symbols.
   b. Characters, roles, and actions: the story of the ad; power relationships and status of the characters; gender, age, or ethnic roles followed or violated; the significance of clothing and accessories, of hair and facial expressions, and of posing, positioning, and gestures.
   c. Photographic effects: lighting, camera angle, cropping, focus?
   d. Language and wording of the ad's copy: its overt message; feelings, mood and values communicated through connotations, double entendres, and so forth; visual layout of copy?
3. Does the analysis interpret the ads convincingly? Do any details of the ads contradict the analysis? Do you disagree with the writer's view of these ads?
4. Do you have any suggestions for making the body of the paper clearer, better organized, or easier to follow? Where might the writer better apply the principles of clarity from Chapter 18 (starting with the big picture; putting points before particulars; using transitions; following the old/new contract)?

D. Sum up what you see as the chief strengths and problem areas of this draft.
   1. Strengths
   2. Problem areas

III. Read the draft one more time. Place a check in the margin wherever you notice problems in grammar, spelling, or mechanics (one check per problem).

TOPIC Guidepost #26

For those using Texas Tech's TOPIC Web-Based assignments:

Direct your web browser to **http://english.ttu.edu:5555**

Guidepost #26 provides full instructions regarding your reading assignment (Chapter 9) and your Journal Entry.

Writing a
Classical Argument

▨ ABOUT CLASSICAL ARGUMENT

The assignment for this chapter introduces you to a classical way of arguing in which you take a stand on an issue, offer reasons and evidence in support of your position, and summarize and respond to alternative views. Your goal is to persuade your audience, who can be initially perceived as either opposed to your position or undecided about it, to adopt your position or at least to regard it more openly or favorably.

The need for argument arises whenever members of a community disagree on an issue. Classical rhetoricians believed that the art of arguing was essential for good citizenship. If disputes can be resolved through exchange of perspectives, negotiation of differences, and flexible seeking of the best solutions to a problem, then nations won't have to resort to war or individuals to fisticuffs.

The study of argumentation involves two components: truth seeking and persuasion. By *truth seeking,* we mean a diligent, open-minded, and responsible search for the best course of action or solution to a problem taking into account all the available information and alternative points of view. By *persuasion,* we mean the art of making a claim on an issue and justifying it convincingly so that the audience's initial resistance to your position is overcome and they are moved toward your position.

These two components of argument seem paradoxically at odds: Truth seeking asks us to relax our certainties and be willing to change our views; persuasion asks us to be certain, to be committed to our claims, and to get others to change their views. We can overcome this paradox if we dispel two common but misleading views of argument. The most common view is that argument is a fight, as in "I just got into a horrible argument with my roommate." This view of argument as a fist-waving shouting match in which you ridicule anyone who disagrees with you (popularized by radio and television talk shows) entirely disregards argument as truth seeking, but it also misrepresents argument as persuasion because it polarizes people rather than promoting understanding, new ways of seeing, and change.

Another common but misleading view is that argument is pro/con debate modeled after high school or college debate matches or presidential debates. Although debating can be an excellent way to develop critical thinking skills, it misrepresents argument as a two-sided contest with winners and losers. Because controversial issues involve many different points of view, not just two, reducing an issue to pro/con positions distorts the complexity of the disagreement. Instead of thinking of *both* sides of an issue, we need to think of *all* sides. Equally troublesome, the debate image invites us to ask, "Who won the debate?" rather than "What is the best solution to the question that divides us?" The best solution might be a compromise between the two debaters or an undiscovered third position. The debate image tends to privilege the confident extremes in a controversy rather than the complex and muddled middle.

From our perspective, the best image for understanding argument is neither "fight" nor "debate" but instead the deliberations of a committee representing a wide spectrum of community voices charged with finding the best solution to a problem. From this perspective argument is both a *process* and *product*. As a process, argument is an act of inquiry characterized by fact finding, information gathering, and consideration of alternative points of view. As a product, it is someone's contribution to the conversation at any one moment—a turn taking in a conversation, a formal speech, or a written position paper such as the one you will write for this chapter. The goal of argument as process is truth seeking; the goal of argument as product is persuasion. When members of a diverse committee are willing to argue persuasively for their respective points of view but are simultaneously willing to listen to other points of view and to change or modify their positions in light of new information or better arguments, then both components of argument are fully in play.

We cannot overemphasize the importance of both truth seeking and persuasion to your professional and civic life. Truth seeking makes you an informed and judicious employee and citizen who delays decisions until a full range of evidence and alternative views are aired and examined. Persuasion gives you the power to influence the world around you, whether through letters to the editor on political issues or convincing position papers for business and professional life. Whenever an organization needs to make a major decision, those who can think flexibly and write persuasively can wield great influence.

◢ EXPLORING CLASSICAL ARGUMENT

An effective way to appreciate argument as both truth seeking and persuasion is to address an issue that is new to you and then watch how your own views evolve. Your initial position will probably reflect what social scientists sometimes call your personal *ideology*—that is, a network of basic values, beliefs, and assumptions that tend to guide your view of the world. However, if you adopt a truth-seeking attitude, your initial position may evolve as the conversation progresses. In fact, the conversation may even cause changes in some of your basic beliefs, since ideologies aren't set in stone and many of us have unresolved allegiance to competing ideologies that may be logically inconsistent (for example, a belief in freedom of speech combined with a belief that hate speech should be banned). In this exercise we ask you to keep track of how your views change and to note what causes the change.

The case we present for discussion involves ethical treatment of animals.

> *Situation:* A bunch of starlings builds nests in the attic of a family's house, gaining access to the attic through a torn vent screen. Soon the eggs hatch, and every morning at sunrise the family is awakened by the sound of birds squawking and wings beating against rafters as the starlings fly in and out of the house to feed the hatchlings. After losing considerable early morning sleep, the family repairs the screen. Unable to get in and out, the parent birds are unable to feed their young. The birds die within a day. Is this cruelty to animals?

1. Freewrite your initial response to this question. Was the family's act an instance of cruelty to animals (that is, was their act ethically justifiable or not)?
2. Working in small groups or as a whole class, share your freewrites and then try to reach a group consensus on the issue. During this conversation (argument as process), listen carefully to your classmates' views and note places where your own initial views begin to evolve.
3. So far we have framed this issue as an after-the-act yes/no question: Is the family guilty of cruelty to animals? But we can also frame it as an open-ended, before-the-fact question: "What should the family have done about the starlings in the attic?" Suppose you are a family member discussing the starlings at dinner prior to the decision to fix the vent screen. Make a list of your family's other options and try to reach class consensus on the two or three best alternative solutions.
4. At the end of the discussion, do another freewrite exploring how your ideas evolved during the discussion. What insights did you get into the twin components of argument: truth seeking and persuasion?

WRITING PROJECT

Write a position paper that takes a stand on a controversial issue. Your introduction will present your issue, provide background, and state the claim you intend to support. The body of your argument will summarize and respond to opposing views as well as present reasons and evidence in support of your own position. You will choose whether to summarize and refute opposing views before or after you have made your own case. Try to end your essay with your strongest arguments.

We sometimes call this assignment an argument in the *classical style* because it is patterned after the persuasive speeches of ancient Greek and Roman orators. In the terms of ancient rhetoricians, the main parts of a persuasive speech are the *exordium*, in which the speaker gets the audience's attention; the *narratio*, which provides needed background; the *propositio*, the speaker's proposition or thesis; the *partitio*, a forecast of the main parts of the speech, equivalent to a blueprint statement; the *confirmatio*, the speaker's arguments in favor of the proposition; the *confutatio*, the refutation of opposing views; and the *peroratio*, the conclusion that sums up the argument, calls for action, and leaves a strong last impression.

We cite these tongue-twisting Latin terms only to assure you that in writing a classical argument you are joining a time-honored tradition that links you to Roman senators on the capitol steps. From their discourse arose the ideal of a democratic society based on superior arguments rather than on superior weaponry. Although there are many other ways to persuade audiences, the classical approach is a particularly effective introduction to persuasive writing.

◢ UNDERSTANDING CLASSICAL ARGUMENT

Having introduced you to argument as both process and product, we now turn to the details of effective argumentation. To help orient you, we begin by describing the typical stages that mark students' growth as arguers.

Stages of Development: Your Growth as an Arguer

We have found that students in our argument classes typically proceed through identifiable stages as their argumentative skills increase. While these stages may or may not describe your own development, they suggest the skills you should strive to acquire.

- *Stage 1: Argument as personal opinion.*   At the beginning of instruction in argument, students typically express strong personal opinions but have trouble justifying their opinions with reasons and evidence and often create short, undeveloped arguments that are circular, lack evidence, and insult those who disagree. The following freewrite, written by a student first confronting the starling case (p. 154), illustrates this stage.

    The family shouldn't have killed the starlings because that is really wrong! I mean that act was disgusting. It makes me sick to think how so many people are just willing to kill something for no reason at all. How are these parents going to teach their children values if they just go out and kill little birds for no good reason?!! This whole family is what's wrong with America!

This writer's opinion is passionate and heartfelt, but it provides no reasons and evidence why someone else should hold the same opinion.

- *Stage 2: Argument structured as claim supported by one or more reasons.*   This stage represents a quantum leap in argumentative skill because the writer can now produce a rational plan containing point sentences (the reasons) and evidence (the particulars). The writer who produced the previous freewrite later developed a structure like this:

The family's act constituted cruelty to animals

- because the starlings were doing minimal harm
- because other options were available
- because the way they killed the birds caused needless suffering

- *Stage 3: Increased attention to truth seeking.*   In Stage 3 students become increasingly engaged with the complexity of the issue as they listen to their classmates' views, conduct research, and evaluate alternative perspectives and stances. They are often willing to change their positions when they see the power of other arguments.
- *Stage 4: Ability to articulate the unstated assumptions underlying their arguments.*   As we show later in this chapter, each reason in a writer's argument is based on an assumption, value, or belief (often unstated) that the audience must accept if the argument is to be persuasive. Often the writer needs to state these assumptions explicitly and support them. At this stage students identify and analyze their own assumptions and those of their intended audiences. Students gain increased skill at accommodating alternative views through refutation or concession.
- *Stage 5: Ability to link an argument to the values and beliefs of the intended audience.*   In this stage writers are increasingly able to link their arguments to their audience's values and beliefs and to adapt structure and tone to the resistance level of their audience. Writers also appreciate how delayed-thesis arguments or other psychological strategies can be more effective than closed-form arguments when addressing hostile audiences.

The rest of this chapter will help you progress through these stages. Although you can read the rest of this chapter in one sitting, we recommend that you break your reading into sections, going over the material slowly and applying it to your own ideas in progress. Let the chapter's concepts and explanations sink in slowly, and return to them periodically for review. This section on "Understanding Classical Argument" contains the chapter's key instructional material and comprises a compact but comprehensive course in argumentation.

Creating an Argument Frame: A Claim with Reasons

Somewhere in the writing process, whether early or late, you need to create a frame for your argument. This frame includes a clear question that focuses the argument, your claim, and one or more supporting reasons. Often your reasons, stated as *because* clauses, can be attached to your claim to provide a working thesis statement.

Finding an Arguable Issue

At the heart of any argument is an issue, which we can define as a question that invites more than one reasonable answer and thus leads to perplexity or disagreement. This requirement excludes disagreements based on personal tastes where no shared criteria could be developed ("Baseball is more fun than soccer"). It also excludes purely private questions because issues arise out of disagreements in communities. When you are thinking of issues, ask what questions are currently being contested in one of the communities to which you belong (your family, neighborhood, religious or social group, workplace, classroom, dormitory, campus, hometown, state, region, nation, and so forth).

Issue questions are often framed as yes/no choices, especially when they appear on ballots or in courtrooms: Should gay marriage be legalized? Should the city pass the new school bond proposal? Is this defendant guilty of armed robbery? Just as frequently, they can be framed openly, inviting many different possible answers: What should our city do about skateboarders in downtown pedestrian areas? How can children be kept from pornography on the internet?

It is important to remember that framing an issue as a yes/no question does not mean that all points of view fall neatly into pro/con categories. Although citizens may be forced to vote yes or no on a proposed ballot initiative, they can support or oppose the initiative for a variety of reasons. Some may vote happily for the initiative, others vote for it only by holding their noses, and still others oppose it vehemently but for entirely different reasons. To argue effectively, you need to appreciate the wide range of perspectives from which people approach the yes/no choice.

How you frame your question will necessarily affect the scope and shape of your argument itself. In our exploratory exercise we framed the starling question in two ways: (1) Was the family guilty of cruelty to animals? and (2) What should the family do about the starlings? Framed in the first way, your argument would have to develop criteria for "cruelty to animals" and then argue whether the family's actions met those criteria. Framed in the second way, you could argue for your own solution to the problem ranging from doing nothing (wait for the birds to grow up, then fix the screen) to climbing into the attic and drowning the birds so that their death is quick and painless. Or you could word the question in a broader, more philosophical way: When are humans justified in killing an animal? Or you could focus on a subissue: When can an animal be labeled a "pest"?

FOR WRITING AND DISCUSSION

1. Working individually, make a list of several communities that you belong to and then identify one or more questions currently being contested within those communities. (If you have trouble, get a copy of your local campus and city newspapers or an organizational newsletter; you'll quickly discover a wealth of contested issues.) Then share your list with classmates.

2. Pick two or three issues of particular interest to you, and try framing them in different ways: as broad or narrow questions, as open-ended or yes/no questions. Place several examples on the chalkboard for class discussion.

Stating a Claim

Your claim is the position you want to take on the issue. It is your brief, one-sentence answer to your issue question:

The family was not ethically justified in killing the starlings.

The city should build skateboarding areas with ramps in all city parks.

You will appreciate argument as truth seeking if you find that your claim evolves as you think more deeply about your issue and listen to alternative views. Be willing to rephrase your claim to soften it or refocus it or even to reverse it as you progress through the writing process.

Articulating Reasons

Your claim, which is the position you take on an issue, needs to be supported by reasons and evidence. A *reason* (sometimes called a *premise*) is a subclaim that supports your main claim. In speaking or writing, a reason is usually linked to the claim with such connecting words as *because, therefore, so, consequently,* and *thus.* In planning your argument, a powerful strategy for developing reasons is to harness the grammatical power of the conjunction *because;* think of your reasons as *because* clauses attached to your claim. Formulating your reasons in this way allows you to create a thesis statement that breaks your argument into smaller parts, each part devoted to one of the reasons.*

Suppose, for example, that you are examining the issue "Should the government legalize hard drugs such as heroin and cocaine?" Here are several different points of view on this issue, each expressed as a claim with because clauses:

One View

Cocaine and heroin should be legalized

- because legalizing drugs will keep the government out of people's private lives.
- because keeping these drugs illegal has the same negative effects on our society that alcohol prohibition did in the 1920s.

Another View

Cocaine and heroin should be legalized

- because the subsequent elimination of the black market would cut down on muggings and robberies.
- because decriminalization would cut down on prison overcrowding and free police to concentrate on dangerous crime rather than finding drug dealers.
- because elimination of underworld profits would change the economic structure of the underclass and promote shifts to socially productive jobs and careers.

---

*The thesis statement for your essay could be your claim by itself or you could include in your thesis statement your main supporting reasons. For advice on how much of your supporting argument you should summarize in your thesis statement, see Chapter 11, pp. 242–244.

Still Another View

The government should not legalize heroin and cocaine

- because doing so will lead to an increase in drug users.
- because doing so will send the message that it is okay to use hard drugs.

Although the yes/no framing of this question seems to reduce the issue to a two-position debate, many different value systems are at work here. The first pro-legalization argument, libertarian in perspective, values maximum individual freedom. The second argument—although it too supports legalization—takes a community perspective valuing the social benefits of eliminating the black market. In the same way, people could oppose legalization for a variety of reasons.

FOR WRITING AND DISCUSSION

Working in small groups or as a whole class, generate a list of reasons for and against one or more of the following yes/no claims. State your reasons as because clauses. Think of as many because clauses as possible by imagining a wide variety of perspectives on the issue.

1. The school year for grades 1–12 should be lengthened to eleven months.
2. Marilyn Manson (and other such iconoclastic entertainers) serves a valuable social function.
3. Women's fashion/style magazines (such as *Glamour* and *Mademoiselle*) are harmful influences on teenage women.
4. The United States should replace its income tax with a national sales tax.
5. Medical insurance should cover alternative medicine (massage therapy, acupuncture, herbal treatments, and so forth).

Articulating Unstated Assumptions

So far, we have focused on the frame of an argument as a claim supported with one or more reasons. Shortly, we will proceed to the flesh and muscle of an argument, which is the evidence you use to support your reasons. But before turning to evidence, we need to look at another crucial part of an argument's frame: its *unstated assumptions.*

What Do We Mean by an Unstated Assumption?

Every time you link together a claim with a reason, you make a silent assumption that may need to be articulated and examined. Consider this argument:

The family was justified in killing the starlings because starlings are pests.

To support this argument, the writer would first need to provide evidence that starlings are pests (examples of the damage they do, and so forth). But the persuasiveness of the argument rests on the unstated assumption that it is okay to kill

pests. If an audience doesn't agree with that assumption, then the argument floun-
ders unless the writer articulates the assumption and defends it. The complete
frame of the argument must therefore include the unstated assumption.

Claim: The family was justified in killing the starlings.

Reason: Because starlings are pests.

Unstated assumption: It is ethically justifiable to kill pests.

It is important to examine the unstated assumption behind any claim with reason
*because you must determine whether your audience will accept that assumption.
If not, you need to make it explicit and support it.* Think of the unstated assumption
as a general principle, rule, belief, or value that connects the reason to the claim.
It answers your reader's question, "Why, if I accept your reason, should I accept
your claim?"

Here are a few more examples.

Claim with reason: Women should be allowed to join combat units because
the image of women as combat soldiers would help society overcome gender stereotyping.

Unstated assumption: It is good to overcome gender stereotyping.

Claim with reason: The government should not legalize heroin and cocaine
because doing so will lead to an increase in drug users.

Unstated assumption: It is bad to increase the number of drug users.

Claim with reason: The family was guilty of cruelty to animals in the starling case because less drastic means of solving the problem were available.

Unstated assumption: A person should choose the least drastic means to
solve a problem.

FOR WRITING AND DISCUSSION

Identify the unstated assumptions for each of the following claims with
reason.

1. Cocaine and heroin should be legalized because legalizing drugs will
   keep the government out of people's private lives.
2. The government should eliminate welfare payments to unwed mothers
   because doing so will reduce the illegitimacy rate.
3. After-school jobs are bad for high school students because they use up
   valuable study time.
4. We should strengthen the Endangered Species Act because doing so
   will preserve genetic diversity on the planet.
5. The Endangered Species Act is too stringent because it severely dam-
   ages the economy.

Using Toulmin Terminology to Describe an Argument's Structure

Our explanation of argument structure is influenced by the work of philosopher Stephen Toulmin, who viewed argumentation as a dynamic courtroom drama where opposing attorneys exchanged arguments and cross-examinations before a judge and jury. The terms used by Toulmin to describe the structure of argument are widely accepted in rhetoric and composition studies and provide a handy vocabulary for discussing arguments. Toulmin called the unstated assumption behind a claim with reason the argument's *warrant*, based on our common word "warranty" for guarantee. If the audience accepts your warrant—that is, if they agree with your unstated assumption—then your argument is sound, or guaranteed. To put it another way, if your audience accepts your warrant, and if you can convince them that your reason is true, then they will accept your claim.

Besides the term *warrant*, Toulmin also uses the terms *grounds, backing, conditions of rebuttal,* and *qualifier.* We will explain these terms to you at the appropriate moments as we proceed.

Using Evidence Effectively

In Chapter 3 we showed you that the majority of words in a closed-form essay are particulars used to support points. If you think of reasons and warrants as the main points of your argument, then think of evidence as the supporting particulars. Each of your reasons will need to be supported by evidence. Toulmin's term for evidence in support of a reason is *grounds,* which we can think of as all the facts, data, testimony, statistics, subarguments and other details a writer can find to support a reason. The evidence and arguments used to support a warrant Toulmin calls *backing.* In this section we survey different kinds of evidence and show you how to incorporate that evidence into an argument, either as grounds to support a reason or as backing to support a warrant. Some arguments can be fleshed out with evidence based on your personal experience and observations. But most arguments require more formal evidence—the kind you gather from library or field research.

Kinds of Evidence

The kinds of evidence most often used for the grounds and backing are the following.

Examples. An example from personal experience can often be used to support a reason. Here is how one student writer, arguing that her church building needs to be remodeled, used a personal example to support a reason.

> Finally, Sacred Heart Church must be renovated immediately because the terrazzo floor that covers the entire church is very dangerous. Four Sundays ago, during 11:00 Mass, nine Eucharistic Ministers went up to the altar to prepare for distributing communion. As they carefully walked to their assigned post on the recently buffed terrazzo floor, a loud crash of crystal echoed through the church.

A woman moving to her post slipped on the recently buffed floor, fell to the ground, hit her head on the marble, and was knocked unconscious. People rushed to her aid, thinking she was dead. Fortunately she was alive, only badly hurt. This woman was my mother.

Besides specific examples like this, writers sometimes invent hypothetical examples, or *scenarios,* to illustrate an issue or hypothesize about the consequences of an event. (Of course, you must signal your reader that the example or scenario is hypothetical.)

Summaries of Research.   Another common way to support an argument is to summarize research studies. Here is how a student writer used a summary statement to support his opposition to mandatory helmet laws for motorcycle riders:

> However, a helmet won't protect against head injury when one is traveling at normal traffic speeds. According to a U.S. Department of Transportation study, "There is no evidence that any helmet thus far, regardless of cost or design, is capable of rejecting impact stress above 13 mph" (Transportation Study, p. 8).*

Statistics.   Another common form of evidence is statistics. Here is how one writer uses statistics to argue that alcohol poses a more serious social problem than heroin or cocaine.

> The uproar about drugs is itself odd. In 1987, according to the Kerry subcommittee, there were 1,400 deaths from cocaine; in 1988, that figure had increased to 3,308. Deaths from *all* forms of illegal drugs total under 6,000. By contrast, 320,000 to 390,000 people die prematurely each year from tobacco and 100,000 to 200,000 from misuse of alcohol. Alcohol is associated with 40 percent of all suicide attempts, 40 percent of all traffic deaths, 54 percent of all violent crimes and 10 percent of all work-related injuries.

Testimony.   Writers can also use expert testimony to bolster a case. The following student essay uses testimony to support "comparable worth"—an economic policy intended to redress salary inequities between traditionally "male" and "female" job fields.

> Barbara Bergmann, professor of economics at the University of Maryland, has studied the comparable worth issue at length. If comparable worth were enacted, she points out, "Nobody's pay need go down. Nor will budgets or profits be wiped out" (9).†

Subarguments.   Sometimes writers support reasons not directly through data but through sequences of subarguments. Sometimes these subarguments develop a

---

*This student is using the APA (American Psychological Association) style for documenting sources. This quotation is found on page 8 of a document listed as "Transportation Study" in the References list at the end of the essay.

†This student is using the MLA (Modern Language Association) style for documenting sources. This quotation will be found on page 9 of an article authored by Barbara Bergmann and listed under Bergman in the Works Cited list at the end of the essay.

persuasive analogy, hypothesize about consequences, or simply advance the argument through a chain of connected points. In the following passage, taken from a philosophic article justifying torture under certain conditions, the author uses a subargument to support one of his main points—that a terrorist holding victims hostage has no "rights":

> There is an important difference between terrorists and their victims that should mute talk of the terrorist's "rights." The terrorist's victims are at risk unintentionally, not having asked to be endangered. But the terrorist knowingly initiated his actions. Unlike his victims, he volunteered for the risks of his deed. By threatening to kill for profit or idealism, he renounces civilized standards, and he can have no complaint if civilization tries to thwart him by whatever means necessary.

Rather than using direct empirical evidence, the author supports his point with a subargument showing how terrorists differ from victims and thus relinquish their claim to rights.

Reliability of Evidence

When you use empirical evidence, you can increase its persuasiveness by monitoring its recency, relevance, impartiality, and scope.

Recency.   As much as possible, and especially if you are addressing current issues in science, technology, politics, or social trends, use the most recent evidence you can find.

Relevance.   Ensure that the evidence you cite is relevant to the point you are making. For example, for many decades the medical profession offered advice about heart disease to their female patients based on studies of male subjects. No matter how extensive or how recent those studies, some of their conclusions are bound to be irrelevant for female patients.

Impartiality.   While all data must be interpreted and hence are never completely impartial, careful readers are aware of how easily data can be skewed. Newspapers, magazines, and journals often have political biases and different levels of respectability. Evidence you take from *Reader's Digest* or *The National Review* is apt to have a conservative bias, whereas evidence from *The Nation* or *Mother Jones* is apt to have a liberal bias. These sources often provide excellent data, but be aware that your readers may be wary of their objectivity. Generally, evidence associated with scientifically conducted studies is more highly regarded than evidence taken from second or third hand sources. Particularly problematic is information gathered from Internet websites, which are often unreliable and highly biased.

Sufficiency.   One of the most common reasoning fallacies is to make a sweeping generalization based on only one or two instances. The criterion of sufficiency (which means having enough examples to justify your point) helps you guard against hasty generalizations.

Addressing Objections and Counterarguments

Having looked at the frame of an argument (claim, reasons, and warrants) and at the kinds of evidence used to flesh out the frame, let's turn now to the important concern of anticipating and responding to objections and counterarguments. In this section, we show you an extended example of a student anticipating and responding to a reader's objection. We then describe a planning schema that can help you anticipate objections and show you how to respond to counterarguments either through refutation or concession. Finally we show how your active imagining of alternative views can lead you to qualify your claim.

Anticipating Objections: An Extended Example

In our earlier discussions of the starling case, we saw how readers might object to the argument "The family is justified in killing the starlings because starlings are pests." What rankles these readers is the unstated assumption (warrant) that it is okay to kill pests. Imagine an objecting reader saying something like this:

> It is *not* okay to get annoyed with a living creature, label it a "pest," and then kill it. This whole use of the term "pest" suggests that humans have the right to dominate nature. We need to have more reverence for nature. The ease with which the family solved their problem by killing living things sets a bad example for children. The family could have waited until fall and then fixed the screen.

Imagining such an objection might lead a writer to modify his claim. But if the writer remains committed to his claim, then he must develop a response. In the following example, in which a student writer argues that it is okay to kill the starlings, note (1) how the writer uses evidence to show that starlings are pests, (2) how he summarizes a possible objection to his warrant, and (3) how he supports his warrant with backing.

Student Argument Defending Reason and Warrant

Claim with reason

The family was justified in killing the starlings because starlings are pests. Starlings are nonindigenous birds that drive out native species and multiply rapidly. When I searched "starlings and pests" on the Alta Vista search engine, I discovered 161 websites dealing with starlings as pests. Starlings are hated by farmers and gardeners because huge flocks of them devour newly planted seeds in spring as well as fruits and berries at harvest. A flock of starlings can devastate a cherry orchard in a few days. As invasive nesters, starlings can also damage attics by tearing up insulation and defecating on stored items. Many of the website articles focused on ways to kill off starling populations. In killing the starlings, the family was protecting its own property and reducing the population of these pests.

Evidence that starlings are pests

Concessionary tone, but.. (handwritten)

Summary of a possible direction

Many readers might object to my argument, saying that humans should have a reverence for nature and not quickly try to kill off any creature they label a pest. Further, these readers might say that even if starlings are pests, the family could have waited until fall to repair the attic or found some other means of protecting their property without having to kill the baby starlings. I too would have waited until fall if the birds in the attic had been swallows or some other native species without starlings' destructiveness and propensity for unchecked population growth. But starlings should be compared to rats or mice. We set traps for rodents because we know the damage they cause when they nest in walls and attics. We don't get sentimental trying to save the orphaned rat babies. In the same way, we are justified in eliminating starlings as soon as they begin infesting our houses. Think of them not as chirpy little songsters but as rats of the bird world.

Response to the objection

In the preceding example, we see how the writer uses grounds to support his reason and then, anticipating his readers' objection to his warrant, summarizes that objection and offers backing. One might not be convinced by the argument, but the writer has done a good job trying to support both the reason and the warrant.

Using a Planning Schema to Anticipate Objections

The arguing strategy used by the previous writer was triggered by his anticipation of objections—what Toulmin calls *conditions of rebuttal*. Under conditions of rebuttal, Toulmin asks arguers to imagine various ways skeptical readers might object to a writer's argument or specific conditions under which the argument might not hold. The Toulmin system lets us create a planning schema that can help writers develop a persuasive argument.

This schema encourages writers to articulate their argument frame (reason and warrant) and then to imagine what could be used for grounds (to support the reason) and backing (to support the warrant). Equally important, the schema encourages writers to anticipate counterarguments by imagining how skeptical readers might object to the writer's reason or warrant or both. To create the schema, you simply make a chart headed by your claim with reason and then make slots for grounds, warrant, backing, and conditions of rebuttal. Then brainstorm ideas to put into each slot. Here is how another student writer used this schema to plan an argument on the starling case:

Claim with reason

The family showed cruelty to animals because the way they killed the birds caused needless suffering.

Grounds

I've got to show how the birds suffered and also how the suffering was needless. The way of killing the birds caused the birds to suffer. The hatchlings starved to death, as did the parent birds if they were trapped inside the attic. Starvation is very slow and agonizing. The suffering was also needless since other means were available such as calling an exterminator who would remove birds and either relocate them or kill them painlessly. If no other alternative was available, someone should have crawled into the attic and found a painless way to kill the birds.

Warrant

If it is not necessary to kill an animal, then don't; if it is necessary, then the killing should be done in the least painful way possible.

Backing

I've got to convince readers it is wrong to make an animal suffer if you don't have to. Humans have a natural antipathy to needless suffering—our feeling of unease if we imagine cattle or chickens caused to suffer for our food rather than being cleanly and quickly killed. If a horse is incurably wounded, we shoot it rather then letting it suffer. We are morally obligated to cause the least pain possible.

Conditions of rebuttal

How could a reader object to my reason? A reader could say that killing the starlings did *not* cause suffering. Perhaps hatchling starlings don't feel pain of starvation or die very quickly. Perhaps a reader could object to my claim that other means were available: There is no other way to kill the starlings—impossibility of catching a bunch of adult starlings flying around an attic. Poison may cause just as much suffering. Cost of exterminator is prohibitive.

How could a reader object to my warrant? Perhaps the reader would say that my rule to cause the least pain possible does not apply to animal pests. In class, someone said that worrying about the baby starlings was sentimental. Laws of nature condemn millions of animals each year to death by starvation or by being eaten alive by other animals. Humans occasionally have to take their place within this tooth-and-claw natural system.

How many of the ideas from this schema would the writer use in her actual paper? That is a judgment call based on the writer's analysis of audience. In every case, the writer should support the reason with evidence because supporting a claim with reasons and evidence is the minimal requirement of argument. But it is not necessary to state the warrant explicitly or provide backing for it unless the writer anticipates readers who doubt it.

The same rule of thumb applies to the need for summarizing and responding to objections and counterarguments: Let your analysis of audience be your guide. If we imagined the preceding argument aimed at readers who thought it was sentimental to worry about the suffering of animal pests, the writer should make her warrant explicit and back it. Her task would be to convince readers that humans have ethical responsibilities that exclude them from tooth-and-claw morality.

FOR WRITING AND DISCUSSION

Working individually or in small groups, create a planning schema for the following arguments: For each claim with reason: (a) imagine the kinds of evidence needed as grounds to support the reason; (b) identify the warrant; (c) imagine a strategy for supporting the warrant (backing); anticipate possible objections to the reason and to the warrant (conditions of rebuttal).

1. *Claim with reason:* Now that we are buying our first car together, we should buy a Jupiter 500 sedan because it is the most economical car on the road. (Imagine this argument aimed at your significant other, who wants to buy a Phantomjet 1000 sports car.)

2. *Claim with reason:* Gay marriage should be legalized because doing so will promote faithful monogamous relationships among gay people. (Imagine this argument aimed at a homophobic audience.)
3. *Claim with reason:* The government should eliminate welfare payments for unwed mothers because doing so would reduce the illegitimacy rate. (Imagine this argument aimed at liberals who support welfare payments to single mothers.)
4. *Claim with reason:* After-school jobs are bad for high school students because they use up valuable study time. (Aim this argument at a middle-class teenager who wants to get a job to earn extra spending money.)

Responding to Objections, Counterarguments, and Alternative Views Through Refutation or Concession

We have seen how a writer needs to anticipate alternative views that give rise to objections and counterarguments. Surprisingly, one of the best ways to approach counterarguments is to summarize them fairly. Make your imagined reader's best case against your argument. By resisting the temptation to distort a counterargument, you demonstrate a willingness to consider the issue from all sides. Moreover, summarizing a counterargument reduces your reader's tendency to say, "Yes, but have you thought of . . . ?" After you have summarized an objection or counterargument fairly and charitably, you must then decide how to respond to it. Your two main choices are to rebut it or concede to it.

Rebutting Opposing Views

When rebutting or refuting an argument, you can question the argument's reasons/grounds or warrant or both. In the following student example, the writer summarizes her classmates' objections to abstract art and then analyzes shortcomings in their reasons and grounds.

> Some of my classmates object to abstract art because it apparently takes no technical drawing talent. They feel that artists turn abstract because they are not capable of the technical drafting skills that appear in Remington, Russell, and Rockwell pieces. Therefore they created an art form that anyone was capable of and that was less time consuming, and then they paraded it as artistic progress. But I object to the notion that these artists turned to abstraction because they lacked the ability to do representative drawing. Many abstract artists, such as Picasso, are excellent draftsmen, and their early pieces show very realistic drawing skill. As his work matured, Picasso became more abstract in order to increase the expressive quality of his work. *Guernica* was meant as a protest against the bombing of that city by the Germans. To express the terror and suffering of the victims more vividly, he distorted the figures and presented them in a black and white journalistic manner. If he had used representational images and color— which he had the skill to do—much of the emotional content would have been

lost and the piece probably would not have caused the demand for justice that it did.

Conceding to Counterarguments

In some cases, an alternative view can be very strong. If so, don't hide that view from your reader; summarize it and concede to it.

Making concessions to opposing views is not necessarily a sign of weakness; in many cases, a concession simply acknowledges that the issue is complex and that your position is tentative. In turn, a concession can enhance a reader's respect for you and invite the reader to follow your example and weigh the strengths of your own argument charitably. Writers typically concede to opposing views with transitional expressions such as the following:

admittedly	I must admit that	I agree that	granted
even though	I concede that	while it is true that	

After conceding to an opposing view, you should shift to a different field of values where your position is strong and then argue for those new values. For example, adversaries of drug legalization argue plausibly that legalizing drugs would increase the number of users and addicts. If you support legalization, here is how you might deal with this point without fatally damaging your own argument:

> Opponents of legalization claim—and rightly so—that legalization will lead to an increase in drug users and addicts. I wish this weren't so, but it is. Nevertheless, the other benefits of legalizing drugs—eliminating the black market, reducing street crime, and freeing up thousands of police from fighting the war on drugs—more than outweigh the social costs of increased drug use and addiction, especially if tax revenues from drug sales are plowed back into drug education and rehabilitation programs.

The writer concedes that legalization will increase addiction (one reason for opposing legalization) and that drug addiction is bad (the warrant for that reason). But then the writer redeems the case for legalization by shifting the argument to another field of values (the benefits of eliminating the black market, reducing crime, and so forth).

Qualifying Your Claim

The need to summarize and respond to alternative views lets the writer see an issue's complexity and appreciate that no one position has a total monopoly on the truth. Consequently, in the argument schema that we have adapted from Toulmin, there is one final term that it is important to know: the *qualifier*. This term refers to words that limit the scope or force of a claim to make it less sweeping and therefore less vulnerable. Consider the difference between the sentences "After-school jobs are bad for teenagers" and "After-school jobs are often bad for teenagers." The first claim can be refuted by one counterexample of a teenager who benefited from an after-school job. Because the second claim admits exceptions, it is much harder to refute. Unless your argument is airtight, you will want to limit your claim with qualifiers such as the following:

perhaps   maybe

in many cases generally

tentatively   sometimes

often   usually

probably   likely

may or might (rather than is)

You can also qualify a claim with an opening "unless" clause ("*Unless* your apartment is well soundproofed, you should not buy such a powerful stereo system.").

Appealing to *Ethos* and *Pathos*

When the classical rhetoricians examined ways that orators could persuade listeners, they focused on three kinds of proofs: *logos,* or the appeal to reason; *ethos,* or the appeal to the speaker's character; and *pathos,* or the appeal to the emotions and the sympathetic imagination. So far in this chapter we have focused on the logical appeals of *logos.* In this section we examine *ethos* and *pathos.* You can see how these three appeals are connected by visualizing a triangle with interrelated points labeled *message, writer/speaker,* and *audience* (Figure 14.1). Effective arguments consider all three points on this *rhetorical triangle.*

Appeal to *Ethos*

A powerful way to increase the persuasiveness of an argument is to gain your reader's trust. You appeal to *ethos* whenever your reader has confidence in your credibility and trustworthiness. In Chapter 4 we discussed how readers develop an image of the writer, the writer's persona, based on features of the writer's prose. For readers to accept your argument, they must perceive a persona that's knowledgeable, trustworthy, and fair. We suggest three ways to enhance your argument's ethos.

1. Demonstrate to your reader that you know your subject well. If you have personal experience with the subject, cite that experience. Reflect thoughtfully on your subject, citing research as well as personal experience, and summarize accurately and carefully a range of viewpoints.
2. Be fair to alternative points of view. Scorning an opposing view may occasionally win you favor with an audience predisposed toward your position, but it will offend others and hinder critical analysis. As a general rule, treating opposing views respectfully is the best strategy.
3. Build bridges toward your audience by grounding your argument in shared values and assumptions. Doing so will demonstrate your concern for your audience and enhance your trustworthiness. Moreover, rooting your argument in the audience's values and assumptions has a strong emotional appeal, as we explain in the next section.

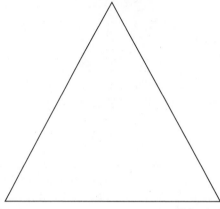

Message

(LOGOS: How can I make the argument internally consistent and logical? How can I find the best reasons and support them with the best evidence?)

Audience

(PATHOS: How can I make the reader open to my message? How can I best engage my readers' emotions and imagination? How can I appeal to my readers' values and interests?)

Writer or Speaker

(ETHOS: How can I present myself effectively? How can I enhance my credibility and trustworthiness?)

FIGURE 14.1   Rhetorical Triangle

Appeals to *Pathos*

Besides basing your argument on appeals to logos and ethos, you might also base it on an appeal to what the Greeks called *pathos.* Sometimes pathos is interpreted narrowly as an appeal to the emotions. This interpretation effectively devalues pathos because popular culture generally values reason above emotion. Although appeals to pathos can sometimes be irrational and irrelevant ("You can't give me a C! I need a B to get into med school, and if I don't I'll break my ill grandmother's heart."), they can also arouse audience interest and deepen understanding of an argument's human dimensions. Here are some ways to use pathos in your arguments.

Use Vivid Language and Examples.   One way to create pathos is to use vivid language and powerful examples. If you are arguing in favor of homeless shelters, for example, you can humanize your appeal by describing one homeless person.

> He is huddled over the sewer grate, his feet wrapped in newspapers. He blows on his hands, then tucks them under his armpits and lies down on the sidewalk with his shoulders over the grate, his bed for the night.

But if you are arguing for tougher laws against panhandling, you might let your reader see the issue through the eyes of downtown shoppers intimidated by "ratty, urine-soaked derelicts drinking fortified wine from a shared sack."

Find Audience-Based Reasons. The best way to see pathos is not as an appeal to emotions but rather an appeal to the audience's values and beliefs. With its emphasis on warrants, Toulmin's system of analysis naturally encourages this kind of appeal. For example, in engineer David Rockwood's argument against wind-generated power (Chapter 1, pp. 12–13), Rockwood's final reason is that constructing wind generation facilities will damage the environment. To environmentalists, this reason has emotional as well as rational power because its warrant ("Preserving the environment is good") appeals to their values. It is an example of an audience-based reason, which we can define simply as any reason whose warrant the audience already accepts and endorses. Such reasons, because they hook into the beliefs and values of the audience, appeal to *pathos.*

When you plan your argument, seek audience-based reasons wherever possible. Suppose, for example, that you are advocating the legalization of heroin and cocaine. If you know your audience is concerned about their own safety in the streets, then you can argue that legalization of drugs will cut down on crime:

> We should legalize drugs because doing so will make our streets safer: It will cut down radically on street criminals seeking drug money, and it will free up narcotics police to focus on other kinds of crime.

If your audience is concerned about improving the quality of life for youths in inner cities, you might argue that legalization of drugs will lead to better lives for the current underclass:

> We should legalize drugs because doing so will eliminate the lure of drug trafficking that tempts so many inner-city youth away from honest jobs and into crime.

Or if your audience is concerned about high taxes and government debt, you might say:

> We should legalize drugs because doing so will help us balance federal and state budgets: It will decrease police and prison costs by decriminalizing narcotics; and it will eliminate the black market in drugs, allowing us to collect taxes on drug sales.

In each case, you would move people toward your position by connecting your argument to their beliefs and values.

Some Advanced Considerations

You have now finished reading what we might call a basic course in argumentation. In this final section, we discuss briefly some more advanced ideas about argumentation. Your instructor may want to expand on these in class, simply ask you to read them, or not assign this section at all. The three concepts we explore briefly are argument types, delayed-thesis and Rogerian arguments, and informal fallacies.

Argument Types

The advice we have given you so far in this chapter applies to any type of argument. However, scholars of argumentation have categorized arguments into several different types, each of which uses its own characteristic structures and ways of development. One way to talk about argument types is to divide them into truth issues and values issues.

Truth issues stem from questions about the way reality is (or was or will be). Unlike questions of fact, which can be proved or disproved by agreed-on empirical measures, issues of truth require interpretation of the facts. Does Linda smoke an average of twenty or more cigarettes per day? is a question of fact, answerable with a yes or a no. But the question, Why did Linda start smoking when she was fifteen? is a question of truth with many possible answers. Was it because of cigarette advertising? Peer pressure? The dynamics of Linda's family? Dynamics in the culture (for example, white American youths are seven times more likely to smoke than are African American youths)? Truth issues generally take one of the three following forms:

1. *Definitional issues.* Does this particular case fit into a particular category? (Is bungee jumping a "carnival ride" for purposes of state safety regulations? Is tobacco a "drug" and therefore under the jurisdiction of the Federal Drug Administration?)
2. *Causal issues.* What are the causes or consequences of this phenomenon? (Does the current welfare system encourage teenage pregnancy? Will the "three strikes and you're out" rule reduce violent crime?*)
3. *Resemblance or precedence issues.* Is this phenomenon like or analogous to some other phenomenon? (Was U.S. involvement in Bosnia like U.S. involvement in Vietnam? Is killing a starling like killing a rat?

Rational arguments can involve disputes about values as well as truth. Family disagreements about what car to buy typically revolve around competing values: What is most important? looks? performance? safety? economy? comfort? dependability? prestige? Similarly, many public issues ask people to choose among competing value systems: Whose values should be adopted in a given situation? Those of corporations or environmentalists? of the fetus or the pregnant woman? of owners or laborers? of the individual or the state? Value issues usually fall in one of the following two categories:

---

*Although we placed our chapter on causes and consequences (Chapter 13) in the "writing to analyze" category, we could have placed it just as logically under "writing to persuade." The difference concerns the writer's perceived relationship to the audience. If you imagine your readers as decidedly skeptical of your thesis and actively weighing alternative theses, then your purpose is persuasive. However, if you imagine your readers as puzzled and curious—reading your essay primarily to clarify their own thinking on a causal question—then your purpose is analytical. The distinction here is a matter of degree, not of kind.

1. *Evaluation issues.* How good is this particular member of its class? Is this action morally good or bad? (How effective was President Clinton's first year in office? Which computer system best meets the company's needs? Is the death penalty morally wrong?)
2. *Policy issues.* Should we take this action? (Should Congress pass stricter gun-control laws? Should health-insurance policies cover eating disorders?)

Delayed-Thesis and Rogerian Argument

Classical arguments are usually closed form with the writer's thesis stated prominently at the end of the introduction. Classical argument works best for neutral audiences weighing all sides of an issue or for somewhat opposed audiences who are willing to listen to other views. However, when you address a highly resistant audience, one where your point of view seems especially threatening to your audience's values and beliefs, classical argument can seem too blunt and aggressive. In such cases, a *delayed-thesis argument* works best. In such an argument you don't state your actual thesis until the conclusion. The body of the paper extends your sympathy to the reader's views, shows how troubling the issue is to you, and leads the reader gradually toward your position.

A special kind of delayed-thesis argument is called *Rogerian argument*, named after the psychologist Carl Rogers, who specialized in helping people with widely divergent views learn to talk to each other. The principle of Rogerian communication is that listeners must show empathy toward each other's world views and make every attempt to build bridges toward each other. In planning a Rogerian argument, instead of asking, "What reasons and evidence will convince my reader to adopt my claim?" you ask, "What is it about my view that especially threatens my reader? How can I reduce this threat?" Using a Rogerian strategy, the writer summarizes the audience's point of view fairly and charitably, demonstrating the ability to listen and understand the audience's views. She then reduces the threat of her own position by showing how both writer and resistant audience share many basic values. The key to successful Rogerian argument, besides the art of listening, is the ability to point out areas of agreement between the writer's and the reader's position. Then the writer seeks a compromise between the two views.

As an example, if you support a woman's right to choose abortion and you are arguing with someone completely opposed to abortion, you're unlikely to convert your reader, but you may reduce the level of resistance. You begin this process by summarizing your reader's position sympathetically, stressing your shared values. You might say, for example, that you also value babies; that you also are appalled by people who treat abortion as a form of birth control; that you also worry that the easy acceptance of abortion diminishes the value society places on human life; and that you also agree that accepting abortion lightly can lead to lack of sexual responsibility. Building bridges like these between you and your readers makes it more likely that they will listen to you when you present your own position.

Avoiding Informal Fallacies

Informal fallacies are instances of murky reasoning that can cloud an argument and lead to unsound conclusions. Because they can crop up unintentionally in anyone's writing, and because advertisers and hucksters often use them intentionally to deceive, it is a good idea to learn to recognize the more common fallacies.

Post Hoc, Ergo Proper Hoc *(After This, Therefore Because of This).* This fallacy involves <u>mistaking sequence for cause.</u> Just because one event happens before another event doesn't mean the first event caused the second. The connection may be coincidental, or some unknown third event may have caused both of these events.

> **Example** For years I suffered from agonizing abdominal itching. Then I tried Smith's pills. Almost overnight my abdominal itching ceased. Smith's pills work wonders.

Hasty Generalization. Closely related to the *post hoc* fallacy is the hasty generalization, which refers to claims based on insufficient or unrepresentative data.

> **Example** The food-stamp program supports mostly freeloaders. Let me tell you about my worthless neighbor.

False Analogy. Analogical arguments are tricky because there are almost always significant differences between the two things being compared. If the two things differ greatly, the analogy can mislead rather than clarify.

> **Example** You can't force a kid to become a musician any more than you can force a tulip to become a rose.

Either/Or Reasoning. This fallacy occurs when a complex, multisided issue is reduced to two positions without acknowledging the possibility of other alternatives.

> **Example** Either you are pro-choice on abortion or you are against the advancement of women in our culture.

Ad Hominem *("Against the Person").* When people can't find fault with an argument, they sometimes attack the arguer, substituting irrelevant assertions about that person's character for an analysis of the argument itself.

> **Example** Don't pay any attention to Fulke's views on sexual harassment in the workplace. I just learned that he subscribes to *Playboy*.

Appeals to False Authority and Bandwagon Appeals. These fallacies offer as support for an argument the fact that a famous person or "many people" already support it. Unless the supporters are themselves authorities in the field, their support is irrelevant.

> **Example** Buy Freeble oil because Joe Quarterback always uses it in his fleet of cars.
>
> **Example** How can abortion be wrong if millions of people support a woman's right to choose?

Non Sequitur (*"It Does Not Follow"*).   This fallacy occurs when there is no evident connection between a claim and its reason. Sometimes a *non sequitur* can be repaired by filling in gaps in the reasoning; at other times, the reasoning is simply fallacious.

> **Example**   I don't deserve a B for this course because I am a straight-A student.

Circular Reasoning.   This fallacy occurs when you state your claim and then, usually after rewording it, you state it again as your reason.

> **Example**   Marijuana is injurious to your health because it harms your body.

Red Herring.   This fallacy refers to the practice of raising an unrelated or irrelevant point deliberately to throw an audience off the track. Politicians often employ this fallacy when they field questions from the public or press.

> **Example**   You raise a good question about my support for continuing the continuing military build-up in Bosnia. Let me tell you about my admiration for the bravery of our soldiers.

Slippery Slope.   The slippery slope fallacy is based on the fear that one step in a direction we don't like inevitably leads to the next with no stopping place.

> **Example**   We don't dare send weapons to these guerrillas. If we do, we will next send in military advisers, then a special forces battalion, and then large numbers of troops. Finally, we will be in all-out war.

▨ COMPOSING YOUR ESSAY

Writing arguments deepens our thinking by forcing us to consider alternative views and to question the assumptions underlying our reasons and claim. Consequently, it is not unusual for a writer's position on an issue to shift—and even to reverse itself—during the writing process. If this happens to you, take it as a healthy sign of your openness to change, complexity, and alternative points of view. If writing a draft causes you to modify your views, it will be an act of discovery, not a concession of defeat.

Generating and Exploring Ideas

The tasks that follow are intended to help you generate ideas for your argument. Our goal is to help you build up a storehouse of possible issues, to explore several of these possibilities, and then to choose one for deeper exploration before you write your initial draft.

Make an Inventory of Issues that Interest You

Following the lead of the discussion exercise on page 157, make a list of various communities that you belong to and then brainstorm contested issues in those communities. You might try a trigger question like this: "When members of [X community] get together, what contested questions cause disagreements?" What decisions need to be made? What values are in conflict? What problems need to be solved?

Explore Several Issues

For this task, choose two or three possible issues from your previous list and explore them through freewriting or idea mapping. Try responding quickly to the following questions:

a. What is my position on this issue and why?
b. What are alternative points of view on this issue?
c. Why do people disagree about this issue? (Do people disagree about the facts of the case? about key definitions? about underlying values, assumptions, and beliefs?)
d. If I were to argue my position on this issue, what evidence would I need to gather and what research might I need to do?

Brainstorm Claims and Reasons

Choose one issue that particularly interests you and work with classmates to brainstorm possible claims that you could make on the issue. Imagining different perspectives, brainstorm possible reasons to support each claim, stating them as because clauses. See pages 158–159.

Conduct and Respond to Initial Research

If your issue requires research, do a quick bibliographic survey of what is available and do enough initial reading to get a good sense of the kinds of arguments that surround your issue and of the alternative views that people have taken. Then freewrite your responses to the following questions.

1. What are the different points of view on this issue? Why do people disagree with each other?
2. Explore the evolution of your thinking as you did this initial reading. What new questions have the readings raised for you? What changes have occurred in your own thinking?

Conduct an In-Depth Exploration Prior to Drafting

The following set of tasks is designed to help you explore your issue in depth. Most students take one or two hours to complete these tasks; the time will pay off, however, because most of the ideas you will need for your rough draft will then be on paper.

1. Write out the issue your argument will address. Try phrasing your issue in several different ways, perhaps as a yes/no question and as an open-ended question. Try making the question broader, then narrower. (See the discussion of issue questions on pages 156–157.) Finally, frame the question in the way that most appeals to you.

2. Now write out your tentative answer to the question. This will be your beginning thesis statement or claim. Put a box around this answer. Next, write out one or more different answers to your question. These will be alternative claims that a neutral audience might consider.

3. Why is this a controversial issue? Is there insufficient evidence to resolve the issue, or is the evidence ambiguous or contradictory? Are definitions in dispute? Do the parties disagree about basic values, assumptions, or beliefs?

4. What personal interest do you have in this issue? How does the issue affect you? Why do you care about it? (Knowing why you care about it might help you get your audience to care about it.)

5. What reasons and evidence support your position on this issue? Freewrite everything that comes to mind that might help you support your case. This freewrite will eventually provide the bulk of your argument. For now, freewrite rapidly without worrying whether your argument makes sense. Just get ideas on paper.

6. Imagine all the counterarguments your audience might make. Summarize the main arguments against your position and then freewrite your response to each of the counterarguments. What are the flaws in the alternative points of view?

7. What kinds of appeals to *ethos* and *pathos* might you use to support your argument? How can you increase your audience's perception of your credibility and trustworthiness? How can you tie your argument to your audience's beliefs and values?

8. Why is this an important issue? What are the broader implications and consequences? What other issues does it relate to? Thinking of possible answers to these questions may prove useful when you write your introduction or conclusion.

Shaping and Drafting

Once you have explored your ideas, create a plan. Here is a suggested procedure.

Begin your planning by analyzing your intended audience. You could imagine an audience deeply resistant to your views or a more neutral, undecided audience acting like a jury. In some cases, your audience might be a single person, as when you petition your department chair to take an upper-division course when you are a sophomore. At other times, your audience might be the general readership of a newspaper, church bulletin, or magazine. When the audience is a general readership, you need to imagine from the start the kinds of reader you particularly want to sway. Here are some questions you can ask:

■ *How much does your audience know or care about your issue?* Will you need to provide background? Will you need to convince them that your issue is important? Do you need to hook their interest? Your answers to these questions will particularly influence your introduction and conclusion.

■ *What is your audience's current attitude toward your issue?* Are they deeply opposed to your position? If so, why? Are they neutral and undecided? If so, what other views will they be listening to? Classical argument works best with neutral or moderately dissenting audiences. Deeply skeptical audiences are best addressed with delayed-thesis or Rogerian approaches (see p. 173).

■ *How do your audience's values, assumptions, and beliefs differ from your own?* What aspects of your position will be threatening to your audience? Why? How does your position on the issue challenge their own world view or identity? What objections will your audience raise toward your argument? Your answers to these questions will help determine the content of your argument and alert you to the extra research you may have to do to respond to audience objections.

■ *What values, beliefs or assumptions about the world do you and your audience share?* Despite your differences with your audience, where can you find common links? How might you use these links to build bridges to your audience?

Your next step is to plan out an audience-based argument by seeking audience-based reasons or reasons whose warrants you can defend. Here is a process you can use:

1. Create a skeleton, tree diagram, outline, or flowchart for your argument by stating your reasons as one or more because clauses attached to your claim. Each because clause will become the head of a main section or *line of reasoning* in your argument.
2. Use the planning schema explained on pages 165–166 to plan each line of reasoning. If your audience accepts your warrant, concentrate on supporting your reason with grounds. If your warrant is doubtful, support it with backing. Try to anticipate audience objections by exploring conditions for rebuttal, and brainstorm ways of addressing those objections.
3. Using the skeleton you created, finish developing an outline or tree diagram for your argument. Although the organization for each part of your argument will grow organically from its content, the main parts of a classical argument are as follows:
   a. *An introduction,* in which you engage your reader's attention, introduce your issue, and state your own position.
   b. *Background and preliminary material,* in which you place your issue in a current context and provide whatever background knowledge and definitions of key terms or concepts that your reader will need. (If this background is short, it can often be incorporated into the introduction.)

c. *Arguments supporting your own position,* in which you make the best case possible for your views by developing your claim with reasons and evidence. This is usually the longest part of your argument, with a separate section for each line of reasoning.

d. *Anticipation of objections and counterarguments,* in which you summarize fairly key arguments against your position. This section not only helps the reader understand the issue more clearly, but also establishes your *ethos* as a fair-minded writer willing to acknowledge complexity.

e. *Response to objections through refutation or concession,* in which you point out weaknesses in opposing arguments or concede to their strengths.

f. *A conclusion,* in which you place your argument in a larger context, perhaps by summarizing your main points and showing why this issue is an important one or by issuing a call to action.

This classical model can be modified in numerous ways. A question that often arises is where to summarize and respond to objections and counterarguments. Writers generally have three choices. One option is to handle opposing positions before you present your own argument. The rationale for this approach is that skeptical audiences may be more inclined to listen attentively to your argument if they have been assured that you understand their point of view. A second option is to place this material after you have presented your argument. This approach is effective for neutral audiences who don't start off with strong opposing views. A final option is to intersperse opposing views throughout your argument at appropriate moments. Any of these possibilities, or a combination of all of them, can be effective.

Another question often asked is the best way to order one's reasons. A general rule of thumb when ordering your own argument is to put your strongest reason last and your second strongest reason first. The idea here is to start and end with your most powerful arguments. If you imagine a quite skeptical audience, build bridges to your audience by summarizing alternative views early in the paper and concede to those that are especially strong. If your audience is neutral or undecided, you can summarize and respond to possible objections after you have presented your own case.

Revising

As you revise your argument, you need to attend both to the clarity of your writing (all the principles of closed-form prose described in Chapter 11) and also to the persuasiveness of your argument. As always, peer reviews are valuable, and especially so in argumentation if you ask your peer reviewers to role-play an opposing audience. The following Guidelines for Peer Reviewers can both assist your peer reviewers and help you with revision.

g u i d e l i n e s

For Peer Reviewers

Instructions for peer reviews, including use of these guidelines, are provided in Chapter 10, pages 195–202. To write a peer review for a classmate, use your own paper, numbering your responses to correspond to the questions on the guidelines. At the head of your paper place the author's name and your own name, as shown.

Author's Name: _____

Peer Reviewer's Name: _____

C. examine
personal
experience
passages
3 suggestion
on improving
appeal to
Pathos

I. Read the draft at a normal reading speed from beginning to end. As you read, do the following:
  A. Place a wavy line in the margin next to any passages that you find confusing, that contain something that doesn't seem to fit, or that otherwise slow down your reading.
  B. Place a "Good!" in the margin next to any passages where you think the writing is particularly strong or interesting.
II. Read the draft again slowly and answer the following questions by writing brief explanations of your answers.
  A. Introduction:
    1. Does the title announce the issue, reveal the writer's claim, or otherwise focus the reader's expectations and pique interest? How could the title be improved?
    2. How effectively does the opening introduce the issue, engage your interest, and convince you that the issue is significant and problematic? What would add clarity or appeal?
    3. Does the end of the introduction adequately forecast the argument and present the writer's claim? Could the statement of the claim be more focused, clear, or risky?
  B. Arguing for the claim:
    1. Consider the overall structure: Does the structure of the argument effectively develop the claim? Can you discern the argument's main parts—background (if needed), supporting reasons (a main section for each line of reasoning), summary and refutation of alternative viewpoints, and conclusion? How could the structure be improved?
    2. Consider the support: For each line of reasoning, does the writer provide adequate grounds in the form of facts, examples, statistics, testimony, or other supporting details? Does the writer need to state warrants and develop backing? Where would you like more support for the writer's reasons?

3. Consider *ethos* and *pathos:* Does the writer establish a trustworthy and credible persona? Where could the writer better appeal to the readers' emotions, beliefs, values?

4. Consider the writer's summary and response to alternative viewpoints: Does the writer summarize opposing arguments fairly? Are there any important differing views that the writer hasn't considered? Does the writer offer adequate refutation of each opposing argument or otherwise respond to it effectively? How might the writer improve his or her treatment of opposing views?

5. Does the conclusion bring a sense of completeness and closure to the argument?

6. How might the writer improve the clarity of the draft? Where might the writer better apply the principles of clarity from Chapter 11?

C. Sum up what you see as the main strengths and problem areas of the draft.

1. Strengths
2. Problem areas

III. Read the draft one more time. Place a check in the margin wherever you notice problems in grammar, spelling, or mechanics (one check per problem).

TOPIC Guidepost #27

For those using Texas Tech's TOPIC Web-Based assignments:

Direct your web browser to **http://english.ttu.edu:5555**

Guidepost #27 provides full instructions regarding your reading assignment (Handbook 209-214) and Draft 4.1.

TOPIC Guidepost #8

For those using Texas Tech's TOPIC Web-Based assignments:

Direct your web browser to **http://english.ttu.edu:5555**

Guidepost #8 provides full instructions regarding your reading assignment (Chapter 10) and Draft 1.2.

Writing as a Problem-Solving Process

I rewrite as I write. It is hard to tell what is a first draft because it is not determined by time. In one draft, I might cross out three pages, write two, cross out a fourth, rewrite it, and call it a draft. I am constantly writing and rewriting. I can only conceptualize so much in my first draft—only so much information can be held in my head at one time; my rewriting efforts are a reflection of how much information I can encompass at one time. There are levels and agenda which I have to attend to in each draft.

　　　　　　　　　　　　　　—Description of revision by an experienced writer

I read what I have written and I cross out a word and put another word in; a more decent word or a better word. Then if there is somewhere to use a sentence that I have crossed out, I will put it there.*

　　　　　　　　　　　　　　—Description of revision by an inexperienced writer

Blot out, correct, insert, refine,
Enlarge, diminish, interline;
Be mindful, when invention fails,
To scratch your head, and bite your nails.

　　　　　　　　　　　　　　　　　　—Jonathan Swift

In Part One of this text we focused on writing as a problem-solving process in which writers pose and solve both subject-matter problems and rhetorical problems. Part Three shows you how to translate these basic principles into effective strategies for composing and revising your writing along the continuum from closed to open forms. The four self-contained chapters, which can be read in whatever sequence best fits your instructor's course plan, will help you compose and revise the essays you write for the assignments in Part Two.

This chapter explains how experienced writers use multiple drafts to manage the complexities of writing and suggests ways for you to improve your own writing

*From Nancy Sommers, "Revision Strategies of Student Writers and Experienced Adult Writers," *College Composition and Communication* 31 (October, 1980): 291–300.

processes. Chapter 11, which takes the form of nine self-contained lessons, focuses on key strategies for composing and revising closed-form prose. Chapter 12 switches from closed to open forms, showing you how, when appropriate, to open your prose by creating surprises of style and structure that engage readers and involve them in the process of completing your text's meaning. Finally, Chapter 13 explains how you can improve your writing processes by working in small groups to solve problems, help each other generate ideas, and provide feedback for revision.

◢ UNDERSTANDING HOW EXPERTS COMPOSE AND REVISE

We begin this chapter with a close look at how experienced writers compose, explaining what they think about when they write and why they often need multiple drafts. In Chapter 3 we quoted Peter Elbow's assertion that "meaning is not what you start out with" but "what you end up with." Thus composing is a discovery process. In the early stages of writing, experienced writers typically discover what they are trying to say, often deepening and complicating their ideas rather than clarifying them. Only in the last drafts will such writers be in sufficient control of their ideas to shape them elegantly for readers.

It's important not to overgeneralize, however, because no two writers compose exactly the same way; moreover, the same writer may use different processes for different kinds of prose. Some writers outline their ideas before they write; others need to write extensively before they can outline. Some write their first drafts very slowly, devoting extensive thought and planning to each emerging paragraph; others write first drafts rapidly, to be sure to get all their ideas on paper, and then rework the material part by part. Some prefer to work independently, without discussing or sharing their ideas; others seek out classmates or colleagues to help them hash out ideas and rehearse their arguments before writing them down. Some seek out the stillness of a library or private room; others do their best writing in noisy cafeterias or coffee shops.

The actual mechanics of composing differ from writer to writer as well. Some writers create first drafts directly at a keyboard, whereas others require the reassuring heft of a pen or pencil. Among writers who begin by planning the structure of their work, some make traditional outlines (perhaps using the flexible outline feature on their word processors), whereas others prefer tree diagrams or flowcharts. Some of those who use word processors revise directly at the computer, whereas others print out a hard copy, revise with pen and ink, and then type the changes into the computer.

Also, writers often vary their composing processes from project to project. A writer might complete one project with a single draft and a quick editing job, but produce a half dozen or more drafts for another project.

What experienced writers do have in common is a willingness to keep revising their work until they feel it is ready to go public. They typically work much harder at drafting and revising than do inexperienced writers, taking more runs at their subject. And experienced writers generally make more substantial alterations in their drafts during revision. (Compare the first two quotations that open this chapter—one from an experienced and one from an inexperienced writer.) An experienced writer will sometimes throw away a first draft and start over; a beginning writer tends to be more satisfied with early drafts and to think of revision as primarily cleaning up errors. Figure 10.1 (on p. 186) shows the first page of a first draft for a magazine article written by an experienced writer.

◢ WHY EXPERIENCED WRITERS REVISE SO EXTENSIVELY

To help you understand the puzzling difference between beginning and experienced writers, let's consider *why* experienced writers revise. If they are such good writers, why don't they get it right the first time? Why so many drafts? To use the language of Part One, experienced writers need multiple drafts to help them pose, pursue, and solve problems—both subject-matter problems and related rhetorical problems. Faced with many choices, experienced writers use multiple drafts to break a complex task into manageable subtasks. Let's look more closely at some of the functions that revising can perform for writers.

Revising to Overcome Limits of Short-Term Memory

A writer's need for multiple drafts results partly from the limitations of memory. Cognitive psychologists have shown that working memory—often called short-term memory—has remarkably little storage space. People use short-term memory to hold the data on which they are actively focusing at any given moment while solving problems, reading texts, writing a draft, or performing other cognitive tasks. People also have long-term memories, which can store an almost infinite amount of material. The trouble is that much of the material held temporarily in short-term memory never gets transferred to long-term memory. (Try closing this book for a moment and writing out this paragraph from memory.)

You can conceptualize short-term memory as a small tabletop surrounded by filing cabinets (long-term memory). To use the ideas and data you generate while writing a draft, you have to place them on the tabletop, which can hold only a few items at once.* As you generate ideas for your draft, you pile on your tabletop more data than it can hold. You need some means of holding on to your thoughts in process, lest ideas spill off the table and become permanently lost.

---

*A famous study conducted by psychologist George Miller revealed that the average person's short-term memory can hold "seven plus or minus two" chunks of information at a time. When given, say, a thirty-item list of random words or numbers, the average person can remember between five and nine of them. The items will quickly be lost from short-term memory unless the person actively rehearses them over and over (as when you repeat a new phone number to yourself so that you won't forget it before you write it down).

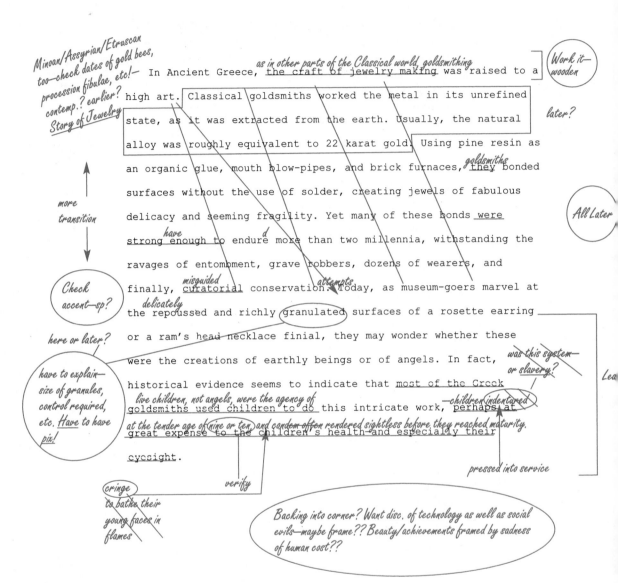

Minoan/Assyrian/Etruscan too—check dates of gold bees, procession fibulae, etc!—contemp.? earlier?

Story of Jewelry

more transition

Check accent—sp?

here or later?

have to explain—size of granules, control required, etc. Have to have pix!

cringe to bathe their young faces in flames

In Ancient Greece, *as in other parts of the Classical world, goldsmithing* ~~the craft of jewelry making~~ was raised to a

Work it—wooden

later?

high art. Classical goldsmiths worked the metal in its unrefined state, as it was extracted from the earth. Usually, the natural alloy was roughly equivalent to 22 karat gold. Using pine resin as an organic glue, mouth blow-pipes, and brick furnaces, *goldsmiths* ~~they~~ bonded surfaces without the use of solder, creating jewels of fabulous delicacy and seeming fragility. Yet many of these bonds _were_

All Later

have strong enough to endure more than two millennia, withstanding the ravages of entombment, grave robbers, dozens of wearers, and finally, *misguided* curatorial conservation. *attempts* Today, as museum-goers marvel at

delicately the repoussé and richly (granulated) surfaces of a rosette earring or a ram's ~~head~~ necklace finial, they may wonder whether these were the creations of earthly beings or of angels. In fact, *was this system—or slavery?*

historical evidence seems to indicate that most of the Greek *live children, not angels, were the agency of* goldsmiths used children to do this intricate work, ~~perhaps at~~ —children indentured

at the tender age of nine or ten, and condemn ~~often rendered sightless before they reached maturity.~~ ~~great expense to the children's health~~ ~~and especially their~~ eyesight.

Lea

pressed into service

verify

Backing into corner? Want disc. of technology as well as social evils—maybe frame?? Beauty/achievements framed by sadness of human cost??

FIGURE 10.1   Draft Page of an Experienced Writer

This analogy illustrates why experienced writers rely on multiple drafts. Because of the limitations of short-term memory, you can actively engage only a few chunks of material at any given moment—a few sentences of a draft or several ideas in an outline. The remaining portions of the evolving essay quickly recede from consciousness without being stored in long-term memory. (Think of your horror when your computer eats your draft or when you accidentally leave your nearly finished term paper on the bus—proof that you can't rely on long-term memory to restore what you wrote.) Writing a draft, however, captures these ideas from short-term memory and stores them on paper. When you reread these stored ideas, you can note problem areas, think of new ideas, see material that doesn't fit, recall additional information, and so forth. You can then begin working on a new draft, focusing on one problem at a time.

What kinds of problems do experienced writers locate in a draft? What triggers further rounds of rewriting? We continue with more reasons why experienced writers revise.

Revising to Accommodate Shifts and Changes in a Writer's Ideas

Early in the writing process, experienced writers often are unsure of what they want to say or where their ideas are leading; they find their ideas shifting and evolving as their drafts progress. Sometimes writing a draft leads the writer to reformulate the initial problem. Just as frequently, the solution that may have seemed exciting at the beginning of the process may seem less satisfactory once it is written out. A writer's ideas deepen or shift under pressure of new insights stimulated by the act of writing. A professional writer's finished product often is radically different from the first draft—not simply in form and style but in actual content.

Revising to Clarify Audience and Purpose

As we noted in Chapter 4, writers need to say something significant to an audience for a purpose. When a writer's sense of audience or purpose shifts, an entire piece may need to be restructured. As they draft, experienced writers pose questions such as these: Who am I picturing as my readers? What is my purpose in writing to them? What effect do I want this piece of writing to have on them? How much background will they need? To which of their values and beliefs should I appeal? What tone and style are appropriate for this audience? What objections will they raise to my argument? In the process of writing, the answers to these questions may evolve so that each new draft reflects a deeper or clearer understanding of audience and purpose.

Revising to Clarify Structure and Create Coherence

Few writers can create detailed outlines before drafting. Those who can, typically set aside their outlines as their drafts take on lives of their own, spilling over the boundaries the writers have laid out. Whereas early drafts usually reflect the order in which writers conceived their ideas, later drafts are often reordered—sometimes radically—in consideration of readers' needs. To help them see their drafts from a reader's perspective, experienced writers regularly put aside those drafts for a time. When they return to a draft, the ideas no longer so familiar, they can more readily see where the material is disjointed, underdeveloped, or irrelevant. Writing teachers sometimes call this transformation a movement from writer-based to reader-based prose.* The lessons in Chapter 11 will help you develop the skills of seeing your drafts from a reader's perspective.

Revising to Improve Gracefulness and Correctness

Finally, writers have to get their grammar right, punctuate effectively, spell correctly, and compose sentences that are concise, clear, graceful, and pleasing to the ear. Late in the revision process, experienced writers focus extensively on these matters. Often this stage of revision involves more than stylistic polishing. Making a single sentence more graceful may entail rewriting surrounding sentences. If an awkward sentence is symptomatic of confused thinking, correcting the sentence may require generating and exploring more ideas.

A WORKING DESCRIPTION OF THE WRITING PROCESS

The writing process we have just described may be considerably different from what you have previously been taught. For many years—before researchers began studying the composing processes of experienced writers—writing teachers typically taught a model something like this:

Old Model of the Writing Process

1. Choose a topic
2. Narrow it
3. Write a thesis
4. Make an outline
5. Write a draft
6. Revise
7. Edit

The major problem with this model is that hardly anyone writes this way. Few experienced writers begin by choosing a topic and then narrowing it—a process that seems passionless, arbitrary, and mechanical. As we explained in Part One, experienced writers begin by looking at the world with a wondering and critical eye; they pose problems and explore ideas; they become dissatisfied with the answers or explanations given by others; they identify questions that impel them to add their own voice to a conversation. Nor is the process neatly linear, as the old model implies. Sometimes writers settle on a thesis early in the writing process. But just as frequently they formulate a thesis during an "Aha!" moment of discovery later in the process, perhaps after several drafts (So *this* is my point! Here is my argument in a nutshell!). Even very late in the process, while checking spelling and

---

*The terms "writer-based" and reader-based" prose come from Linda Flower, "Writer-Based Prose: A Cognitive Basis for Problems in Writing." *College English*, 1979, 41.1, 19–37.

punctuation, experienced writers are apt to think of new ideas, thus triggering more revision.

Rather than dividing the writing process into distinct, sequential steps, let's review the kinds of things experienced writers are likely to do early, midway, and late in the process of writing an essay.

Early in the Process

The activities in which writers engage early in the process are recursive—writing a draft sends the writer back for further exploring, researching, and talking.

Writers Sense a Question or Problem. Initially, the question or problem may not be well-defined, but the writers sense something unknown about the topic, see it in an unusual way, disagree with someone else's view of it, doubt a theory, note a piece of unexplained data, or otherwise notice something confusing or problematic. In college, the instructor often assigns the problem or question to be addressed. Sometimes, the instructor assigns only a general topic area, leaving writers to find their own questions or problems.

Writers Explore the Problem, Seeking Focus. The writers gather data from various sources, including readings, laboratory or field research, experience, conversation, and memory. Through exploratory writing and talking, writers analyze, compare, puzzle, and probe, searching for an effective response to the problem. They consider why they are writing, what they want their readers to know about the topic, and how their ideas might surprise the readers, given the readers' background knowledge and point of view. Often writers explore ideas in a journal, research log, Internet chat room, or conversations with colleagues. Writers may also take time off from the problem and do other things, letting ideas cook in the unconscious.

Writers Compose a First Draft. At some point writers put ideas on paper in a whole or partial draft. Some writers make an informal outline or tree diagram prior to writing. Others discover direction as they write, putting aside concerns about coherence to pursue different branches of ideas. In either case, they don't try to make the draft perfect as they go. One of the major causes of writer's block among less experienced writers is the inability to live with temporary imperfection and confusion. Experienced writers know their first drafts are often times awful, and they lower their expectations accordingly. Writing a first draft often leads writers to discover new ideas, to complicate or refocus the problem, to reimagine audience or purpose, and sometimes to change directions.

Midway Through the Process

Writers Begin to Revise and Reformulate. Once they have written a first draft, writers are in a better position to view the whole territory and are better able to recognize relationships among the parts. Some writers begin again, selecting insights and perspectives from the first draft and reshaping them into a new draft with a different approach and structure; others keep much of the original draft, but incorporate their newfound perspectives. Writers often find that the conclusion of the first draft is much clearer than its introduction—proof that they discovered and clarified their ideas as they wrote. At this point writers begin a second draft, often by going slowly through the first draft, adding, deleting, reordering, or completely rewriting passages. As writers revise, they ask themselves questions such as, What is my point here? Does this material really fit? What am I really trying to say? To help them see the relationship between the parts and the whole, writers often make new outlines or tree diagrams to clarify the shape of their thinking.

Writers Increasingly Consider the Needs of Readers. As writers clarify their ideas for themselves, they increasingly focus on their readers' needs. They reorganize material and insert mapping statements, transitions, and cue words to help readers follow their ideas. In particular, they try to write effective introductions to hook readers' attention, explain the problem to be examined, and preview the whole of the essay.

Writers Seek Feedback from Readers. Midway through the writing process, experienced writers often ask colleagues to read their drafts and offer feedback. They seek readers' responses to such questions as these: Where do you get lost or confused? Where do you disagree with my ideas? Where do I need to put in more evidence or support?

Writers Rewrite in Response to Feedback from Readers. Readers' responses can often help writers locate confusing spots and better anticipate readers' objections or the need for background. Different readers sometimes respond differently to a draft and offer conflicting advice. Considering the differing responses of multiple readers may allow writers to formulate their own ideas more clearly and may lead to further revisions.

Late in the Process

Writers begin to shift from discovery, shaping, and development to editing. Eventually, the writer's sense of purpose and audience stabilizes and the ideas become increasingly clear, well organized, and developed. At this point writers begin shifting their attention to the craft of writing—getting each word, phrase, sentence, and paragraph just right, so that the prose is clear, graceful, lively, and correct. Even as writers struggle with issues of style and correctness, however, they may discover new meanings and intentions that impel them to rethink parts of the essay.

FOR WRITING AND DISCUSSION

When you write, do you follow a process resembling the one we just described? Have you ever

- had a writing project grow out of your engagement with a problem or question?
- explored ideas by talking with others or by doing exploratory writing?

- made major changes to a draft because you changed your mind or otherwise discovered new ideas?
- revised a draft from a reader's perspective by consciously trying to imagine and respond to a reader's questions, confusions, and other reactions?
- road tested a draft by trying it out on readers and then revising it as a result of what they told you?

Working in groups or as a whole class, share stories about previous writing experiences that match or do not match the description of experienced writers' processes. To the extent that your present process differs, what strategies of experienced writers might you like to try?

▨ IMPROVING YOUR OWN WRITING PROCESSES

The previous section describes the many ways in which experienced writers compose. Although it is difficult for beginning writers simply to duplicate these processes, which evolve from much experience and practice, trial and error, beginning writers can take steps to develop more effective composing habits. Some nuts-and-bolts suggestions for improving your writing processes are given next.

Recognizing Kinds of Changes Typically Made in Drafts

We begin by classifying the kinds of changes writers typically make in drafts and explaining their reasons for making each sort of change.

Kinds of Changes	Reasons for Change
Crossing out whole passage and rewriting from scratch	Original passage was unfocused; ideas have changed.
	New sense of purpose or point meant whole passage needed reshaping.
	Original passage was too confused or jumbled merely to be edited.
Cutting and pasting; moving parts around	Original was disorganized.
	Points weren't connected to particulars.
	Conclusion was clearer than introduction; part of conclusion had to be moved to introduction.
	Rewriting introduction led to discovery of more effective plan of development; new forecasting required different order in body.

Kinds of Changes *(cont.)*	Reasons for Change *(cont.)*
Deletions	Material not needed or irrelevant.
	Deleted material was good but went off on a tangent.
Additions	Supporting particulars needed to be added: examples, facts, illustrations, statistics, evidence (usually added to bodies of paragraphs).
	Points and transitions needed to be supplied (often added to openings of paragraphs).
	New section needed to be added or a brief point expanded.
Recasting of sentences (crossing out and rewriting portions of sentences; combining sentences; rephrasing; starting sentences with a different grammatical structure)	Passage violated old/new contract (see pp. 232–38).
	Passage was wordy or choppy.
	Passage lacked rhythm and voice.
	Grammar was tangled, diction odd, meaning confused.
Editing sentences to correct mistakes	Words were misspelled or mistyped.
	Writer found comma splices, fragments, dangling participles, other grammatical errors.

FOR WRITING AND DISCUSSION

Choose an important paragraph in the body of a draft you are currently working on. Then write out your answers to these questions about that paragraph.

1. Why is this an important paragraph?
2. What is its main point?
3. Where is that main point stated?

Now—as an exercise only—write the main point at the top of a blank sheet of paper, put away your original draft, and, without looking at the original, write a new paragraph with the sole purpose of developing the point you wrote at the top of the page.

When you are finished, compare your new paragraph to the original. What have you learned that might help you revise your original?

Here are some typical responses of writers who have tried this exercise:

I recognized that my original paragraph was unfocused. I couldn't find a main point.

I recognized that my original paragraph was underdeveloped. I had a main point but not enough particulars supporting it.

> I began to see that my draft was scattered and that I had too many short paragraphs.
>
> I recognized that I was making a couple of different points in my original paragraph and that I needed to break it into separate paragraphs.
>
> I recognized that I hadn't stated my main point (or that I buried it in the middle of the paragraph).
>
> I recognized that there was a big difference in style between my two versions and that I had to choose which version I liked best (it's not always the "new" version!).

Practice the Composing Strategies of Experienced Writers

In addition to knowing the kinds of changes writers typically make in drafts, you can improve your composing processes by practicing the strategies used by experienced writers.

Use Expressive Writing for Discovery and Exploration

Use the exploratory strategies described in detail in Chapter 2. Don't let your first draft be the first time you put your ideas into written words. Long before writing a draft, experienced writers typically write extensive notes in the margins of books and articles, explore ideas in journals or research logs, exchange ideas with colleagues on e-mail, and do extensive notetaking, scratch outlining, and idea mapping. Each assignment chapter in Part Two includes exploratory exercises that will help you generate ideas and overcome writer's block.

Talk About Your Ideas; Talk Your Draft

Good writing grows out of good talking. Seek out opportunities to talk about your ideas with classmates or friends. Exchange ideas on topics so that you can appreciate alternative points of view. Whenever possible, talk through your draft with a friend; rehearse your argument in conversation as practice for putting it in writing.

Invent with Research

Depending on your topic, audience, purpose, and genre, you will frequently need to do outside reading and research. In the process of finding new information and exploring the multisided conversation surrounding your subject, you will be deepening your understanding of the topic and reshaping your thinking.

Schedule Your Time

Plan for exploration, drafting, revision, and editing. Don't begin your paper the night before it is due. Talk about your ideas and do exploratory writing before writing a rough draft. Give ideas time to ruminate in your mind. Recognize that your ideas will shift, branch out, even turn around as you write. Allow some time off between writing the first draft and beginning revision. Experienced writers build in time for revision.

Exchange Drafts with Others

Get other people's reactions to your work in exchange for your reactions to theirs. The next section explains procedures for peer review of drafts.

Discover What Methods of Drafting Work Best for You

Some people compose rough drafts directly on a computer; others write longhand. Of those who write longhand, some find that a certain kind of paper or pen best stimulates thought. Different people prefer different surroundings, also. One of the writers of this text works best in a noisy bagel shop or coffeehouse; the other prefers sitting on a sofa with a legal pad in hand. Discover what works best for you.

Revise on Double- or Triple-Spaced Hard Copy

Although some people can revise directly at the computer, research suggests that writers are more apt to make large-scale changes in a draft if they work from hard copy. Double- or triple-space your drafts and write on one side of the page only. Cross out text to be changed and write new text in the blank spaces between the lines. When a draft gets too messy, write revised passages on a separate sheet and tape that sheet to the hard-copy draft. Then, if you are working on a computer, enter your changes into the computer and print out another hard copy for another round of revision.

Save Correctness for Last

To revise productively, concentrate first on the big questions: Do I have good ideas in this draft? Am I responding appropriately to the assignment? Are my ideas adequately organized and developed? Save questions about exact wording, grammar, and mechanics for later. These concerns are important, but they cannot be efficiently attended to until after higher-order concerns are met. Your first goal is to create a thoughtful, richly developed draft.

To Meet Deadlines and Bring the Process to a Close, Learn How to *Satisfice*

Our description of the writing process may seem pretty formidable. Potentially, it seems, you could go on revising forever. How can you ever know when to stop? There's no ready answer to that question, but in our opinion it is much more a psychological than a technical problem. The best advice we can offer is to "satisfice."

Satisficing doesn't require that you be perfectly satisfied with your writing. To *satisfice* is to make it as good as you can under the circumstances—your rhetorical situation, your time constraints, and the pressures of other demands on you. The best advice we can give you for finishing a project is to write a rough draft as early in the process as possible and to allow time for feedback from peers or other readers. Then let the deadline give you the energy for intensive revision. From lawyers preparing briefs for court to engineers developing design proposals, writers have used deadlines to help them put aside doubts and anxieties and to conclude their work, as every writer must. "Okay, it's not perfect, but it's the best I can do" (a good definition of *satisficing*).

◢ USING PEER REVIEWS TO STIMULATE REVISION

One of the best ways to become a better reviser is to see your draft from a *reader's* rather than a writer's perspective. As writer, you know what you mean; you are already inside your own head. But you need to see what your draft is like to someone outside your head.

The best way to learn this skill is to practice reading your classmates' drafts and have them read yours. In this section we offer advice on how to respond candidly to your classmates' drafts and how to participate in peer reviews.

Becoming a Helpful Reader of Classmates' Drafts

When you respond to a writer's draft, learn to make readerly rather than writerly comments; describe your mental experience in trying to understand the draft rather than pointing out problems or errors in the draft. For example, instead of saying, "Your draft is disorganized," say, "I got lost when. . . ." Instead of saying, "This paragraph needs a topic sentence," say, "I had trouble seeing the point of this paragraph."

When you help a writer with a draft, your goal is both to point out where the draft needs more work and to brainstorm with the writer possible ways to improve the draft. Begin by reading the draft all the way through at a normal reading speed. As you read, take mental notes to help focus your feedback. We suggest that you make wavy lines in the margin next to passages that you find confusing; write "Good!" in the margin where you like something; and write "?" in the margin where you want to ask questions.

After you have read the draft, use the following strategies for making helpful responses.

If the ideas in the draft seem thin or undeveloped, or if the draft is too short:

- ■ help the writer brainstorm for more ideas.
- ■ help the writer add more examples, better details, more supporting data or arguments.

If you get confused or lost:

- ■ have the writer talk through ideas to clear up confusing spots.
- ■ help the writer sharpen the thesis: suggest that the writer view the thesis as the answer to a controversial or problematic question; ask the writer to articulate the question that the thesis answers.

- help the writer create an outline, tree diagram, or flow chart (see Chapter 11, pp. 213–15).
- help the writer clarify the focus by asking him or her to complete these statements about purpose:
    My purpose in this paper is _____.
    My purpose in this section (paragraph) is _____.
    Before reading my paper, the reader will have this view of my topic: _____; after reading my paper, my reader will have this different view of my topic: _____.
- show the writer where you get confused or miscued in reading the draft ("I started getting lost here because I couldn't see why you were giving me this information" or "I thought you were going to say X, but then you said Y").

If you can understand the sentences but can't see the point:

- help the writer articulate the meaning by asking "So what?" questions, making the writer bring the point to the surface by stating it directly ("I can understand what you are saying here but I don't quite understand why you are saying it. I read all these facts, and I say 'So what?' What do these facts have to do with your thesis?").

If you disagree with the ideas or think the writer has avoided alternative points of view:

- play devil's advocate to help the writer deepen and complicate ideas.
- show the writer specific places where you had queries or doubts.

FOR WRITING AND DISCUSSION

In the following exercise, we ask you to respond to a student's draft ("Should the University Carpet the Dorm Rooms?," on pp. 431–32). The assignment asked students to take a stand on a local campus issue. Imagine that you have exchanged drafts with this student and that your task is to help this student improve the draft.

Read the draft carefully; make wavy lines in the margins where you get confused, write "Good!" for something you like, and write "?" where you want to ask questions.

On your own, complete the following tasks:

1. Identify one specific place in the draft where you got confused. Freewrite a brief explanation for why you got confused. Make readerly rather than writerly comments.
2. Identify one place in the draft where you think the ideas are thin or need more development.
3. Identify one place where you might write "So what?" in the margins. These are places where you understand the sentences but don't see what the writer is getting at, the point.
4. Identify at least one place where you could play devil's advocate or otherwise object to the writer's ideas. Freewrite your objections.

In groups or as a whole class, share your responses. Then turn to the following tasks:

1. With the instructor serving as a guide, practice explaining to the writer where or how you got confused while reading the draft. Readers often have difficulty explaining their reading experience to a writer. Let several class members role-play being the reader. Practice using language such as "I like the way this draft started because . . ." "I got confused when . . ." "I had to back up and reread when . . ." "I saw your point here, but then I got lost again because . . . ." Writing theorist Peter Elbow calls such language a "movie of your mind."
2. Have several class members role-play being devil's advocates by arguing against the writer's thesis. Where are the ideas thin or weak?

Should the University Carpet the Dorm Rooms?

Tricia, a University student, came home exhausted from her work-study job. She took a blueberry pie from the refrigerator to satisfy her hunger and a tall glass of milk to quench her thirst. While trying to get comfortable on her bed, she tipped her snack over onto the floor. She cleaned the mess, but the blueberry and milk stains on her brand new carpet could not be removed.

Tricia didn't realize how hard it was to clean up stains on a carpet. Luckily this was her own carpet.

A lot of students don't want carpets. Students constantly change rooms. The next person may not want carpet.

Some students say that since they pay to live on campus, the rooms should reflect a comfortable home atmosphere. Carpets will make the dorm more comfortable. The carpet will act as insulation and as a soundproofing system.

Paint stains cannot be removed from carpets. If the university carpets the rooms, the students will lose the privilege they have of painting their rooms any color. This would limit students' self-expression.

The carpets would be an institutional brown or gray. This would be ugly. With tile floors, the students can choose and purchase their own carpets to match their taste. You can't be an individual if you can't decorate your room to fit your personality.

According to Rachel Jones, Assistant Director of Housing Services, the cost will be $300 per room for the carpet and installation. Also the university will have to buy more vacuum cleaners. But will vacuum cleaners be all that is necessary to keep the carpets clean? We'll need shampoo machines too.

What about those stains that won't come off even with a shampoo machine? That's where the student will have to pay damage deposit costs.

There will be many stains on the carpet due to shaving cream fights, food fights, beverage parties, and smoking, all of which can damage the carpets.

Students don't take care of the dorms now. They don't follow the rules of maintaining their rooms. They drill holes into the walls, break mirrors, beds, and closet doors, and leave their food trays all over the floor.

If the university buys carpets our room rates will skyrocket. In conclusion, it is a bad idea for the university to buy carpets.

Conducting a Peer Review Workshop

If you are willing to respond candidly to a classmate's draft—in a readerly rather than a writerly way—you will be a valuable participant in peer review workshops. In a typical workshop, classmates work in groups of two to six to respond to each other's rough drafts and offer suggestions for revisions.* These workshops are most helpful when group members have developed sufficient levels of professionalism and trust to exchange candid responses. A frequent problem in peer review workshops is that classmates try so hard to avoid hurting each other's feelings that they provide vague, meaningless feedback. Saying, "Your paper's great. I really liked it. Maybe you could make it flow a little better" is much less helpful than saying, "Your issue about environmental pollution in the Antarctic is well defined in the first paragraph, but I got lost in the second paragraph when you began discussing penguin coloration."

---

*Chapter 13 discusses additional ways to use groups and strategies to improve the dynamics of groups.

Responsibilities of Peer Reviewers and Writers

Learning to respond conscientiously and carefully to others' work may be the single most important thing you can do to improve your own writing. When you review a classmate's draft, you should prepare as follows:

1. ***Understand how experienced writers revise their drafts.***   Prior to reviewing a classmate's draft, review the material in this chapter. Pay particular attention to pages 195–96, which provide general guidelines about what to look for when reading a draft and to pages 191–92, which summarize the kinds of changes writers often make in response to reviews: additions, deletions, reordering, complete refocusing and rewriting, and so forth.
2. ***Understand the assignment and the guidelines for peer reviewers.***   For assignments in Part Two of this text, carefully read both the assignment itself and the guidelines for peer reviewers at the end of the chapter in which the assignment appears. These guidelines will help both the writer and you, as peer reviewer, to understand the demands of the assignment and the criteria on which it should be evaluated.
3. ***Understand that you are not acting as a teacher.***   A peer reviewer's role is that of a fresh reader. You can help the writer appreciate what it's like to encounter his or her text for the first time. Your primary responsibility is to articulate your understanding of what the writer's words say to you and to identify places where you get confused, where you need more details, where you have doubts or queries, and so on. Although the specific kinds of evaluations called for in the Guidelines for Peer Reviewers will be helpful, you don't need to be an expert who is offering solutions to every problem.

When you play the role of writer during a workshop session, your responsibilities parallel those of your peer reviewers. You need to provide a legible rough draft, preferably typed and double-spaced, which doesn't baffle the reader with illegible handwriting, cross-outs, arrows, and confusing pagination. Your instructor may ask you to bring photocopies of your draft for all group members. During the workshop, your primary responsibility is to *listen*, taking in how others respond to your draft without becoming defensive.

Exchanging Drafts

An excellent method of exchanging drafts is to have each writer read his or her draft aloud while group members follow along in their own photocopies. We value reading drafts aloud when time allows. Reading expressively, with appropriate emphasis, helps writers distance themselves from their work and hear it anew. When you read your work silently to yourself, it's all too easy to patch up bits of broken prose in your head or to slide through confusing passages. But if you stumble over a passage while reading aloud, you can place a check in the margin to indicate where further attention is needed. Another benefit to reading aloud is perhaps more symbolic than pragmatic. Reading your work to others means that you are claiming responsibility for it, displaying your intention to reach a range of readers other than the teacher. And knowing that you will have to read your work aloud will encourage you to have that work in the best possible shape before bringing it to class.

Types of Peer Review Workshops

After you've read your draft aloud, the next stage of your peer review may take one of several forms, depending on your instructor's preference. We describe here three basic strategies: response-centered workshops, advice-centered workshops, and out-of-class reviews. Additional strategies often build on these approaches.

Response-Centered Workshops.   This process-oriented, nonintrusive approach places maximum responsibility on the writer for making decisions about what to change in a draft. After the writer reads the draft aloud, group members follow this procedure.

1. All participants take several minutes to make notes on their copies of the manuscript. We recommend using the "Good!" wavy line, "?" system described in the Guidelines for Peer Reviewers.
2. Group members take turns describing to the writer their responses to the piece—where they agreed or disagreed with the writer's ideas, where they got confused, where they wanted more development, and so forth. Group members do not give advice; they simply describe their own personal response to the draft as written.
3. The writer takes notes during each response but does not enter into a discussion. The writer listens without trying to defend the piece or explain what he or she intended.

No one gives the writer explicit advice. Group members simply describe their reactions to the piece and leave it to the writer to make appropriate changes.

Advice-Centered Workshops.   In this more product-oriented and directive approach, peer reviewers collaborate to give advice to the writer. This method works best if group members use the Guidelines for Peer Reviewers that conclude each chapter in Part Two. For advice-centered reviews, students typically work in pairs, exchanging drafts with each other. But many students prefer the following approach, which allows each class member to collaborate with a partner.

1. The instructor divides the class into groups of four. Each student reads his or her paper aloud to the group. (This step can be omitted if time is limited.)
2. Each group divides into pairs; each pair exchanges drafts with the other pair.
3. The members of each pair collaborate to compose jointly written reviews of the two drafts they have received. These reviews should present the pair's collaborative responses to the questions in the Guidelines for Peer Reviewers in the assignment's chapter.
4. The drafts and the collaboratively written reviews are then returned to the original writers. If time remains, the two pairs meet jointly to discuss their reviews.

Since advice-centered reviews take longer than response-centered reviews, the instructor may ask writers to supply copies of their drafts to their peer reviewers at the class meeting prior to the workshop. The reviewers can read the drafts carefully and come to the review session with critiques already in mind. When two students work together to share observations about a draft, they often produce more useful and insightful reviews than when working alone.

Out-of-Class Peer Reviews

A variation on the advice-centered approach can be used for out-of-class reviews.

1. The instructor divides the class into pairs; each pair exchanges drafts with another pair.
2. Each pair meets outside class to write its collaborative review based on the Guidelines for Peer Reviewers. Then pairs exchange their reviews the next day in class.

This method allows reviewers to spend as long as they need on their reviews without feeling rushed by in-class time constraints.

Responding to Peer Reviews

After you and your classmates have gone over each others' papers and walked each other through the responses, everyone should identify two or three things about his or her draft that particularly need work. Before you leave the session, you should have some notion about how you want to revise your paper.

You may get mixed or contradictory responses from different reviewers. One reviewer may praise a passage that another finds confusing or illogical. Conflicting advice is a frustrating fact of life for all writers, whether students or professionals. Such disagreements reveal how readers cocreate a text with a writer: each brings to the text a different background, set of values, and way of reading.

It is important to remember that you are in charge of your own writing. If several readers offer the same critique of a passage, then no matter how much you love that passage, you probably need to follow their advice. But when readers disagree, you have to make your own best judgment about whom to heed. In our own writing—including the writing of this text—we tend to follow the advice that is presented to us most fully and rationally. We value most a well-explained sense of the reader's difficulty, an explanation of what causes the problem, and a specific suggestion about how to solve it.

Once you have received advice from others, sit down alone and reread your draft again slowly, "re-visioning" it in light of that feedback. Note especially how different readers responded to different sections of the draft. Then, based on your own responses as well as theirs, develop a revision plan, allowing yourself time to make sweeping, global changes if needed. You also need to remember that you can never make your draft perfect. Plan when you will bring the process to a close so that you can turn in a finished product on time and get on with your other classes and your life (see our advice on *satisficing* on pp. 1948–95).

◢ CHAPTER SUMMARY

This chapter has focused on the writing processes of experts, showing how experienced writers use multiple drafts to solve subject matter and rhetorical problems. We have also offered advice on how to improve your own writing processes. Particularly, beginning college writers need to understand the kinds of changes writers typically make in drafts, to role-play a reader's perspective when they revise, and to practice the revision strategies of experts. Because peer reviewing is a powerful strategy for learning how to revise, we showed you how to make "readerly" rather than "writerly" comments on a rough draft and how to participate productively in peer review workshops.

TOPIC Guidepost #15

For those using Texas Tech's TOPIC Web-Based assignments:

Direct your web browser to **http://english.ttu.edu:5555**

Guidepost #15 provides full instructions regarding your reading assignment (Chapter 12) and your Interactive Tree Diagram.

Nine Lessons in Composing and Revising Closed-Form Prose

> [Form is] an arousing and fulfillment of desires. A work has form insofar as one part of it leads a reader to anticipate another part, to be gratified by the sequence.
>
> —Kenneth Burke, *Rhetorician*

> I think the writer ought to help the reader as much as he can without damaging what he wants to say; and I don't think it ever hurts the writer to sort of stand back now and then and look at his stuff as if he were reading it instead of writing it.
>
> —James Jones, *Writer*

Chapter 10 explained the composing processes of experienced writers and suggested ways that you could improve your own writing processes. In this chapter we present nine lessons in composing and revising closed-form prose. This chapter is not intended to be read in one sitting, lest you suffer from information overload. To help you cover the material efficiently, we have made each lesson a self-contained unit that can be read comfortably in a half-hour or less and discussed in class as part of a day's session. You will benefit most from these lessons if you return to them periodically as you progress through the term because their advice becomes increasingly meaningful and relevant as you gain experience as a writer.

The first lesson—on reader expectations—is intended as an overview to the rest of the chapter. The remaining eight lessons can then be assigned and read in any order your instructor desires. You will learn how to think like a reader (Lesson 1); how to convert loose structures into thesis/support structures (Lesson 2); how to use expert strategies for planning and developing your argument (Lessons 3 and 4); how to use point sentences, transitions, and other strategies to guide your readers through the twists and turns of your prose (Lessons 5, 6, and 7); and how to write effective introductions and conclusions (Lessons 8 and 9). Together the lessons will teach you strategies for making your closed-form prose friendly to readers, well structured, clear, and persuasive.

◪ LESSON 1: UNDERSTANDING READER EXPECTATIONS

In this opening lesson, we show you how to think like a reader. Imagine for a moment that your readers have only so much *reader energy*, which they can use either to follow and respond to your ideas (the result you want) or to puzzle over what you are trying to say (the result you don't want).* Skilled readers make predictions about where a text is heading based on clues provided by the writer. When readers get lost, the writer has often failed to give clues about where the text is going or has failed to do what the reader predicted. "Whoa, you lost me on the turn," a reader might say. "How does this passage relate to what you just said?" To write effective closed-form prose, you need to help readers see how each part of your text is related to what came before. (Sometimes with open-form prose, surprise or puzzlement may be the very effect you want to create. But with closed-form prose this kind of puzzlement is fatal.)

In this lesson we explain what readers of closed form prose need in order to predict where a text is heading. Specifically we will show you that readers need three things in a closed-form text:

- They need unity and coherence.
- They need old information before new information.
- They need forecasting and fulfillment.

Let's look at each in turn.

Unity and Coherence

Together the terms *unity* and *coherence* are defining characteristics of closed-form prose. *Unity* refers to the relationship between each part of an essay and the larger whole. *Coherence* refers to the relationship between adjacent sentences, paragraphs, and parts. The following thought exercise will illustrate your own expectations for unity and coherence:

Thought Exercise 1

Read the following two passages and try to explain why each fails to satisfy your expectations as a reader:

A. Recent research has given us much deeper—and more surprising—insights into the father's role in childrearing. My family is typical of the east side in that we never had much money. Their tongues became black and hung out of their

---

*For the useful term *reader energy*, we are indebted to "The Science of Scientific Writing" by George Gopen and Judith Swan, *American Scientist* 78 (1990): 550–559. In addition, much of our discussion of writing in this chapter is indebted to the work of Joseph Williams, George Gopen, and Gregory Colomb. See especially Gregory G. Colomb and Joseph M. Williams, "Perceiving Structure in Professional Prose: A Multiply Determined Experience," in *Writing in Nonacademic Settings*, eds. Lee Odell and Dixie Goswamie (New York: The Guilford Press, 1985), pp. 87–128.

mouths. The back-to-basics movement got a lot of press, fueled as it was by fears of growing illiteracy and cultural demise.

B. Recent research has given us much deeper—and more surprising—insights into the father's role in childrearing. Childrearing is a complex process that is frequently investigated by psychologists. Psychologists have also investigated sleep patterns and dreams. When we are dreaming, psychologists have shown, we are often reviewing recent events in our lives.

If you are like most readers, Passage A comically frustrates your expectations because it is a string of random sentences. Because the sentences don't relate either to each other or to a larger point, Passage A is neither unified nor coherent.

Passage B frustrates expectations in a subtler way. If you aren't paying attention, Passage B may seem to make sense because each sentence is linked to the one before it. But the individual sentences don't develop a larger whole; the topics keep switching from a father's role in childrearing to psychology to sleep patterns to the function of dreams.

To fill a reader's expectations, then, a closed-form passage must be both unified and coherent:

C *(Unified and coherent)*. Recent research has given us much deeper—and more surprising—insights into the father's role in childrearing. It shows that in almost all of their interactions with children, fathers do things a little differently from mothers. What fathers do—their special parenting style—is not only highly complementary to what mothers do but is by all indications important in its own right. [The passage continues by showing the special ways that fathers contribute to childrearing.]

This passage makes a unified point—that fathers have an important role in childrearing. Because all the parts relate to that whole (unity) and because the connections from sentence to sentence are clear (coherence), the passage satisfies our expectations: It makes sense.

Because achieving unity and coherence is a major goal in revising closed-form prose, we'll refer frequently to these concepts in later lessons.

Old Before New

One dominant way that readers process information and register ideas is by moving from already known (old) information to new information. In a nutshell, this concept means that new material is meaningful to a reader only if it is linked to old material that is already meaningful. To illustrate this concept, consider the arrangement of names and numbers in a telephone directory. Because we read from left to right, we want people's names in the left column and the telephone numbers in the right column. A person's name is the old, familiar information we already know and the number is the new, unknown information that we seek. If the numbers were in the left column and the names in the right, we would have to read backwards.

You can see the same old-before-new principle at work in the following thought exercise:

Thought Exercise 2

You are a passenger on an airplane flight into Chicago and need to transfer to Flight 29 to Atlanta. As you descend into Chicago, the flight attendant announces transfer gates. Which of the following formats is easier for you to process? Why?

Option A				Option B
To Memphis on Flight 16	Gate B20		Gate B20	Flight 16 to Memphis
To Dallas on Flight 35	Gate C25		Gate C25	Flight 35 to Dallas
To Atlanta on Flight 29	Gate C12		Gate C12	Flight 29 to Atlanta

If you are like most readers, you will prefer Option A, which puts old information before new. In this case, the old/known information is our destination and perhaps our flight number (To Atlanta on Flight 29). The new/unknown information is Gate C12. Option B causes us to expend more energy than does Option A because it forces us to hold the number of each gate in memory until we hear its corresponding city and flight number. Whereas Option A allows us to relax until we hear the word "Atlanta," Option B forces us to concentrate intensely on each gate number until we find the meaningful one.

The principle of old before new has great explanatory power for writers. At the level of the whole essay, this principle helps writers establish the main structural frame and ordering principle of their argument. An argument's frame derives from the writer's purpose to change some aspect of the reader's view of the topic (see Chapter 3). The reader's original view of the topic—what we might call the common, expected, or ordinary view—constitutes old/known/familiar material. The writer's surprising view constitutes the new/unknown/unfamiliar material. The writer's hope is to move readers from their original view to the writer's new and different view. By asking what constitutes old/familiar information to readers, the writer can determine how much background to provide, how to anticipate readers' objections, and how to structure material by moving from the old to the new. We discuss these matters in more depth in Lesson 8, on writing effective introductions.

At the sentence level, the principle of old before new also helps writers create coherence between adjacent parts and sentences. Most sentences in an essay should contain both an old element and a new element. To create coherence, the writer begins with the old material, linking back to something earlier, and then puts the new material at the end of the sentence. (See the discussion of the old/new contract in Lesson 7.)

Forecasting and Fulfillment

Finally, readers of closed-form prose expect writers to forecast what is coming and then to fulfill those forecasts. To appreciate what we mean by forecasting and fulfillment, try one more thought exercise:

Thought Exercise 3

Although the following paragraph describes a simple procedure in easy-to-follow sentences, most readers still scratch their heads in bewilderment. Why? What makes the passage difficult to understand?

> The procedure is actually quite simple. First, you arrange things into different groups. Of course, one pile may be sufficient depending on how much there is to do. If you have to go somewhere else due to lack of facilities, that is the next step; otherwise, you are pretty well set. Next you operate the machines according to the instructions. After the procedure is completed, one arranges the materials into different groups again. Then they can be put in their appropriate places. Eventually, they will be used once more and the whole cycle will have to be repeated. However, that is part of life.

Most readers report being puzzled about the paragraph's topic. Because the opening sentence doesn't provide enough context to tell them what to expect, the paragraph makes no forecasts that can be fulfilled. Now try rereading the paragraph, but this time substitute the following opening sentence:

> The procedure for washing clothes is actually quite simple.

With the addition of "for washing clothes," the sentence provides a context that allows you to predict and understand what's coming. In the language of cognitive psychologists, this new opening sentence provides a schema for interpretation. A *schema* is the reader's mental picture of a structure for upcoming material. The new opening sentence allows you as reader to say mentally, "This paragraph will describe a procedure for washing clothes and argue that it is simple." When the schema proves accurate, you experience the pleasure of prediction and fulfillment. In the language of rhetorician Kenneth Burke, the reader's experience of form is "an arousing and fulfillment of desire."

What readers expect from a closed-form text, then, is an ability to predict what is coming and regular fulfillment of those predictions. Writers forecast what is coming in a variety of ways: through titles and thesis statements; through point sentences at the heads of sections and paragraphs; through transitions and mapping passages; and so forth. To meet their readers' needs for predictions and fulfillment, closed-form writers start and end with the big picture. They tell readers where they are going before they start the journey, they refer to this big picture at key transition points, and they refocus on the big picture in their conclusion.

Summary

In this lesson we explained that to think like a reader you need to understand a reader's needs and expectations. The three needs we explained—unity and coherence, old before new, and forecasting and fulfillment—all work together when a reader construes meaning from a text. Your knowledge of these expectations will give you a theoretical basis for understanding the practical advice in the lessons that follow.

◪ LESSON 2: CONVERTING LOOSE STRUCTURES INTO THESIS/SUPPORT STRUCTURES

In Lesson 1 we described readers' expectations for unity and coherence, old information before new, and forecasting and fulfillment. In academic contexts, readers also expect closed-form prose to have a thesis/support structure. As we explained in Chapter 3, closed-form academic writing is governed by a thesis statement, which needs to be contestable and surprising. Because developing and supporting a risky thesis is complex work, requiring much critical thought, writers sometimes retreat into loose structures that are easier to compose than a thesis-based argument with points and particulars.

In this lesson we help you better understand thesis-based writing by contrasting it with prose that looks like thesis-based writing but isn't. We show you three common ways in which inexperienced writers give the appearance of writing thesis-based prose while actually retreating from the rigors of making and developing an argument. Avoiding the pitfalls of these loose structures can go a long way toward improving your performance on most college writing assignments.

And Then Writing, or Chronological Structure

Chronological structure, often called *narrative*, is the most common organizing principle of open-form prose. It may also be used selectively in closed-form prose to support a point. But sometimes the writer begins recounting the details of a story until chronological order takes over, driving out the thesis-based structure of points and particulars.

To a large degree, chronological order is the default mode we fall into when we aren't sure how to organize material. For example, if you were asked to analyze a fictional character, you might slip into a plot summary instead. In much the same way, you might substitute historical chronology ("First A happened, then B happened . . .") for historical analysis ("B happened because A happened . . ."); or you might give a chronological recounting of your research ("First I discovered A, then I discovered B . . .") instead of organizing your material into an argument ("I question A's account of this phenomenon on the grounds of B's recent findings . . .").

The tendency toward loose chronological structure is revealed in the following example from a student's essay on Shakespeare's *The Tempest*. This excerpt is from the introduction of the student's first draft:

Plot Summary—*And Then* Writing

Prospero cares deeply for his daughter. In the middle of the play Prospero acts like a gruff father and makes Ferdinand carry logs in order to test his love for Miranda and Miranda's love for him. In the end, though, Prospero is a loving father who rejoices in his daughter's marriage to a good man.

Here the student seems simply to retell the play's plot without any apparent thesis. (The body of her rough draft primarily retold the same story in more detail.) However, during an office conference, the instructor discovered that the student regarded her sentence about Prospero's being a loving father as her thesis. In fact, the student had gotten in an argument with a classmate over whether Prospero was a good person or an evil one. The instructor helped her convert her draft into a thesis/support structure:

Revised Introduction—Thesis/Support Structure

Many persons believe that Prospero is an evil person in the play. They claim that Prospero exhibits a harsh, destructive control over Miranda and also, like Faust, seeks superhuman knowledge through his magic. However, I contend that Prospero is a kind and loving father.

This revised version implies a problem (What kind of father is Prospero?), imagines a view that the writer wishes to change (Prospero is harsh and hateful), and asserts a contestable thesis (Prospero is a loving father). The body of her paper can now be converted from plot summary to an argument with reasons and evidence supporting her claim that Prospero is loving.

This student's revision from an *and then* to a thesis/support structure is typical of many writers' experience. Because recounting events chronologically is a natural way to organize, many writers—even very experienced ones—lapse into long stretches of *and then* writing in their rough drafts. In fact, researchers have shown that chronological thinking is a normal strategy for retrieving ideas and details from the writer's long-term memory. But experienced writers have learned to recognize these *and then* sections in their drafts and to rework this material into a closed-form, thesis-based structure.

All About Writing, or Encyclopedic Structure

Whereas *and then* writing turns essays into stories by organizing details chronologically, *all about* writing turns essays into encyclopedia articles by piling up details in heaps. When *all about* writing organizes these heaps into categories, it can appear to be well organized: "Having told you everything I learned about educational opportunities in Cleveland, I will now tell you everything I learned about the Rock and Roll Hall of Fame." But the categories do not function as points and particulars in support of a thesis. Rather, like the shelving system in a library, they are simply ways of arranging information for convenient retrieval, not a means of building a hierarchical structure.

If you've ever paraphrased an encyclopedia for a report on "earthquakes" or "North Dakota," you'll know what we mean by *all about* writing. Because such reports don't require a contestable thesis, they invite you simply to crank out information.

To illustrate the differences between *all about* writing and thesis-based writing, consider the case of two students asked to write term papers on the subject of, for example, female police officers. One student is asked simply to write "all about" the topic; the other is asked to pose and investigate some problem related to female police officers and to support a thesis addressing that problem. In all likelihood, the first student would produce an initial outline with headings such as the following:

I. History of women in police roles
   A. female police or soldiers in ancient times

    B. 19th century (Calamity Jane)
    C. 1900s–1960
    D. 1960–present
  II. How female police officers are selected and trained
 III. A typical day in the life of a female police officer
 IV. Achievements and acts of heroism of female police officers
  V. What the future holds for female police officers

Such a paper is a data dump that places into categories all the information the writer has uncovered. It is riskless, and, except for occasional new information, surpriseless. In contrast, when a student focuses on a significant question—one that grows out of the writer's own interests and demands engagement—the writing can be quite compelling.

    Consider the case of a student, Lynnea, who wrote a research paper entitled "Women Police Officers: Should Size and Strength Be Criteria for Patrol Duty?" Her essay begins with a group of male police officers complaining about being assigned to patrol duty with a new female officer, Connie Jones (not her real name), who is four feet ten inches tall and weighs ninety pounds. Here is the rest of the introduction to Lynnea's essay.

> Connie Jones has just completed police academy training and has been assigned to patrol duty in _____. Because she is so small, she has to have a booster seat in her patrol car and has been given a special gun, since she can barely manage to pull the trigger of a standard police-issue .38 revolver. Although she passed the physical requirements at the academy, which involved speed and endurance running, situps, and monkey bar tests, most of the officers in her department doubt her ability to perform competently as a patrol officer. But nevertheless she is on patrol because men and women receive equal assignments in most of today's police forces. But is this a good policy? Can a person who is significantly smaller and weaker than her peers make an effective patrol officer?

Lynnea examined all the evidence she could find—through library and field research (interviewing police officers) and arrived at the following thesis: "Because concern for public safety overrides all other concerns, police departments should set stringent size and strength requirements for patrol officers, even if these criteria exclude many women." This thesis has plenty of tension because it sets limits on equal rights for women. Because Lynnea considers herself a feminist, it caused her considerable distress to advocate setting these limits and placing public safety ahead of gender equity. The resulting essay is engaging precisely because of the tension it creates and the controversy it engenders.

Engfish Writing, or Structure Without Surprise

Unlike the chronological story and the *all about* paper, the *engfish* essay has a thesis.* But the thesis is a riskless truism supported with predictable reasons—

---

*The term *engfish* was coined by the textbook writer Ken Macrorie to describe a fishy kind of canned prose that bright but bored students mechanically produce to please their writing teachers. See *Telling Writing* (Rochelle Park, NJ: Hayden Press, 1970).

often structured as three supports in a traditional five-paragraph theme. It is fill-in-the-blanks writing: "The food service is bad for three reasons. First, it is bad because the food is not tasty. Blah, blah, blah about tasteless food. Second, it is bad because it is too expensive. Blah, blah, blah about the expense." And so on. The writer is on autopilot and is not contributing to a real conversation about a real question. In some situations, writers use engfish intentionally: bureaucrats and politicians may want to avoid saying something risky; students may want to avoid writing about complex matters that they fear they do not fully understand. In the end, using engfish is bad not because what you say is *wrong;* it's because what you say couldn't *possibly be* wrong. To avoid engfish, stay focused on the need to surprise your reader.

Summary

This lesson has explained strategies for converting *and then, all about,* and engfish writing into thesis/support writing. Your goal as a closed-form academic writer is to pose a problematic question about your topic and, in response to it, assert a contestable thesis that you must support with points and particulars.

FOR WRITING AND DISCUSSION

As a class, choose a topic from popular culture such as TV talk shows, tattooing, eating disorders, rock lyrics, or something similar.

1. Working as a whole class or in small groups, give examples of how you might write about this topic in an *and then* way, an *all about* way, and an engfish way.
2. Then develop one or more questions about the topic that could lead to thesis/support writing. What contestable theses can your class create?

◢ LESSON 3: PLANNING AND VISUALIZING YOUR STRUCTURE

We have explained so far how closed-form writing supports a contestable thesis through a hierarchical network of points and particulars. One way to visualize this structure is to outline its skeleton, as we did in Chapter 3 for an argument about a hypothetical college administration that did not care for its students (see p. 46). As the outline makes visually clear, not all points are on equal levels. The highest level point is an essay's thesis statement, which is usually supported by several main points that are in turn supported by subpoints and subsubpoints, all of which are supported by their own particulars. In this lesson we want to show you how to create such a hierarchical structure for your own papers and how to visualize this structure through an outline, tree diagram, or flow chart.

At the outset, we want to highlight two important points. First, think of your structural diagrams as flexible planning devices that evolve as your thinking shifts and changes. The outline of your final draft may be substantially different from your initial and intermediate structural sketches. In fact, we want to show you how to use your outlines or diagrams to help you generate more ideas and reshape your structure.

Second, note that in all our examples of outlines, diagrams, and flowcharts we write *complete sentences* in the high-level slots. We do so because the writer's task is to organize *meanings* rather than topics. Any point—whether a thesis, a main point, or a subpoint—is a contestable assertion that requires its own particulars for support. By using complete sentences rather than topic phrases, the writer is forced to articulate the point of each section of the emerging argument. (We'll have more to say on the value of sentences over phrases later in this lesson.)

With this background, we now proceed to a sequence of stages you can use to plan and visualize a structure.

Articulate the Change You Want to Make in Your Audience's View of Your Subject

Through exploratory writing and talking, you begin to see how your view of a subject differs from that of your imagined audience. You are then ready to plan out the outer frame or "big picture" of your argument. As a planning strategy, we suggest that you write out answers to the following prompts:

1. Before reading my paper, my readers will think this about (my topic):
2. But after reading my paper, my readers will think this about (my topic):
3. The purpose of my paper is: [finish this sentence]
4. The question my paper addresses is:

Here is how one student, Dao (whose Vietnamese heritage will become relevant in later lessons), answered these questions:

1. Before reading my paper my readers will believe that euthanasia is often justified, particularly if someone is elderly and suffering and has no good quality of life.
2. But after reading my paper my readers will believe that euthanasia is wrong.
3. The purpose of my paper is to show that euthanasia cannot be justified.
4. Is euthanasia right or wrong?

Articulate a Working Thesis and Main Points

Once you have articulated your purpose and the kind of change you want to bring about in your audience, you are ready to compose a working thesis statement and develop your main supporting points. This isn't a neatly linear process; often you have to write one or more rough drafts aimed primarily at exploring ideas before you are finally clear about your thesis. But once you have a thesis, you need to visualize a structure of supporting ideas arranged in sections (steps, stages, pieces, paragraphs, parts), each of which is headed by a main point. Try answering these questions:

4. *My working thesis (claim) is:*
5. *My main supporting points are:*

Here are Dao's answers to these questions:

4. Despite my classmate Martha's arguments for legalizing euthanasia, it is wrong.
5. (a) It primarily benefits survivors; (b) it has bad consequences; (c) it doesn't recognize the good aspects of suffering.

Sketch Your Structure Using an Outline, Tree Diagram, or Flowchart

At this point you can make an initial structural sketch of your argument and use the sketch to plan out the subpoints and particulars that will be necessary to support the main points. We offer you three different ways to visualize your argument: outlines, tree diagrams, and flowcharts. Use whichever strategy best fits your way of thinking and perceiving.

Outlines

The most common way of visualizing structure is the traditional outline, which uses letters and numerals to indicate levels of points, subpoints, and particulars. If you prefer outlines, we recommend that you use the outliner feature of a modern word processing program, which allows you to move and insert material and change heading levels with great flexibility. Here is an outline of Dao's argument:

Thesis: Despite Martha's strong argument for legalizing euthanasia, euthanasia is wrong for several reasons.

I. First, I object to euthanasia because it benefits survivors more than the sick person.
   A. Pain can be controlled by modern drugs so sick people don't have to suffer.
   B. Euthanasia most benefits survivors because it saves them worry and money.
II. Second, I oppose euthanasia because of its unfavorable consequences.
   A. Euthanasia would tempt people to murder for inheritance.
   B. Euthanasia would lead to discrimination against those with "unpopular diseases," such as AIDS.
III. Third, I oppose euthanasia because it fails to see the value in suffering (supported by example of my grandmother's caring for my crippled uncle in Vietnam).

Tree Diagrams

A tree diagram displays a hierarchical structure visually, using horizontal and vertical space instead of letters and numbers. Figure 11.1 shows Dao's argument as a tree diagram. Her introduction is at the top of the tree, above the thesis. Her main reasons, written as point sentences, appear as branches beneath her claim. Supporting evidence and arguments are displayed as subbranches beneath each reason.

Unlike outlines, tree diagrams allow us to *see* the hierarchical relationship of points and particulars. When you develop a point with subpoints or particulars, you move down the tree. When you switch to a new point, you move across the tree to make a new branch. Our own teaching experience suggests that for many writers this visual/spatial technique, which engages more areas of the brain than the more purely verbal outline, produces fuller, more detailed, and more logical arguments than does a traditional outline.

Flowcharts

Many writers prefer an informal, hand-sketched flowchart as an alternative to an outline or tree diagram. The flowchart sketches out the sequence of sections as separate boxes, inside which (or next to which) the writer notes the material needed to fill each box. A flowchart of Dao's essay is shown in Figure 11.2.

FIGURE 11.1   Dao's Tree Diagram

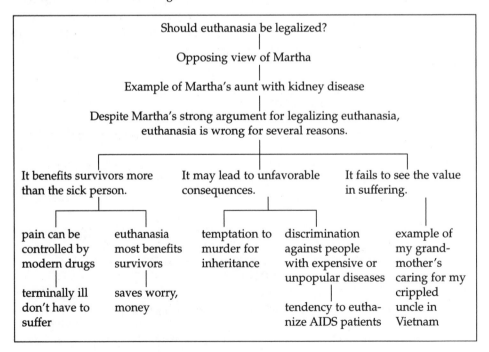

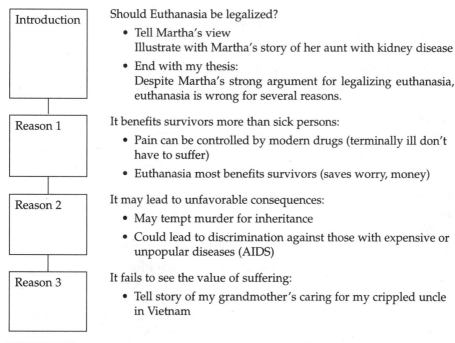

| Introduction | Should Euthanasia be legalized?
| | • Tell Martha's view
| | Illustrate with Martha's story of her aunt with kidney disease
| | • End with my thesis:
| | Despite Martha's strong argument for legalizing euthanasia, euthanasia is wrong for several reasons.

Introduction

Should Euthanasia be legalized?
- Tell Martha's view
  Illustrate with Martha's story of her aunt with kidney disease
- End with my thesis:
  Despite Martha's strong argument for legalizing euthanasia, euthanasia is wrong for several reasons.

Reason 1

It benefits survivors more than sick persons:
- Pain can be controlled by modern drugs (terminally ill don't have to suffer)
- Euthanasia most benefits survivors (saves worry, money)

Reason 2

It may lead to unfavorable consequences:
- May tempt murder for inheritance
- Could lead to discrimination against those with expensive or unpopular diseases (AIDS)

Reason 3

It fails to see the value of suffering:
- Tell story of my grandmother's caring for my crippled uncle in Vietnam

FIGURE 11.2   Dao's Flowchart

Let the Structure Evolve

Once you have sketched out an initial structural diagram, use it to generate ideas. Tree diagrams are particularly helpful because they invite you to place question marks on branches to "hold open" spots for new points or for supporting particulars. If you have only two main points, for example, you could draw a third main branch and place a question mark under it to encourage you to think of another supporting idea. Likewise, if a branch has few supporting particulars, add question marks beneath it. The trick is to think of your structural diagrams as evolving artist's sketches rather than rigid blueprints. As your ideas grow and change, revise your structural diagram, adding or removing points, consolidating and refocusing sections, moving parts around, or filling in details.

Articulate Points, Not Topics

As we noted at the start of this lesson, we recommend complete sentences rather than topic phrases at the higher levels of a structural diagram. You can see why we make this recommendation if you compare the tree diagram in Figure 11.1 (p. 214) with the phrase-only version in Figure 11.3.

Phrases identify topics, but they don't create meanings. Sentences combine topic-identifying subjects with assertion-making predicates. The *meaning* arises from the assertion-making predicate, as in the following examples:

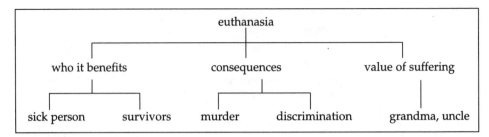

FIGURE 11.3   Dao's Phrase-Only Tree Diagram

Name Something	Make an Assertion About It
Fat	is an essential dietary ingredient without which we would die.
Justice	is hard to get if you are poor or black.
Television	may cause some children to act violently.

Because topic phrases don't have predicates, they don't have clear meanings. If you already know what you intend to say, a phrase-only tree or outline can be useful as a shorthand way to jog your memory. But if you are trying to discover and create meanings, writing out complete sentences for main points and subpoints makes a tree diagram or an outline a far more powerful tool.

Summary

This lesson has shown you the value of framing your argument by articulating the change you are trying to bring about in your reader and then by identifying your purpose, your thesis, and your main supporting points. You can then use outlines, tree diagrams, or flowcharts to help you visualize your structure and use it to develop new ideas.

FOR WRITING AND DISCUSSION

1. Working individually or in small groups, make a traditional outline, a tree diagram, and a flowchart of David Rockwood's argument against wind-generated electricity on pages 10–11. Which method of representing structure works best for you?
2. Working individually or in groups, make a tree diagram with place-holding question marks to guide a next draft for the carpets essay on pages 197–98.

▨ LESSON 4: LEARNING FOUR EXPERT MOVES FOR ORGANIZING AND DEVELOPING IDEAS

In this lesson we show you that writers of closed-form prose often employ a conventional set of moves to organize parts of an essay. In using the term *moves,* we are making an analogy with the "set moves" or "set plays" in such sports as basketball, volleyball, and soccer. For example, a common set move in basketball is the "pick," in which an offensive player without the ball stands motionless in order to block the path of a defensive player who is guarding the dribbler. Similarly, certain organizational patterns in writing occur frequently enough to act as set plays for writers. These patterns set up expectations in the reader's mind about the shape of an upcoming stretch of prose, anything from a few sentences to a paragraph to a large block of paragraphs. As you will see, these moves also stimulate the invention of ideas. Next, we describe four of the most powerful set plays.*

The For Example Move

Perhaps the most common set play occurs when a writer makes an assertion and then illustrates it with one or more examples, often signaling the move explicitly with transitions such as *for example, for instance,* or *a case in point is. . . .* Once the move starts, readers can anticipate how it will unfold, just as experienced basketball fans can anticipate a pick as soon as they see a dribbler swerve toward a stationary teammate. You can probably sense this move unfolding now as you wait for us to give an example of the *for example move.* We have aroused an expectation; now we will fulfill it.

A good example of the for example move occurs in the paragraph Dao wrote to support her third reason for opposing euthanasia (see Figure 11.1, p. 216, for the tree diagram of Dao's essay).

For Example Move

My third objection to euthanasia is that it fails to see the value in suffering. *— Point sentence*
Suffering is a part of life. We only see the value of suffering if we look deeply within our suffering. <u>For example</u>, I never thought my crippled uncle from Viet-nam was a blessing to my grandmother until I talked to her. My mother's little *— Transition signaling the move*
brother was born prematurely. As a result of oxygen and nutrition deficiency, he was born crippled. His tiny arms and legs were twisted around his body, preventing him from any normal movements such as walking, picking up things, and lying down. He could only sit. Therefore, his world was very limited, for it consisted of his own room and the garden viewed through his window. Because of his disabilities, my grandmother had to wash him, feed him, and watch him constantly. It was hard, but she managed to care for him for forty-three years. He *— Extended example supporting point*
passed away after the death of my grandfather in 1982. Bringing this situation out of Vietnam and into Western society shows the difference between Viet-namese and Western views. In the West, my uncle might have been euthanized as a baby. Supporters of euthanasia would have said he wouldn't have any quality of life and that he would have been a great burden. But he was not a burden on my grandmother. She enjoyed taking care of him, and he was always her company after her other children got married and moved away. Neither one of them saw his defect as meaningless suffering because it brought them closer together.

---

*You might find it helpful to follow the set plays we used to write this section. This last sentence is the opening move of a play we call *division into parts*. It sets up the expectation that we will develop four set plays in order. Watch for the way we chunk them and signal transitions between them.

This passage uses a single, extended example to support a point. You could also use several shorter examples or other kinds of illustrating evidence, such as facts or statistics. In all cases the for example move creates a pattern of expectation and fulfillment. This pattern drives the invention of ideas in one of two ways: it urges the writer either to find examples to develop a generalization or to formulate a generalization that shows the point of an example.

FOR WRITING AND DISCUSSION

Working individually or in groups, develop a plan for supporting one or more of the following generalizations using the for example move.

1. Another objection to state sales taxes is that they are so annoying.
2. Although assertiveness training has definite benefits, it can sometimes get you into real trouble.
3. People say large cars are generally safer than small ones, but that is not always the case.
4. Sometimes effective leaders are indecisive.
5. Sometimes writing multiple drafts can make your essay worse rather than better.

The Summary/However Move

This move occurs whenever a writer sums up another person's viewpoint in order to qualify or contradict it or to introduce an opposing view. Typically, writers use transition words such as *but, however, in contrast,* or *on the other hand* between the parts of this move. This move is particularly common in academic writing, which often contrasts the writer's new view with prevailing views. Here is how Dao uses a *summary/however move* in the introduction of her essay opposing euthanasia.

Summary/However Move

Issue over which there is disagreement

Summary of opposing viewpoint

Transition to writer's viewpoint

Statement of writer's view

Should euthanasia be legalized? My classmate Martha and her family think it should be. Martha's aunt was blind from diabetes. For three years she was constantly in and out of the hospital, but then her kidneys shut down and she became a victim of life supports. After three months of suffering, she finally gave up. Martha believes this three-month period was unnecessary, for her aunt didn't have to go through all of that suffering. If euthanasia were legalized, her family would have put her to sleep the minute her condition worsened. Then, she wouldn't have had to feel pain, and she would have died in peace and with dignity. However, despite Martha's strong argument for legalizing euthanasia, I find it wrong.

The first sentence of this introduction poses the question that the essay addresses. The main body of the paragraph summarizes Martha's opposing view on euthanasia, and the final sentence, introduced by the transition "however," presents Dao's thesis.

FOR WRITING AND DISCUSSION

For this exercise, assume that you favor development of wind-generated electricity. Use the summary/however move to acknowledge the view of civil engineer David Rockwood, whose letter opposing wind-generated electricity you read in Chapter 1 (pp. 12–13). Assume that you are writing the opening paragraph of your own essay. Follow the pattern of Dao's introduction: (a) begin with a one-sentence issue or question; (b) summarize Rockwood's view in approximately one hundred words; and (c) state your own view, using *however* or *in contrast* as a transition. Write out your paragraph on your own, or work in groups to write a consensus paragraph. Then share and critique your paragraphs.

The Division-into-Parallel-Parts Move

Among the most frequently encountered and powerful of the set plays is the *division-into-parallel-parts move*. To initiate the move, a writer begins with an umbrella sentence that forecasts the structure and creates a frame. (For example, "Freud's theory differs from Jung's in three essential ways" or "The decline of the U.S. space program can be attributed to several factors.") Typical overview sentences either specify the number of parts that will follow by using phrases such as "two ways," "three differences," "five kinds," or they leave the number unspecified, using words such as *several, a few,* or *many*. Alternatively, the writer may ask a rhetorical question that implies the frame: "What are some main differences, then, between Freud's theory and Jung's? One difference is. . . ."

To signal transitions from one part to the next, writers use two kinds of signposts: transition words or bullets and parallel grammatical structure.* The first kind of signpost can use transition words to introduce each of the parallel parts.

first . . . , second . . . , third . . . , finally. . . .

first . . . , another . . . , still another . . . , finally. . . .

to begin . . . , likewise . . . , in addition . . . , lastly. . . .

either . . . or. . . .

one . . . , in addition . . . , furthermore . . . , also. . . .

Or, instead of transition words, writers can also use a series of bullets followed by indented text.

The Wolf Recovery Program is strictly opposed by a large and vociferous group of ranchers who pose numerous objections to increasing wolf populations.

- They perceive wolves as a threat to livestock.
- They fear the wolves will attack humans.
- etc.

---

*Note how this sentence itself initiates a division-into-parallel-parts move.

The second kind of signpost uses the same grammatical structure to begin each parallel part, creating a parallel, echolike effect.

> I learned several things from this class. First, *I learned that.* . . . Second, *I learned that.* . . . Finally, *I learned that.* . . .

A typical version of this move is embedded in the following single paragraph taken from a long professional essay. The author is discussing the impact of an article in which psychologist George Miller shows that a person's short-term memory capacity is "seven plus or minus two" pieces of information.* This paragraph uses a rhetorical question as the umbrella sentence that initiates the move.

> Why did this apparently simple point have a decidedly major impact within [cognitive psychology]? First, Miller's essay brought together a large amount of hitherto dispersed data and suggested that they pointed to a common conclusion. Second, it suggested that the number 7 was no mere accident: it designated genuine limitations in human information-processing capacities. . . . Third, as indicated, the message in the paper was not without hope, for Miller indicated ways by which humans ingeniously transcend this limitation.
>
> —Howard Gardner, *The Mind's New Science: A History of the Cognitive Revolution*

Using the Parallel-Parts Move on a Large Scale

The division-into-parallel-parts move is also frequently used to control larger stretches of text in which a dozen or more paragraphs may work together to complete a parallel series of parts. For example, you are currently in part three of a stretch of text introduced by the mapping sentence on page 451: "Next we describe four of the most powerful set plays." In fact, the division-into-parallel-parts move often forms the major organizational strategy of the whole essay. Here are some examples of common situations in which writers use this move on a large scale.

Classification.   When writers want to divide a concept into various categories—a thinking process often called *classification*—they regularly devote a major piece of the essay to each of the classes or categories.

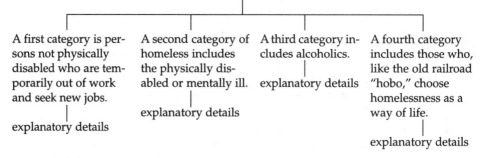

*We demonstrated the significance of Miller's article for writers in the discussion of why writers revise in Chapter 10.

Exemplification. A process sometimes called *exemplification* or *illustration* occurs when a writer illustrates a point with several extended examples.

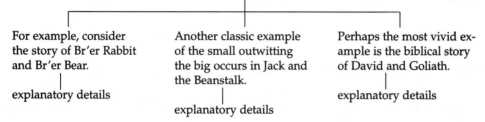

Many of our stories and legends depict cunning little guys outwitting dull-brained big guys.

For example, consider the story of Br'er Rabbit and Br'er Bear.

explanatory details

Another classic example of the small outwitting the big occurs in Jack and the Beanstalk.

explanatory details

Perhaps the most vivid example is the biblical story of David and Goliath.

explanatory details

Causal Analysis. Writing that analyzes causes of a phenomenon is also often organized into parallel parts, with each part developing a single cause.

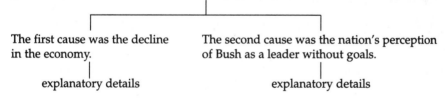

Despite George Bush's enormous popularity following the Gulf War, he nevertheless lost the presidency to Bill Clinton. His decline in popularity can be attributed to two causes.

The first cause was the decline in the economy.

explanatory details

The second cause was the nation's perception of Bush as a leader without goals.

explanatory details

Process Analysis. Writers often explain a process by dividing it into a number of separate stages or steps.

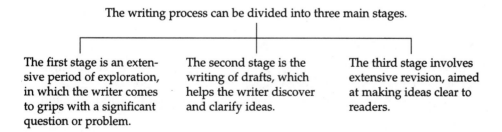

The writing process can be divided into three main stages.

The first stage is an extensive period of exploration, in which the writer comes to grips with a significant question or problem.

The second stage is the writing of drafts, which helps the writer discover and clarify ideas.

The third stage involves extensive revision, aimed at making ideas clear to readers.

Argumentation. When writers of arguments offer two or more parallel reasons for adhering to a particular view or course of action, they typically use the division-into-parallel-parts move. Dao used this large-scale strategy to organize her argument against euthanasia.

Despite Martha's strong argument for legalizing euthanasia,
I find it is wrong for several reasons.

First, euthanasia is wrong because it benefits survivors more than the sick person.	Second, euthanasia is wrong because of its unfavorable consequences.	Third, euthanasia is wrong because it fails to see the value in suffering.

Using the Parallel-Parts Move to Generate Ideas

The division-into-parallel-parts move can serve as a particularly powerful engine for idea generation. When displayed in a tree diagram, the parallel branches created by the move invite you to think of ideas that will fit laterally and vertically into the diagram. For example, in your first draft you might identify two causes of a phenomenon, but in the act of drafting you might think of a third or even a fourth cause. Simultaneously, you might think of more or stronger ways to develop each of the causes. The number of main branches and supporting branches can be expanded or contracted as you think of new ideas or see ways to combine or recombine old ones.

Ordering the Parallel Parts

Whenever you create two or more parallel parts, you must decide which to put first, which to put in the middle, and which to put last. If the parts are of equal weight and interest, or if you are just exploring their significance, the order doesn't much matter. But if the parts are of different importance, significance, or complexity, their order can be rhetorically important. As a general rule, save the best for last. What constitutes "best" depends on the circumstances. In an argument, the best reason is usually the strongest or the one most apt to appeal to the intended audience. In other cases, the best is usually the most unusual, the most surprising, the most thought provoking, or the most complex, in keeping with the general rule that writers proceed from the familiar to the unfamiliar, from the least surprising to the most surprising.

FOR WRITING AND DISCUSSION

Working individually or in small groups, use the division-into-parallel-parts move to create, organize, and develop ideas to support one or more of the following point sentences. Try using a tree diagram to help guide and stimulate your invention.

1. To study for an exam effectively, a student should follow these (specify a number) steps.
2. Why do U.S. schoolchildren lag so far behind European and Asian children on standardized tests of mathematics and science? One possible cause is . . . (continue).

3. There are several ways for an individual to help the homeless without giving money to panhandlers.
4. TV advertisements for male-oriented products, such as beer, razors, and aftershaves, reflect several different kinds of gender stereotypes.
5. Constant dieting is unhealthy for several reasons.

The Comparison/Contrast Move

A common variation on the division-into-parallel-parts move is the *comparison/contrast move.* To compare or contrast two items, you must first decide on the points of comparison (or contrast). If you are contrasting the political views of two presidential candidates, you might choose to focus on four points of comparison: differences in their foreign policy, differences in economic policy, differences in social policy, and differences in judicial philosophy. You then have two choices for organizing the parts: the *side-by-side pattern,* in which you discuss all of candidate A's views and then all of candidate B's views; or the *back-and-forth pattern,* in which you discuss foreign policy, contrasting A's views with B's views, then move on to economic policy, then social policy, and then judicial philosophy. Here is how these two patterns would appear on a tree diagram.

Side-by-side pattern

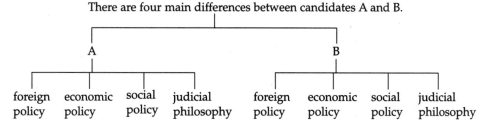

Back-and-forth pattern

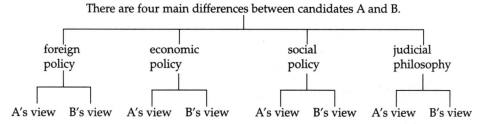

There are no cut-and-dried rules that dictate when to use the side-by-side pattern or the back-and-forth pattern. However, for lengthy comparisons the back-and-forth pattern is often more effective because the reader doesn't have to store great amounts of information in memory. The side-by-side pattern requires readers to remember all the material about A when they come to B, and it is sometimes difficult to keep all the points of comparison clearly in mind.

FOR WRITING AND DISCUSSION

Working individually or in groups, create tree diagrams for possible paragraphs or essays based on one or more of the following point sentences, all of which call for the comparison/contrast move. Make at least one diagram follow the back-and-forth pattern and make at least one diagram follow the side-by-side pattern.

1. There are several significant differences between childbirth as it is practiced by middle-class American women today and childbirth as it was practiced by middle-class American women prior to the women's liberation movement.
2. To understand U.S. politics, an outsider needs to appreciate some basic differences between Republicans and Democrats.
3. Although they are obviously different on the surface, there are many similarities between the Boy Scouts and a street gang.
4. There are several important differences between closed-form and open-form writing.
5. There are significant differences between the classic 1931 film *Frankenstein* and Mary Shelley's original novel by the same title. (You can substitute any other film/novel comparison.)

Summary

In this lesson we have shown you how practicing experts' set moves extends your repertoire of strategies for organizing and developing ideas. In particular, we have explained how to add an example to support a point; how to sum up an alternative view and then switch to your own; how to develop an idea by announcing a series of parallel subparts; and how to compare or contrast two ideas or phenomena. These moves can be used on a large or small scale, wherever appropriate in a paper.

◪ LESSON 5: PLACING POINTS BEFORE PARTICULARS

In our lesson on outlining (Lesson 3), we suggested that you write *point sentences* rather than topic phrases for the high level slots of the outline in order to articulate the *meaning* or *point* of each section of your argument. In this lesson, we show you how to place those point sentences where readers need them: near the front of the sections or paragraphs they govern. When you place points before particulars, you help readers in all three of the important ways we described in Lesson 1. You create unity by relating each new section back to your thesis or next higher point; you forecast what is coming in the section, thereby satisfying your reader's desire for forecasting and fulfillment. And finally, you place old material before new material. The point sentence links back to preceding material but also states the point of what is coming so that keywords in the point sentence can then serve as old information for the rest of the section.

Put Point Sentences at the Beginning of Paragraphs

Although readers expect closed-form paragraphs to open with point sentences (often called *topic sentences*), writers' early drafts often lack them because writers, while drafting, are often unsure of their points and are still searching for them (see Chapter 17 on the writing process). In their rough draft paragraphs, writers often omit point sentences entirely or place them at the end of paragraphs, or they write point sentences that misrepresent what the paragraph actually does or says. In such cases, readers momentarily lose the connection between what they are currently reading and the writer's intended meaning. During revision, then, you should check your body paragraphs carefully to be sure you have placed accurate point sentences near the beginning.

What follows are examples of the kinds of revisions writers typically make. Note how the annotations in the examples that follow identify changes that help the paragraphs become unified and clear to readers. Our first example is from a later draft of the student essay opposing carpeting dorm rooms (Chapter 17, pp. 197–98).

Revision—Point Sentence First

Another reason for the university not to buy carpets is the cost.
According to Rachel Jones, Assistant Director of Housing Services, *Point sentence placed first*

the initial purchase and installation of carpeting would cost $300 per

room. Considering the number of rooms in the three residence halls,

carpeting amounts to a substantial investment. Additionally, once the

carpets are installed, the university would need to maintain them through

the purchase of more vacuum cleaners and shampoo machines. This money

would be better spent on other dorm improvements that would benefit more

residents, such as expanded kitchen facilities and improved recreational

space. ~~Thus carpets would be too expensive.~~

In the original draft, the writer states the point at the end of the paragraph. In his revision he states the point in an opening topic sentence that links back to the thesis statement, which promises "several reasons" that the university should not buy carpets for the dorms. The words "another reason" thus link the topic sentence to the argument's big picture.

Revise Paragraphs for Unity

In addition to placing topic sentences at the heads of paragraphs, writers often need to revise topic sentences to better match what the paragraph actually says, or revise the paragraph to better match the topic sentence. Paragraphs have unity when all of their sentences develop what is forecast in the topic sentence. Paragraphs in rough drafts are often not unified because they reflect the writer's shifting, evolving, thinking-while-writing process. Consider the following paragraph from an early draft of Dao's argument (see Lessons 3 and 4) against euthanasia. Her peer reviewer labeled it "confusing." What makes it confusing?

Early Draft—Confusing

First, euthanasia is wrong because no one has the right to take the life of another person. Some people say that euthanasia or suicide will end suffering and pain. But what proofs do they have for such a claim? Death is still mysterious to us; therefore, we do not know whether death will end suffering and pain or not. What seems to be the real claim is that death to those with illnesses will end *our* pain. Such pain involves worrying over them, paying their medical bills, and giving up so much of our time. Their deaths end our pain rather than theirs. And for that reason, euthanasia is a selfish act, for the outcome of euthanasia benefits us, the nonsufferers, more. Once the sufferers pass away, we can go back to our normal lives.

The paragraph opens with an apparent topic sentence: "Euthanasia is wrong because no one has the right to take the life of another person." But the rest of the paragraph doesn't focus on that point. Instead, it focuses on how euthanasia benefits the survivors more than the sick person. Dao had two choices: to revise the paragraph to fit the topic sentence or to revise the topic sentence to fit the paragraph. Here is her revision, which includes a different topic sentence and an additional sentence mid-paragraph to keep particulars focused on the opening point.

```
                    Revision for Unity
```

First, euthanasia is wrong because it benefits the survivors more than the sick person. ◄——————— *Revised point*
~~First, euthanasia is wrong because no one has the right to take the~~   *sentence better*
     forecasts focus
~~life of another person.~~ Some people say that euthanasia or suicide will   *of paragraph*
  the sick person's ◄——————————————————————
end suffering and pain. But what proofs do they have for such a claim?   *Keeps focus on*
  "sick person"
Death is still mysterious to us; therefore, we do not know whether death
     Moreover, modern pain killers can relieve most of the pain a sick person has to endure. ◄—— *Concludes sub-*
will end suffering and pain or not. What seems to be the real claim is   *point about*
    sick person
that death to those with illnesses will end *our* pain. Such pain involves

worrying over them, paying their medical bills, and giving up so much of   *Makes subpoint*
   about how
our time. Their deaths end our pain rather than theirs. And for that   *euthanasia*
   benefits survivors
reason, euthanasia is a selfish act, for the outcome of euthanasia bene-

fits us, the nonsufferers, more. Once the sufferers pass away, we can go

back to our normal lives.

Dao unifies this paragraph by keeping all its parts focused on her main point: "Euthanasia . . . benefits the survivors more than the sick person." You may not be persuaded by her argument, but at least her point is now clear.

A paragraph may lack unity for a variety of reasons. It may shift to a new direction in the middle, or one or two sentences may simply be irrelevant to the point. The key is to make sure that all the sentences in the paragraph fulfill the reader's expectations based on the point sentence.

Add Particulars to Support Points

Just as writers of rough drafts often omit point sentences from paragraphs, they sometimes leave out the particulars needed to support a point. In such cases, the writer needs to make a *for example move* (see Lesson 4) or add other kinds of particulars such as facts, statistics, quotations, research summaries, or further subpoints. Consider how adding additional particulars to the following draft paragraph strengthens the student's argument.

Draft Paragraph: Particulars Missing

One reason that it is not necessary to log old-growth forests is that the timber industry can supply the world's lumber needs without doing so. For example, we have plenty of new-growth forest from which timber can be taken (Sagoff 89). We could also reduce the amount of trees used for paper products by using other materials besides wood for paper pulp. In light of the fact that we have plenty of trees and ways of reducing our wood demands, there is no need to harvest old-growth forests.

Revised Paragraph: Particulars Added

One reason that it is not necessary to log old-growth forests is that the timber industry can supply the world's lumber needs without doing so. For example, we have plenty of new-growth forest from which timber can be taken as a result of major reforestation efforts all over the United States (Sagoff 89). In the Northwest, for instance, Oregon law requires every acre of timber harvested to be replanted. According to Robert Sedjo, a forestry expert, the world's demand for industrial wood could be met by a widely implemented tree farming system (Sagoff 90). We could also reduce the amount of trees used for paper products by using a promising new innovation called Kenaf, a fast growing annual herb which is fifteen feet tall and is native to Africa. It has been used for making rope for many years, but recently it was found to work just as well for paper pulp. In light of the fact that we have plenty of trees and ways of reducing our wood demands, there is no need to harvest old-growth forests.

Added particulars support subpoint that we have plenty of new-growth forest

Added particulars support second subpoint that wood alternatives are available

Summary

Point sentences form the structural core of an argument. In this lesson, we stressed the reader's need to have point sentences placed at the heads of sections and paragraphs. In revising, writers often have to recast point sentences or restructure paragraphs to create unity. We also stressed the reader's need for particulars, which make points vivid and persuasive.

FOR WRITING AND DISCUSSION

Look again at the student draft arguing against university-provided carpets for dorm rooms (Chapter 10, pp. 197–98). Working as individuals or in small groups, write the next draft of this essay, focusing on creating a closed-form piece with unified, coherent, and sufficiently developed body paragraphs headed by topic sentences. You can reshape or combine paragraphs as needed and invent your own plausible particulars to flesh out a point.

▨ LESSON 6: SIGNALING RELATIONSHIPS WITH TRANSITIONS

As we have explained in previous lessons, when readers read closed-form prose, they expect each new sentence, paragraph, and section to link clearly to what they have already read. They need a well-marked trail with signposts signaling the twists and turns along the way. They also need resting spots at major junctions where they can review where they've been and survey what's coming. In this lesson, we show you how transition words, summary and forecasting passages, and headings and subheadings can keep your reader securely on the trail.

Use Common Transition Words to Signal Relationships

One of the best ways to keep readers on track is to signal the relationship between sentences and larger parts with transitions. Transitions are like signposts that signal where the road is turning. Without them, a reader can't predict where an argument might be headed. Transitions limit the possible directions that an unfolding argument might take. Consider how the use of "therefore" and "nevertheless" limits the range of possibilities in the following examples:

> While on vacation, Suzie caught the chicken pox. Therefore, _____.
>
> While on vacation, Suzie caught the chicken pox. Nevertheless, _____.

"Therefore" signals to the reader that what follows is a consequence. Most readers will imagine a sentence similar to this one:

> Therefore, she spent her vacation lying in bed itching, feverish, and miserable.

In contrast, "nevertheless" signals an unexpected or denied consequence, so the reader might anticipate a sentence such as this:

> Nevertheless, she enjoyed her two weeks off, thanks to a couple of bottles of calamine lotion, some good books, and a big easy chair overlooking the ocean.

Here is a list of the most common transition words and phrases and what they signal to the reader*:

Words or Phrases	What They Signal
first, second, third, next, finally, earlier, later, meanwhile, afterwards	*sequence*—First we went to dinner; then we went to the movies.
that is, in other words, to put it another way, — (dash) , : (colon)	*restatement*—He's so hypocritical that you can't trust a word he says. To put it another way, he's a complete phony.
rather, instead	*replacement*—We shouldn't use the money to buy opera tickets; rather, we should use it for a nice gift.
for example, for instance, a case in point	*example*—Mr. Carlysle is very generous. For example, he gave the janitors a special holiday gift.
because, since, for	*reason*—Taxes on cigarettes are unfair because they place a higher tax burden on the working class.
therefore, hence, so, consequently, thus, then, as a result, accordingly, as a consequence	*consequences*—I failed to turn in the essay; therefore I flunked the course.
still, nevertheless	*denied consequence*—The teacher always seemed grumpy in class; nevertheless, I really enjoyed the course.

*Although all the words on the list serve as transitions or connectives, grammatically they are not all equivalent; some are coordinating conjunctions, some are subordinating conjunctions, and some are transition adverbs. Each different kind of word requires a different grammatical construction and punctuation.

Words or Phrases *(cont.)*	What They Signal *(cont.)*
although, even though, granted that (with still)	*concession*—Even though the teacher was always grumpy, I still enjoyed the course.
in comparison, likewise, similarly	*similarity*—Teaching engineering takes a lot of patience. Likewise, so does teaching accounting.
however, in contrast, conversely, on the other hand, but	*contrast*—I disliked my old backpack immensely; however, I really like this new one.
in addition, also, too, moreover, furthermore	*addition*—Today's cars are much safer than those of ten years ago. In addition, they get better gas mileage.
in brief, in sum, in conclusion, finally, to sum up, to conclude	*conclusion or summary*—In sum, the plan presented by Mary is the best choice.

FOR WRITING AND DISCUSSION

This exercise is designed to show you how transition words govern relationships between ideas. Working in groups or on your own, finish each of the following statements using ideas of your own invention. Make sure what you add fits the logic of the transition word.

1. Writing is difficult; therefore _____.
2. Writing is difficult; however, _____.
3. Writing is difficult because _____.
4. Writing is difficult. For example, _____.
5. Writing is difficult. To put it another way, _____.
6. Writing is difficult. Likewise, _____.
7. Although writing is difficult, _____.
8. _____. In sum, writing is difficult.

In the following paragraph, various kinds of linking devices have been omitted. Fill in the blanks with words or phrases that would make the paragraph coherent. Clues are provided in brackets.

Writing an essay is a difficult process for most people. _____ [contrast] the process can be made easier if you learn to practice three simple techniques. _____ [sequence] learn the technique of nonstop writing. When you are first trying to think of ideas for an essay, put your pen on your paper and write nonstop for ten or fifteen minutes without ever letting your pen leave the paper. Stay loose and free. Let your pen follow the waves of thought. Don't worry about grammar or spelling. _____ [concession] this technique won't work for everyone, it helps many people get a good cache of ideas to draw on. A _____ [sequence] technique is to write your rough draft rapidly without worrying about being perfect. Too many writers try to get their drafts right the first time. _____ [contrast] by learning to live with imperfection, you will save yourself headaches and a wastepaper basket full of crumpled paper. Think of your first rough draft as a path hacked out of the jungle—as part of an exploration, not as a completed highway. As a _____ [sequence] technique, try printing out a triple-spaced copy to allow space for revision. Many beginning writers don't leave enough space to revise. _____ [consequence] these writers never get in the habit of crossing out chunks of their rough draft and writing revisions in the blank spaces. After you have revised your rough draft until it is too messy to work from any more, you can _____ [sequence] enter your changes into your word processor and print out a fresh draft, again setting your text on triple space. The resulting blank space invites you to revise.

Write Major Transitions Between Parts

In long closed-form pieces, writers often put *resting places* between major parts—transition passages that allow readers to shift their attention momentarily away from the matter at hand to a sense of where they've been and where they're going. Often such passages sum up the preceding major section, refer back to the essay's thesis statement or opening blueprint plan, and then preview the next major section. The longer the essay, the more readers appreciate such passages. Here are three typical examples.

> So far I have looked at a number of techniques that can help people identify debilitating assumptions that block their self-growth. In the next section, I examine ways to question and overcome these assumptions.

> Now that the difficulty of the problem is fully apparent, our next step is to examine some of the solutions that have been proposed.

> These, then, are the major theories explaining why Hamlet delays. But let's see what happens to Hamlet if we ask the question in a slightly different way. In this next section, we shift our critical focus, looking not at Hamlet's actions, but at his language.

Signal Transitions with Headings and Subheadings

In many genres, particularly scientific and technical reports, government documents, business proposals, textbooks, and other long articles in magazines or scholarly journals, writers conventionally break up long stretches of text with headings and subheadings. Headings are often set in different type sizes and fonts, and mark transition points between major parts and subparts of the argument.

Headings serve some of the same purposes served by the title of the essay or article; they encapsulate the big picture of a part or section and preview its contents. They may also relate back to the thesis statement, but sometimes, especially in scientific and social scientific articles, they are generic section markers, such as "Introduction," "Methods," "Findings," and so forth. Writers are apt to compose their headings late in the writing process, and the act of doing so may lead to further revisions. When you add headings, ask yourself questions such as these: Just where *are* the major transition points in the text? What would be a good title or umbrella that summarizes or previews this part? How clearly do my levels of headings relate to each other?

Writing descriptive headings is almost as demanding as writing a thesis statement. Because composing headings and subheadings is such a powerful exercise, we often ask our students to write headings for their papers, even if headings are not conventionally used for the type of writing they are doing.

Summary

In this brief lesson we explained some simple yet effective strategies for keeping your reader on track:

- Mark your trail with appropriate transition words
- Write major transitions between sections
- If the genre allows, use headings and subheadings

Effective use of these strategies will help your reader follow your ideas with ease and confidence.

◢ LESSON 7: BINDING SENTENCES TOGETHER BY FOLLOWING THE OLD/NEW CONTRACT

In the previous lesson we showed you how to mark the reader's trail with transitions. In this lesson we show you how to build a smooth trail without potholes or washed out bridges that force your reader to jump over gaps between sentences.

An Explanation of the Old/New Contract

A powerful way to prevent gaps is to follow the old/new contract—a writing strategy derived from the principle of old before new that we explained and illustrated in Lesson 1. Simply put, the old/new contract asks writers to begin sentences with something old—something that links back to what has gone before—and then to end sentences with new information.

The following examples illustrate how following the old/new contract creates a smooth trail for readers; in contrast, violating the contract creates potholes that the reader must leap over. We'll start with a passage that violates the contract. Note in Passage A how difficult it is to follow the writer's ideas when the writer violates the principle of old-before-new. Each sentence seems unconnected to the one that went before it; the ideas seem disjointed.

Passage A: Violates Old/New Contract

Play is an often overlooked dimension of fathering. From the time a child is born until its adolescence, caretaking is emphasized less by fathers than play. Egalitarian feminists may be troubled by this, and spending more time in caretaking may be wise for fathers. There seems to be unusual significance in the father's style of play. Physical excitement and stimulation are likely to be part of it. With older children more physical games and teamwork that require the competitive testing of physical and mental skills are also what it involves. Resemblance to an apprenticeship or teaching relationship is also a characteristic of father's play: Come on, let me show you how.

Now note how much easier it is to follow the writer's ideas when each sentence opens with something old:

Passage B: Follows Old/New Contract

An often-overlooked dimension of fathering is play. From their children's birth through adolescence, fathers tend to emphasize play more than caretaking. This may be troubling to egalitarian feminists, and it would indeed be wise for most fathers to spend more time in caretaking. Yet the fathers' style of play seems to have unusual significance. It is likely to be both physically stimulating and exciting. With older children it involves more physical games and teamwork that require the competitive testing of physical and mental skills. It frequently resembles an apprenticeship or teaching relationship: Come on, let me show you how.

If you are like most readers, you have to concentrate much harder to understand Passage A than Passage B because it violates the old-before-new way that our minds normally process information. If a writer doesn't begin a sentence with old material, readers have to hold the new material in suspension until they have figured out how it connects to what has gone before. They can stay on the trail, but they have to keep jumping over the potholes between sentences.

To follow the old/new contract, you place old information near the beginning of sentences in what we call the *topic position* and new information that advances the argument in the predicate or *stress position* at the end of the sentence. We associate topics with the beginnings of sentences simply because in the standard English sentence the topic (or subject) comes before the predicate. Hence the notion of a *contract* by which we agree not to fool or frustrate our readers by breaking with the "normal" order of things. The contract says that the old, backward-linking material comes at the beginning of the sentence and the new argument-advancing material comes at the end.

But what exactly do we mean by "old" or "familiar" information? In the context of sentence-level coherence, we mean everything in the text the reader has read so far. Any upcoming sentence is new information, but once the reader reads it, it becomes old information. For example, when a reader is halfway through a text, everything previously read—the title, the introduction, half the body—is old information to which you can link back to meet your readers' expectations for unity and coherence.

In making these backward links, writers have three targets:

1. They can link back to a key word or concept in the immediately preceding sentence (creating coherence).
2. They can link back to a key word or concept in a preceding point sentence (creating unity).
3. They can link back to a preceding forecasting statement about structure (helping readers map their location in the text).

Writers have a number of textual strategies for making these links. In Figure 11.4 our annotations show how a professional writer links back to old information within the first five or six words of each sentence. What follows is a compendium of these strategies:

- **Repeat a key word.**   The most common way to open with something old is to repeat a key word from the preceding sentence or an earlier point sentence. In our example, note the number of sentences that open with *father*, *father's*, or *fathering*. Note also the frequent repetitions of *play*.
- **Use a pronoun to substitute for a key word.**   In our example, the second sentence opens with the pronouns *it*, referring to *research* and *their* referring to *fathers*. The last three sentences open with the pronoun *it*, referring to *father's style of play*.

FIGURE 11.4   How a Professional Writer Follows the Old/New Contract

Recent research has given us much deeper—and more surprising—insights into the father's role in childrearing. It shows that in almost all of their interactions with children, fathers do things a little differently from mothers. What fathers do—their special parenting style—is not only highly complementary to what mothers do but is by all indications important in its own right.

For example, an often over-looked dimension of fathering is play. From their children's birth through adolescence, fathers tend to emphasize play more than caretaking. This may be troubling to egalitarian feminists, and it would indeed be wise for most fathers to spend more time in caretaking. Yet the fathers' style of play seems to have unusual significance. It is likely to be both physically stimulating and exciting. With older children it involves more physical games and teamwork that require the competitive testing of physical and mental skills. It frequently resembles an apprenticeship or teaching relationship: Come on, let me show you how.

(David Popenoe, "Where's Papa?" from *Life Without Father: Compelling New Evidence that Fatherhood and Marriage Are Indispensable for the Good of Children and Society.*)

Annotations (left margin):
- Refers to fathers in previous sentence
- Transition tells us new paragraph will be an example of previous concept
- Refers to fathers
- Pronoun sums up previous concept
- It refers to fathers' style of play

Annotations (right margin):
- Refers to research in previous sentence
- Rephrases idea of "childrearing"
- Repeats fathers from previous sentence
- Rephrases concept in previous paragraph
- New information that becomes topic of this paragraph
- Repeats words father and play from paragraph point sentence

■ *Summarize, rephrase, or restate earlier concepts.*   Writers can link back to a preceding sentence by using a word or phrase that summarizes or restates a key concept. In the second sentence, "interactions with children" restates the concept of childrearing. Similarly, the phrase "an often-overlooked dimension" refers to a concept implied in the preceding paragraph—that recent research reveals something significant (rephrased as a *dimension*) and not widely known (rephrased as *overlooked*) about a father's role in childrearing. An "often-overlooked dimension" sums up this idea. Finally, note that the pronoun *this* in the second paragraph sums up the main concept of the previous two sentences. (But see our warning on p. 236 about the overuse of *this* as a pronoun.)

■ *Use a transition word.*   Writers can also use transition words such as *first . . . , second . . . , third . . .* or *therefore* or *however* to cue the reader about the logical relationship between an upcoming sentence and the preceding ones. Note how the second paragraph opens with *For example,* indicating that the upcoming paragraph will illustrate the concept identified in the preceding paragraph.

These strategies give you a powerful way to check and revise your prose. Comb your drafts for gaps between sentences where you have violated the old/new contract. If the opening of a new sentence doesn't refer back to an earlier word, phrase, or concept, your reader could derail, so use what you have learned to repair the tracks.

FOR WRITING AND DISCUSSION

Here is an early draft paragraph from a student's essay in favor of building more nuclear reactors for electricity. This paragraph attempts to refute an argument that building nuclear power plants is prohibitively expensive. Read the draft carefully and then do the exercises that follow.

[1] One argument against nuclear power plants is that they are too expensive to build. [2] But this argument is flawed. [3] On March 28, 1979, Three Mile Island (TMI) Nuclear Station suffered a meltdown. [4] It was the worst accident in commercial nuclear power operation in the United States. [5] During its investigation of TMI the Presidential Commission became highly critical of the U.S. Nuclear Regulatory Commission (NRC), which responded by generating hundreds of new safety regulations. [6] These regulations forced utility companies to modify reactors during construction. [7] Since all the changes had to be made on half-completed plants, the cost of design time, material, and personnel had to be very large. [8] The standards set by the NRC would not be acceptable to a utility company. [9] All reactors now being built had been ordered before 1973. [10] With all the experience gained by research here in the U.S. and overseas, the licensing process can be cut in half without reducing the safety of the plant. [11] A faster approval rate could lower the cost of

the construction of a plant because it eliminates all the delays and cost overruns.

1. Working on your own, place a vertical slash in front of any sentence that doesn't open with some reference back to familiar material.
2. See if your class or small group agrees on the location of these slashes. In each case, how does the writer's violation of the old/new contract create confusion?
3. Working individually or in small groups, try to revise the paragraph by filling in gaps created by violation of the old/new contract.

As we discussed in Lesson 1, the principle of old before new has great explanatory power in helping writers understand their choices when they compose. In this last section, we give you some further insights into the old/new contract.

Avoid Ambiguous Use of "This" to Fulfill the Old/New Contract

Some writers try to fulfill the old/new contract by frequent use of the pronoun *this* to sum up a preceding concept. Occasionally this usage* is effective, as in our example passage on fathers' style of play when the writer says: "*This* may be troubling to egalitarian feminists." But frequent use of *this* as a pronoun creates lazy and often ambiguous prose. Consider how our example passage might read if many of the explicit links were replaced by *this.*

Lazy Use of *This* as Pronoun

Recent research has given us much deeper—and more surprising—insights into **this.** It shows that in doing **this,** fathers do things a little differently from mothers. **This** is not only highly complementary to what mothers do but is by all indications important in its own right.

For example, an often-overlooked dimension of **this** is play.

Perhaps this passage helps you see why we refer to *this* (used by itself as a pronoun) as "the lazy person's all-purpose noun-slot filler."

How the Old/New Contract Modifies the Rule "Avoid Weak Repetition"

Many students have been warned against repetition of the same word (or *weak repetition,* as your teacher may have called it). Consequently, you may not be aware that repetition of key words is a vital aspect of unity and coherence. The repeated words create what linguists call *lexical strings* that keep a passage focused on a particular point. Note in our passage about the importance of fathers' style of play the

---

*It's okay to use *this* as an adjective, as in "this usage"; we refer only to *this* by itself as a pronoun.

frequent repetitions of the words *father* and *play*. What if the writer worried about repeating *father* too much and reached for his thesaurus?

Unnecessary Attempt to Avoid Repetition

Recent research has given us much deeper—and more surprising—insights into the **male parent's** role in childrearing. It shows that in almost all of their interactions with children, **patriarchs** do things a little differently from mothers. What **sires** do . . .

For example, an often-overlooked dimension of **male gender parenting** is . . .

You get the picture. Keep your reader on familiar ground through repetition of key words.

How the Old/New Contract Modifies the Rule "Prefer Active over Passive Voice"

Another rule that you may have learned is to use the active voice rather than the passive voice. In the active voice the doer of the action is in the subject slot of the sentence and the receiver is in the direct object slot, as in the following examples:

The dog caught the Frisbee.

The women wrote letters of complaint to the boss.

The landlord raised the rent.

In the passive voice the receiver of the action becomes the subject and the doer of the action either becomes the object of the preposition *by* or disappears from the sentence.

The Frisbee was caught by the dog.

Letters of complaint were written (by the women) to the boss.

The rent was raised (by the landlord).

Other things being equal, the active voice is indeed preferable to the passive because it is more direct and forceful. But in some cases other things *aren't* equal, and the passive voice is preferable. *What the old/new contract asks you to consider is whether the doer or the receiver represents the old information in a sentence.* Consider the difference between the following passages.

Second Sentence, Active Voice	My great-grandfather was a skilled cabinet-maker. He made this dining-room table near the turn of the century.
Second Sentence, Passive Voice	I am pleased that you stopped to admire our dining-room table. It was made by my great-grandfather near the turn of the century.

In the first passage, the opening sentence is about *my great-grandfather*. To begin the second sentence with old information (*he*, referring to *grandfather*), the writer uses the active voice. The opening sentence of the second passage is about the dining-room table. To begin the second sentence with old information (*it*, referring to *table*), the writer must use the passive voice, since the table is the receiver of the action. In both cases, the sentences are structured to begin with old information.

Summary

This lesson has focused on the power of the old/new contract to bind sentences together and eliminate gaps that the reader must leap over. We have shown various ways that writers can link back to old information by repeating key words, using a pronoun, summarizing or restating an earlier concept, or using a transition word. Additionally, we have advised against the ambiguous use of *this* as a pronoun to link back to old information and have shown how the principle of old before new modifies rules about the avoidance of *weak repetition* and *passive voice*.

FOR WRITING AND DISCUSSION

A helpful technique for understanding how skilled writers keep their readers on track is to reorder a *scrambled* paragraph. The following passage is a paragraph from science writer Carl Sagan's *Broca's Brain*. However, the order of the sentences has been scrambled. Working individually or in small groups, place the sentences in correct order. Try to articulate the thinking processes you used to link the sentences correctly. What cues helped you reconstruct the correct order?

(1) There are also a number of cases where one or two people claim to have been taken aboard an alien spaceship, prodded and probed with unconventional medical instruments, and released. (2) To the best of my knowledge there are no instances out of hundreds of thousands of UFO reports filed since 1947 in which many people independently and reliably report a close encounter with what is clearly an alien spacecraft. (3) Flying saucers, or UFOs, are well known to almost everyone. (4) It might, for example, be an automobile headlight reflected off a high-altitude cloud, or a flight of luminescent insects, or an unconventional aircraft, or a conventional aircraft with unconventional lighting patterns, such as a high-intensity searchlight used for meteorological observations. (5) But seeing a strange light in the sky does not mean that we are being visited by beings from the planet Venus or a distant galaxy named Spectra. (6) But in these cases we have only the unsubstantiated testimony, no matter how heartfelt and seemingly sincere, of one or two people.

◢ LESSON 8: WRITING EFFECTIVE TITLES AND INTRODUCTIONS

In our experience, writers often have trouble writing titles and introductions—so much so that we often advise waiting until late in the writing process to write them (although trying to imagine a title early on can help you nutshell your ideas).

In this lesson, we hope to reduce your anxiety about titles and introductions by explaining some of the principles behind them. Titles and introductions need to include old information that links back to your readers' interests and new information that promises something surprising or challenging. The function of introductions is to hook your readers' interest, tie into their current state of knowledge, orient them to the problem you will investigate, and finally forecast the new surprising material to be presented and supported in the body of your paper. It follows, then, that to write a good introduction you need to know the background knowledge and interests of your readers and the big picture of your own argument.

Writing Effective Titles

A good title has an old-information element that hooks into a reader's existing knowledge and interests and a new-information element that promises something surprising. It is the reader's first indication of an essay's big picture. Typically, readers scan tables of contents, bibliographies, and indexes to select what they want to read by title alone. In a magazine's table of contents, imagine how unhelpful a title such as "My Paper," "Essay 3," or "Democracy" would be. Yet inexperienced writers, forgetting to think about how readers use titles, sometimes select ones such as these.

Your title should provide a brief but detailed overview of what your paper is about. Academic titles are typically longer and more detailed than are titles in popular magazines. They usually follow one of four conventions.

1. Some titles simply state the question that the essay addresses ("Will Patriarchal Management Survive Beyond the Twentieth Century?").
2. Some titles state, often in abbreviated form, the essay's thesis ("The Writer's Audience Is Always a Fiction").
3. Very often the title is a summary of the essay's purpose statement ("The Relationship Between Client Expectation of Improvement and Psychotherapy Outcome").
4. Many titles consist of two parts separated by a colon. To the left of the colon the writer presents key words from the essay's issue or problem or a "mystery phrase" that arouses interest; to the right the author places the essay's question, thesis, or summary of purpose ("Money and Growth: An Alternative Approach"; "Deep Play: Notes on a Balinese Cockfight"; or "Fine Cloth, Cut Carefully: Cooperative Learning in British Columbia").

Although such titles might seem stuffy or overly formal to you, they indicate how much a closed-form writer wishes to preview an article's big picture. Although their titles may be more informal, popular magazines often use these same strategies. Here are some titles from recent issues of *Redbook* and the business magazine *Forbes*.

"Is the Coffee Bar Trend About to Peak?" (question)

"A Man *Can* Take Maternity Leave—And Love It" (abbreviated thesis)

"Why the Department of Education Shouldn't Take Over the Student Loan Program" (summary of purpose statement)

"Feed Your Face: Why Your Complexion Needs Vitamins" (two parts linked by colon)

Composing a title for your essay can help you find your focus when you get bogged down in the middle of a draft. When students come to our offices for help with a draft, we usually begin by asking them their proposed title. Such a question forces them to *nutshell* their ideas—to see their project's big picture. Talking about the title inevitably leads to a discussion of the writer's purpose, the problem to be addressed, and the proposed thesis. Having invested all this conceptual effort, students can appreciate how much information their title provides their readers.

Planning an Introduction

Introductions serve two purposes—to engage the reader's interest and then to pick up where the title leaves off in sketching in the big picture. Closed-form introductions typically describe the problem to be addressed, provide needed background, state the essay's thesis or purpose, and preview the essay's structure, sometimes including a summary of its argument. In a short essay, the introduction may comprise simply the opening paragraph, but in longer essays introductions typically require several paragraphs. Writers often wait until late in the writing process to draft an introduction because, as you saw in Chapter 10, these big-picture features are often in flux during the writer's early drafts.

Whether you do it early in the process as a way to focus your initial plan or late in the process after your ideas have solidified, writing the introduction forces you to focus on your essay's big picture. If you have trouble writing introductions—and many writers do—guide questions can help. Before writing your introduction, take fifteen minutes or so to write out exploratory answers to the following questions.

1. What is your thesis statement?
2. What question does your thesis answer?
3. Why is this a problematic and significant question? What attempts have others made to answer it (include your own previous attempts)? (Freewrite for at least three to four minutes on this one.)
4. Do you imagine that your reader is already interested in this question? If not, how could you make this question interesting for your reader? (Freewrite for several minutes.)
5. How much prior knowledge do you think your reader has about this topic? How much background information will your reader need to understand the problem and appreciate the conversation that your paper is joining?
6. Finish this sentence: My purpose in this paper is

_____.

7. Fill in the blanks: Before reading my paper, I expect my reader to believe this about my topic: _____;

After reading my paper, I want my reader to believe this about my topic:
_____.

8. Finish this sentence: I can describe the structure of my paper as follows:
_____.

These questions will help you get unstuck because they generate all the information you will need to write an initial draft of your introduction.

Typical Features of a Closed-Form Introduction

A typical introduction to an academic article has the following features (for further discussion of academic introductions, see Chapter 2, pages 25–27):

Feature 1: An Opening Lead or Hook Appropriate to Your Rhetorical Context. The lead or hook comprises the opening sentences of the essay and is aimed at capturing the reader's interest in the subject. Academic writers generally assume a reader is already interested in the general topic area and ready to be informed about the specific problem to be addressed. But when you are writing for general audiences, you may need to hook your readers in the opening sentences through a dramatic vignette, a startling fact or statistic, an arresting quotation, or an interesting scene. *Reader's Digest* articles are famous for their interest-grabbing leads. Here is a typical opening from a *Reader's Digest* article.

> The first faint tremor rippled through the city just before ten o'clock that warm summer night. Then came the sound—as if something heavy was rolling along the ground. The tremor intensified into a rapid jerking, sending dishes crashing and tables and chairs dancing. Thousands of frightened people ran out of their houses into the darkness.
>
> Dawn's light showed the earthquake's horror. At least 60 lay dead, many buried under collapsed buildings. Virtually every home was damaged.
>
> This wasn't just another trembler along one of California's many faults, like the devastating quake that shook the Los Angeles area last January 17. It was one that rocked Charleston, S.C., on August 31, 1886.
>
> While many Americans believe serious earthquakes happen only in California, scientific research confirms that the risk in other states may be higher than anyone thought.

Opening lead used as a hook

Thesis

—Lowell Ponte, "Earthquakes: Closer than You Think"

Most academic writing opens less dramatically than does this example. Typically, academic writers begin with old information by describing something familiar about the topic to be investigated and summarizing the current state of knowledge or belief about it—what we might call the ordinary or common view. (This section can be based on your answer to question 7 on p. 240: "Before reading my paper, I expect my reader to believe this about my topic: _____ .") The writer then makes a crucial move by raising a problem or question about this common ground. At this point the introduction moves to the next stage—the problem or question to be investigated.

Feature 2: Explanation of the Question to Be Investigated. Readers are intrinsically interested in questions. Once they become engaged with your question, they will look forward to your answer. The question is thus the starting place for your argument; it summarizes the conversation that your essay joins. Academic writers often state the question directly, but sometimes they imply it, letting the reader formulate it from context.

Unless the problem or question is a very familiar one, you will need to show your readers both what makes the question problematic—that is, why it hasn't already been solved—and what makes it significant—that is, why it is a problem worth solving. To demonstrate why a question is problematic, writers often summarize differing views among experts, show why a commonly posed answer to the question is unsatisfactory, or otherwise show what aspects of the problem need more attention, often through a review of the literature. To reveal a problem's significance, writers point either to the benefits that will come from solving it or to the bad consequences of leaving it unsolved. Sometimes these benefits or consequences are measured in practical, real-world terms; at other times they are measured by how much the solution advances knowledge. (See Chapters 1 and 2 for further discussion of academic problems.)

Feature 3: Background Information. Sometimes your readers may need background information before they can appreciate the problem that your paper addresses or the approach you take—perhaps a definition of key terms; a summary of events leading up to the problem at issue; factual details needed for basic understanding of the problem; and so forth. When readers need extensive information, writers sometimes place it in the first main section of the paper *following* the introduction.

Feature 4: A Preview of the Whole. One of the crucial functions of a closed-form introduction is to sketch the big picture by giving readers a sense of the whole. Initially new information, this preview, once read, becomes part of the old information readers will use to locate their position in the journey; simultaneously, by forecasting what's coming, the preview triggers the pleasure of prediction/fulfillment that we discussed in Lesson One. How writers lay out the whole is the subject of the next section.

Laying Out the Whole with a Thesis Statement, Purpose Statement, or Blueprint Statement

The most succinct way to lay out the whole is to state your thesis directly. Think of your thesis statement as your one-sentence answer to the question your paper addresses. In a prototypical short academic paper, your thesis statement is the last sentence of your introduction, in accordance with the principle of old before new. Thus you begin your introduction with the reader's common view (the old) and end with your thesis (the new).

Student writers often ask how detailed their thesis statements should be and whether it is permissible, sometimes, to delay revealing their thesis until the conclusion—an open-form move that gives their paper a more exploratory, mystery novel feel. You have a number of choices for kinds of thesis statements. For an illustration of a writer's options, we will use Dao's essay on euthanasia that we first introduced in Lesson 3:

- **Short thesis:** Your briefest option is simply to state your claim without a summary of your supporting argument or a forecasting of your structure:

  Euthanasia is wrong.

- **Short thesis with structural forecasting:** You can also state your claim but add to it a phrase that predicts structure:

  Euthanasia is wrong for several reasons. [*Or*] Euthanasia is wrong for three reasons.

- **Detailed thesis:** Using this option you not only state your claim but also succinctly summarize your whole argument. Sometimes you begin with an *although* clause that summarizes the view you are trying to change:

  Although my friend Martha argues that euthanasia is justified for terminally ill patients who have lost all quality of life, I am opposed to euthanasia because it benefits the living more than the sick, because it leads to dangerous consequences, and because it fails to appreciate the value of suffering.

- **Purpose statement:** A purpose statement announces a writer's purpose or intention without actually summarizing the argument. A purpose statement typically begins with a phrase such as "My purpose is to . . . " or "In the following paragraphs I wish to . . .":

  My purpose in this essay is to show the flaws in Martha's argument.

- **Blueprint or mapping statement:** A blueprint or mapping statement describes the form of the upcoming essay, usually announcing the number of main parts and describing the function or purpose of each one.

  First I show how euthanasia benefits the living more than the sick; then I discuss the bad consequences of euthanasia; finally I argue that euthanasia fails to acknowledge the value of suffering.

- **Multisentence summary:** In long articles, academic writers often use all three kinds of statements—a purpose statement, thesis statement, and blueprint statement—and also include a detailed summary of the whole argument. This sort of extensive forecasting is common in academic and business writing but occurs less frequently in informal or popular essays. Dao's paper is too short to justify a multisentence summary.

- **Thesis question:** When writers wish to delay their thesis, letting their argument slowly unfold and keeping their final stance a mystery, they often end the introduction with a question. Using this approach, Dao wouldn't tell readers where she stood until late in the paper, treating the body of the paper as an exploration. This powerful open-form strategy invites readers to join the writer in a mutual search for the answer.

  Although I instinctively oppose any sort of mercy killing, I find myself deeply moved by Martha's story about her dying aunt. The question of euthanasia leaves me baffled and troubled. Should euthanasia be legalized or not?

Which of these options should a writer choose? There are no firm rules to help you answer this question. How much you decide to forecast in the introduction and where you reveal your thesis is a function of your purpose, audience, and genre. The more you forecast, the clearer your argument is and the easier it is to read quickly. You minimize your demands on readers' time by giving them the gist of your argument in the introduction, making it easier to skim your essay if they haven't time for a thorough reading. The less you forecast, the more demands you make on readers' time; you invite them, in effect, to accompany you through the twists and turns of your own thinking process, and you risk losing them if they ever get confused, lost, or bored. For these reasons, academic writing is generally closed form and aims at maximum clarity. In many rhetorical contexts, however, more open forms are appropriate (see Chapter 4).

If you choose a closed-form structure, we can offer some advice on how much to forecast. Readers sometimes feel insulted by too much forecasting, so include only what is needed for clarity. For short papers, readers usually don't need the complete supporting argument forecast in the introduction. In longer papers, however, or in especially complex ones, readers appreciate having the whole argument forecast at the outset. Academic writing in particular tends to favor explicit and often detailed forecasting.

Summary

In this lesson we have shown that both titles and introductions must include old information that links back to your readers' interests and background knowledge and new information that predicts what is new, surprising, or challenging in your essay. The key features of a closed-form introduction are the opening lead; explanation of the problem to be investigated; background information (optional); and a forecasting of the whole by means of a thesis statement, purpose statement, blueprint statement, or predictive question.

FOR WRITING AND DISCUSSION

What follows is the introduction to a closed-form essay by paleontologist Stephen Jay Gould. Gould writes for general audiences interested in the philosophy and history of science, especially the field of evolutionary biology. Read the introduction carefully. Then, working in small groups or as a whole class, answer the questions that follow.

The human mind delights in finding pattern—so much so that we often mistake coincidence or forced analogy for profound meaning. No other habit of thought lies so deeply within the soul of a small creature trying to make sense of a complex world not constructed for it. [. . .] No other error of reason stands so doggedly in the way of any forthright attempt to understand some of the world's most essential aspects—the tortuous paths of history, the unpredictability of complex systems, and the lack of causal connection among events superficially similar.

Numerical coincidence is a common path to intellectual perdition in our quest for meaning. We delight in catalogs of disparate items united by the same number, and often feel in our gut that some unity must underlie it all. [Gould then gives numerous examples of people's fascination with certain "mystical" numbers, such as the numbers seven and five.]

In this essay, I shall discuss two taxonomic systems [theories of classification of organisms] popular in the decades just before Darwin published the *Origin of the Species*. Both assumed reasons other than evolution for the ordering of organisms; both proposed a scheme based on the number five for placing organisms into a hierarchy of groups and subgroups. Both argued that such a simple numerical regularity must record an intrinsic pattern in nature, not a false order imposed by human hope upon a more complex reality. I shall describe these systems and then discuss how evolutionary theory undermined their rationale and permanently changed the science of taxonomy by making such simple numerical schemes inconsistent with a new view of nature. This important change in scientific thought embodies a general message about the character of history and the kinds of order that a world built by history, and not by preordained plan, can (and cannot) express.

—Stephen Jay Gould, "The Rule of Five"

1. What question or problem does this article address?
2. What makes this problem both problematic and significant? In Gould's view, why should anyone care that scientists used to interpret the universe as governed by a preordained plan based on the number five?
3. What strategy does Gould use in the opening lead to engage readers' interest?
4. Identify the previewing features in this introduction (thesis statement, purpose statement, blueprint statement, partial summary of what's coming).
5. What is the predicted organization of Gould's article?

The following passage occurred at the end of the introduction for a college research paper on theories of education. Using cues about structure and meaning in this previewing passage, create the top branches of a tree diagram for this essay.

My purpose in the following paragraphs is to reveal the complexity of the arguments surrounding the open curriculum controversy. I will examine first the view of three educators influenced by Rousseau—A. S. Neill, John Holt, and Jerry Farber. Each of these people believes that the goal of education should be the joyful pursuit of self-discovery and that children should be free to explore their own natural interests. I will then turn to two opponents of the open curriculum—Max Rafferty and B. F. Skinner. Rafferty believes that the goal of education is the acquisition of intellectual skills rather than self-discovery. B. F. Skinner believes that the concept of freedom is an illusion and thus opposes the notion that students can "choose" their own curriculum.

▰ LESSON 9: WRITING EFFECTIVE CONCLUSIONS

Conclusions can best be understood as complements to introductions. In both the introduction and the conclusion, writers are concerned with the essay as a whole more than with any given part. In a conclusion, the writer attempts to bring a sense of completeness and closure to the profusion of points and particulars laid out in the body of the essay. The writer is particularly concerned with helping the reader move from the parts back to the big picture and to understand the importance or significance of the essay.

If you are having trouble figuring out how to conclude an essay, consider the following guide questions, which are designed to stimulate thought about how to conclude and to help you determine which model best suits your situation.

1. How long and complex is your essay? Is it long enough or complex enough that readers might benefit from a summary of your main points?
2. What's the most important point (or points) you want your reader to remember about your essay? How long ago in the essay did you state that point? Would it be useful to restate that point as succinctly and powerfully as possible?
3. Do you know of an actual instance, illustration, or example of your main point that would give it added weight?
4. What larger principle stands behind your main point? Or what must your audience accept as true in order to accept your main point? How would you defend that assumption if someone were to call it into question?
5. Why is your main point significant? Why are the ideas in your paper important and worth your audience's consideration? What larger issues does your topic relate to or touch on? Could you show how your topic relates to a larger and more significant topic? What might that topic be?
6. If your audience accepts your thesis, where do you go next? What is the next issue or question to be examined? What further research is needed? Conversely, do you have any major reservations, unexpressed doubts, or "All bets are off if X is the case" provisos you'd like to admit? What do you *not* know about your topic that reduces your certainty in your thesis?
7. How much antagonism or skepticism toward your position do you anticipate? If a great deal, would it be feasible to delay your thesis, solution, or proposal until the very end of the paper?

Because many writers find conclusions challenging to write, we offer the following six possible models.

The Simple Summary Conclusion

The most common, though often not the most effective, kind of conclusion is a simple summary, in which the writer recaps what has just been said. This approach is useful in a long or complex essay or in an instructional text that focuses on concepts to be learned. We use summary conclusions for most of the chapters in this text. In a short, easy-to-follow essay, however, a summary conclusion can

be dull and may even annoy readers who are expecting something more significant, but a brief summary followed by a more artful concluding strategy can often
be effective.

The Larger Significance Conclusion

A particularly effective concluding strategy is to draw the reader's attention
to the *larger significance* of your argument. In our discussion of academic problems
(see Chapter 1), we explained that a good academic question needs to be significant (worth pursuing). Although readers need to be convinced from the outset that
the problem investigated in your paper is significant, the conclusion is a good
place to elaborate on that significance by showing how your argument now leads
to additional benefits for the reader. If you started off asking a pure knowledge
question, you could show in your conclusion how your thesis leads to potential
understanding of a larger, more significant question. If you asked an applied
knowledge question, your conclusion could point out the practical benefits of your
ideas. If you posed a values question, you could show how your argument clari-
fies the stance you might take when facing a related problem. Your goal in writing this kind of conclusion is to show how your answer to the question posed in
your paper leads to a larger or more significant understanding.

The Proposal Conclusion

Another option, often used in analyses and arguments, is a *proposal conclusion*,
which calls for action. A proposal conclusion states the action that the writer believes needs to be taken and briefly demonstrates the advantages of this action
over alternative actions or describes its beneficial consequences. If your paper analyzes the consequences of shifting from a graduated to a flat-rate income tax,
your conclusion may recommend an action, such as adopting, modifying, or opposing the flat tax. A slight variation is the *call-for-future-study conclusion*, which indicates what else needs to be known or resolved before a proposal can be offered.
Such conclusions are especially common in scientific writing.

The Scenic or Anecdotal Conclusion

Popular writers often use a *scenic* or *anecdotal conclusion*, in which a scene or
brief story illustrates a theme's significance without stating it explicitly. A paper
examining the current trend against involuntary hospitalization of the mentally ill
homeless might end by describing a former mental patient, now an itinerant
homeless person, collecting bottles in a park. Such scenes can help the reader experience directly the emotional significance of the topic analyzed in the body of
the paper.

The Hook and Return Conclusion

A related variety of conclusion is the *hook and return,* in which the ending of
the essay returns to something introduced in the opening hook or lead. If the lead

of your essay is a vivid illustration of a problem—perhaps a scene or an anec-
dote—then your conclusion might return to the same scene or story, but with some
variation to illustrate the significance of the essay. This sense of return can give
your essay a strong feeling of unity.

The Delayed-Thesis Conclusion

This type of conclusion delays the thesis until the end of the essay. Rather than
stating the thesis, the introduction merely states the problem, giving the body of
the essay an open, exploratory, "let's think through this together" feel. Typically,
the body of the paper examines alternative solutions or approaches to the problem and leaves the writer's own answer—the thesis—unstated until the end. This
approach is especially effective when writing about highly complex or divisive
issues on which you want to avoid taking a stand until all sides have been fairly
presented.

Summary

These six types of conclusion are neither exhaustive nor mutually exclusive. It
is possible to imagine a conclusion that mixes several of these types—a few sentences summarizing your essay, a short passage showing the relationship of your
topic to some broader issues, a brief call to action, and a final concluding scene. In
determining an effective conclusion, you need to assess your audience's attitude
toward your thesis, its understanding of your topic, the length and complexity of
your essay, and what you want to happen as a result of people's reading your
essay. Review the guide questions at the beginning of this section to help determine the most appropriate conclusion for you.

TOPIC Guidepost #16

For those using Texas Tech's TOPIC Web-Based assignments:

Direct your web browser to **http://english.ttu.edu:5555**

Guidepost #16 provides full instructions regarding your reading
assignment (Handbook pages 181-190) and Draft 2.1.

TOPIC Guidepost #7

For those using Texas Tech's TOPIC Web-Based assignments:

Direct your web browser to **http://english.ttu.edu:5555**

Guidepost #7 provides full instructions regarding your reading assignment (Chapter 12) and Critique of Draft 1.1.

Composing
and Revising
Open-Form Prose

More and more I think I've entirely lost the knack of identifying issues, making arguments, and joining the debate. I've veered off toward the particular, the peripheral, accelerating so fast in that direction that sometimes I feel myself lost in a kind of aphasia, my left hemisphere almost dormant. All I'm interested in, all I seem to process, are moods and moments, atmosphere, sudden scenes and faces. I'm swept along at the market*, dazed, sometimes elated, and the fish are flying around me and the ferries are coming and going and sometimes the mountain appears from behind the clouds and sometimes it doesn't. . . .

My reading has become purely "literary" in the sense of dwelling in the kind of visceral world only literary detail can re-create, the impulse for meaning and extraction suspended. I sit in the easy chair in the livingroom, in front of the maple tree and the picture window, the trees all around me, and I drink coffee and read and the afternoon fades to evening and I reach up to turn on the light.

—Chris Anderson, *English Teacher and Writer*

Like Chris Anderson in this epigraph, we probably all share the desire at times to do writing that does not meet the requirements of tightly argued, thesis-governed, closed-form prose intended to inform, analyze, or persuade. We understand his longing to let the particulars of his experience—ferries, mountains, flying fish, and the dimming late-afternoon light—into his prose.

Here, we too shift our attention from closed- to open-form writing. In this chapter, we develop some of the concepts introduced in Chapter 7, seeking both to clarify and complicate your understanding of open-form features. This chapter focuses on the main distinctions between the closed and open ends of the form continuum. But we need to acknowledge at the outset that whereas closed-form prose is governed by a few widely accepted conventions, one of the main features of open-form prose is its freedom to play with conventions in a bewildering

---

*Pike Place Market in Seattle, Washington, famous for its fish merchants who throw fish from one station to the next as the fish are being cleaned and iced for sale.

variety of ways. Consequently, our discussion of open-form writing seeks more to introduce you to options rather than to treat open-form writing exhaustively. In this chapter we have two main purposes: (1) to draw your attention to and give you illuminating examples of features and techniques that you can think about as you are composing and revising open-forms; and (2) to make some suggestions about how to enliven your prose when your purpose, audience, and genre call for open-form features. To this end, we begin by reviewing the major differences between closed- and open-form writing.

UNDERSTANDING OPEN-FORM FEATURES

Open-form prose differs from closed-form prose in its basic features, in the challenges and options it presents writers, in the demands it places on its readers, and in the mental and emotional pleasures it creates. For our purposes throughout this chapter, when we speak of open-form prose, we are referring to *literary nonfiction,* which is nonfiction writing that uses, in the words of rhetorician Chris Anderson, "the *modes* of fiction for nonfictive *aims,* either the communication of information or the dramatization of a point of view."*

As we discussed in Chapters 4 and 11, closed-form writing seeks to be efficient and reader friendly. By forecasting what's coming, placing points first, using clear transitions, and putting old information before new, closed-form writers place maximum emphasis on delivering clear ideas that readers can grasp quickly. In contrast, open-form writers, by violating or simply stretching those same conventions, set up a different kind of relationship with readers. Open-form writing often demands patience and tolerance for ambiguity from readers. Yet open-form prose yields its own special rewards, for readers and for writers. What follows are some of the main features of open-form writing.

Narrative Base and Reader Involvement

Both the difficulties and the pleasures of open-form writing derive from its narrative base: the tendency to convert explicit themes and conceptual issues into stories with dramatic tensions and implicit themes. This narrative base forces readers to have a different sort of engagement with the text than they have with closed-form writing. Open-form reading affords pleasures akin to solving puzzles, playing games, and making surprising discoveries. The price readers pay for this recreation is the expenditure of considerable intellectual energy. Because ideas are

---

*For the definition of literary nonfiction and the focus on the rhetorical effect of gaps, we are indebted to Chris Anderson, "Teaching Students What Not to Say: Iser, Didion, and the Rhetoric of Gaps," *Journal of Advanced Composition* 7 (1987): 10–22.

embedded in a story's events rather than handed to readers in straightforward statements, readers are asked to become mentally active in a specific way with open-form prose.

The Writer's Role and Reader Involvement

Open-form prose also sets up its own kind of relationship between writer and reader. Thesis-based writers typically discover their ideas offstage. They analyze particulars and test ideas during drafting, delete irrelevant and unsuccessful notions, and then rearrange their remaining ideas and particulars under a hierarchy of points and subpoints in a final draft. Closed-form writers typically begin by telling the audience what conclusion they've reached about the topic, and then use most of the rest of the paper to justify that conclusion.

Open-form writers, in contrast, are just as likely to take readers backstage to share the process that led to their conclusion. They often cast themselves in the role of narrators or characters reporting their quest for understanding and all the coincidences, disappointments, snatches of conversation, puzzling advice, and confusion they experienced along the way. In this process of sharing and in making the readers co-discoverers with the writer, open-form prose may draw more attention than closed-form prose to the writer's persona. In addition, readers become participants in the writer's experiences and reflections.

Artistic Language and Reader Involvement

Open-form prose is also characterized by its emphasis on an aesthetic use of language: that is, language used to please and entertain. Without the benefit of a thesis or a points-first structure to convey meaning, open-form prose depends on the very specificity of words, the ability of words to create mental pictures, to appeal to readers' senses and emotions, and to conjure up memories. Along with the literary features of plot, character, and setting, open-form prose employs language artistically to generate meaning and evoke pleasure. Open-form prose gives prominence to the particulars that writers experience. As Anderson comments, "details make sense. The trivial has meaning." Figurative language—such as metaphors, similes, and personifications—appeals to readers' imaginations, eliciting emotional as well as mental responses.

Of the many kinds of open-form prose, one of the most common and one that you will probably have the most occasion to write is an autobiographical narrative. A personal narrative combines an expressive purpose (writing that emphasizes the writer's experiences and feelings) with a literary purpose (writing that uses strategies of literature for an aesthetic effect.) To help you see the possibilities and demands of open-form writing, we begin with an example of an autobiographical narrative written by a student.

After reading the essay, respond to the questions that follow.

READING

▼
PATRICK KLEIN

BERKELEY BLUES

[handwritten marginal note: very discriptive doesn't give thesis so writing makes you want to keep reading to see point of story.]

It was a cold night. That is nothing new in San Francisco, but something made this   1
night particularly frigid. It was early February and the whole city, including the Berkeley section where we were staying, was still held tight in the firm grip of winter. It had
also rained that afternoon and the air, having been cleared by the storm, was cold and
sharp. It hurt the back of your throat when you inhaled and turned into mist when you
exhaled. As the six of us hurriedly walked in a huddled mass, the water that was lying
in puddles on the dimly lit sidewalk jumped out of our way as we slammed our dress
shoes down into its dregs. We silently decided on our destination and slipped into the
grungy, closet-like pizza joint. We took the only seats the place had and as we pulled
them into a circle, we all breathed a sigh of relief.

This was our first night at Berkeley. We were there for a debate tournament to be   2
held the next day at the university. On this night, however, we were six high school
sophomores in search of food. So, dressed in our suits and ties (we were required to
wear them) and heavy coats, we ventured out of the university and entered the city of
Berkeley.

Berkeley is an interesting place. Many might have romantic notions of a bunch of   3
shaggy intellectuals discussing French existentialism while sipping cappuccino, but
while this might have been the case a few decades ago, the reality is that Berkeley is
a ghetto. The place is filled with grungy closet shops while newspapers cover the sidewalks and the people lying on them. The university is divided from this ghetto by a two-
lane street.

As the six of us crossed the two-lane street that fateful night, my thoughts drifted   4
to my own neighborhood, which up until that moment had been the extent of my world.

McCormick Ranch, Arizona, is a sheltered place. To a certain extent it's mostly   5
white, with little crime and few domestic problems. Everybody has a pool, at least two
cars, and a beautiful desert sunset every night. I had everything I ever wanted. It
seemed very gentle and dreamlike compared to the harsh slum we found ourselves in.

When we made it into the pizza place and moved the chairs into a protective cir-   6
cle around a square table, anxiety about our "hostile" environment was quickly swept
away with hot, greasy pizza. We ate until we were content and were trying to decide
how to divide the few remaining pieces among ourselves when it happened.

The pizza place was separated from the rest of humanity by a large window. Our   7
table was directly in front of that window and two feet from the door. People had been
passing the window and probably remarking on the six well-dressed kids inside, but we
paid them no mind and they all walked by without incident. Still, our hearts were seized
with terror every time a human being would pass that window, and we hoped with all
that we could muster that every one of them would continue on. We were almost right.

On this night, when six young yuppie kids from an upper middle-class world de-   8
cided to risk it and go eat pizza in a ghetto, he walked by. He didn't look any different
from others we'd seen that night. Black. Dirty. Tired. Cold. His clothes consisted of a

grimy, newspaper-stained jacket, a T-shirt with who-knows-how-old dirt on it, flimsy pants with holes at the knees, and tattered excuses for shoes. He was not quite up to par with our Gucci loafers and Armani jackets.

9   He shuffled past the window and glanced in. We didn't notice. He stopped. We noticed. Twelve eyes glanced up as casually as they could and six hearts stopped beating for a second. Yep, still there. All eyes went back to the floor, except for two. Those eyes belonged to Chad, and in some act of defiance, his eyes met the poor man's eyes and glared.

10   The man opened the door. "We're all going to die," I thought. "All my hopes and dreams are going to end here, in a stupid pizza place, at the hands of a crazy black bum."

11   He took something out of his pocket.

12   It was shiny.

13   I couldn't look.

14   A knife.

15   No. It was a flask. He took a swig from it, and, still propping the door open with his sagging frame, spoke the most jolting, burning words I've ever heard.

16   "I love you," he said. "All of you." He glanced at Chad, "Even you." He stepped back and said, "I know what you think of me, but I still love you." I will probably never forget those words or how he said them with a steady, steely voice.

17   Then he left. That was it. Gone. It took about five minutes for anyone to talk. When the talking started, we exchanged jokes and responded with empty, devastating laughter.

18   We soon left the shop. It had grown colder outside and we quickly returned to our climate-controlled hotel room. We had just eaten a filling meal and paid for it with our own money. We were all about fifteen. The man we had encountered was probably in his fifties. He had no roof, no money, or food. It seemed strange that I owned more than an adult, but in truth, he had more than I. He was able to love us when we ostracized him and thought stereotypically about him.

19   ¶ I remember later trying to rationalize my sickening behavior by thinking that there is nothing wrong with being and acting afraid in a strange environment. I tried to use my age as an excuse. Nothing worked. I was guilty of fearing a fellow human being because of his color and my preset notions of bums.

20   To this day I still think about what difference, if any, it would have made if we had given him our leftover pizza. It might have eased my conscience. It was a very cold night and we had made it colder.

2) Significance is he realizes his unnecessary fear of blacks & "bums".

Thesis

FOR WRITING AND DISCUSSION

1. A piece of advice often given to open-form writers is "Above all else, be interesting." How does student writer Patrick Klein hook and sustain readers' interest? *intriging observations of surroundings*

2. This essay does not assert a thesis statement in the introduction, yet the narrative has a focus and a theme that becomes increasingly clear near the end. What do you see as the theme of significance of this essay?

3. According to his instructor, Patrick was at first unable to think of a topic to write about. (The assignment was to write an autobiographical

narrative about an event that made a difference in your life.) "But I can't think of anything that made a big difference in my life!" he commented. Then his teacher asked him to write a journal entry in which he looked at some event, situation, or behavior, however minor, that he now regretted. This journal entry led him to remember the incident in the pizza joint, which he still thought was no big deal and too minor to write about. What Patrick came to understand is the point that Chris Anderson made about open-form writing: "Details make sense. The trivial has meaning." How has Patrick invested a seemingly trivial event with meaning?

[handwritten marginalia: He looked at his life & thought twice about his actions & reactions to people]

[handwritten annotation: related event to how you treat people and your judgements of people based on the way you're brought up. His opinion toward "bums".]

■ IDENTIFYING AND CREATING A MINIMAL STORY

In open-form prose, where you do not have a thesis upon which to build a hierarchy of points and subpoints, you need to use other structures to convey meaning. Open-form writing relies heavily on narrative for its substance and form. Another word for the term *narrative* is story. As we show in this section, what distinguishes a story from *and then* writing, which also follows chronological order, is *significance* conveyed through and embodied in a writer's conscious shaping of events and meaning. *And then* writing becomes a story when it has certain features: depicted events, connectedness, tension, and resolution. We say that to be a *minimal story*—a narrative must depict connected events that create a sense of tension or conflict that is resolved through insight, understanding, or action.

Depiction of Events

The depiction of events is the defining feature of narrative. Whereas thesis-based writing descends from problem to thesis to supporting reasons and evidence, stories unfold linearly, temporally, from event to event over time. Consider the sequence of events in the following fable.

Minimal Story: Depiction of Events

A crow stole a large chunk of cheese off a windowsill and flew away to a high tree to eat it. A fox witnessed the theft and trotted over beneath the tree. As the crow prepared to eat the cheese, the fox watched quietly. Finally, the fox cleared his throat and caught the crow's attention.

"Excuse me, sir. I couldn't help but notice the lovely black sheen of your feathers. Really quite striking. And the graceful lines of your body, the perfect proportions. One just doesn't see that sort of beauty around here everyday."

The crow listened closely, puffing himself up with each of the fox's compliments.

"I also can't help wondering if your voice is as beautiful as your body. If it is, you are, to be sure, the king of birds in these woods."

The crow, eager to affirm the fox's high opinion of him, broke out in a raucous, cawing serenade. The moment he opened his beak, the cheese fell to the ground at the fox's feet. The fox promptly ate the morsel and trotted away, calling out over his shoulder as he left:

"So much for your beauty; next time we meet, let's discuss your brains."

Moral: "It is a maxim in the schools,
    That Flattery's the food of fools;"
And whoso likes such airy meat
Will soon have nothing else to eat.

—Oliver Goldsmith, "The Crow and the Fox," *Aesop's Fables*

This story recounts the events of a crow stealing a piece of cheese and a wily fox cajoling the crow into forfeiting the cheese.

In addition to the temporal unfolding of events in a story, the events should convey a sense of "onceness." Things that happen at a point in time happen only once, as the classic fairytale opening, "Once upon a time," suggests. To be sure, many people enter college or get married every day, but no one else's account of that experience can be substituted for your account of your own experience of universal events. Composing and revising your narrative involves the challenge of depicting your experience as a series of events that capture the "onceness" of that experience.

Connectedness

To be a minimal story, the events of a narrative must also be connected—not merely spatially or sequentially connected, but causally or thematically related as well. They must affect one another. Stories are more than just chronicles of events. Novelist E. M. Forster offered the simplest definition of a true narrative when he rejected "The King dies and then the queen died," but accepted "The king died and then the queen died . . . of grief." The last two words in the second version connect the two events to each other in a causal relationship, converting a series of events into a patterned, meaningfully related sequence of events. Now examine the following passage to see the kinds of connections the writer establishes between the scenes he describes.

Minimal Story: Thematic and Causal Connectedness

I have been so totally erased from nature lately, like a blackboard before school starts, that yesterday when I was in the Japanese section of San Francisco, Japantown, I saw the sidewalk littered with chocolate wrappers.

There were hundreds of them. Who in the hell has been eating all these chocolates? I thought. A convention of Japanese chocolate eaters must have passed this way.

Then I noticed some plum trees on the street. Then I noticed that it was autumn. Then I noticed that the leaves were falling as they will and as they must every year. Where had I gone wrong?

—Richard Brautigan, "Leaves"

Brautigan's narrative becomes a story only when you realize that the "chocolate wrappers" are really plum leaves; the two images are connected by the writer's changed perception, which illuminates the thematic question raised at the beginning and the end: Why has the writer become "so totally erased from nature"? As you write, make the elements of your narrative connect causally and thematically.

Tension or Conflict

The third criterion for a minimal story—tension or conflict—creates the anticipation and potential significance that keeps the reader reading. In whodunit stories, the tension follows from attempts to identify the murderer or to prevent the murderer from doing in yet another victim. In many comic works, the tension is generated by confusion or misunderstanding that drives a wedge between people who would normally be close. Tension always involves contraries, such as those between one belief and another, between opposing values, between the individual and the environment or the social order, between where I am now and where I want to be or used to be. In the following passage, see how the contraries create dramatic tension that engages readers.

Minimal Story: Dramatic Tensions

Straddling the top of the world, one foot in China and the other in Nepal, I cleared the ice from my oxygen mask, hunched a shoulder against the wind, and stared absently down at the vastness of Tibet. I understood on some dim, detached level that the sweep of earth beneath my feet was a spectacular sight. I'd been fantasizing about this moment, and the release of emotion that would accompany it, for many months. But now that I was finally here, actually standing on the summit of Mount Everest, I just couldn't summon the energy to care.

It was early in the afternoon of May 10, 1996. I hadn't slept in fifty-seven hours. The only food I'd been able to force down over the preceding three days was a bowl of ramen soup and a handful of peanut M&Ms. Weeks of violent coughing had left me with two separated ribs that made ordinary breathing an excruciating trial. At 29,028 feet up in the troposphere, so little oxygen was reaching my brain that my mental capacity was that of a slow child. Under the circumstances, I was incapable of feeling much of anything except cold and tired.

—Jon Krakauer, *Into Thin Air*

Notice how this passage presents several contraries or conflicts: the opposition between the narrator's expectation of what it would be like to stand on the top of Mount Everest and the actuality once he's there; and the opposition between the physical strength and stamina of the climber and the extreme danger of climbing this mountain. The reader wonders how Krakauer reached the summit with no sleep, almost no food, and a violent and agonizing cough; more important, the reader wonders why he kept on climbing. We can ask this important query of any narrative: What conflicts and tensions are prompting readers' ongoing questions and holding their interest?

Resolution, Recognition, or Retrospective Interpretation

The final criterion for a minimal story is the resolution or retrospective interpretation of events. The resolution may be stated explicitly or implied. Fables typically sum up the story's significance with an explicit moral at the end. In contrast, the interpretation of events in poetry is almost always implicit. Note how the following haiku collapses events and resolution.

> A strange old man
> stops me,
> Looking out of my deep mirror.
>
> —Hitomaro, *One Hundred Poems from the Japanese*

In this minimal story, two things happen simultaneously. The narrator is stopped by a "strange old man" and the narrator looks into a mirror. The narrator's *recognition* is that he is that same old man. This recognition—"That's I in the mirror; when I wasn't looking, I grew old!"—in turn ties the singular event of the story back to more universal concerns and the reader's world.

The typical direction of a story, from singular event(s) to general conclusion, reverses the usual points-first direction of closed-form essays. Stories force readers to read inductively, gathering information and looking for a pattern that's confirmed or disconfirmed by the story's resolution. This resolution is the point *toward* which readers read. It often drives home the significance of the narrative. Typically, a reader's satisfaction or dissatisfaction with a story hinges on how well the resolution manages to explain or justify the events that precede it. Writers need to ask: How does my resolution grow out of my narrative and fit with the resolution the reader has been forming?

FOR WRITING AND DISCUSSION

1. Working as a whole class or in groups, explain how the student essay "Berkeley Blues" (pp. 250–51) qualifies as a minimal story. How does it meet the four basic criteria for a minimal story: depiction of events, connectedness, tension, and resolution?

2. In contrast, how does the following *and then* narrative fail to meet the criteria for a minimal story? How does your experience as a reader differ as you ponder "Berkeley Blues" versus "The Stolen Watch?"

```
                       The Stolen Watch


    Last fall and winter I was living in Spokane with my brother, who

during this time had a Platonic girlfriend come over from Seattle

and stay for a weekend. Her name was Karen, and we became interested

in each other and I went over to see her at the first of the year.
```

She then invited me to, supposedly, the biggest party of the year, called the Aristocrats' Ball. I said sure and made my way back to Seattle in February. It started out bad on Friday, the day my brother and I left Spokane. We left town an hour late, but what's new. Then my brother had to stop along the way and pick up some parts; we stayed there for an hour trying to find this guy. It all started out bad because we arrived in Seattle and I forgot to call Karen. We were staying at her brother's house and after we brought all our things in, we decided to go to a few bars. Later that night we ran into Karen in one of the bars, and needless to say she was not happy with me. When I got up the next morning I knew I should have stayed in Spokane, because I felt bad vibes. Karen made it over about an hour before the party. By the time we reached the party, which drove me crazy, she wound up with another guy, so her friends and I decided to go to a few bars. The next morning when I was packing, I could not find my watch and decided that someone had to have taken it. We decided that it had to have been the goon that Karen had wound up with the night before, because she was at her brother's house with him before she went home. So how was I going to get my watch back?

We decided the direct and honest approach to the problem would work out the best. We got in contact and confronted him. This turned out to be quite a chore. It turned out that he was visiting some of his family during that weekend and lived in Little Harbor, California. It turned out that Karen knew his half brother and got some information on him, which was not pretty. He had just been released by the army and was trained in a special forces unit, in the fields of Martial Arts. He was a trained killer! This information did not help matters at all, but the next bit of information was just as bad if not worse. Believe it or not, he was up on charges of attempted murder and breaking and entering. In a way, it turned out lucky for me, because he was in enough trouble with the police and did not need any more. Karen got in contact with him and threatened him that I would bring him up on charges, if he did not return the watch. His mother decided that he was in enough trouble and sent me the watch. I was astounded, it was still working and looked fine. The moral of the story is don't drive 400 miles to see a girl you hardly know, and whatever you do, don't leave your valuables out in the open.

CONSIDERING STRUCTURAL OPTIONS FOR OPEN-FORM WRITING

The epigraph to Chapter 11 by the philosopher Kenneth Burke speaks about form as "an arousing and fulfillment of desires." In closed-form prose, we can easily see this process at work: The writer previews what he or she is going to say, arousing the reader's desire to see the general statement translated into specifics, and then fulfills that desire speedily through a presentation of pertinent points and particulars.

In more open-form prose, the fulfillment of desire follows a less straightforward path. Writers offer fewer overviews and clues, leaving readers less sure of where they're headed; or writers mention an idea and then put it aside for a while as they pursue some other point, whose relevance may seem tenuous. Rather than establish the direction or point of their prose, writers suspend that direction, waiting until later in the prose to show how the ideas are meaningfully related. In other words, the period of arousal is longer and more drawn out; the fulfillment of desire is delayed until the end, when the reader finally sees how the pieces fit together.

Open-form prose gives you the opportunity to overlay your narrative core with other patterns of ideas—to move associatively from idea to idea, to weave a complex pattern of meaning in which the complete picture emerges later. Often the way you achieve these surprising twists and turns of structure and meaning is by playing with the conventions of closed-form prose. For example, in the autobiographical narrative "Berkeley Blues," Patrick Klein breaks the cardinal closed-form rule that pronouns should refer only to previously stated antecedents; he introduces the stranger only as *he* and gradually reveals that person's identity. This violation creates an aura of mystery and suspense. Here we describe some of your open-form options to surprise your readers and delay their fulfillment of desires.

Suspending and Disrupting Readers' Desire for Direction

Open-form writers frequently violate the principle of forecasting and mapping that we stressed in Chapter 11. Consider the following introduction to an essay.

Passage with Suspended Direction

Whose bones?
What feathers?
Birds? What
birds?

I suppose their little bones have years ago been lost among the stones and winds of those high glacial pastures. I suppose their feathers blew eventually into the piles of tumbleweed beneath the straggling cattle fences and rotted there in the mountain snows, along with dead steers and all the other things that drift to an end in the corners of the wire. I do not quite know why I should be thinking of birds over the *New York Times* at breakfast, particularly the birds of my youth half a continent away. It is a funny thing what the brain will do with memories and how it will treasure them and finally bring them into odd juxtapositions with other things, as though it wanted to make a design, or get some meaning out of them, whether you want it or not, or even see it.

What do birds
have to do with
the working of the
brain? Where is
this writer going?

—Loren Eisley, "The Bird and the Machine"

Note the sequence of ideas from bones to birds to breakfast over the *New York Times* to comments about the workings of the brain. In fact, in this essay it takes Eisley six full paragraphs in which he discusses mechanical inventions to return to the birds with the line: ". . . or those birds, I'll never forget those birds. . . ."

Throughout these paragraphs, what drives the reader forward is curiosity to discover the connections between the parts and to understand the meaning of the essay's title "The Bird and the Machine." Actually, Eisley's comment about the brain's "odd juxtaposition" of memories with "other things, as though it wanted to make a design, or get meaning out of them" could be a description of this open-form technique we've called *suspending direction.* Open-form writers can choose when "odd juxtapositions" are an appropriate strategy for inviting the reader to accompany the discovering, reflecting writer on a journey toward meaning.

Leaving Gaps

An important convention of closed-form prose is the old/new contract, which specifies that the opening of every sentence should link back in some way to what has gone before. Open-form prose often violates this convention, leaving *gaps* in the text, forcing the reader to puzzle over the connection between one part and the next.

The following passage clearly violates the old/new contract. This example recounts the writer's thoughts after startling a weasel in the woods and exchanging glances with it.

Passage with Intentional Gaps

What goes on in [a weasel's brain] the rest of the time? What does a weasel think about? He won't say. His journal is tracks in clay, a spray of feathers, mouse blood and bone: uncollected, unconnnected, loose-leaf, and blown.

I would like to learn, or remember, how to live. I come to Hollins Pond not so much to learn how to live as, frankly, to forget about it.

—Annie Dillard, "Living like Weasels"

Gap caused by unexplained or unpredicted shift from weasel to philosophic musing

Dillard suddenly switches, without transition, from musing about the mental life of a weasel to asserting that she would like to learn how to live. What is the connection between her encounter with the weasel and her own search for how to live? Dillard's open-form prose leaves these gaps for readers to ponder and fill in, inviting us to participate in the process of arriving at meaning. Just as open-form writers can deliberately avoid predicting or mapping statements, they also have the liberty to leave gaps in a text when it suits their purpose.

Employing Unstable or Ironic Points of View

Whereas the closed-form style encourages a single sort of viewpoint—rational, trustworthy, thoughtful—the open-form style tolerates a variety of viewpoints, including some that are more perplexing than reassuring. In open-form prose, writers are free to don masks and play around with different personae, including some that the writer may question or even loathe. A particular favorite of open-form writers is the ironic point of view. In this context, *irony* means saying one thing while intending other things, one of which may be the exact opposite of what's being said.

Consider the following bit of irony from eighteenth-century writer Jonathan Swift:

> I have been assured by a very knowing American of my acquaintance in London, that a young healthy child well nursed is at a year old a most delicious, nourishing, and wholesome food, whether stewed, roasted, baked, or boiled; and I make no doubt that it will equally serve in a fricassee or a ragout.

The shock of this passage comes in part from the narrator's sudden change of direction. The opening seemingly points toward some elevating discussion of child wellness. Then, without warning, the reader is plunged into a grotesque treatise on the tastiness of cooked children.

Clearly the narrator's values are not shared by Swift, a religious Irishman who spent much of his life protesting the very sort of inhumanity he presents in this passage. What does Swift gain by adopting the persona of a moral monster and proposing that poor Irish people sell their children to English gentry for food in order to reduce Ireland's population and make some money? For one thing, he gains immediacy.

By stepping inside the persona that he reviles, Swift dramatizes what he sees as the snobbish, self-assured, and predatory English "gentleman." He doesn't talk about his enemy; he *becomes* that enemy so that the reader can see him as Swift sees him. Swift could have written an essay condemning the callous attitudes that were causing the Irish people so much suffering. But consider what would happen to the passage if Swift were to speak for himself.

> The landed English gentry who control Ireland treat the Irish people like consumer goods to be bought, sold, and used up in the service of their self-interests. For all the English care, we Irish could be chunks of mutton to be tossed into their nightly stew.

That's still pretty strong, but it leaves the reader outside the evil that Swift describes. The audience hears about "landed English gentry" but doesn't experience their attitudes, values, and language directly, as in the original passage. The difference in the two passages is the difference between being told that someone is really hideous and spending half an hour trapped in a phone booth with that person.

Unstable viewpoints aren't always this dramatic. But they always offer writers the freedom to present directly, through dialogue and perspective, points of view that they might otherwise have to re-present via summary and argument. Such viewpoints also require readers to be more attentive in order to distinguish the author's point of view from that of the narrator.

◤ USING LANGUAGE ARTISTICALLY FOR MEANING AND PLEASURE

Perhaps the first thing you notice about open-form prose is its great range of styles. In many cases, you can read a paragraph of open-form prose and identify the writer solely by the style. The primacy of style in open-form prose results from the writer's desire to use language artistically for meaning and pleasure. In open-form writing, you may well be arrested by a writer's peculiar use of language—an evocative word, a striking phrase, an unexpected metaphor, or an unusual construction.

Let us consider more closely some of the ways that open-form writers play with the medium of language.

Using Specific Words

According to the poet William Blake, "To Generalize is to be an Idiot." Open-form writers don't usually go that far, but they do tend to stay at a fairly low level of abstraction, typically eschewing a hierarchy of points and subpoints in favor of an artful array of particulars.

To illustrate what might constitute "an artful array of particulars," consider the case of writer John McPhee. When asked why he wrote the sentence "Old white oaks are rare because they had a tendency to become bowsprits, barrel staves, and queen-post trusses" instead of a more generic sentence, such as "Old white oaks are rare because they used to be so valuable as lumber," he responded in a way that reveals his love of the particular.

> There isn't much life in [the alternative version of the sentence]. If you can find a specific, firm, and correct image, it's always going to be better than a generality, and hence I tend, for example, to put in trade names and company names and, in an instance like this, the names of wood products instead of a general term like "lumber." You'd say "Sony" instead of "tape recorder" if the context made it clear you meant to say tape recorder. It's not because you're on the take from Sony, it's because the image, at least to this writer or reader, strikes a clearer note.

Some readers might complain that the particulars "bowsprits, barrel staves, and queen-post trusses" aren't helpful in the way that particulars in closed-form prose are. In closed-form prose, examples clarify and support points. McPhee, on the other hand, uses three unusual examples that will give most readers a moment's pause. Today most barrel staves and bowsprits are made of metal, not oak, and few contemporary readers encounter them on a regular basis no matter what they're made of. Furthermore, few readers at any time could readily identify "queen-post trusses," a technical term from the building trade. Instead of smoothly completing the reader's understanding of a point, McPhee's particulars tend to arrest and even sidetrack, sending the reader in pursuit of a dictionary.

But if McPhee's examples momentarily puzzle, it's the sort of puzzlement that can lead to greater understanding. Precisely because they are exotic terms, these words arouse the reader's curiosity and imagination. "Exotic language is of value," says McPhee. "A queen-post truss is great just because of the sound of the words and what they call to mind. The 'queen,' the 'truss'—the ramifications in everything."

For McPhee, the fact that these words trip up the reader is a point in their favor. If McPhee had said that old white oaks are rare these days because they became parts of "floors, buckets, and fences" no one would blink or notice. If you were to visualize the items, you'd probably call up some ready-made pictures that leave little trace in your mind. You also wouldn't hear the sounds of the words. (In this regard, notice McPhee's emphasis on images sounding "a clearer note.") Your forward progress toward the point would be unimpeded, but what would be lost? A new glimpse into a lost time when oak trees were used to make exotic items that today exist mostly in old books and memories.

Another quality also recommends words that readers trip over, words such as *bowsprit, barrel stave,* and *queen-post truss*: their power to persuade the reader to believe in the world being described. Tripping over things, whether they're made of steel or words, forces the reader to acknowledge their independence, the reality of a world outside the reader's own head. For this reason, writers of formula fiction—thrillers, westerns, romances, and the like—will load their texts with lots of little details and bits of technical information from the time and place they describe. Because their stories are otherwise implausible (e.g., the description of the Evil Empire's doomsday machine) they need all the help they can get from their details (the size of the toggle bolts used to keep the machine in place while it's blasting out intergalactic death rays) to convince readers that the story is real.

Using Revelatory Words

We use the term *revelatory words* for specific details that reveal the social status, lifestyle, beliefs, and values of people. According to writer Tom Wolfe, carefully chosen details can reveal a person's *status life*—"the entire pattern of behavior and possessions through which people express their position in the world or what they think it is or hope it to be."

Wolfe favors writing that records "everyday gestures, habits, manners, customs, styles of furniture, clothing, decoration, styles of traveling, eating, keeping house, modes of behaving toward children, servants, superiors, inferiors, peers, plus the various looks, glances, poses, styles of walking and other symbolic details that might exist within a scene." For example, Patrick Klein and his classmates are economically revealed as middle class by their attire—"Armani jackets" and "Gucci loafers."

FOR WRITING AND DISCUSSION

Try your own hand at using descriptive details that reveal status life. Working in small groups or as a whole class, create a list of specific details that you might associate with each of the following: junior-high boys standing on a street corner; college professor's office; the kitchen of an upscale apartment of a two-professional couple; the kitchen of a lower-middle-class blue-collar family; the kitchen of an apartment shared by college students.

Example: Junior high boys standing on a street corner might be associated with baggy pants with crotch at the knee level and exposed boxer shorts; Nike Air Jordans with the top laces loose; Marlboro cigarettes; Chicago Bulls cap on backwards.

Using Memory-Soaked Words

Wolfe offers a psychological explanation for the pleasure people take in exotic or revelatory language: "Print (as opposed to film or theater) is an indirect medium that does not so much 'create' images or emotions as jog the reader's memories." The best way to jog that memory and evoke sensations, according to Wolfe, is through careful selection of very specific words and images that evoke complex responses in the brain; the "human memory seems to be made up of *sets of meaningful data*" (emphasis ours) as opposed to separate bits of data that people consciously combine. In the following passage, Wolfe describes the complex interplay between writers' words and readers' responses.

> These memory sets often combine a complete image and an emotion. The power of a single image in a story or song to evoke a complex feeling is well known. I have always enjoyed the opening lines of a country and western song by Roger Miller called "King of the Road." "Trailers for Sale or Rent," it begins, "Room to Let Fifty Cents." It is not the part about trailers that I enjoy so much as the "Room to Let." This is the sort of archaic wording that, in my experience, is found only in windows or on door frames in the oldest and most run-down section of a city. It immediately triggers in my memory a particular view of a particular street near Worcester Square in New Haven, Connecticut. The emotion it calls up is one of loneliness and deprivation but of a rather romantic sort (bohemia). One's memory is apparently made up of millions of such sets, which work together. . . . The most gifted writers are those who manipulate the memory sets of the reader in such a rich fashion that they create within the mind of the reader an entire world that resonates with the reader's own real emotions.
>
> —Tom Wolfe, *New Journalism*

Had Miller opened his song with "Room *for Rent* Fifty Cents," there would have been no loss of clarity; if anything, most people would process the more familiar "rent" more rapidly than "let." The loss would have been associational and emotional. "For Rent" signs are too common to evoke any particular set of associations for most people. "To Let" signs, however, are rare enough that they are much more likely to evoke particular times and places for those who've encountered them. People who have never heard the phrase "to let" will either puzzle over it and eventually experience the pleasure of making sense of it or not notice the substitution and pass over it.

FOR WRITING AND DISCUSSION

Make a list of specific words and names associated with your childhood that you now rarely hear or use. Share your list with others in your group and identify the items that provoke the strongest associations. Examples include *Flexible Flyer* for those who remember those old sleds; *tetherball,* for those who have played that game on a playground; *Cookie Monster* from *Sesame Street; Pez guns; Mister Bill;* or *8-track tapes.* The idea is to think of specific words that are soaked with memories. Identify the emotions you associate with these words.

Using Figurative Words

Open-form writers often use figurative language in situations in which closed-form writers would use literal language. When journalist Nicholas Tomalin describes a captured Vietnamese prisoner as young and slight, the reader understands him in a literal way, but when he compares the prisoner to "a tiny, fine-boned wild animal," the reader understands him in a different way; the reader understands not only what the subject looks like—his general physical attributes—but how that particular boy appears in that moment to those around him—fierce, frightened, trapped.

Metaphors abound when literal words fail. When writers encounter eccentric people or are overwhelmed by the strangeness of their experiences, they use *figurative language*—imaginative comparisons—to explain their situation and their reactions to it. Figurative language—similes, metaphors, and personifications—enables the writer to describe an unfamiliar thing in terms of different, more familiar things. The surprise of yoking two very unlike things evokes from the reader a perception, insight, or emotional experience that could not otherwise be communicated. The originality and vividness of the imaginative comparison frequently resonates with meaning for readers and sticks in their minds long afterwards.

In the following passage, Isak Dinesen describes an experience that most of us have not had—seeing iguanas in the jungle and shooting one. After reading this passage, however, we have a striking picture in our minds of what she saw and a strong understanding of what she felt and realized.

Passage Using Figurative Language

Similes heaped up

Simile

Metaphor of dying applied to color simile

Metaphor

Simile

In the Reserve I have sometimes come upon the Iguana, the big lizards, as they were sunning themselves upon a flat stone in a river-bed. They are not pretty in shape, but nothing can be imagined more beautiful than their coloring. They shine like a heap of precious stones or like a pane cut out of an old church window. When, as you approach, they swish away, there is a flash of azure, green and purple over the stones, the color seems to be standing behind them in the air, like a comet's luminous tail.

Once I shot an Iguana. I thought that I should be able to make some pretty things from his skin. A strange thing happened then, that I have never afterwards forgotten. As I went up to him, where he was lying dead upon his stone, and actually while I was walking a few steps, he faded and grew pale, all color <u>died</u> out of him as in one long sigh, and by the time that I touched him he was gray and dull like a lump of concrete. It was the live impetuous blood pulsating within the animal, which had radiated out all that glow and splendor. Now that the flame was put out, and the soul had flown, the Iguana was as dead as a sandbag.

—Isak Dinesen, "The Iguana"

The figurative language in this passage enables readers to share Dinesen's experience. It also compacts a large amount of information into sharp, memorable images.

To see how structural and stylistic options contribute to the effectiveness of a piece of literary nonfiction, read the following essay, "Living like Weasels," by nature writer and essayist Annie Dillard from her book *Teaching a Stone to Talk: Expeditions and Encounters*. After you have read the essay, address the questions that follow.

READING

ANNIE DILLARD

LIVING LIKE WEASELS

1   A weasel is wild. Who knows what he thinks? He sleeps in his underground den, his tail draped over his nose. Sometimes he lives in his den for two days without leaving. Outside, he stalks rabbits, mice, muskrats, and birds, killing more bodies than he can eat warm, and often dragging the carcasses home. Obedient to instinct, he bites his prey at the neck, either splitting the jugular vein at the throat or crunching the brain at the base of the skull, and he does not let go. One naturalist refused to kill a weasel who was socketed into his hand deeply as a rattlesnake. The man could in no way pry the tiny weasel off, and he had to walk half a mile to water, the weasel dangling from his palm, and soak him off like a stubborn label.

2   And once, says Ernest Thompson Seton—once, a man shot an eagle out of the sky. He examined the eagle and found the dry skull of a weasel fixed by the jaws to his throat. The supposition is that the eagle had pounced on the weasel and the weasel swiveled and bit as instinct taught him, tooth to neck, and nearly won. I would like to have seen that eagle from the air a few weeks or months before he was shot: was the whole weasel still attached to his feathered throat, a fur pendant? or did the eagle eat what he could reach, gutting the living weasel with his talons before his breast, bending his beak, cleaning the beautiful airborne bones?

3   I have been reading about weasels because I saw one last week. I startled a weasel who startled me, and we exchanged a long glance.

4   Twenty minutes from my house, through the woods by the quarry and across the highway, is Hollins Pond, a remarkable piece of shallowness, where I like to go at sunset and sit on a tree trunk. Hollins Pond is also called Murray's Pond; it covers two acres of bottomland near Tinker Creek with six inches of water and six thousand lily pads. In winter, brown-and-white steers stand in the middle of it, merely dampening their hooves; from the distant shore they look like miracle itself, complete with miracle's nonchalance. Now, in summer, the steers are gone. The water lilies have blossomed and spread to a green horizontal plane that is terra firma to plodding blackbirds, and tremulous ceiling to black leeches, crayfish, and carp.

5   This is, mind you, suburbia. It is a five-minute walk in three directions to rows of houses, though none is visible here. There's a 55 mph highway at one end of the pond, and a nesting pair of wood ducks at the other. Under every bush is a muskrat hole or a beer can. The far end is an alternating series of fields and woods, fields and woods, threaded everywhere with motorcycle tracks—in whose bare clay wild turtles lay eggs.

6   So. I had crossed the highway, stepped over two low barbed-wire fences, and traced the motorcycle path in all gratitude through the wild rose and poison ivy of the pond's shoreline up into high grassy fields. Then I cut down through the woods to the mossy fallen tree where I sit. This tree is excellent. It makes a dry, upholstered bench at the

upper, marshy end of the pond, a plush jetty raised from the thorny shore between a shallow blue body of water and a deep blue body of sky.

The sun had just set. I was relaxed on the tree trunk, ensconced in the lap of lichen, watching the lily pads at my feet tremble and part dreamily over the thrusting path of a carp. A yellow bird appeared to my right and flew behind me. It caught my eye. I swiveled around—and the next instant, inexplicably, I was looking down at a weasel, who was looking up at me.   7

Weasel! I'd never seen one wild before. He was ten inches long, thin as a curve, a muscled ribbon, brown as fruitwood, soft-furred, alert. His face was fierce, small and pointed as a lizard's; he would have made a good arrowhead. There was just a dot of chin, maybe two brown hairs' worth, and then the pure white fur began that spread down his underside. He had two black eyes I didn't see, any more than you see a window.   8

The weasel was stunned into stillness as he was emerging from beneath an enormous shaggy wild rose bush four feet away. I was stunned into stillness twisted backward on the tree trunk. Our eyes locked, and someone threw away the key.   9

Our look was as if two lovers, or deadly enemies, met unexpectedly on an overgrown path when each had been thinking of something else: a clearing blow to the gut. It was also a bright blow to the brain, or a sudden beating of brains, with all the charge and intimate grate of rubbed balloons. It emptied our lungs. It felled the forest, moved the fields, and drained the pond; the world dismantled and tumbled into that black hole of eyes. If you and I looked at each other that way, our skulls would split and drop to our shoulders. But we don't. We keep our skulls. So.   10

He disappeared. This was only last week, and already I don't remember what shattered the enchantment. I think I blinked, I think I retrieved my brain from the weasel's brain, and tried to memorize what I was seeing, and the weasel felt the yank of separation, the careening splashdown into real life and the urgent current of instinct. He vanished under the wild rose. I waited motionless, my mind suddenly full of data and my spirit with pleadings, but he didn't return.   11

Please do not tell me about "approach-avoidance conflicts." I tell you I've been in that weasel's brain for sixty seconds, and he was in mine. Brains are private places, muttering through unique and secret tapes—but the weasel and I both plugged into another tape simultaneously, for a sweet and shocking time. Can I help it if it was a blank?   12

What goes on in his brain the rest of the time? What does a weasel think about? He won't say. His journal is tracks in clay, a spray of feathers, mouse blood and bone: uncollected, unconnected, loose-leaf, and blown.   13

I would like to learn, or remember, how to live. I come to Hollins Pond not so much to learn how to live as, frankly, to forget about it. That is, I don't think I can learn from a wild animal how to live in particular—shall I suck warm blood, hold my tail high, walk with my footprints precisely over the prints of my hands?—but I might learn something of mindlessness, something of the purity of living in the physical senses and the dignity of living without bias or motive. The weasel lives in necessity and we live in choice, hating necessity and dying at the last ignobly in its talons. I would like to live as I should, as the weasel lives as he should. And I suspect that for me the way is like the weasel's: open to time and death painlessly, noticing everything, remembering nothing, choosing the given with a fierce and pointed will.   14

I missed my chance. I should have gone for the throat. I should have lunged for that streak of white under the weasel's chin and held on, held on through mud and into the wild rose, held on for a dearer life. We could live under the wild rose wild as weasels,   15 mute and uncomprehending. I could very calmly go wild. I could live two days in the den, curled, leaning on mouse fur, sniffing bird bones, blinking, licking, breathing musk, my hair tangled in the roots of grasses. Down is a good place to go, where the mind is single. Down is out, out of your ever-loving mind and back to your careless senses. I remember muteness as a prolonged and giddy fast, where every moment is a feast of utterance received. Time and events are merely poured, unremarked, and ingested directly, like blood pulsed into my gut through a jugular vein. Could two live that way? Could two live under the wild rose, and explore by the pond, so that the smooth mind of each is as everywhere present to the other, and as received and as unchallenged, as falling snow?

16   We could, you know. We can live any way we want. People take vows of poverty, chastity, and obedience—even of silence—by choice. The thing is to stalk your calling in a certain skilled and supple way, to locate the most tender and live spot and plug into that pulse. This is yielding, not fighting. A weasel doesn't "attack" anything; a weasel lives as he's meant to, yielding at every moment to the perfect freedom of single necessity.

17   I think it would be well, and proper, and obedient, and pure, to grasp your one necessity and not let it go, to dangle from it limp wherever it takes you. Then even death, where you're going no matter how you live, cannot you part. Seize it and let it seize you up aloft even, till your eyes burn out and drop; let your musky flesh fall off in shreds, and let your very bones unhinge and scatter, loosened over fields, over fields and woods, lightly, thoughtless, from any height at all, from as high as eagles.

FOR WRITING AND DISCUSSION

Working in small groups or as a whole class, use the questions that follow to guide your close examination of Dillard's structural and stylistic choices.

1. How does Dillard's essay meet the requirements for a minimal story? What are the events depicted in this piece? How are they connected? What are the contraries that give the story tension and conflict? What resolution or interpretation does Dillard offer?
2. To what extent do the opening paragraphs of this essay predict its focus and meaning? How does she create a design of ideas through juxtapositions? What would you say is the theme or meaning of this piece? What is it about?
3. Choose *three* consecutive paragraphs in this essay and examine how Dillard employs gaps between sentences to stimulate readers to think actively with her about the questions she is raising. Try tracking her ideas from sentence to sentence in these paragraphs. Where are the biggest gaps?
4. How does Dillard experiment with viewpoint, and how is this shifting of perspective part of the significance of her narrative?
5. Find *ten* examples of Dillard's use of specific words and *ten* examples of figurative language and explain how these are particularly effective

> in holding the reader's interest and in portraying the intensity of her experience. Can you find examples of memory-soaked words? What possible memories does Dillard appeal to?

◪ COMBINING CLOSED AND OPEN ELEMENTS

So far we have been talking about features of open-form prose in its purer forms. Sometimes, however, writers wish simply to loosen basically closed-form prose by combining it with some features of open-form prose. If, for example, an academic wanted to share new developments in a field with a popular audience, he or she would be well advised to leaven his or her prose with some elements of open-form writing. In this final section, we offer several pieces of advice for loosening up closed-form prose.

Introducing Some Humor

Humor is rare in tightly closed prose because humor is nonfunctional—it doesn't *have* to be there for a writer to make a point—and closed-form prose values efficiency, getting what you have to say said in the most economical fashion. Also, closed-form writers are concerned with being taken seriously, and for some readers, serious writing and humorous writing are incompatible. Writers who make people laugh may find themselves being taken less seriously, no matter how unfair that may be.

Humor is closely related to one of the mainsprings of open-form style, surprise. Humor typically depends on sudden twists and abrupt changes in direction. In physical comedy, pratfalls are funny in direct proportion to the audience's inability to see them coming. In verbal humor, the less clearly the audience sees the punch line coming, the more it makes the audience laugh.

Humor is particularly valuable in that it can make imposing subjects more manageable for readers. Just as humor can deflate pretensions and bring down the high and the mighty in an instant, it can make difficult and foreign subjects less anxiety producing. Formal, abstract language can put readers off, estranging them from the subject; humor has the power to "de-strange" a subject, to allow the audience to look at it long enough to understand it. Many popular books on science and many of the best instructional books on car repair, cooking, money management, and other of life's drearier necessities use a humorous style to help their phobic readers get on with life.

To appreciate the effect of humor, consider the following passages from two different instructional books on how to operate the database program Paradox. The first passage, from *Windows in 21 Days,* uses a clear, humor-free, closed-form style.

> In this book, you learn by following detailed step-by-step exercises based on real-world problems in database application design. Every exercise leads you

further into the power of "Paradox for Windows" as you develop the components of an automated application. This section does the following: explains the assumptions and conventions used in this book; lists the hardware and software requirements and setup needed to run Paradox for Windows and use this book efficiently; and offers some suggestions for strategies to get the most from this book. The step-by-step exercises make it easy.

Now note the different effect produced by the following passage from one of the hugely popular *Dummies* books:

> Welcome to *Paradox for Windows for Dummies*, a book that's not afraid to ask the tough questions like "When's lunch?" and "Who finished the cookie dough ice cream?" If you're more interested in food (or Australian Wombats, for that matter) than you are in Paradox for Windows, this book is for you. If you're more interested in Paradox for Windows, please get some professional help before going out into society again.
>
> My goal is to help you get things done despite the fact that you're using Paradox. Whether you're at home, in your office, or at home in your office (or even if you just *feel* like you live at work) *Paradox for Windows for Dummies* is your all-in-one guidebook through the treacherous, frustrating, and appallingly technical world of the relational database.

FOR WRITING AND DISCUSSION   *answer for journal 4*

1. Which of these two instructional books would you prefer to read?
2. The second passage says that the world of relational databases is "treacherous, frustrating, and appallingly technical," whereas the first stresses that the "step-by-step exercises [in the book] make it easy." Why do you suppose the humorous passage stresses the difficulty of databases whereas the humorless passage stresses the ease of a step-by-step approach? Is it good strategy for the humorous writer to stress the difficulty of Paradox?
3. Under what rhetorical circumstances are humorous instructions better than strictly serious instructions? When is a strictly serious approach better?

Using Techniques from Popular Magazines

Writers who publish regularly for popular audiences develop a vigorous, easy-reading style that differs from the style of much academic writing. The effect of this difference is illustrated by the results of a famous research study conducted by Michael Graves and Wayne Slater at the University of Michigan. For this study, teams of writers revised passages from a high school history textbook.* One team consisted of linguists and technical writers trained in producing closed-form texts using the strategies discussed in Chapter 11 (forecasting structure, putting points

*The study involved three teams, but for purposes of simplification we limit our discussion to two.

first, following the old/new contract, using transitions). A second team consisted of two *Time-Life* book editors.

Whereas the linguists aimed at making the passages clearer, the *Time-Life* writers were more concerned with making them livelier. The result? One hundred eleventh grade students found the *Time-Life* editors' version both more comprehensible and more memorable. Lack of clarity wasn't the problem with the original textbook; unbearable dryness was the problem. According to the researchers, the *Time-Life* editors did not limit themselves

> to making the passages lucid, well-organized, coherent, and easy to read. Their revisions went beyond such matters and were intended to make the texts interesting, exciting, vivid, rich in human drama, and filled with colorful language.

To see how they achieved this effect, let's look at their revision. Here is a passage about the Vietnam War taken from the original history text.

Original History Text

The most serious threat to world peace developed in Southeast Asia. Communist guerrillas threatened the independence of the countries carved out of French Indo-China by the Geneva conference of 1954. In South Vietnam, Communist guerrillas (the Viet Cong) were aided by forces from Communist North Vietnam in a struggle to overthrow the American-supported government. . . .

Shortly after the election of 1964, Communist gains prompted President Johnson to alter his policy concerning Vietnam. American military forces in Vietnam were increased from about 20,000 men in 1964 to more than 500,000 by 1968. Even so, North Vietnamese troops and supplies continued to pour into South Vietnam.

Here is the *Time-Life* editors' revision.

History Presented in Popular Magazine Style

In the early 1960's the greatest threat to world peace was just a small splotch of color on Kennedy's map, one of the fledgling nations sculpted out of French Indo-China by the Geneva peacemakers of 1954. It was a country so tiny and remote that most Americans had never uttered its name: South Vietnam. . . .

Aided by Communist North Vietnam, the Viet Cong guerrillas were eroding the ground beneath South Vietnam's American-backed government. Village by village, road by road, these jungle-wise rebels were waging a war of ambush and mining: They darted out of tunnels to head off patrols, buried exploding booby traps beneath the mud floors of huts, and hid razor-sharp bamboo sticks in holes. . . .

No sooner had Johnson won the election than Communist gains prompted Johnson to go back on his campaign promise. The number of American soldiers in Vietnam skyrocketed from 20,000 in 1964 to more than 500,000 by 1968. But in spite of GI patrols, leech-infested jungles, swarms of buzzing insects, and flash floods that made men cling to trees to escape being washed away—North Vietnamese troops streamed southward without letup along the Ho Chi Minh Trail.

What can this revision teach you about loosening up prose? What specifically are the editors doing here?

First, notice how far the level of abstraction drops in the revision. The original is barren of sensory words; the revision is alive with them ("South Vietnam" becomes a "small splotch of color on Kennedy's map"; "a struggle to overthrow the American-supported government" becomes "[They] buried exploding booby traps beneath the mud floors of huts and hid razor-sharp bamboo sticks in holes").

Second, notice how much more dramatic the revision is. Actual scenes, including a vision of men clinging to trees to escape being washed away by flash floods, replace a chronological account of the war's general progress. According to the editors, such scenes, or "nuggets"—vivid events that encapsulate complex processes or principles—are the lifeblood of *Time-Life* prose.

Finally, notice how the revision tends to delay critical information for dramatic effect, moving information you would normally expect to find early on into a later position. In the first paragraph, the *Time-Life* writers talk about "the greatest threat to world peace" in the early 1960s for five lines before revealing the identity of that threat—South Vietnam.

FOR WRITING AND DISCUSSION

Here is a passage from a student argument opposing women's serving on submarines. Working individually or in small groups, enliven this passage by using some of the techniques of the *Time-Life* writers.

> Not only would it be very expensive to refit submarines for women personnel, but having women on submarines would hurt the morale of the sailors. In order for a crew to work effectively, they must have good morale or their discontent begins to show through in their performance. This is especially crucial on submarines, where if any problem occurs, it affects the safety of the whole ship. Women would hurt morale by creating sexual tension. Sexual tension can take many forms. One form is couples' working and living in a close space with all of the crew. When a problem occurs within the relationship, it could affect the morale of those directly involved and in the workplace. This would create an environment that is not conducive to good productivity. Tension would also occur if one of the women became pregnant or if there were complaints of sexual harassment. It would be easier to deal with these problems on a surface ship, but in the small confines of a submarine these problems would cause more trouble.

Delaying Your Thesis

In Chapter 7, we described a strategy for taking your reader on an exploratory journey toward a thesis rather than stating the thesis explicitly in the introduction. The effect is twofold. First, the *problem,* not the writer's solution, is put in the foreground. Second, readers are invited to co-investigate the mystery, which increases their delight in discovering a resolution. When making an argument, the writer might propose several opposing theses or review several other people's theses without committing to one until late in the essay. Or, the writer might simply reject all the arguments and choose to end in a quandary. In either case, the writer enlists the reader in a hunt for closure. Although such essays still have theses at their hearts, they follow the pattern of quest narratives and can possess all the compelling readability of a mystery tale.

◢ CHAPTER SUMMARY

Open-form writing tries to do more with language than state a thesis and support it. We have shown how open-form writing uses a narrative base. When narrative is effective, it meets the criteria for a minimal story—depiction of events, connectedness, tension, and resolution. Typically, open-form writers create surprising structural twists by suspending and disrupting the direction of their ideas, by leaving intentional gaps in the text, and by adopting various points of view, including, on occasion, unstable viewpoints, such as irony. Open-form writers also have a penchant for concrete, sensory language—specific details, revelatory words, memory-soaked words and figurative words. We suggested several ways of loosening up closed-form prose by writing midway along the continuum: using humor, trying out some of the strategies of popular writers (using concrete language and dramatic construction), or delaying the thesis.

TOPIC Guidepost #3

For those using Texas Tech's TOPIC Web-Based assignments:

Direct your web browser to http://english.ttu.edu:5555

Guidepost #4 provides full instructions regarding your reading assignment (Chapter 13) and Critique of Microtheme 0.1.

c h a p t e r 13

Working in Groups to Pose and Solve Problems

The consensual process of truth seeking is based on the simple assumption that all of us thinking together are smarter than any one of us thinking alone.

—Parker Palmer, Educator

For excellence, the presence of others is always required.

—Hannah Arrendt, Philosopher

There are many reasons why writers benefit from working in groups. As we have stressed throughout this book, thinking and writing are social acts. At first, this notion may contradict certain widely accepted stereotypes of writers and thinkers as solitary souls who retreat to cork-lined studies where they conjure great thoughts and works. But in most cases the works they produce have grown out of intense conversations with others. For this reason, writers tend to belong to communities of peers with whom they test and share ideas, theories, and work.

Writing communities are especially important in academic, business, and professional settings. The vast majority of scientific and technical articles are team written, often by three or more authors. And few major reports or proposals in the business or academic world are the product of a single author. Increasingly, legal briefs, ad campaigns, professional proposals, research reports, brochures to stockholders, and so forth are team-produced efforts.

The reasons for this trend are not hard to trace. First, much contemporary work is so complex and technical that no single person has enough expertise to compose a nonroutine document. Second, many large businesses now use self-directed teams, as opposed to middle managers overseeing a hierarchically organized staff, to accomplish tasks, most of which require the production of documents. And perhaps most important, much professional writing is now produced on networked computers. Writers on a network can easily transfer files to multiple team members, each of whom can enter changes electronically without converting the file to paper or redoing the entire draft.

Clearly, the ability to write effectively as part of a team is an increasingly critical skill for career advancement. Many businesses now regard group skills as one of the three or four most important determinants of employee success. But the ability to form writing communities is important for reasons that transcend economics and career ambitions.

Humans construct knowledge through interaction with others. Throughout this text we have said that to write an essay is to join a conversation about a topic; the back-and-forth dialogue involved in group work is a real time version of the conversations embodied in printed texts. Through discourse with others, you gather multiple perspectives on phenomena, which you synthesize through the filter of your own perspective. In other words, you construct your knowledge by exposing yourself to alternative views. Moreover, purposeful, thoughtful group interaction is a source not only for knowledge of the world around you, but also for self-knowledge. It allows you to stand outside yourself—to see the products of your mind the way that others see them. The kind of thinking that you practice in groups, therefore, is the kind you must exhibit in writing.

In the rest of this chapter, we offer advice on how to work effectively in groups and to become more adept at critical thinking, composing, and revising. We examine some basic principles of group interaction, explore typical problems small groups encounter, and then provide several strategies for thinking in groups. Perhaps the most common kind of group activity in a writing classroom—conducting peer reviews of drafts—we have covered earlier in Chapter 10 on revision (pp. 195–202).

◪ BASIC PRINCIPLES OF SUCCESSFUL GROUP INTERACTION

If the thought of group work makes you uncomfortable, you are not alone. Most people have had unpleasant or unproductive experiences working in groups. Jokes about committees ("Committees keep minutes and waste hours," or "A zebra is a horse designed by a committee") attest to the innate distrust of groups felt by most born in the United States. Middle-class popular literature, film, and media all lionize the exploits of the single individual working apart from the herd.

Keep in mind, however, that small groups in writing classrooms are less like unwieldy, bureaucratic committees than they are like problem-solving design teams analogous to the engineering teams that design cars or the marketing teams that plan new sales strategies. And recall that one of the world's most influential documents—the Declaration of Independence—was written as a small-group project.

To help you form efficient and productive teams, we recommend that you and your teammates practice the following principles.

Avoid Clone-Think and Ego-Think

Many group tasks ask you to propose and justify a solution to a problem by consensus. As we will show later in this chapter, a group consensus is not the same as a majority view. Although a consensus is a form of agreement, a good one grows out of respectful and productive *disagreement.* The best small groups build solutions thoughtfully, beginning with different points of view and encouraging dissent along the way. Weak groups either reach closure too early or bicker endlessly, never building on disagreement to reach consensus.

To steer a middle ground between early closure and endless bickering, you need to avoid two common problems of group interaction: clone-think and ego-think. When groups lapse into *clone-think,* discussions degenerate into "feel-good sessions" guaranteed to produce safe, superficial solutions. Everyone agrees with the first opinion expressed to avoid conflict and difficult work. At the other extreme is the *ego-think* group, in which group members go their own way, producing a collection of minority views. Whereas clone-thinkers view their task as conformity to a norm, ego-thinkers see their goal as safeguarding the autonomy of individual group members. At both extremes, group members fail to take one another's ideas seriously.

When we talk about taking other people's ideas seriously or about reaching consensus, we don't mean that group discussions should transform people's fundamental values and attitudes. But we do mean that they should bring about realistic changes: softening a position, complicating an understanding, or simply acknowledging an alternative possibility. These sorts of changes in understanding happen only when people learn how to present and consider alternative views in a constructive, nonthreatening manner. One approach to avoiding both clone-thinking and ego-thinking is to practice our next principle, empathic listening.

Listen Empathically

Sometimes called Rogerian listening, after the psychologist Carl Rogers, who popularized the technique, empathic listening is a powerful strategy for helping people resolve conflicts. To be *empathic* is to try to stand in the other person's shoes—to understand the values, beliefs, and fears underlying that person's position. Empathic listeners are *active,* not passive; they interpret not only the speaker's words, but also the speaker's tone of voice, body language, and even silences. Empathic listeners invite speech from others by maintaining eye contact, avoiding disapproving frowns or gestures, asking clarifying questions, and nodding or taking notes.

The rules of empathic listening are simple. Before you respond to someone else's position on an issue, summarize that person's viewpoint fairly in your own words. Carl Rogers discovered that when negotiating parties in a dispute (or couples in marital therapy) were required to summarize each other's views, the experience often defused their anger and encouraged them toward compromise or synthesis. In small groups, empathic listening can deepen conversation. If there is a dispute, the acting group leader might ask one disputant to summarize the other's position. For example: "Irwin, what do you understand Beth's position to be here and how do you see your position differing from hers?" Once Irwin and Beth understand their differences, they will be better able to reconcile them.

When a group becomes skilled at listening, here's what happens.

1. *There are fewer interruptions.*   Group members have more "space" in which to complete their thoughts. They take turns speaking. To get the floor, one person doesn't have to interrupt another.
2. *Participation is more equitable.*   Group discussions are less apt to be dominated by one or two group members. The group draws out shy or quiet group members and values their contributions.
3. *Discussions are more connected.*   Speakers are apt to begin their contributions by referring to what previous speakers have said. "I really liked Pam's point about . . ." or "I see what Paul was saying when . . . , but. . . ."

FOR WRITING AND DISCUSSION

Freewrite your response to the following questions:

1. In the group work we have done so far in this class, how well do I think the group members have listened to and understood my views?
2. How good a listener have I been?
3. What might our group do differently to promote better listening?

Then share your freewrites in groups and take turns summarizing each other's views. Reach consensus on several ways in which the group might improve its listening skills.

Play Assigned Roles

Writing groups accomplish tasks more efficiently when members take turns playing two distinct roles.

1. *Leader/Coordinator.*   This person's job is to ensure that the assigned task is clearly understood by all, to set clear goals for the session, to monitor the time, to keep the group on task, and to make sure that the group has its assigned product completed in the time allocated by the instructor. To prevent early closure or endless bickering, the leader/coordinator must draw out divergent views, promote good listening, and help the group achieve a consensus, without ever being dictatorial.
2. *Recorder/reporter.*   The recorder keeps notes on the group's decision-making process, constantly asking group members for clarification, and reads back what he or she understands group members to have said and decided. The recorder also synthesizes the group's deliberations and reports the results to the class.

In writing classrooms, we have found that groups work best when each student takes a rotation in each of these roles. Some instructors prefer to combine the two roles so that a group recorder serves as both leader and note taker.

Be Sensitive to Body Language

Groups can often learn to function more effectively by reading body language. Groups that draw their chairs close together are more effective than groups that maintain distance from each other or marginalize some members through irregular placement of chairs. Group members should note potential problems signaled by body language. A person who sits with arms folded across the chest staring out a window is signaling alienation. Other signs of dysfunction include side conversations, division of the group into subgroups, and domination of the discussion by one or two people who ignore others.

Invest Time in Group Maintenance

Group members periodically need to reflect on and think critically about their performance, a process called *group maintenance*. Group maintenance may be as simple as taking several minutes at the completion of a task to discuss the things the group did well or not so well and to identify steps for improvement.

Occasionally a more extensive and formal sort of group-maintenance task is required. One such task calls for each member to do a self-assessment by freewriting responses to questions such as the following:

Our group performs best when _____.

Our group's effectiveness could be improved if _____.

My greatest strength as a group member is _____.

Another thing I could contribute is _____.

The members then share these self-assessments with the whole group.

An even more ambitious group-maintenance project involves an ethnographer, a student from another group who observes the group in action and writes up a report on his or her observations. Figure 13.1 is a list of items we ask ethnographers to look for when observing a group.

FIGURE 13.1   Ethnographer's Questionnaire

1. How much time did the group spend reviewing the instructions before plunging into discussion?
2. How were the coordinator and recorder chosen? Had they fulfilled these responsibilities previously?
3. Describe how the group undertook its task. How did it begin the actual work?
4. On average, how long did each group member speak? What was the total amount of time that each group member spoke during the entire session?
5. How many times did group members interrupt each other?
6. How often did group members refer to what others had said before presenting their own contributions?
7. How were disagreements resolved or not resolved?
8. How well did the coordinator and recorder perform their functions?

After responding to these questions, the ethnographers should present the observations to the group and answer any questions the group may have about them. Later, the group should discuss the report on its own. Finally, the group should present to the whole class a brief summary of what it learned from being observed and how it intends to improve its processes.

◼ SOME SPECIAL PROBLEMS IN MAKING GROUPS WORK

How groups handle problem situations is crucial to their success. In this section we suggest how an understanding of the effects of learning style and cultural background on group behavior can alleviate potential problems. We also discuss ways of handling an "impossible" group member.

Recognizing How Personality and Culture Affect Group Participation

Group interaction can often be improved if group members understand the influence of personality and culture on a person's behavior in a group. Psychologists have discovered that people with different personality types have different reactions to working in groups. According to interpreters of the Myers-Briggs Type Indicator,* one of the most highly regarded personality assessment tests, people who test as *extroverts* like to think through an issue by talking out their ideas with others; they tend to be vocal and highly engaged during group discussions. People who test as *introverts* prefer thinking privately about an issue before talking about it and are often uncomfortable discussing their ideas in groups, although they listen carefully and take in what everyone is saying. Often, quiet group members are listening more carefully and thinking more deeply than more vocal people realize. Until the group gently encourages them to contribute, however, they may be silent.

Judgers like to reach decisions rapidly, and they often grow impatient if the group wants to extend discussion of an issue. In contrast, *perceivers* resist early closure and want to talk through all possible points of view on an issue before reaching a decision. If you understand such personality differences, then you might better tolerate classmates' behaviors that are different from your own.

Other important differences are related to culture. Most U.S.-born students are used to talking in class, holding class debates, and even disagreeing with the teacher. In many cultures, however, it is disrespectful to argue with the teacher or to speak in class unless called on. Students are socialized to listen and not to talk. They can find group work in a North American college extremely painful.

---

*The Myers-Briggs Type Indicator locates persons along four different continuums: introversion/extroversion, thinking/feeling, sensing/intuition, perceiving/judging. Composition researchers have used the Myers-Briggs inventory to reveal fascinating differences among writers that throw valuable light on students' behavior in groups. See G. H. Jensen, and J. K. DiTiberio, *Personality and the Teaching of Composition* (Norwood, NJ: Ablex, 1989).

Speech habits also vary widely. Typically, North Americans state their desires bluntly and assertively in ways that would seem rude to people from Asian cultures, who are taught to mask their statements of desire in roundabout conversation. Some cultures have a strong oral tradition of storytelling or speech making, whereas others have a tradition of silence. If your institution has a diverse student body that includes members of ethnic minority groups and international students, then group work can be a fascinating laboratory for the study of cultural differences.

FOR WRITING AND DISCUSSION

Your instructor or institution might arrange for your class to take the Myers-Briggs Type Indicator or the Kolb Learning Style Inventory. If so, then you can share what these tests reveal about you with other members of your group. If not, then you can take your own mini-inventory by checking off the description in Table 13.1 that best represents you for each of the pairs listed. After you have made your choices, share your self-assessment with other members of your group. How do the differences in your responses account for the different ways in which you behave in the group?

Dealing with an "Impossible Group Member"

Occasionally groups face a critical test of their ability to manage conflict: the Impossible Group Member, or IGM. IGMs may dominate group discussions; they may be rude or intimidating, trying to turn every discussion into a conflict; they may

TABLE 13.1 Mini–Personality Inventory

Do you like to:

_____ Organize the discussion	_____ Go with the flow
_____ Assert your own views and rights	_____ Compromise
_____ Stick to the central issue	_____ Examine all facets of a problem
_____ Reach a firm decision	_____ See merit in all sides of an issue
_____ Think out your own position before talking	_____ Think by talking now
_____ Reason problems out logically	_____ Trust your instincts and feelings
_____ Get serious	_____ Lighten up
_____ Show passion	_____ Stay calm
_____ Reach a resolution	_____ Talk for talk's sake
_____ Follow teacher's instructions carefully	_____ Value spontaneity
_____ Apply rules rigorously	_____ Allow exceptions to rules
_____ Stay on the assigned task	_____ Digress; engage in off-topic talk

sit sullenly, draining off group enthusiasm; or they may be generally unprepared or fail to do the work assigned to them outside class.

Although it's not easy to deal with an IGM (sometimes the instructor has to intervene), most impossible group members are really possible group members who need encouragement and direction. The root of most IGMs' problems is their difficulty in recognizing the effects they're having on other people. Direct criticism of their behaviors will likely surprise them—they won't see it coming—and cause them to react defensively. IGMs need to see the consequences of their actions and they need to see positive behaviors modeled for them. If IGMs dominate discussions, they need to learn to listen. If they are sullenly silent, they need to have their input actively solicited and their responses taken seriously. They have to take their turns in leadership positions and learn to appreciate the difficulties of consensus building and decision making. And they must be made aware that their actions are bothering the other group members.

The best way to deal with IGMs is to discuss the problem candidly, perhaps during a group-maintenance session (see pp. 277–78). If group members reflect on and evaluate *how* the group did its task, focusing on group shortcomings ("What could we do better next time?") rather than on individuals' failures ("Martine, you drive me crazy!"), then it becomes easier for errant group members to accept responsibility for their actions. In explaining a problem to an IGM, try using what communication experts call *I statements* rather than *you statements*. Keep the focus on your own feelings and avoid launching accusations. Note the different tones in the following examples:

You **Statement**	Martine, you're always insulting us by looking out the window.
I **Statement**	Martine, when you look out the window, it makes me feel like I'm a boring person.
You **Statement**	Pete and Valencia are always dominating the discussion.
I **Statement**	On some days I want to say something in the group but there is never a break in the conversation where I can join.

Using *I* statements helps defuse defensiveness by calling attention to the consequences of behaviors without attaching blame or censure.

We are now ready to turn to productive group strategies for addressing three kinds of tasks: consensus-seeking, brainstorming, and orally rehearsing drafts.

◤ THINKING IN GROUPS

Group work is one of the most effective ways to practice critical thinking. This section examines three ways that groups can think together.

Seeking Consensus

Most of the problems posed in the For Writing and Discussion exercises in this text have alternative solutions—there is no single "right" answer. Seeking a consensus answer—especially when group members have different views—can lead to highly productive critical thought. When different group members propose different answers to the same problem, how does a group reach a consensus?*

First, don't assume that every group member has to be completely satisfied with the group's final solution. Instead, everyone should agree that the proposed solution is feasible and rationally supportable. Your solution must be achieved through *consensus* rather than through majority vote, coin flip, or turn taking. This approach means that each group member has veto power over the final solution. But this option should be used sparingly, and only if a person truly cannot live with the proposed solution. After an initial discussion to be sure that everyone understands the task, you can use the following guidelines to embark on a problem-solving procedure that encourages consensus:

1. *Ask every group member to propose at least one tentative solution for discussion.* Members should present justifying arguments as well, so that group members can appreciate the reasoning behind each approach.
2. *Once you have presented a possible solution, avoid arguing for it a second time.* Your goal is now to be flexible and listen to other viewpoints rather than to press for adoption of your own position. Remember, however, not to give up your viewpoint quickly just to avoid conflict. Yield only if you see legitimate strengths in other approaches.
3. *If none of the proposed solutions wins everyone's approval, begin brainstorming for alternatives that synthesize good features from various proposals.* Sometimes you can formulate a lowest-common-denominator solution—one that everyone grudgingly accepts but that no one really likes—and brainstorm ways to improve it.
4. *Don't think in terms of winners and losers* ("If Lenore's solution wins, then Pete's must lose"). Rather, try to negotiate win/win solutions in which all parties give up something but also retain something.
5. *Accept disagreement and conflict as a strength rather than a weakness.* Chances are that the disagreements in your group mirror disagreements in the larger community to which your solution must appeal. From these disagreements you can forge a synthesis that is much stronger than any individual's private solution. As Parker Palmer says in the epigraph to this chapter, "The consensual process of truth seeking is based on the simple assumption that all of us thinking together are smarter than any one of us thinking alone."

Brainstorming

Group brainstorming uses intuitive, unstructured thinking. During a brainstorming session, everyone is encouraged to suggest ideas, however outlandish they may seem on the surface, and to build on, without criticizing or questioning,

*The discussion of consensus making is adapted from Parker Palmer, *To Know as We Are Known: Education as a Spiritual Journey* (San Francisco: Harper & Row, 1983), pp. 94–96.

all other suggestions generated by group members. Groups often begin brainstorming by asking individual members to take turns offering ideas. Frequently, a high-energy, almost frantic atmosphere develops. In its zanier moments, brainstorming crosses over into free association.

For a writer exploring topic ideas, brainstorming sessions can provide a variety of options to consider as well as clues about an audience's potential reaction to a topic and ideas about how the writer might change those views. Brainstorming can also generate arguments in support of a thesis. When the class is assigned a persuasive paper, playing the believing and doubting game with each group member's proposed thesis can help writers anticipate alternative possibilities and counter-evidence as well as new support for a position (see Chapter 2, pp. 35–37).

Oral Rehearsal of Drafts

Rehearsing a draft orally is an excellent way to generate and clarify ideas. A good procedure for doing so is to interview one another in pairs or in groups of three early in the writing process. One-on-one or one-on-two interviews that enable writers to talk through their ideas can help clarify their sense of direction and stimulate new ideas. When you are the interviewer, use the set of generic questions in Figure 13.2, modifying them to fit each assignment.

When you conduct your interview, get the writer to do most of the talking. Respond by offering suggestions, bringing up additional ideas, playing devil's advocate, and so forth. The goal is for the writer to rehearse the whole paper orally. Whenever the writer gets stuck for ideas, arguments, or supporting details, help to brainstorm possibilities.

During these sessions, it is best for writers not to look at notes or drafts. They should try to reformulate their ideas conversationally. We recommend that each student talk actively for fifteen to twenty minutes as the interviewer asks probing questions, plays devil's advocate, or helps the writer think of ideas.

FIGURE 13.2   Guide Questions for Interviewers

- What problem or question is your paper going to address?
- Why is this an interesting question? What makes it problematic and significant?
- How is your paper going to surprise your readers?
- What is your thesis statement? (If the writer doesn't have a good thesis statement yet, go on to the next question and then come back to this one. Perhaps you can help the writer figure out a thesis.)
- Talk me (us) through your whole argument or through your ideas so far.

◪ CHAPTER SUMMARY

This chapter has focused on the value of small groups for writers, both student and professional. Because to write is to join a conversation, working in groups teaches us to appreciate the dialectic nature of knowledge and to practice the kind of dialectic thinking that writers need. Specifically, we looked at basic principles of group interaction, special problems in making groups work, and ways that groups can think together to vary perspectives and build consensus, to brainstorm, and to conduct interviews that help classmates rehearse their drafts orally. An additional use of groups—providing peer reviews of drafts—is covered in Chapter 17, pages 429–35.

TOPIC Guidepost #5

For those using Texas Tech's TOPIC Web-Based assignments:

Direct your web browser to http://english.ttu.edu:5555

Guidepost #5 provides full instructions regarding your reading assignment (Handbook, pages 199-208) and TOPIC Mail Interviews.

TOPIC Guidepost #29

For those using Texas Tech's TOPIC Web-Based assignments:

Direct your web browser to **http://english.ttu.edu:5555**

Guidepost #29 provides full instructions regarding your reading assignment (Chapter 14) and Critique of Draft 4.2.

c h a p t e r 14

Focusing a Problem and Finding Sources

College writers regularly use research information in their work, whether it is a short analytical or persuasive piece that cites one or two sources or a longer research paper that cites dozens of sources. A research paper, although longer than many other kinds of papers, follows the same principles of writing discussed throughout this text. In a research paper, the writer poses an interesting and significant problem and responds to it with a surprising thesis. However, in a formal research paper, the writer is expected to use extensive research data for support and to cite and document all sources in a formal academic style.

Much popular writing takes on the characteristics of a research paper, but without the documentation. Consider the following excerpt from an article in *Glamour*.

> Subliminal self-help tapes—which promise everything from instant relaxation to higher earning power—are a big business: Industry watchers estimate they generate about $60 million in sales annually. But a number of recent studies show no evidence that they work.
>
> . . . Philip Merkle, Ph.D., of the University of Waterloo, analyzed commercially available tapes using a spectrograph that reveals patterns of auditory signals. He found no evidence of speech-associated patterns on the tapes. The messages embedded in the tapes are so completely masked by the other sounds that they cannot be heard *even subliminally.*
>
> —Pamela Erens, "Are Subliminal Self-Help Tapes a Hoax?"

As does a good research paper, this article has a thesis (subliminal self-help tapes are not effective) and uses research data for development and support (a statistic about the size of the subliminal self-help tape industry and a summary of the research by Philip Merkle). But if you doubt the figure of $60 million, you have no way to check the author's accuracy. Nor can you find Merkle's work to read it for yourself. You might be able to contact the researcher at the University of Waterloo, but that would be an inefficient approach to tracking down his work.

The purpose of citing sources and giving complete bibliographic information in academic research papers is to enable readers to follow the trail of the author's research. Although the conventions for documentation seem cumbersome at first, they are designed to give readers essential information about a source quickly and efficiently.

■ WHAT DO WE MEAN BY SOURCES?

Before starting a research project, you need to know what researchers mean by the word *sources*. There are two kinds of sources. *Primary sources* include newspaper articles, letters, diaries, eyewitness accounts, laboratory notes, interviews, court records, government data, historical documents, and the like, and *secondary sources* are articles and books written by investigators who have themselves analyzed and evaluated the primary sources. For Mary Turla's research project on mail-order brides, for example, a catalog distributed by a mail-order bride service would be a primary source, whereas a book on culture in the Philippines would be a secondary source.

Understanding how secondary sources get published may also be helpful to you. When scholars undertake a research project, they generally record their findings first as field notes, exploratory entries in research logs, write-ups of interviews, computer spreadsheets of statistics, and so forth. Other scholars can occasionally access these immediate data if the researcher is willing to share it informally in personal letters, e-mail postings, interviews, or casual discussions. The first formal sharing of research data often takes place at academic conferences, when scholars with similar interests get together to present papers orally and to participate in discussions. A paper presented orally often becomes a first draft, which the researcher will revise as an article for a scholarly journal. Sometimes conferences publish their proceedings in a microfilm format or in an electronic forum, such as a World Wide Web site. Conference presentations usually occur within six months to a year following completion of the research.

Research results deemed important by the scholar's research community are often published as articles in specialized scholarly journals, usually one to three years after completion of the research. Most academic research is published in scholarly journals rather than in books. Scholarly journals are usually refereed— an editorial board evaluates submissions and accepts or rejects them on the basis of their scholarly merit. Because prestigious journals have a high rejection rate, acceptance of an article by an important journal marks a high point in a scholar's academic career.

Later—three to six years after completion of the research—a fraction of the research published in journals finds its way into books. Many scholarly books are reworkings of material originally published as articles in scholarly journals. These books are typically aimed at more general audiences than are scholarly articles and usually integrate more material, giving readers a more complete view of a topic and a much richer sense of context. The bibliographies in the back of scholarly books are often an excellent resource for further research.

Finally, when ideas and information have been established as central to a discipline, they are published in reference sources, such as encyclopedias. Later in this chapter we list a variety of specialized encyclopedias that will enable you to get a quick overview of any topic.

In summary, you will find the newest information on a topic in the papers presented at recent scholarly conferences. The next most recent sources are articles in academic journals, and then information and ideas in recent scholarly books. The currently accepted ideas of a field—its established and less controversial tenets—can be found in reference books, such as encyclopedias. In addition, much of the research generated by academic institutions is picked up by the popular media and reported in newspapers or integrated into feature articles in popular magazines, such as *Scientific American, Psychology Today,* or *The Atlantic Monthly.*

FOR WRITING AND DISCUSSION

Prior to class, go to your college's library and ask the reference librarian for a recently acquired scholarly book in a field you find interesting. (Many libraries have special shelves for new acquisitions.) Look at the copyright date of the book. Then look at the bibliography in the back of the book. What is the most recent date of the sources cited in the bibliography? What can you surmise about the lag time between the last research the writer was able to do and the time the book was actually published? Peruse the book's preface to see if the writer gives any overview of his or her research process. Whom does the writer thank in the acknowledgments section, usually placed near the end of the preface? Does the writer mention debts to previous researchers? What can you surmise about how this book came to be published?

In class, share your findings with your classmates.

BEGINNING A RESEARCH PAPER

Your first goal in writing a research paper is to convert a general topic area into a research question. The research question focuses your investigation, and later, when your answer to that question emerges as a thesis, it focuses your writing.

Developing Your Research Question

How do you choose a topic and develop it into a significant research question? First, you need to choose something that interests you. Your initial interest in a subject is likely to be broad and unfocused. For instance, you may be interested in eating disorders, say, or homelessness, but you may not be ready or able to pose specific research questions. To formulate questions, you need to do some preliminary reading. We recommend the following strategy:

- Read an overview of your topic in an encyclopedia.
- Skim a recent book related to your topic, looking carefully at its table of contents and examining the titles in its bibliography.
- Locate and read a recent scholarly article related to your topic (later in this chapter we show you how to find articles in academic journals). Note carefully the problem that the article addresses, and peruse the titles in its bibliography.
- Find and read a popular article related to your topic from the kinds of magazines indexed in *The Reader's Guide to Periodical Literature* or INFOTRAC.

This preliminary reading should give you some initial insights into the kinds of questions or controversies that writers are investigating or debating. The bibliographies in your sources may lead you to other books or articles that spark your interest. After doing this preliminary reading, try freewriting your answers to probe questions.

- What problems, questions, or issues about my topic are examined in the material I have read?
- What problems or questions does this material raise for me?
- When people discuss my topic, what questions do they ask or what do they argue about?

Another way to develop a research question is to discuss your topic with friends, trying to discover issues that particularly interest you. You don't need to know the answer to your question right away; your research will help you find a response. But until you settle on a research question, you won't know what part of your reading will be useful in your paper. Once you develop a research question—for example, "What is the current thinking about in-patient versus out-patient treatment of anorexia nervosa?" or "Should eating disorders be covered by insurance policies?" or "What role did the deinstitutionalization of the mentally ill play in the increase in homelessness?"—your research efforts can become focused and efficient.

In Chapter 1 we illustrated the development of a research question by following the exploratory process of student writer Mary Turla, who had selected the topic "mail-order brides." As we explained, Mary was attracted to this topic by a notorious murder case in Seattle in which an American husband gunned down his Filipina mail-order bride outside the courtroom where she was filing for divorce. Mary's initial abhorrence of the mail-order bride industry was later tempered when her mother commented that becoming a mail-order bride might be the only way for many young Filipina woman to escape abject poverty in the Philippines.

Mary then posed her research problem this way: Should the mail-order bride industry be made illegal? (See Chapter 1, pp. 7–8.)

Evaluating Your Research Question

Once you have posed an initial research question (remember that your question may evolve considerably as your research progresses), test it for feasibility by considering the following questions:

■ Are you personally interested in this question?
■ Is the question both problematic and significant?
■ Is the question limited enough for the intended length of your paper?
■ Is there a reasonable possibility of finding information on this question?

This last question is particularly crucial. Good research writers depend on their skill at sleuthing out sources from a wide variety of places—college library, specialized libraries in the community, government and industry reports, nonprint media such as radio and television, the Internet, personal correspondence and interviews, or your own field research using observation and questionnaires. The rest of this chapter shows you how to unlock the resources of your library and your community.

FOR WRITING AND DISCUSSION

Review the criteria for evaluating research questions. Working as a whole class or in small groups, discuss each of the following research questions, evaluating them against the criteria. Does the question seem interesting? Is it problematic and significant? Is it limited enough for a short research project? Will there be information available on the topic? Is the question clear and precise? If a question doesn't meet the criteria, try revising it.

1. Do students work better if they don't work for grades?
2. Should pregnant women receive prenatal care?
3. Are helmet laws for motorcyclists effective in preventing injuries?
4. Is education good for children?
5. Why are there so many wars?
6. Why don't we do something about the welfare system?
7. Does a low-fat diet increase life expectancy?
8. Is Western medicine superior to traditional nonwestern medicine?
9. Should the United States limit immigration?
10. Does birth order affect children's development?

◼ FINDING LIBRARY SOURCES

To be a good researcher, you need to know how to find materials in your college's or university's library. Because most people think "books" when they enter a library, they tend to focus on the bookshelves and neglect the wealth of other resources available. Much of the valuable—and the most up-to-date—information in a library resides in articles in newspapers and periodicals (magazines and academic journals). Libraries also contain a wealth of special reference tools, ranging from specialized encyclopedias to vital statistics.

Searching for Books

Until recently, a library's holdings were listed in a card catalog. Today, most libraries use online catalogs. A library's catalog, whether accessed by cards or by computer, is the guidepost to its books as well as to its magazines, journals, newspapers, dissertations, major government documents, and multimedia (videos, cassettes, and microform collections).

The basic logic of card catalogs—author cards, title cards, and subject cards—is retained in online systems. In both systems, books are listed by author, title, and subject. Our discussion of card catalogs highlights the logic of this approach.

In a card catalog, the author card (the main entry card) displays the author's name in the top left just under the call number. Other cards for the same work are identical to the author card but have a line added above for the title or subject. Because many famous authors not only write books but also have books written about them, their names may be on cards both as authors and as subjects. On a subject card the subject heading—in this case, a proper name—is written in capital letters or typed in red above the author of the work. Author cards—books by a person—are filed in front of subject cards—books about a person. In a library with a large collection, remembering how to navigate around these similar-looking cards can help you avoid becoming confused. Sometimes files include cards for editors, coauthors, illustrators, or translators as well. Individual essays, stories, or plays in an anthology may also have separate cards.

Making Shrewd Use of Subject Headings

At the start of a research project, when you have only a topic area in mind, the subject cards (or subject entries in an online catalog) are probably your most important resource. Subject headings used for the subject entries are logical, uniform, and consistent. Most libraries use the headings established by the Library of Congress, which you can find listed in a four-volume reference book entitled *Library of Congress Subject Headings* (ask your librarian where this source is located in your library). This book can be especially helpful if you have trouble finding a subject heading that fits your topic.

Suppose that you are researching the effectiveness of state-run alcohol-treatment programs for street people. What subject heading do you start with? Alcoholism? Treatment programs? Homeless? Let's say you decide to begin with "alcoholism." You discover in the *Library of Congress Subject Headings* that "alcoholism" is a mammoth topic, with more than a page of subheadings. You then try "street people." Under that heading you find the instruction "USE Homeless persons." So you look up "homeless persons," where you find the following listing:

Homeless persons *(May Subd Geog)*

    UF Homeless adults

        Homeless people

        Street people

Means that the subject heading "homeless persons" is used for (UF) these other three terms.

    BT Persons

Means that "persons" is a broader term (BT).

    RT Homelessness

Means that "homelessness" is a related term (RT).

    NT Church work with the homeless

        Homeless aged

Means that all these headings are narrower terms (NT).

        Homeless children

        Homeless students

        Homeless veterans

        Homeless women

        Homeless youth

        Libraries and the homeless

        Police services for the homeless

        Rogues and vagabonds

        Shelters for the homeless

        Social work with the homeless

        Tramps

        Underground homeless persons

Mental health services *(May Subd Geog)*

Law and legislation *(May Subd Geog)*

Indicates subheadings under "homeless persons."

These listings use several abbreviations. *(May Subd Geog)* stands for "may be subdivided geographically" and indicates that listings under this category may be further subdivided by state or region. UF means "used for." The remaining abbreviations classify other subject headings that you might want to call up in your search: BT = "broader term"; RT = "related term"; and NT = "narrower term." In this case, because you are interested in treatment programs for homeless alcoholics, you might decide to try the subject headings "Social work with the homeless" and "Homeless mental health services."

In traditional card catalogs, subject headings place the most important or general word first and list specific qualities or subdivisions next. For example, the topic "the government of France" is listed under "France—Politics and government." Be creative as you look for subject headings, and use the helpful hints provided by the card or online catalog. A "See" or "Use" reference will lead you from an unused heading to a used heading. A "See also" reference suggests other related subject headings. Finally, when you find a book on your topic, look at the bottom of the card, which lists all the subject headings under which your book is filed. An online catalog usually provides the same information, but its location on the screen may vary from library to library. These other subject headings may lead you to other books.

In an online catalog, you don't need to worry about alphabetizing. With a card catalog, however, the following alphabetizing rules will be helpful.

- Headings are alphabetized word by word rather than letter by letter. For example, *New Zealand* comes before *Newark.* Remember the rule "Nothing before something."
- Articles (*a, an,* and *the*) at the beginning of headings or titles are ignored.
- Abbreviations are alphabetized as if they were spelled out. For example, *St.* is filed under *Saint.*
- Names beginning with *Mc* and *M'* are grouped with names beginning with *Mac.*
- Chronological order is used for historical subheadings. "Great Britain—Literature—Sixteenth Century" precedes "Great Britain—Literature—Eighteenth Century."

The Logic of Shelving Systems

Once you have found a book in your library's catalog, you use the call number to locate the book in the library. Most libraries have open stacks, allowing you to go to the shelf and pick up a book yourself. Take advantage of your trip to the shelf to browse through the nearby volumes because other books on the same subject will be housed in the same area. Often your best sources turn up through casual browsing.

The call number will be either a Dewey Decimal number, generally used in elementary, high school, and local public libraries, or a Library of Congress (LC) number, generally used in academic libraries. Some older libraries have books shelved under both systems. Following is an overview of each system.

Dewey Decimal System

000	General Works
100	Philosophy and Related Disciplines
200	Religion
300	Social Sciences
400	Language
500	Pure Science
600	Technology and Applied Science
700	The Arts
800	Literature and Rhetoric
900	General Geography and History

Library of Congress System

A	General Works
B	Philosophy, Psychology, and Religion

C	Auxiliary Sciences of History
D	General and Old World History (except America)
E–F	American History
G	Geography, Anthropology, Manners and Customs, Folklore, Recreation
H	Social Science, Statistics, Economics, Sociology
J	Political Science
K	Law
L	Education
M	Music
N	Fine Arts
P	Language and Literature
Q	Science
R	Medicine
S	Agriculture, Plant and Animal Industry, Fish Culture, Fisheries, Hunting, Game Protection
T	Technology
U	Military Science
V	Naval Science
Z	Bibliography and Library Science

These numbers and letters represent general categories that are further subdivided as other letters and numerals are added. A book titled *Familiar Trees of America,* by William C. Grimm, for instance, has the Library of Congress call number QK481 (Q = science; K = botany; 481 = North American trees). If you are aware of the system's logic, you can browse more productively.

Searching for Articles in Periodicals

Most of the information in periodicals (magazines and academic journals) and newspapers never finds its way into books. You can find articles in these important sources either through computerized indexes or through traditional printed indexes. This section explains traditional indexes, which remain an important resource even if your library offers online searching of periodicals.

Before discussing how to use the indexes, let's review some of the most useful ones. We have divided them into two categories. The indexes listed under Current Affairs cover a variety of subjects and lead the researcher to current controversies and issues in numerous fields. The specialized indexes focus on individual areas of study.

Current Affairs

Readers' Guide to Periodical Literature.   The best-known index, the *Readers' Guide,* covers popular magazines for a general audience including such topics as current events, famous people, movie reviews, and hobbies. It focuses primarily on nonscholarly publications, such as *Time, Newsweek, Popular*

Mechanics, and *People,* but it also indexes many highly respected intellectual sources such as *Foreign Affairs* and *Scientific American.*

New York Times Index. The subject index to the *New York Times* includes brief synopses of articles and gives exact references to date, page, and column. Its wide circulation, comprehensive coverage, and extensive indexing make this publication especially useful. Once you have found the date of an event through this index, you can search the back issues of other papers for their coverage of the same event.

Wall Street Journal Index. A monthly and annual guide to the *Wall Street Journal,* this index is organized in two parts: (1) corporate news indexed by name of company and (2) general news indexed by subject.

Business Periodical Index. This index leads you to articles on marketing, management, public relations, advertising, and economics.

Biography Index. This quarterly and annual index lists biographical material in current books and periodicals.

Public Affairs Information Service (P.A.I.S.) Bulletin. Serving as a guide to articles, pamphlets, and books on economic and social issues, public administration, politics, and international relations, this index is useful for finding information on current public policy, both domestic and international.

General Science Index. This index to general science periodicals covers topics such as biology, botany, chemistry, environment and conservation, medicine and health, physics, and zoology.

Education

Education Index. This index includes more than 300 periodicals, proceedings, and yearbooks covering all phases of education, organized by author and subject. It also has good coverage of sources related to children and child development.

Current Index to Journals in Education. This index lists more than seven hundred education and education-related journals, organized by author and subject.

History and Literature

MLA (Modern Language Association) International Bibliography of Books and Articles in Modern Language and Literature. This comprehensive index of scholarly articles on languages and literature of various countries is arranged by national literatures with subdivisions by literary periods.

Annual Bibliography of English Language and Literature. A subject index of scholarly articles on English language and literature, this index covers major writers and is arranged chronologically.

Humanities Index. This subject index covers topics in archeology, classics, folklore, history, language and literature, politics, performing arts, philosophy, and religion. It was called the *Social Sciences and Humanities Index* until 1974.

Historical Abstracts.   This work includes abstracts of scholarly articles on world history, excluding the United States and Canada, covering the period from 1775 to 1945.

America: History and Life.   This work comprises abstracts of scholarly articles on the history of the United States and Canada.

Nursing and Medical Sciences

Cumulative Index to Nursing and Allied Health Literature.   This major index covers topics on nursing and public health.

Index Medicus.   This monthly subject index includes periodical literature on medicine and related topics published in all principal languages.

Philosophy and Religion

Philosophers' Index.   Scholarly articles in books and periodicals are indexed by author and subject. The subject section includes abstracts.

Religion Index One: Periodicals.   This index has a Protestant viewpoint but includes Catholic and Jewish periodicals as well. It provides a subject and author index of scholarly articles on topics in religion.

Physical and Social Sciences

Social Sciences Index.   This index covers all subjects and disciplines in the social sciences, including anthropology, area studies, psychology, political science, and sociology. It concentrates on scholarly journals, but includes some popular magazines. The title was *Social Sciences and Humanities Index* until 1974.

Psychological Abstracts.   This subject and author index covers books, journals, technical reports, and scientific documents and includes an abstract of each item.

Applied Science and Technology Index.   This work is a subject index to periodicals in the fields of aeronautics and space sciences, automation, earth sciences, engineering, physics, telecommunications, transportation, and related topics.

Biological and Agricultural Index.   This subject index covers English-language periodicals in agricultural and biological sciences.

General Science Index.   See under Current Affairs.

Using Periodical Indexes

Although there are many periodical indexes, they are all organized similarly and include clear directions for use in the front of each volume. The key to using these indexes efficiently is thinking of good subject headings. Be creative and persistent. Most indexes have extensive cross-references that will eventually lead you to the heading you need. Keeping a list of the subject headings you use can save you time if you return to the indexes a second time or if you use more than one index for the same topic.

Once you have found appropriate articles listed under a subject heading, copy the bibliographic information you will need to find the articles. The library will have a list of its periodicals; check that list to see whether the journal or magazine you need is in the library. If it is, note its call number. Periodicals are often shelved by call number in the stacks just as books are shelved, although some libraries have a separate periodicals section arranged alphabetically.

Your library may also store some periodicals on microfiche (a small card containing page-by-page photographic negatives of a journal or magazine) or microfilm (a roll of film, similar to a traditional filmstrip). Your librarian will help you use machines that allow you easily to read the text and even copy pages that you will need for further reference. If your library does not have the article you need in any form, ask your librarian about getting the article through an interlibrary loan—an increasingly quick and common practice.

Finding Information in Special Reference Materials

Reference works are usually kept in a special section for use in the library only. They offer excellent help, ranging from background information as you begin your reading to statistics that provide hard evidence related to your thesis. The following list gives you some examples of reference works. Be sure to ask your librarian for other suggestions.

Encyclopedias.   Encyclopedias are extremely helpful for background reading in the initial stages of research. By giving you the big picture, encyclopedias provide a context for better understanding articles and books. In addition to general encyclopedias, you will find many specialized encyclopedias, among them the *Dictionary of American History, The International Encyclopedia of the Social Sciences,* the *McGraw-Hill Encyclopedia of Science and Technology,* and the *Encyclopedia of World Art.*

Book Review Digest.   This reference work provides a summary of the reviewed book and excerpts from a variety of reviews so that you can gain an understanding of controversies and issues in a given field. To use the *Book Review Digest* efficiently, you need to know the publication date of the book in question, as reviews are published the year the book is published and in the two to three succeeding years.

Congressional Record.   The *Congressional Record* contains the transcript of what is said on the floors of the Senate and the House of Representatives. It also contains an appendix of materials that members have asked to be included as part of the permanent record. Its index allows you to trace every reference to a given subject and to find out who discussed or acted on a bill. Many reference libraries carry this useful tool for people interested in history, politics, biography, and current events.

Statistical Abstract of the United States.   This publication dates back to 1879 and contains statistical tables on birthrates, abortion, marriage, divorce, health care, employment, nutrition, and so forth. It is a good primary source on life in the United States.

Facts on File.   Summaries of news stories in this publication show the development of events so that you see how they played out over the space of a year. Stories are arranged by subject, person, and country.

At each step of your library search, remember that your best aid is your librarian. Librarians are experienced in helping you find the right subject headings, pointing out nonbook holdings in the library, leading you through the interlibrary loan process, and introducing you to less-known resources in the library. Librarians will also steer you to the most helpful of the various reference tools designed for research projects such as yours.

FOR WRITING AND DISCUSSION

Working in groups, choose a current issue about public affairs (for example, global warming, gangs, or the federal deficit) that will allow you to use a wide range of library resources, including the *New York Times Index* and *Congressional Record.* With your group, go to your college library and use indexes to find titles of articles on the issue you selected; also locate relevant information from specialized references, such as encyclopedias, *Facts on File*, and *Statistical Abstracts of the United States.* You will probably want to divide up the work, having each group member become familiar with several sources in order to teach them to the rest of the group. When the group has finished, everyone should have a good idea of how to use these sources.

◣ SPECIALIZED LIBRARIES AND LOCAL ORGANIZATIONS

Sometimes a search of your college library doesn't give you the information you need. In these cases, don't give up too quickly. Mary Turla, whose freewriting on mail-order brides we have been following, found little information in two academic libraries, even though one of them is the largest academic library in her part of the country. Instead, she was able to find the material she needed at a small specialized library devoted to Filipino culture and history. The public libraries in many cities house directories of specialized libraries.

Businesses and organizations also have libraries and information services. Public relations departments can provide brochures and pamphlets. For example, if you were writing about diabetes, you could ask the American Diabetes Association for books and articles available to the public. Check the Yellow Pages of your telephone directory for businesses or organizations that might be good sources of information. Student writer Sheridan Botts, who wrote an exploratory paper and a research paper on the funding of hospices, obtained much of her information from materials provided by local hospices and insurance companies.

Be aware, however, that businesses and organizations that provide information to the public do so for a reason. Often the reasons are benign. The American

Diabetes Association, for example, wants to provide helpful information to persons afflicted with diabetes. But it is wise to keep in mind the bias of any organization whose information you use. Bias does not mean that the information is wrong, but bias will affect the slant of writing and the choice of aspects of a question that will be discussed. A good researcher looks at many points of view with an open and questioning mind. If you are researching whether to cut old-growth timber, you will want to read publications of both the environmentalists and the timber industry, keeping in mind the goals and values of each group. If the "facts" of either group seem hazy, you will need to seek more reliable data from a disinterested source. In one respect, you have an advantage when working with data provided by organizations because their biases are readily visible.

◤ FINDING INFORMATION THROUGH INTERVIEWS AND PERSONAL CORRESPONDENCE

Interviews and personal correspondence can often provide special perspectives as well as the most current look at what is happening in an area.

Interviews

An interview is often a highly effective way to gather specialized information. Although asking a busy professional for an interview can be intimidating, many experts are generous with their time when they encounter a student who is truly interested in their work. Depending on circumstances, your interview can be formal or informal; you may even conduct an interview over the telephone, without a face-to-face meeting. No matter what the format, all interviews benefit from the following practices:

1. *Be prepared for the interview.* Be professional as well as friendly. Explain what you are working on and why you are asking for an interview. Know in advance what you hope to learn from the interview.
2. *Be sure you have done background reading before the interview.* Ideally, interviews should give you knowledge or perspectives unavailable in books or articles. The interview should supplement what you have learned from your reading, not take the place of your reading. Although you needn't be an expert at the time of the interview, you should be conversant about your subject.
3. *Have well-thought-out questions ready.* Be as thorough with your questions as possible. Most likely you will have only one chance to interview this person. Although you may include some short-answer questions, such as "How long have you been working in this field?" the heart of your interview should focus on open-ended questions, such as "What changes have

you seen in this field?" "What solutions have you found to be most successful in dealing with . . . ? or "What do you see as the causes of . . . ?" Questions framed in this way will elicit the information you need but still allow
the interviewee to range freely. Avoid yes-or-no questions that can stall conversation with a one-word answer. Also try to avoid leading questions. For
example, instead of asking a social worker, "What do you think about in-
fringing on the rights of the homeless by making some of them take antipsychotic medication?" ask instead, "What are your views on requiring the
mentally ill homeless to take antipsychotic medications as a condition for
welfare assistance?" The more you lead the interviewee to the answers you
want, the less valid your research becomes.

4. *If the interviewee rambles away from the question, don't jump in too fast.*
   You may learn something valuable from the seeming digression. You may
   even want to ask unanticipated questions once you have delved into new
   ideas. In short, be prepared, but also be flexible.

Before you conduct an interview, consider how you plan to record the information. Many people like to use a portable tape recorder, but be sure to ask your
interviewee's permission if you plan to do so. You may still want to take notes, but
taping allows you to focus all your attention on the interaction, following the
speaker's train of thought and asking yourself what else you need to know. If
you do not tape-record the interview, try to get all the main ideas down on paper
and to be accurate with quotable material. Don't hesitate to ask if you are unsure
about a fact or statement or if you need to double check what the person intended
to say.

You will probably leave the interview feeling immersed in what you heard.
No matter how vivid the words are in your mind, take time *very* soon after the interview to go over your notes or to transcribe your tape. What may seem unfor-
gettable at the moment is all too easy to forget later. If you do your checking soon,
you can usually fill in gaps in your notes or explain unclear passages on the tape.
Do not trust your memory alone.

FOR WRITING AND DISCUSSION

You can practice interview techniques by interviewing fellow students.
Imagine that your class is conducting field research to answer the following
question: What are the chief problems that students encounter in producing
college-level research papers? Working in small groups, develop a short sequence of interview questions that will elicit the information you seek. Outside class, each class member should interview a fellow student, preferably
one not in your current writing class. The next day, you should all report the
results of your interviews to the class, discussing any difficulties in conducting the interviews and sharing insights into how to improve interviewing
techniques.

Personal Correspondence

Occasionally, it is appropriate to write a letter requesting information from an individual or organization. In the letter, state who you are and explain the purpose of your request. Make your request clear and concise. Enclose a stamped, self-addressed envelope for the reply.

◢ GATHERING INFORMATION THROUGH QUESTIONNAIRES

The results of a questionnaire can often add weight to your argument. Although questionnaires always raise problems of bias and statistical validity, careful planning, decision making, and accurate reporting can alleviate most of the problems. You must first decide whether to make your questionnaire anonymous. Although respondents are likely to answer more honestly when the questionnaire is anonymous (for instance, a person is not likely to admit having plagiarized a paper if you are watching him or her fill out the questionnaire), anonymous questionnaires often have a low rate of return. Typically, those who feel strongly on an issue are most likely to fill out and return an anonymous questionnaire, so the returned questionnaires may not accurately reflect a random sampling of opinions. Choose carefully what group of people receive your questionnaire. In your paper, you have an obligation to describe your sample accurately and to state your rate of return.

Finally, the construction of the questionnaire is crucial to its success. Experts work days or weeks perfecting survey questions to avoid bias in answers. Including your questionnaire as an appendix to your paper will lend credibility to your evidence because readers will then be able to check the quality of your questions. Keep your questionnaire clear and easy to complete. Proofread it carefully, and try it out on a guinea pig respondent before you make your final version. Once your questionnaire is complete, type it neatly and write an introduction that explains its purpose. If possible, encourage response by explaining why the knowledge gained from the questionnaire will be beneficial to others.

◢ CONCLUDING YOUR INFORMATION GATHERING

Once you have posed an interesting research question, your search for sources can take on the fascination of a detective puzzle. For many students it is difficult to bring the process of information gathering to a close and to begin the process of reading, note taking, exploratory writing, and drafting. But it is important to do some actual writing early in the process because only by producing a preliminary draft will you detect gaps in your knowledge that require additional research. Exploratory writing and drafting help you focus and increase the efficiency of your information gathering.

◢ CHAPTER SUMMARY

This chapter has discussed the purpose of citing sources and introduced the terms *primary source* and *secondary source*. We presented strategies for converting a general topic into a research question, including preliminary reading and discussions with friends. Once a research question has been chosen, we suggested testing it by posing a series of questions, considering especially the availability of sources. We also described library sources and suggested ways to use them effectively. We pointed out additional sources of information, such as specialized libraries and local organizations. Finally, we addressed strategies for information gathering through interviewing, correspondence, and questionnaires.

TOPIC Guidepost #30

For those using Texas Tech's TOPIC Web-Based assignments:

Direct your web browser to **http://english.ttu.edu:5555**

Guidepost #30 provides full instructions regarding Draft 4.3.

INDEX